HOLES IN THE SAFETY NET

While the United States continues to recover from the 2008 Great Recession, the country still faces unprecedented inequality as increasing numbers of poor families struggle to get by with little assistance from the government. *Holes in the Safety Net: Federalism and Poverty* offers a grounded look at how states and the federal government provide assistance to poor people. With chapters covering everything from welfare reform to recent efforts by states to impose work requirements on Medicaid recipients, the book avoids unnecessary jargon and instead focuses on how programs operate in practice. This timely work should be read by anyone who cares about poverty, rising inequality, and the relationship between state, local, and federal levels of government.

Ezra Rosser is a law professor at American University Washington College of Law, where he teaches poverty law, property law, and federal Indian law. He is a co-author of the leading poverty law textbook and is the editor of the Poverty Law Blog.

T0384639

Holes in the Safety Net

FEDERALISM AND POVERTY

Edited by

EZRA ROSSER

American University Washington College of Law

CAMBRIDGE
UNIVERSITY PRESS

University Printing House, Cambridge CB2 8BS, United Kingdom

One Liberty Plaza, 20th Floor, New York, NY 10006, USA

477 Williamstown Road, Port Melbourne, VIC 3207, Australia

314-321, 3rd Floor, Plot 3, Splendor Forum, Jasola District Centre, New Delhi - 110025, India

79 Anson Road, #06-04/06, Singapore 079906

Cambridge University Press is part of the University of Cambridge.

It furthers the University's mission by disseminating knowledge in the pursuit of education, learning and research at the highest international levels of excellence.

www.cambridge.org
Information on this title: www.cambridge.org/9781108468848
DOI: 10.1017/9781108631662

© Cambridge University Press 2019

This publication is in copyright. Subject to statutory exception and to the provisions of relevant collective licensing agreements, no reproduction of any part may take place without the written permission of Cambridge University Press.

First published 2019
First paperback edition 2020

A catalogue record for this publication is available from the British Library

Library of Congress Cataloging in Publication data
NAMES: Rosser, Ezra, editor.
TITLE: Holes in the safety net : federalism and poverty / edited by Ezra Rosser.
DESCRIPTION: 1 Edition. | New York : Cambridge University Press, 2019. |
Includes bibliographical references and index.
IDENTIFIERS: LCCN 2018058442 | ISBN 9781108475730 (hardback) | ISBN 9781108468848 (paperback
SUBJECTS: LCSH: Public welfare–United States. | Poverty–Government policy–United States. |
Legal assistance to the poor–United States. | Federal government–United States. |
State governments–United States. | BISAC: LAW / Constitutional.
CLASSIFICATION: LCC HV95 .H625 2019 | DDC 362.5/560973–dc23
LC record available at https://lccn.loc.gov/2018058442

ISBN 978-1-108-47573-0 Hardback
ISBN 978-1-108-46884-8 Paperback

Additional resources for this publication at www.cambridge.org/delange

Cambridge University Press has no responsibility for the persistence or accuracy of URLs for external or third-party internet websites referred to in this publication, and does not guarantee that any content on such websites is, or will remain, accurate or appropriate.

To Mateo and Mario with love.

Contents

Contributors

Dhruv Aggarwal is a second-year student at Yale Law School who studies corporate law, tax policy, and law and inequality.

Wendy Bach is an associate professor at the University of Tennessee College of Law. Before entering the academy, Bach was director of the Homelessness Outreach and Prevention Project at the Urban Justice Center in New York City and a staff attorney with the Legal Aid Society of Brooklyn. Her scholarship focuses on participatory democracy, social welfare policy, race, gender, and poverty law.

Monica Bell is an Associate Professor of Law and Sociology at Yale University who writes on criminal justice, poverty and inequality, and race in the law.

Peter Edelman is the Carmack Waterhouse Professor of Law and Public Policy at Georgetown University Law Center, where he teaches constitutional law and poverty law and is faculty director of the Georgetown Center on Poverty and Inequality. During President Clinton's first term he was Counselor to HHS Secretary Donna Shalala and then Assistant Secretary for Planning and Evaluation. He was a Legislative Assistant to Senator Robert F. Kennedy and was Issues Director for Senator Edward Kennedy's Presidential campaign in 1980. Earlier, he was a Law Clerk to Supreme Court Justice Arthur J. Goldberg and before that to Judge Henry J. Friendly on the U.S. Court of Appeals for the Second Circuit. Professor Edelman's recent books include *Not a Crime to Be Poor: The Criminalization of Poverty in America* (2017) and *So Rich So Poor: Why It's So Hard to End Poverty in America* (2012).

Michelle Gilman is the Venable Professor of Law and Director of Clinical Education at the University of Baltimore School of Law. Previously, Professor Gilman was a trial attorney in the Civil Rights Division at the Department of Justice; an associate at Arnold and Porter in Washington, DC; a law clerk to United States District Court

Judge Frank A. Kaufman of the District of Maryland; and an editor of the Michigan Law Review. Professor Gilman directs the Saul Ewing Civil Advocacy Clinic and is a co-director of the Center on Applied Feminism.

Andrew Hammond is Senior Lecturer in the College and Lecturer in Law at the University of Chicago, where he serves as the Associate Director of the Law, Letters, and Society program. His research and teaching interests include civil procedure, administrative law, and poverty law. Andrew has worked for several anti-poverty organizations, most recently as a Skadden Fellow at the Sargent Shriver National Center on Poverty Law, where he remains Of Counsel.

Daniel Hatcher is a professor of law at the University of Baltimore School of Law where he teaches in the Saul Ewing Civil Advocacy Clinic. Before joining the faculty in 2004, Hatcher worked at the Maryland Legal Aid Bureau, Legal Aid in the Baltimore Child Advocacy Unit, and the Children's Defense Fund. Hatcher is the author of *The Poverty Industry: The Exploitation of America's Most Vulnerable Citizens* (2016).

Nicole Huberfeld is a Professor of Law at Boston University School of Law and Professor of Health Law, Ethics & Human Rights at Boston University School of Public Health. Her scholarship focuses on the cross-section of health care law and constitutional law with emphasis on the role of federalism and spending power in federal health care programs, especially Medicaid. Huberfeld authored the first new casebook on health care law in a generation, *The Law of American Health Care*, with Elizabeth Weeks and Kevin Outterson.

Clare Huntington is the Joseph M. McLaughlin Professor of Law and Associate Dean for Research at Fordham Law School. She previously served an Attorney Advisor in the Justice Department's Office of Legal Counsel and was a law clerk for Justice Harry A. Blackmun and Justice Stephen Breyer of the Supreme Court of the United States. Huntington is the author of *Failure to Flourish: How Law Undermines Family Relationships* (2014).

Francine J. Lipman is the William S. Boyd Professor of Law at UNLV William S. Boyd School of Law. Prior to joining the academy, Francince practiced law with O'Melveny & Myers LLP and Irell & Manella LLP. Professor Lipman is an elected member of the American Law Institute, the American College of Tax Counsel, and the American Bar Foundation, and an editor and former committee chair for the Tax Section of the American Bar Association.

Lisa R. Pruitt is Martin Luther King, Jr., Professor of Law at UC Davis School of Law. She writes and teaches about gender, race, class, and rurality. Pruitt is a member of the interdisciplinary Poverty and Geography Network of the Institute for Research on Poverty and a faculty affiliate of the UC Davis Center for Poverty Research. She is the co-chair of the Rural Task force of the California Commission on Access to Justice.

Ezra Rosser is a professor of law at American University Washington College of Law. He writes about poverty law, property law, and Navajo economic development. Ezra is a co-author *Poverty Law, Policy, and Practice* (2014) (with Juliet Brodie, Clare Pastore & Jeff Selbin) and was a co-editor of *The Poverty Law Canon* (2014) (with Marie Failinger) and *Tribes, Land, and the Environment* (2012) (with Sarah Krakoff).

David Super is a professor of law at Georgetown University Law Center. His research focuses on Administrative Law, Constitutional Law, Legislation (including the federal budget), Local Government Law, and Public Welfare Law. Prior to entering the legal academy, he served for several years as the general counsel for the Center on Budget and Policy Priorities and worked for the National Health Law Program and Community Legal Services in Philadelphia.

Isra Syed is a third-year student at Yale Law School who studies law, political economy, and critical approaches to civil rights.

Andrea Taverna is a second-year student at Yale Law School who studies the interaction between law and public policy.

Rebecca H. Williams is a 2019 J.D. candidate at UC Davis, Martin Luther King Jr. School of Law. She received her undergraduate degree in International Studies (Political Science & Sociology) at UC San Diego.

Acknowledgments

This book is a product of the poverty law scholarly community. I would not have considered working on it if I had not been confident that I would find a great group of scholars willing to participate in this project. This is my third collaborative poverty law book project and it truly is wonderful to be part of a community that is primarily motivated by concern for the poor. My confidence was justified and I would like to thank especially the great group of contributors who wrote chapters for this book.

This book grew out of a conference hosted by American University Washington College of Law (WCL). I would like to thank Dean Camille Nelson, as well as Jennifer Dabson, Shayan Davoudi, and Karina Wegman for their support not only of the biannual poverty law conference but also of the Economic Justice Program at WCL. Daniel Hatcher's eye-opening book, *The Poverty Industry: The Exploitation of America's Most Vulnerable Citizens* (2016), inspired both that conference and this edited volume. Hatcher's book is well worth reading in its own right.

I would like to give a special shout-out to my phenomenal research assistant, Oliver Jury. Often it was Oliver who caught the stray period mark or came up with the best way to fix a troublesome sentence. His attention to detail and skills as a writer are truly impressive.

Finally, I owe a big thank you to all those who cared for my young children while I worked on this project. In the United States, I want to thank Glenda, Onestina, and the staff at Play, Work or Dash; in El Salvador, thanks to my mother-in-law and to Elba. And everywhere, at all points in time, and for everything, thanks to Elvia. This book is dedicated to our children, Mateo and Mario. May they realize both the value of hard work and tremendous privileges they enjoy, and may their lives be filled with happiness and meaning. Un fuerte abrazo.

Introduction

Ezra Rosser

This is a book about the relationship between antipoverty programs and federalism. It is also a book about the politics of aid to the poor. Poverty and federalism are difficult topics that invite instinctive reactions. The very use of the term *federalism* pushes the conversation from the lived experience of poverty to the structure of antipoverty programs and the balance between state sovereignty and federal control. Given the ways in which rhetoric of "states' rights" served in the past, and continues to serve, as cover for systematic discrimination against African Americans and Latinos, including the differential provision of poor relief, federalism's ugly side readily comes to mind. However, advocates for vulnerable populations often turn to state and local governments to provide support and relief when the federal government is unable or unwilling to fund antipoverty efforts or recognize the rights of the poor. For many antipoverty efforts, the dynamic is not an "either the federal government or state governments" one, but a complicated, interdependent relationship of cooperative, and uncooperative, federalism.

There is no single model of federalism when it comes to antipoverty work. It is nearly impossible to find an example of either a purely federal (though the federal earned income tax credit comes close) or a purely state program. The federal government provides funding to states but attaches conditions on that funding, in the form of matching payments, program conditions, and administrative requirements. For their part, states often take on the primary role administering the programs and determining program eligibility requirements and benefit levels for recipients. Even federally defined standards are subject to deviation because many programs allow states to seek waivers so they can operate their programs differently. It is important to note that reliance on federalism and allowance for significant state variation is a choice. It is a choice that reflects the traditional justification for federalism, that states are the laboratories of democracy, as well as the unwillingness of the United States to recognize a broad set of socioeconomic rights as is common in other developed countries.

BRIEF HISTORY OF THE WELFARE STATE

Until the New Deal, assistance to the poor was traditionally a local matter. Borrowing from the poor laws of England, the colonies, and later the states, distinguished between the deserving and undeserving poor and provided different forms of relief depending on that classification. Those not part of the community were turned away. The New Deal changed things, to a point. The sense that something had to be done in response to the widespread hardship of the Great Depression created a political environment in which it was possible to pass the Social Security Act. Joined by an alphabet soup of other New Deal programs, such as the Federal Emergency Relief Act, the Civilian Conservation Corps, and the Works Progress Administration, the Social Security Act marked an important milestone in federal assistance. The Social Security Act established a national contribution-based pension system, a national unemployment insurance program, and federal aid to mothers with children. The New Deal was the "formative moment of the American national welfare state,"[1] but it did not sweep aside state interests. Southern states, concerned that generous socioeconomic rights would undermine the Jim Crow economic structure of the South, were allowed – through carve outs for agricultural and domestic workers, as well as through deference to state administration – to exclude blacks from coverage. The New Deal might have created federal welfare rights, but the benefited population largely did not include poor African Americans, Latinos, or Native Americans.

It took the combined pressure of the Cold War, the civil rights movement, and the War on Poverty for welfare to begin to take seriously the truth of the Declaration of Independence's assertion that "all men are created equal." Poverty, especially multigenerational poverty connected with discrimination against minorities, was an international embarrassment that undermined the country's claim to the rest of the world that American-style capitalism had more to offer than communism. Aside from the propaganda problem, it was hard to fight the Cold War's proxy fights that were supposedly about freedom when minorities could not find equal treatment at home. The civil rights movement inserted itself in the postwar period, demanding an end to institutionalized racism, not only from the de jure segregation found throughout the South but also from the institutionalized inequality of the North. It is worth recalling that Martin Luther King famously spoke about his "dream deeply rooted in the American dream" at the March on Washington for Jobs and Freedom. President Lyndon Johnson, pushed along by the civil rights movement, used his 1964 State of the Union Address to declare a War on Poverty. The declaration led to the founding of the food stamps program in 1964, the creation of Medicare and

---

[1] Robert C. Lieberman, *Race and the Limits of Solidarity: American Welfare State Development in Comparative Perspective, in* RACE AND THE POLITICS OF WELFARE REFORM (Sanford F. Schram et al. eds., 2003), at 28.

Medicaid (through amendments to the Social Security Act) in 1965, as well as other significant programs such as Head Start, Job Corps, and the Office of Economic Opportunity. Cold War pressure, civil rights victories, and the War on Poverty came together at a critical moment in American history in terms of both economics and law.

The widely shared economic growth that followed World War II laid the groundwork for the country to imagine a better, more inclusive future. Between the end of the war and the first oil crisis of the 1970s, the US economy charged along, delivering not only sustained growth but also growth shared by large segments of the population across the income spectrum. Published in 1962, Michael Harrington's *The Other America* brought attention to the plight of the poor, especially those poor in areas that the postwar period had left behind: Appalachia, inner cities, the Black Belt, and Indian reservations. It challenged the cookie-cutter, *Leave It to Beaver*, version of American life and exposed the extent to which the poor were struggling. The War on Poverty reflected the optimism of the period; optimism born out of the country's sustained economic growth and optimism that the federal government could tackle poverty. The Supreme Court briefly joined the fight. In 1968,[2] the Court held that Alabama could not strip Sylvester Smith of her welfare benefits under the Aid to Families with Dependent Children (AFDC) program simply because she was cohabitating with a man.[3] A year later, the Court struck down a Pennsylvania residency requirement for welfare, protecting the welfare rights of the poor as well as their freedom of movement.[4] And in 1970, the Supreme Court – relying in part on a law review article by Charles Reich that argued that welfare was a new form of property – found in *Goldberg* v. *Kelly* that New York had violated the due process rights of welfare recipients by removing them from the welfare rolls without first providing them an in-person hearing.[5] This was a robust understanding of aid to the poor built on an expanding list of federal programs and Court-protected federal requirements.

The Supreme Court retreated from the War on Poverty and from federal protections quickly. Just two weeks after *Goldberg*, the Supreme Court handed states a huge victory when it upheld Maryland's family cap, an upper limit on a family's welfare benefit that would not increase if more children were born, using the highly deferential rational basis review.[6] According to the *Dandridge* v. *Williams* decision, states have the authority to make such distinctions even though a family cap policy

[2]   *King* v. *Smith*, 392 U.S. 309 (1968).
[3]   For more on the case and on Sylvester Smith, see Henry Freedman, *Sylvester Smith, Unlikely Heroine*, in THE POVERTY LAW CANON: EXPLORING THE MAJOR CASES (Marie A. Failinger & Ezra Rosser eds., 2016), at 51–71.
[4]   *Shapiro* v. *Thompson*, 394 U.S. 618 (1969).
[5]   *Goldberg* v. *Kelly*, 397 U.S. 254 (1970). *See also* Charles Reich, *The New Property*, 73 YALE L. J. 733 (1964).
[6]   *Dandridge* v. *Williams*, 397 U.S. 471 (1970).

harms families and children. Three years later, the Supreme Court ruled against minority poor families who challenged unequal public school funding in San Antonio, holding that "wealth" was not a suspect classification and education was not a fundamental right.[7] *San Antonio v. Rodriguez* allowed states to continue relying upon local tax funding of education, even though it guaranteed students in poor districts would continue to receive dramatically fewer resources than students in wealthy districts. Though there were occasional victories for the poor in the decades that followed *Dandridge* and *Rodriguez*, the Supreme Court effectively closed the poor out of the federal courts. To find judicial relief, the poor would have to rely upon state courts and state constitutions.

The legislative retreat from the War on Poverty took longer, with public debates in the 1980s leading eventually to the 1996 welfare reform bill. The backlash against welfare and against the poor grew out of a potent combination of racism and a belief that the poor were undeserving of support.[8] Though aid for the poor takes many forms, from health care coverage to food stamps, cash welfare has pride of place in the public imagination of how the government helps the needy. The deconstruction of racial barriers to welfare receipt and increased recognition of welfare rights resulted in a growth in the number of people on welfare. Even though the number of whites on welfare exceeded the figures for other races, African Americans received welfare disproportionately; the rolls darkened. The public, with the help of biased media depictions of the poor, came to think of poverty in black-and-white terms. Had the shared economic growth of the postwar period continued, the expansion in the welfare rolls might not have created a political crisis. By the end of the 1970s, things had changed. The US economy continued to expand but the gains were not widely shared. The early 1980s were marked by a rise in unemployment and downward pressure on the economy as President Reagan worked to tame inflation. Though the Reagan administration promoted the idea of trickle-down economics, inequality increased as the rich got richer and everyone else stagnated. This was not an environment in which the public was prepared to accept large numbers of black and brown people receiving "free" money from the government. Ronald Reagan, using racially coded language, rallied white voters by telling stories of "welfare queens" and welfare cheats. Conservative commentators – most notably Charles Murray – argued that welfare hurt the poor by permitting them to make "bad" decisions and provided intellectual cover for the welfare backlash.[9]

Antipoor and antiwelfare rhetoric worked. Welfare became a deeply unpopular program, leaving politicians scrambling to offer a new direction. In 1992, Bill Clinton used a pledge to "end welfare as we know it" as a signal to voters that he

---

[7] *San Antonio Indep. Sch. Dist. v. Rodriguez*, 411 U.S. 1 (1973).

[8] *See, e.g.*, Bertrall L. Ross II & Terry Smith, *Minimum Responsiveness and the Political Exclusion of the Poor*, 72 LAW & CONTEMP. PROBS. 197, 206–7 (2009).

[9] *See* CHARLES MURRAY, LOSING GROUND: AMERICAN SOCIAL POLICY, 1950–1980 (1984).

was a different type of Democrat, one not driven to protect the legacy of the New Deal or Johnson's Great Society, nor beholden to the party's traditional constituencies.[10] It worked. Candidate Clinton became President Clinton, and his pledge took on new urgency after Republicans won the 1994 midterm elections in a landslide. Newt Gingrich led the resurgent conservative charge with his Contract with America, which had as its third provision the imposition of family caps, work requirements, and time limits on welfare recipients. Facing a tough reelection, Clinton signed the Personal Responsibility and Work Opportunity Reconciliation Act of 1996. Welfare reform had arrived.

WELFARE REFORM

The challenge when it comes to cash welfare is the tremendous imbalance between the number of people it serves and the hold it has on the discourse about poverty. The 1996 welfare reform act had three major components: work requirements, time limits, and block grants. The first two received most of the attention. Welfare recipients were expected to work. This expectation was based on the linked ideas that all (poor) people, even single parents of young children, should work and that work is inherently a good thing. The work requirement was not grounded in an understanding of the sort of jobs and the limited possibility of upward mobility available to welfare recipients. Time limits were imposed in a similar fashion. The AFDC program was replaced by the Temporary Assistance for Needy Families (TANF) program, and the act explicitly rejected the notion that recipients had a "right" to welfare. TANF promised that the poor would face a lifetime five-year limit on receiving welfare paid with federal funds and allowed states to impose even stricter limits. Though many states would find various methods to avoid strictly enforcing – through use of state funds, credits for reducing the overall rolls that could excuse continued welfare payments, etc. – the message was clear: Welfare is not a right and it is not a way of life. Though work requirements and time limits fill the welfare reform headlines, arguably it was the third component, block grants capped at pre–welfare reform levels, that was the most significant change. The move from a federally funded, rights-based cash welfare system to a block grant system that gave tremendous latitude to states fundamentally rewrote the relationship between federalism and antipoverty efforts.

The conservative take on welfare reform is that it was a success. Large numbers of poor recipients left welfare. Buoyed along by the strong economy of Clinton's second term, many found work. Even if they did not find work, states had an incentive to get them off the welfare rolls. States were given tremendous flexibility in how they were to use their block grants, bound only by four broad goals:

[10] *See* Peter Edelman, *The Worst Thing Bill Clinton Has Done*, THE ATLANTIC, Mar. 1997.

(1) provide assistance to needy families so that children may be cared for in their own homes or in the homes of relatives; (2) end the dependence of needy parents on government benefits by promoting job preparation, work, and marriage; (3) prevent and reduce the incidence of out-of-wedlock pregnancies and establish annual numerical goals for preventing and reducing the incidence of these pregnancies; and (4) encourage the formation and maintenance of two-parent families.[11]

As a practical matter, TANF's block grant structure meant that states got to keep – and use elsewhere – whatever money they did not pay out as welfare. The incentives were there and states complied, toughening their eligibility standards, increasing the administrative hurdles associated with the program, and penalizing recipients who failed to strictly comply with the requirements. As a Congressional Research Services' report highlights, "TANF is not a program per se, but a flexible funding stream," which has replaced the prior federal cash welfare program.[12]

Today, less than a quarter of all people in poverty receive cash assistance from TANF, compared to 68 percent in 1996.[13] State-determined maximum benefit levels vary considerably. In July 2013, for example, the maximum monthly family benefit for a single parent with two kids was $170 in Mississippi, $389 in Virginia, and $638 in California.[14] In 2017, there were 2.5 million people receiving cash assistance from TANF nationwide, but New York and California accounted for more than 40 percent of the total caseload.[15] In Wyoming, a state with a population of 579,000, only 1,257 people received cash welfare in 2017.[16] This is not because there are not poor people but because states have been successful in creating barriers to welfare. When the Great Recession hit, the welfare rolls only slight budged, increasing from 1.7 million in 2008 to 2.0 million families in 2010.[17] If welfare is supposed to provide a safety net when things get tough, there should have been a much bigger change. However, the number of people receiving Supplemental Nutrition Assistance Program (SNAP) benefits did take off, with 46 million people receiving SNAP benefits in 2012, a 76 percent increase from when the recession began.[18] Federalism largely explains the different trajectories of these two programs. While TANF is state-administered and the block grant framework means that assistance to the poor

[11] 42 U.S.C. § 601(a) (2012).
[12] Gene Falk, Cong. Research Serv., R40946, The Temporary Assistance for Needy Families (TANF) Block Grant: An Introduction, (2013) at Summary.
[13] Ife Floyd et al., Center on Budget and Policy Priorities, TANF Reaching Few Poor Families (2017).
[14] Gene Falk, Cong. Research Serv., RL32760, The Temporary Assistance for Needy Families (TANF) Block Grant: Responses to Frequently Asked Questions (2016).
[15] Office of Family Assistance, TANF: Total Number of Recipients: Fiscal and Calendar Year 2017, www.acf.hhs.gov/sites/default/files/ofa/2017_recipient_tan.pdf.
[16] Id.
[17] Gene Falk, Cong. Research Serv., RL32760, The Temporary Assistance for Needy Families (TANF) Block Grant: Responses to Frequently Asked Questions, (2016).
[18] Sheila Zedlewski et al., Urban Institute, SNAP's Role in the Great Recession and Beyond (2012).

comes at the expense of other state budget priorities, SNAP benefits paid to individuals come out of the federal budget. The same states that seek to divert the poor from TANF recognize the benefit of increasing SNAP enrollment. Differences in how antipoverty programs are structured, in terms of federalism, can have a significant impact on their reach, effectiveness, and political resonance.

POVERTY AND ANTIPOVERTY PROGRAMS TODAY

The future of antipoverty policy is in flux and depends in part on the degree to which the welfare debates of the 1980s and 1990s continue to define the terms of debate about assistance to the poor. Although TANF benefits are crucial for those who receive them, the safety net is much broader than just cash welfare. The lives of the poor are affected by everything from tax policy to health care coverage. Federalism challenges are pervasive. What should the respective roles of the federal and state governments be in the various programs? How much flexibility should states have? What rights or practices should be uniform nationwide? To what degree should advocates accept second-best solutions when it comes to federalism because of political considerations? If questions about antipoverty programs are answered, as they were in the mid-1990s, by blaming the poor for their own poverty and turning a blind eye to the way that potential reforms structure the relationship between the federal government and state governments, then we will have talked a great deal about welfare reform but learned very little. Put differently, antipoverty efforts have to prioritize both the lived experiences of the poor and the structural challenges of federalism. At the moment, the road forward is obscured by both the welfare reform debates and new dark clouds on the horizon.

In July 2018, the Council of Economic Advisors concluded that "War on Poverty is largely over and a success."[19] Based on an alternative consumption-based standard of poverty, the Council of Economic Advisors' conclusion was remarkable in several respects. Not only was the conclusion problematically driven by the arbitrary selection of 1980 as the fixed (and dated) consumption standard, but also Trump's appointed council seemed to be undercutting a long-standing conservative talking point – that the country wastes money spending on the poor. A 2012 Cato Institute report claiming that "the United States spends nearly $1 trillion every year to fight poverty" became the basis for Congressman Paul Ryan's provocative claim that "$15 trillion had been spent fighting poverty since 1964" with very little to show for it.[20] Both figures were falsely inflated and failed to acknowledge that many antipoverty

---

[19] COUNCIL OF ECONOMIC ADVISORS, EXPANDING WORK REQUIREMENTS IN NON-CASH WELFARE PROGRAMS (2018).

[20] MICHAEL TANNER, CATO INSTITUTE, THE AMERICAN WELFARE STATE: HOW WE SPEND NEARLY $1 TRILLION A YEAR FIGHTING POVERTY – AND FAIL (2012); *see also* Glenn Kessler, *Paul Ryan's Claim That $15 Trillion Has Been Spent in the War on Poverty*, WASH. POST, AUG. 2, 2013.

programs "are both very efficient and effective at reducing poverty."[21] Indeed, it is this last point that makes the Council of Economic Advisors' conclusion so surprising: By declaring the War on Poverty a success, it seemed to indicate a rhetorical course reversal.

The Republican Party has long made attacking means-tested programs an important plank of the party's national platform. A 2014 Heritage Foundation headline provocatively declared, "The War on Poverty: 50 Years of Failure."[22] Not to be outdone, a *Forbes* headline from the same year went even further, "The War on Poverty Wasn't a Failure – It Was a Catastrophe."[23] And in 2011, *Business Insider* published an op-ed that purported to show that "LBJ's War on Poverty Is the Greatest Policy Failure of Modern America."[24] Such hyperbolic language about the War on Poverty fits the long tradition of politicians attempting to score political points by attacking the poor as undeserving and antipoverty programs as misguided. One of Trump's first actions explicitly about poverty, the euphemistically titled "Executive Order Reducing Poverty in America by Promoting Opportunity and Economic Mobility," called for "strengthening existing work requirements for work-capable people and introducing new work requirements when legally permissible."[25] This is not to say that Democrats have not done the same – after all, it was President Clinton who signed welfare reform into law – but it is especially noteworthy that Trump's Council of Economic Advisors declared victory over poverty. As the Urban Institute's Gregory Acs noted, while the council was wrong "to declare the War on Poverty over, it is important to recognize the progress we have made and the important role our antipoverty programs such as SNAP and EITC [Earned Income Tax Credit] have played in that success."[26]

The problem with declaring national victory over poverty is that it is self-evidently untrue. Poverty continues to exist in the United States, despite the size and strength of the country's overall economy. The homeless can be found in every major city, too many schoolchildren still do not have enough food at home, and families often cannot afford the cost of basic necessities. But just as Trump and his surrogates insisted against all evidence that the size of the crowd at his inauguration exceeded

[21] Mike Konczal, *No, We Don't Spend $1 Trillion on Welfare Each Year*, WASH. POST, Jan. 12, 2014.

[22] Robert Rector, *The War on Poverty: 50 Years of Failure*, THE HERITAGE FOUNDATION, Sept. 23, 2014, www.heritage.org/marriage-and-family/commentary/the-war-poverty-50-years-failure.

[23] Louis Woodhill, *The War on Poverty Wasn't a Failure – It Was a Catastrophe*, FORBES, Mar. 19, 2014.

[24] Walter Russell Mead, *LBJ's War on Poverty Is the Greatest Policy Failure of Modern America*, BUSINESS INSIDER, July 6, 2011.

[25] Proclamation No. 13,828, 83 Fed. Reg. 15,941 (Apr. 10, 2018); *see also* Ezra Rosser, *Pulling from a Dated Playbook: President Trump's Executive Order on Poverty*, HARV. L. REV. BLOG (Aug. 20, 2018, 10:04 PM), https://blog.harvardlawreview.org/pulling-from-a-dated-playbook-president-trumps-executive-order-on-poverty/.

[26] Gregory Acs, *Have We Won the War on Poverty? Not Yet*, URBAN INSTITUTE, July 26, 2018, www.urban.org/urban-wire/have-we-won-war-poverty-not-yet.

that of Obama's, his administration has doubled down on its insistence that poverty affects a tiny percentage of the population. After the United Nations issued a country visit report that found that in United States "40 million live in poverty, 18.5 million in extreme poverty, and 5.3 million live in Third World conditions of absolute poverty," the US Ambassador to the United Nations Nikki Haley called it "patently ridiculous for the United Nations to examine poverty in America."[27] Instead of 18.5 million in extreme poverty, "there are only approximately 250,000 persons in 'extreme poverty' circumstances," according to the official State Department response.[28] The response, leveraging the same consumption-based study that the Council of Economic Advisors relied upon, also argued that "poverty is down by 77 percent since 1980."[29] These are extraordinary claims by the State Department, unsupported by those government agencies tasked with tracking poverty in the United States.

According to the Census Bureau's standard measure of poverty, there were 40.6 million people in poverty in the United States in 2016, or 12.7 percent of the population.[30] If the Census Bureau used the Supplemental Poverty Measure, a poverty measure based on recommendations by the National Academy of Sciences, the figures would be 44.8 million people, or 14 percent of the population.[31] But these figures tell only part of the story. A total of 18.5 million people, 5.8 percent of the population, have an income under half of the poverty line, including 6 million children.[32] As the *New York Times* reported in 2010, "About one in 50 Americans now lives in a household with a reported income that consists of nothing but a food-stamp card."[33] Kathryn Edin and Luke Shaefer found that if food stamps are not taken into account, 3.55 million children in the United States lived in extreme poverty – in households living on less than $2 per person a day – in mid-2011.[34] Even taking into account food stamps, 1.17 million children lived in extreme poverty.[35] Edin and Shaefer explain, "The bottom line is that extreme poverty has grown

[27] Jenny Jarvie, *Nikki Haley Calls U.N. Report on Poverty in U.S. "Misleading and Politically Motivated,"* L.A. TIMES, June 21, 2018.

[28] US Dept. of State, *Country Concerned Statement in Response to SR Alston's Country Report on the United States*, June 22, 2018, https://geneva.usmission.gov/2018/06/22/country-concerned-statement-in-response-to-sr-alstons-country-report-on-the-united-states/.

[29] *Id.*

[30] Jessica L. Semega et al., U.S. BUREAU OF THE CENSUS, INCOME AND POVERTY IN THE UNITED STATES: 2016 (2017) at 12.

[31] LIANA FOX, U.S. BUREAU OF THE CENSUS, THE SUPPLEMENTAL POVERTY MEASURE: 2016 (2017) at 20 (Appendix Table A-1, "Number and Percentage of People in Poverty Using the Supplemental Poverty Measure: 2016 and 2015").

[32] Jessica L. Semega et al., U.S. BUREAU OF THE CENSUS, INCOME AND POVERTY IN THE UNITED STATES: 2016 (2017) at 17.

[33] Jason DeParle & Robert M. Gebeloff, *Living on Nothing but Food Stamps*, N.Y. TIMES, Jan. 20, 2010.

[34] H. Luke Shaefer & Kathryn Edin, *The Rise of Extreme Poverty in the United States*, PATHWAYS, Summer 2014, at 28.

[35] *Id.*

sharply since welfare reform."[36] Whatever the supposed justifications were for
welfare reform, these are shocking statistics about how the country fails to protect
children. Had the State Department looked around the world, it would have
discovered that other developed countries, including countries with lower per capita
resources, use tax-and-transfer policies to lift a far larger percentage of their population out of poverty.[37]

But poverty is about more than just income, it is also about the lives people are
forced to live. More than 2 million Americans with yearlong, full-time jobs live in
poverty.[38] For many working poor, jobs offer little by way of pay or security. Even a
set work schedule is often asking too much, making work especially demanding for
parents of young children. In Richmond, Virginia, more than 10 percent of renters
are evicted each year,[39] starting a chain of negative consequences that harm
families, disrupt children's schooling, and can lead to homelessness.[40] Those "fortu-
nate" enough to have public housing often have to deal with poor conditions,
deferred maintenance, and invasions of their privacy.[41] As the UN Special
Rapporteur noted, not only do American "citizens live shorter and sicker lives
compared to those living in all other rich democracies" but also the country "has
one of the lowest rates of intergenerational social mobility of any of the rich
countries."[42] The country's limited response to poverty means that poor parents
not only have to suffer the indignities and hardships of poverty but can also expect
their children to live similar lives when they grow up.

National poverty statistics disguise the fact that poverty affects some communities
and groups more than others. While 42.5 percent of all poor people in the United
States were non-Hispanic whites in 2016, the white poverty rate was only 8.8
percent.[43] In contrast, 22.0 percent of blacks and 19.4 percent of Hispanics were
below the poverty line.[44] The group with the highest, 26.2 percent, poverty rate:
American Indians and Alaska Natives.[45] Though the poverty rate for the United
States as a whole was 13.5 percent in 2016, the rate in the Midwest was 11.7 percent,

[36] *Id.*
[37] Orsetta Causa & Mikkel Hermansen, *Income Redistribution through Taxes and Transfers across OECD Countries*, 85 (Org. for Econ. Co-operation and Dev., Working Paper No. 1453, 2018).
[38] Jay Shambaugh et al., Brookings, Who is Poor in the United States? (2017).
[39] Eviction Lab, *Eviction Rankings*, https://evictionlab.org/rankings/#/evictions?r=United%20States&a=0&d=evictionRate&l=1.
[40] *See generally* Matthew Desmond, Evicted: Poverty and Profit in the American City (2016).
[41] *See generally* Khiara M. Bridges, The Poverty of Privacy Rights (2017).
[42] U.N. GAOR, 38th Sess., U.N. Doc. A/HRC/38/33/Add. 1 (May 4, 2018) at 3–5.
[43] Semega, *supra* note 29, at 13 Table 3, "People in Poverty by Selected Characteristics: 2015 and 2016."
[44] *Id.*
[45] U.S. Bureau of the Census, CB17-FF.20, American Indian and Alaska Native Heritage Month: November 2017 (based on 2016 figures from the American Community Survey).

while the rate in the South was 15.3 percent. The confluence of race and place can result in areas of notably concentrated poverty at the local level, as can be seen in two areas of the nation's capital. For the last decade, almost 50 percent of the predominantly African American residents of Washington, DC's Anacostia neighborhood have been below the poverty line.[46] In contrast, the poverty rate for the wealthy, white neighborhood of Ward 3 in upper northwest DC was less than 3 percent for the same period (2006–15).[47] The same basic contrast exists between Oakland and San Francisco, California, North and South Milwaukee, Wisconsin, and Ferguson and Ladue, Missouri. Though we as a nation have moved away from de jure segregation, the struggle of poor minority families in poor communities continues. It has been more than 50 years since the Kerner Commission's famous words, "Our nation is moving toward two societies, one black, one white – separate and unequal," but, sadly, such a conclusion still holds for much of the country.[48]

That struggle continues does not mean the fight against poverty has been in vain. But for existing forms of government assistance, it is estimated that double the number of people in the United States would be in poverty.[49] The elderly provide a good example of what can happen when we no longer tolerate high levels of poverty for a given population. Owing in large part to Social Security and Medicare, the poverty rate for those age 65 or older is only 8.8 percent, compared to a rate of 19.7 percent for those under age 18.[50] A common complaint on the right is that government does not work; that government programs are wasteful and ineffective. But consider SNAP for a moment. Food stamps reduce poverty, extreme poverty, and food insecurity; if anything, the effectiveness of the SNAP program is limited not by its implementation but by the need to increase funding for the program so that recipient benefits do not run out at the end of the month.[51] Even though antipoverty spending is likely to always face political headwind, it is inaccurate to say that antipoverty programs are failures or do not make a difference.

---

[46] DC Kids Count, *Ward Snapshots: Tracking Child Well-Being in Your Ward*, Wash. Post (Aug. 20, 2018, 11:51 PM), http://apps.washingtonpost.com/g/documents/local/dc-action-for-children/2407/.

[47] *Id.*

[48] U.S. Riot Commission, Report of the National Advisory Commission on Civil Disorders 1 (1968).

[49] David Cooper & Julia Wolfe, *Poverty Declined Modestly in 2016; Government Programs Continued to Keep Tens of Millions Out of Poverty*, Economic Policy Institute, Sept. 12, 2017, www.epi.org/blog/poverty-declined-modestly-in-2016-government-programs-continued-to-keep-tens-of-millions-out-of-poverty/ (based on calculations done in connection with the Supplemental Poverty Measure).

[50] Semega, *supra* note 29, at 13 Table 3, "People in Poverty by Selected Characteristics: 2015 and 2016."

[51] Council of Economic Advisors, Long-Term Benefits of the Supplemental Nutrition Assistance Program (2015).

OUTLINE OF THE BOOK

Though the chapters in this book vary considerably in their focus, the authors all
share the belief that government can and should act to help those in poverty. This
shared assumption allows the chapters to focus on the relationship between federalism and the safety net, freed from the need to justify assistance for the poor. Ranging
from chapters that explore the history of antipoverty efforts abstractly to chapters that
delve deeply into the workings of individual programs, each chapter offers a different
way of understanding the practical impacts of federalism on the most vulnerable.
Each individually offers a window on how states and localities interact with the
federal government; read together, the chapters shed considerable light on how
federalism operates in practice. This book, grounded as it is in the relationship
between federalism and poverty, provides a layer of realism to the highly theoretical
discussions about federalism that fill academic works.

The question each of the chapters is asking, in one way or another, is whether
federalism is working for or against the poor. Of course, the answer is often not black
or white. Or, for that matter, red or blue. The chapters show that state governments
have made very different choices about how to help the poor. Often, these choices
mirror normative assumptions about how red states or blue states behave. But
sometimes state policy does not fit so easily into standard political boxes when it
comes to helping the poor. All states, regardless of which party dominates their
politics, have figured out how to take advantage of block grants and other cooperative federalism arrangements to serve their own ends, often to the detriment of the
poor. Put differently, this book is less about what states, as the "laboratories of
democracy," might do, and more about what states are doing.[52] Similarly, the
chapters focus more on the politics of the relative authority of states versus the
federal government when it comes to poverty programs than on the abstract reasons
to favor cooperative federalism. As this book shows, the decision to have states
implement and administer federal programs that assist the poor has significant
consequences in terms of both the effectiveness of those programs and how the
poor are treated.

Federalism is a fundamental part of governance in the United States. While it is
easy to think of moments when states did little to protect the poor, especially the
minority poor, at other points, states have stepped up to help the poor or protect
antipoverty programs when the federal government seemed either powerless or
determined to act against the interests of the poor. The goal of this book is not to
convince anyone that all antipoverty programs should be nationalized nor to
demonize states or localities. Federalism has its place, but the chapters in this book

[52] For a critique of theoretical assertions of devolution as an independently valuable governance
move, see David A. Super, *Laboratories of Destitution: Democratic Experimentalism and the
Failure of Antipoverty Law*, 157 U. PENN. L. REV. 541 (2008).

suggest ways states and the federal government could do a better job managing the dynamics of federalism when it comes to antipoverty programs. Though united in their commitment to the poor, it is impossible to imagine that antipoverty advocates (much less all the contributors to this book) would come together and agree on a single best model of federalism in terms of helping the poor. Perhaps the best approach is to narrow the space in which states are allowed to experiment or implement state-specific choices regarding eligibility and benefit levels. Some scholars have argued that poverty programs, even ones that rely on state administration, should be structured around hard national baselines below which states cannot deviate.[53] Perhaps the best approach is to nudge states toward good governance through the use of soft power such as reporting and rankings mechanisms. Or perhaps full nationalization of all welfare programs should be on the table after all. The point of this book is not to provide a single answer but to bring out ways to improve how federalism in the antipoverty context works in practice. Full agreement about an ideal version of federalism may be impossible, but, without question, there is a need to pay more attention to the tremendous power that the particular version of federalism built into particular programs has to shape whether federalism helps or hurts the poor.

Holes in the Safety Net begins with three chapters that set the stage for many of the other chapters in the book. Debates about cash welfare play an outsized role in public perception of antipoverty programs and of the poor, and Part I, Chapters 1 through 3, focuses on such assistance and shows the extensive reach of welfare rhetoric. Part II, Chapters 4 through 8, looks at state antipoverty efforts and at state administration of various antipoverty programs. The chapters in Part II cover diverse topics, ranging from the imposition of work requirements on rural poor populations to the bureaucratic interests behind state administration of the federal food stamp program. Collectively they show the way federalism, as it operates in practice, helps and hurts the poor. Part III focuses on advocacy. Chapter 9 focuses on health care reform and Chapter 10 focuses on the work of poverty lawyers, but both chapters share an appreciation for expanding protections for the poor within the federal structure. The last chapter, Chapter 11, provides a holistic vision of antipoverty advocacy going forward.

Before introducing each chapter, it is worth acknowledging that the topics covered in particular chapters defy easy characterization and bleed across the book's loose three-part structure. There is no right way to read *Holes in the Safety Net*. The chapters can be read individually and out of sequence. That being said, the complexity of the relationship between poverty and federalism comes across best

---

[53] *See, e.g.,* Jamila Michener, Fragmented Democracy: Medicaid, Federalism, and Unequal Politics 15, 168 (2018); Sheryll D. Cashin, Federalism, *Welfare Reform and the Minority Poor: Accounting for the Tyranny of State Majorities*, 99 Colum. L. Rev. 552, 618–26 (1999).

from reading the book as a whole. Aspects of federalism that may work well for one program may contribute to a race to the bottom in another, and the conservative versus liberal politics of one program may be reversed when it comes to a different form of aid to the poor. Although the chapters vary in their approach, with some focused on policy changes over time and others focused on how federalism impacts the poor today, together they paint a vivid picture of the relationship between federalism and the major antipoverty programs. The hope is that this book, written by some of the leading poverty law scholars in the United States, contributes to the work of poverty advocates at both the national and state levels.

Part I: Welfare and Federalism

Professor Wendy Bach argues in Chapter 1, "Federalism, Entitlement, and Punishment across the US Social Welfare State," that poverty programs are wrongly treated as separate and distinct from the way the government provides subsidies across the income spectrum. As Bach shows, government benefits enjoyed by the nonpoor such as favorable tax treatment of employment-based health insurance are normalized and operate largely behind the scenes. In contrast, assistance to the poor is closely monitored and often punitive. The form that federalism takes, the chapter argues, changes from joint federal and state administration when it comes to the poor, to largely federal for those subsidies that flow to the wealthy.

Chapter 2, "Laboratories of Suffering: Toward Democratic Welfare Governance," written by Monica Bell, Andrea Taverna, Dhruv Aggarwal, and Isra Syed, details the policies and politics behind the TANF program. The chapter provides a history of cash welfare programs and details the broad authority Congress granted states when it passed welfare reform. Using Illinois and Kentucky as examples, the authors highlight the divergent paths states are allowed to follow under TANF. The chapter ends by arguing that if federalism is to live up to its promise of supporting democratic participation, more needs to be done to protect the participation rights of the poor, who are currently sidelined when it comes to welfare policy.

Unfortunately for the poor, states, particularly conservative "red" states, are extending the punitive policies of welfare reform and applying them to other means-tested programs. Chapter 3, "The Difference in Being Poor in Red States versus Blue States," shows how work requirements, family caps, and drug testing have migrated from TANF to other programs in what Michelle Gilman labels "welfare creep." Federalism, Gilman argues, creates space for conservative politicians at the national and state level to punish the poor, the result being a patchwork of policies that make poor people's rights and benefits highly dependent on where they happen to live. Though federalism promises innovation, Chapter 3 highlights that in practice it has created a split in benefit levels between more generous blue states and more punitive red states.

Part II : States, Federalism, and Antipoverty Efforts

Chapters 4 through 8 offer in-depth explorations of the interplay between antipoverty efforts and federalism, with an emphasis on the role of states. The chapters focus on the nuts and bolts, how programs work in practice – how they benefit the poor and how levels of government interact – not on the theoretical benefits of cooperative federalism.

Chapter 4, "States' Rights and State Wrongs: Supplemental Nutritional Assistance Program Work Requirements in Rural America," highlights the mismatch between work requirements and the limited employment options available in rural parts of the country. Rebecca H. Williams and Lisa Pruitt show that the recent push to impose work requirements on SNAP beneficiaries seems to be divorced from the barriers to employment in rural areas. The chapter uses Maine's experience with work requirements to show how such policies harm the poor.

Any discussion of government assistance to the poor is incomplete if the analysis does not include tax policies. Part of the justification given for welfare reform, at the time and after the fact, is that the EITC expanded to provide substitute aid to the working poor. But federal tax policies are only part of the story, as Professor Francine Lipman shows in Chapter 5, "State and Local Tax Takeaways." Though federal taxes are mildly progressive, meaning the wealthy pay more than the poor, state and local taxes are regressive for a variety of reasons. For those committed to helping the poor but with limited knowledge of tax, the chapter serves as tax primer, focusing on the way state and local taxes burden the poor. As Lipman highlights, in addition to state efforts that build upon federal initiatives, such as state-level EITC programs, there is a great deal that states and localities can do to help the poor and move away from their dependence on regressive tax structures.

Chapter 6, "Early Childhood Development and the Replication of Poverty," highlights the importance of early childhood education and experiences on human development and explores the different ways states help (or fail to help) poor children during this crucial period. After providing a summary of the scientific studies finding that support, stability, and interactions from birth until age five provide the foundation for later outcomes in life, Professor Clare Huntington notes that experiences of poverty in early childhood can have lasting impacts on school readiness and lifetime earnings. Effective state interventions exist, and Huntington emphasizes that whether a state is predominantly Republican or Democrat does not seem to be determinative when it comes to state funding for early childhood programs.

While Chapter 6 includes some hopeful examples of red and blue states stepping up to help the poor, Chapter 7, "States Diverting Funds from the Poor," describes the dark side of poverty programs and federalism. Professor Daniel Hatcher presents example upon example of states behaving badly. As Hatcher shows, states routinely divert money meant for the poor to fill holes in their general budgets. Contracting with private firms that specialize in maximizing federal outlays, states treat poor people as sources of revenue but do not use those revenue streams to benefit the poor. Hatcher argues that states revenue maximization and diversionary strategies must be stopped, as they are antagonistic to the purposes of these federal-state antipoverty programs.

Though SNAP (formerly food stamps) is thought of as a federal program, Chapter 8, "States' Evolving Role the Supplemental Nutritional Assistance Program," details the important role states play administering the program. Though benefits are federally funded, administration of SNAP is left to the states. Professor David Super's in-depth exploration focuses on the history of state SNAP administration and on the groups that support and attempt to influence the direction of the program. The chapter challenges common understandings of federalism in antipoverty efforts by showing the importance of state administration even in the context of SNAP, a supposedly "federal" program.

Part III: Advocacy

Chapter 9, "Federalism in Health Care Reform," focuses on the most controversial part of the safety net over the past decade. It examines the history of incrementally expanding health care coverage for the poor and the political compromises in the name of federalism that expansion has required. Professor Nicole Huberfeld shows that states often are granted authority to deviate from the standards and priorities of national health care programs such as Medicaid, not because such deviation furthers health care goals, but because of political expediency. Huberfeld considers whether the political trade-offs have been worthwhile and highlights the way the Trump administration has used waivers to undercut the Affordable Care Act.

In Chapter 10, "Poverty Lawyering in the States," Andrew Hammond describes the often state-centric practice of poverty lawyering and the many constraints on poverty lawyers. As the chapter shows, ever since the US Supreme Court balked at expanding the rights of the poor after *Goldberg*, state-level practice has become central to the work of poverty lawyers. Hammond notes that limited funding, practice area restrictions, and even the limited legislative capacity of many state governments make the work of poverty lawyers today particularly challenging. Whether pushing for state enforcement of existing rights under the various poverty programs or pushing for the recognition of rights as a matter of state law, much of the "action" in the field involves state law and administrative decisions at the state level.

The book ends with a broad look at the history and future of the nation's antipoverty efforts. Chapter 11, "Conclusion: A Way Forward," argues that the Left needs to coalesce around economics as a way to promote economic justice, not just for the poor and near poor but also for the middle class. The chapter emphasizes that antipoverty programs lift large numbers of people out of poverty. Though universal basic income proposals seem to be popular right now, Professor Peter Edelman urges caution because of the danger that such proposals will be co-opted as a way to weaken existing programs. This final chapter calls for increased attention to the connections between poverty and race and poverty and place, and illustrates the point through examples of successful, multifaceted community efforts. Successful efforts, Edelman shows, are dynamic, network based, and responsive to the needs of the poor.

CONCLUSION

Debates about the nature of poverty can seem a bit tired, mere reflections of the political fights of the 1990s. But since welfare reform, much has been learned about how cooperative federalism works in practice. This book seeks to bring our understanding of the importance of the structure of antipoverty efforts into the present and to highlight how program design affects poor people. By connecting history with ongoing debates about the role of the federal government and the states in responding to poverty, *Holes in the Safety Net* provides concrete examples of how poverty federalism functions in practice. The many competing interests at stake when it comes to states, the federal government, cooperation across levels of government, program flexibility, and the rights of the poor mean that the relationship between poverty and federalism is destined to be contested territory far into the future.

The relationship between federalism and antipoverty efforts cannot be reduced to a simple preference for federal or for state authority. The advantages of federalism – the ability to bring decisions down to lower levels of government, the possibility such devolution will further democratic participation, and the possibility that state involvement will lead to innovation – have powerful rhetorical appeal. They may even prove true in some circumstances. By contrast, the federalism of antipoverty programs is not without disadvantages. States have taken advantage of federalism to redirect federal money away from the poor and politicians have weakened the country's safety net by disguising their intentions behind the rhetoric of federalism. The way in which the country helps the poor is up for grabs as politicians debate radical proposals to undermine the basic structure of the social safety net under the banner of federalism. Since the New Deal, providing for the poor has been a joint effort of federal, state, and local governments, but welfare reform showed that politicians can replace long-standing federal protections for the poor with block grants to the states. Armed with that lesson, conservatives in Congress are using the rhetoric of states' rights and local control to challenge the welfare state.

The Great Recession brought increasing attention to the struggles of the poor, but not necessarily agreement about what should be done to aid them. The promise and danger of state primacy when it comes to protecting the most vulnerable cannot be ignored, nor should federalism be treated as a matter of secondary importance when policy reforms are debated. In practice, federalism is not singular. It is instead dynamic, it is contested, and its contours vary across programs and across time. Most importantly, questions of federalism matter because of the significant impact they can have on the lives of the poor.

PART I

Welfare and Federalism

Federalism, Entitlement, and Punishment across the US Social Welfare State

Wendy Bach

The agency encourages "meritorious innovations that build on the human dignity that comes with training, employment and independence."

Tom Price, Secretary of Health and Human Services, and
Seema Verma, Administrator, Centers for Medicare and Medicaid Services

In the 2018 letter[1] quoted in the preceding text, the Trump administration announced that it was open to proposals to include work requirements and other changes in state Medicaid programs. These proposals came in the form of administrative waiver requests that would allow particular states the flexibility to change the rules of Medicaid eligibility in their state. They were seeking permission to condition the receipt of Medicaid on compliance with work requirements and to "align" the Medicaid program with programs like Temporary Assistance to Needy Families (TANF). The Obama administration had consistently rejected such requests on the grounds that work requirements did not further the aims of the Medicaid program, but the Trump administration felt no such qualms, likening Medicaid to TANF (colloquially welfare) and arguing that, just like welfare recipients, Medicaid recipients needed to be incentivized to work to "build" their dignity. This contest, like many others in the field of social welfare policy, plays out on the terrain of federalism. It is, on the surface, a battle over control among levels of government and over the appropriate rules and structures for particular programs. But, this chapter argues that these controversies over legal structures, legal rules, and the location of governance, are better understood as arguments about both deservingness and control played out through controversies about administrative structure. In short, programs are called "welfare," or are urged by some to be more

---

[1] Letter from Tom Price, Secretary of Health and Human Services, and Seema Verma, Administrator of the Centers for Medicare and Medicaid Services, to state governors regarding their openness to innovation in the Medicaid Program (Mar. 14, 2017), www.hhs.gov/sites/default/files/sec-price-admin-verma-ltr.pdf.

like "welfare," when what is really meant is that we wish to use the administrative mechanisms of federalism to control, stigmatize, punish, and deter recipients. In contrast, when we perceive recipients as entitled, these mechanisms fall away to be replaced by purely federally controlled, far less visible, and far more inviting administrative structures. To make this process visible, this chapter describes the administrative tools of benefit programs as well as the corresponding cultural assumptions tied to each program and then contextualizes a debate like the one over Medicaid work rules using this context.

To begin, it is crucial to provide a brief theoretical background, to situate conversations about US poverty programs within a larger frame of social support across socioeconomic class, and to challenge some basic and common assumptions about who does and does not receive benefits. This chapter begins with that theoretical framework, proceeds to a (re)description of the US social welfare state to include not only poverty-based programs but also significant support programs targeted at those of substantial wealth. The chapter then demonstrates that the administrative structures of US social welfare provisions operate on a continuum from highly stigmatizing and restrictive mechanisms for the poor to nearly invisible entitlement structures for the wealthy.[2] The chapter then returns to the preceding example and to the argument that these contests over rules and structure are best understood as arguments about deservingness being played out through deceptively neutral-seeming rhetoric and on the terrain of federalism and administrative law. The chapter concludes by arguing that advocates must do more than just respond to these arguments on their face (by demonstrating, for example, that the vast majority of Medicaid recipients already work). In addition, advocates must counter these moral arguments by laying bare the privileging and subordinating assumptions and mechanisms on which they are built. They must assert that, contrary to the assumptions embedded in these arguments, those in poverty, like those of means, are not people in need of our help to acquire dignity but are instead people, deserving of dignity, who should be treated accordingly.

CRITICAL THEORY AND SOCIAL SUPPORT

Critical scholarship plays a key role in describing the state's role in perpetuating and exacerbating the vast economic inequality that characterizes US society. Scholarship focused on these issues identifies ways that the state plays a role in subordinating those at the bottom and facilitating the privilege of those at the top. Not only do these analyses reveal the way that structures operate but they also reveal that arguments about legal rules (for example whether benefit programs should drug

---

[2]   This chapter is based on a more detailed presentation of these arguments in Wendy A. Bach, *Poor Support/Rich Support: (Re)Viewing the American Social Welfare State*, 20 FL. TAX. REV 495 (2017) [hereinafter Bach, *Poor Support/Rich Support*]. Several brief passages within the chapter are taken from that text without inserting quotation marks.

test applicants) – though presented as justified by seemingly neutral and benign ideas – are in fact deeply embedded in cultural constructs about the worthiness of those with and without economic and racial privilege.

Turning first to structurally supported subordination, a wide variety of scholars have described the way that poverty-focused support programs stigmatize, control, and punish the poor. In short, while programs like TANF and public housing do provide some support, they do so at a tremendously high cost. These mechanisms can be understood as part of what I have previously called the *hyperregulatory state* – a set of "mechanisms of social support [that] are targeted, by race, class, gender and place, to exert punitive social control over [disproportionately] poor, African-American women, their families and their communities."[3] So, for example, conditioning welfare on drug testing both conveys the (incorrect) assumption that the poor are more likely to use drugs and exposes women to a heightened of risk of child welfare intervention. Similarly, Kaaryn Gustafson's work on the criminalization of welfare shows that programs are administered in similarly to criminal processing;[4] Dorothy Roberts' scholarship shows the ways in which structures of support subordinate poor, African American women;[5] and Priscilla Ocen's work highlights how community decisions to "police" Section 8 families terrorizes those poor families who had the temerity to relocate into predominantly white suburbia.[6]

Scholars have also laid bare how administrative structures and practices both arise from, and reinforce, deeply held social beliefs about the worthiness of poor families. Scholars like Michele Gilman[7] and Ann Cammett,[8] highlight the powerful role that racially coded cultural imagery of welfare has played in justifying intrusive and punitive policies aimed at poverty-based support programs. More recently, Khiara Bridges's *The Poverty of Privacy Rights* provides detailed and persuasive evidence that the intrusive policies that characterize welfare programs, as well as the constitutional doctrines that consistently fail to protect women from these intrusions, are grounded in cultural beliefs that poor women are fundamentally unworthy of privacy and the dignity it supports.[9]

---

[3] Wendy A. Bach, *The Hyperregulatory State: Women, Race, Poverty and Support*, 25 YALE J. L. & FEMINISM 319 (2014).

[4] KAARYN S. GUSTAFSON, CHEATING WELFARE: PUBLIC ASSISTANCE AND THE CRIMINALIZATION OF POVERTY 1 (2011).

[5] *See, e.g.*, Dorothy E. Roberts, *Prison, Foster Care and the Systemic Punishment of Black Mothers*, 59 UCLA L. REV. 1474 (2012).

[6] Priscilla A. Ocen, *The New Racially Restrictive Covenant: Race, Welfare and the Policing of Black Women in Subsidized Housing*, 59 UCLA L. REV. 1540 (2012).

[7] Michele Gilman, *The Return of the Welfare Queen*, 22 AM. U. J. GENDER & SOC. POL'Y & L. 247(2014).

[8] Ann Cammett, *Deadbeat Dads and Welfare Queens: How Metaphor Shapes Poverty Law*, 34 B.C. J. L. & SOC. JUST. 233 (2014).

[9] KHIARA M. BRIDGES, THE POVERTY OF PRIVACY RIGHTS (2017).

The focus on the way poverty programs reinforce subordination is complemented by another body of critical scholarship focused on those with economic privilege. Our benefit structures do not simply subordinate those in poverty, they also reinforce the privilege of those at the top. Martha McClusky's scholarship on the rhetoric of neoliberalism and welfare programs is emblematic of this work. As she explains, "[N]eoliberalism embraces a racialized, genderized, and class-biased vision of social equity and community solidarity that favors the interests of the most privileged members of society."[10] The state favors those interests by actively enabling the interests of privileged actors through the seemingly neutral concepts of efficiency and moral hazard. McClusky unmasks the central efficiency arguments of neoliberalism by asking a crucial question: efficient for whom? She then encourages those who defend welfare to broaden their arguments:

> [D]efenders of welfare should challenge the double standard underlying the neoliberal double bind, and the hierarchical vision of citizenship it both obscures and promotes. This double standard identifies some people's interests in increasing their share of the pie as part of an efficient and naturalized market that benefits the public, while others' interests in increasing their share of the pie are instead labeled redistributive, and therefore potentially harmful to the public well-being.[11]

As McClusky demonstrates, the idea that the provision of social welfare to the poor is "inefficient" and results in "moral hazard" is entirely dependent on whose interests are centered. If the central good being promoted is participation in the low-wage labor market, then the provision of welfare is inefficient. Welfare is both inefficient and creates a moral hazard by enabling and perhaps incentivizing recipients to stay out of the market. But if one redefines the social goal as promoting a society in which jobs provide a living wage, welfare starts to look different. By providing economic support, welfare is efficient and creates a moral benefit by strengthening the bargaining position of poor workers and incentivizing employers to provide a living wage. Turning to another example, McClusky contrasts the societal approbation for welfare with support for tax cuts for the wealthy. McClusky argues that these are moral rather than economic judgments. "By identifying welfare recipients' gains as inefficient moral hazard and tax cuts for the wealthy as promoting an efficient market, [scholars] implicitly [affirm] a citizenship vision in which the poor have subordinate moral status."[12] McClusky's analysis also suggests that, rather than continuing to look solely at state structures that function to subordinate, we also need to look at the structures that elevate or sustain privilege. Heeding McClusky's call, the following section turns to this wider view of the US social welfare state.

---

[10] Martha McClusky, Efficiency and Social Citizenship: Challenging the Neoliberal Attack on the Welfare State, 78 Ind. L. J. 783, 785 (2003).
[11] *Id.* at 806.
[12] *Id.* at 832.

THE US SOCIAL WELFARE STATE: LARGER AND LESS PROGRESSIVE
THAN YOU MIGHT THINK

Since at least the 1970s, a variety of scholars have sought to redefine the US social welfare state to include not only traditional benefit programs but also a variety of tax benefits that are "hidden"[13] or "submerged"[14] forms of "Welfare for the Wealthy."[15] Including these benefits in the overall picture of US social welfare reveals a system that is larger in size than popularly believed and that distributes significant benefits regressively, to households with substantial wealth.

In popular culture, the benefits we collectively think about as "welfare" are means tested and heavily stigmatized. TANF (formerly Aid to Families with Dependent Children, or AFDC), the Supplemental Nutrition Assistance Program (SNAP, formerly food stamps), and public housing dominate the national conversation about poverty and social welfare provision. However, these programs fit but one of the three distinct categories of social welfare provision that comprise the US welfare state. The categories, for the purposes of this chapter, are (1) means-tested, nontax-based benefits that individuals receive if they fall below a particular income threshold; (2) social insurance benefits for retirees, their spouses, and dependents, as well as for some disabled individuals; and (3) benefits – like tax expenditures, students loans, and parts of Medicare – that flow largely invisibly to individuals and families through the tax code and other support programs.

Although means-tested benefits and social insurance are the most visible forms of cash and near-cash assistance, the United States also dispenses significant financial assistance to individuals and families in other ways. These benefits have been described by Suzanne Mettler as benefits within the "Submerged State."[16] Mettler contrasts visible benefits, which include both social insurance and means-tested benefits, with other benefits structured to be significantly less visible. According to Mettler, "The 'submerged state' includes a conglomeration of federal policies that function by providing incentives, subsidies, or payment to private organizations or households to encourage or reimburse them for conducting activities deemed to serve a public purpose."[17]

Chief among submerged state programs are tax provisions that simultaneously reduce tax collection and meet social welfare objectives. Often referred to as *tax expenditures*, these provisions are tax rules that are functionally identical to social

---

[13] Christopher Howard, The Hidden Welfare State: Tax Expenditures and Social Policy in the United States 3 (1997).

[14] Suzanne Mettler, The Submerged State: How Invisible Government Policies Undermine American Democracy 16–17 (2011).

[15] Christopher G. Faricy, Welfare for the Wealthy: Parties, Social Spending and Inequality in the United States (2015).

[16] Mettler, *supra* note 14, at 4.

[17] *Id.* at 4.

welfare spending programs in that they provide a financial benefit and "promote some socially desirable objective."[18] As explained by the Congressional Budget Office, "Both tax expenditures and spending programs provide financial assistance for particular activities, entities, or groups of people. Through that assistance, tax expenditures and spending programs alter people's behavior, change the allocation of resources in the economy, and transfer income among households."[19]

The argument that legal rules, colloquially known as "tax breaks," are functionally equivalent to a welfare payment is counterintuitive. Tax breaks, so the argument goes, allow a taxpayer to "keep their own money" whereas welfare is a "handout." But from a budgetary perspective, the two are identical. Both result in a net reduction in revenue to the state and a net cash benefit to the taxpayer. As Christopher Howard explains:

> [W]ith tax expenditures, the government is essentially collecting what taxpayers would owe under a "pure" tax system and simultaneously cutting some taxpayers a check for behaving in certain desired ways, such as buying a home. In a pure system, everyone with the same income would pay the same amount of income tax. In the real world, people with the same income often do not pay the same tax, because some are able to take advantage of tax expenditures while others are not.[20]

When one takes this wider view of the US social welfare state, the extent of spending appears quite different. In 2018, the US government is projected to spend approximately $560 billion on the largest cash and near-cash benefit programs for housing, food, cash assistance, medical care, and child care.[21] The United States will spend approximately $1.67 trillion on social insurance ($615 billion on Medicare and $1.052 trillion on old age and disability insurance).[22] Finally in 2013,[23] the

---

[18] HOWARD, *supra* note 13, at 3.

[19] CONG. BUDGET OFFICE, THE DISTRIBUTION OF MAJOR TAX EXPENDITURES IN THE INDIVIDUAL INCOME TAX SYSTEM 8 (2013).

[20] *Id.*

[21] OFFICE OF MGMT. & BUDGET, FISCAL YEAR 2016 ANALYTICAL PERSPECTIVES OF THE US GOVERNMENT, at Table 25–12 (2017), www.gpo.gov/fdsys/pkg/BUDGET-2016-PER/pdf/BUDGET-2016-PER-9-6-2.pdf (table for "Baseline Net Budget Authority by Function, Category, and Program") [hereinafter Table 25–12]. This figure includes 2018 outlays (all in millions) for Medicaid ($381,521); the Children's Health Insurance Program ($5,700); Supplemental Nutrition Assistance ($83,536); the Supplemental Food Program for Women, Infants and Children ($6,954); state child nutrition programs ($23,196); federally funded housing programs ($45,440); Temporary Assistance to Needy Families ($17,347); Supplemental Security Income ($56,511); the Childcare and Development Block Grant ($2,579). *Id.* Not included in this number are transfer programs focusing on education and training, energy assistance, Veteran's benefits, programs funded to provide services to low-income individuals and communities, and some smaller mean-tested programs. Also excluded, to prevent double counting, are means-tested tax expenditures, the two most significant of which are the EITC ($62,615) and the CTC ($21,508).

[22] *Id.*

[23] For this calculation, despite the obvious downside of using 2013 rather than 2018 data, I have chosen to use these figures because of complications involved in calculating the value of tax

United States provided more than $900 billion to individuals and families through the 10 largest tax expenditures.[24] This figure represents approximately two-thirds of overall tax expenditure spending, roughly 5.6 percent of GDP. Clearly, inclusion of tax expenditures in the category of social welfare spending significantly affects the size of the US social welfare state.

Moreover, although benefit provision remains progressive to a certain degree, it is significantly less progressive than generally assumed.[25] The three categories of social welfare programs benefit very different groups in society. The majority of means-tested benefits go to those in poverty; social insurance goes to nearly all with a progressive distribution overall. In contrast, tax expenditures flow primarily to those in the top quintiles of the economic distribution. While a small percentage of the provisions that the Congressional Budget Office deems tax expenditures benefit those in lower-income quintiles, the vast majority benefit the richest taxpayers – those in the top 20 percent. For the 10 largest tax expenditures in 2013, which again totaled more than $900 billion or 5.6 percent of GDP, "more than half of the combined benefits ... accrue to households in the highest income quintile ... with 17% going to households in the top 1 percent of the population."[26] At this point it should be clear that social welfare programs exist and benefit those across the US income spectrum. But while this is true, what is also true is that these programs are structured quite differently. The following section explores those differences.

---

expenditures. While one can calculate outlays for direct spending programs simply by adding budget items, the calculation of tax expenditures is far more complicated. This is due to a variety of important factors. First, although one can calculate the revenue lost through a particular tax provision, this figure only represents the revenue that the state would gain if the particular provision was repealed and there were no other effects. It therefore does not account for behavioral and market changes that might result. So, for example, it does not contemplate the housing market effects on a repeal of the home mortgage interest deduction, although presumably its repeal would potentially lower market prices and/or lower the amount that a particular family spends on a home. In addition, as explained by the Congressional Budget Office, "the estimated magnitude of a collection of tax expenditures may differ from the sum of the estimate magnitudes of the separate expenditures because of the interactions that arise among expenditures." CONG. BUDGET OFFICE, *supra* note 19, at 9. Finally, estimations "are measured relative to a comprehensive income tax system. If tax expenditures were evaluated relative to an alternative tax system ... some of the 10 major tax expenditures [included in the CBO report] would not be considered tax expenditures." *Id.*

[24] CONG. BUDGET OFFICE, *supra* note 19, at 1. The 10 tax expenditures included in this analysis were exclusions for employer-sponsored health insurance, net pension contributions and earnings, capital gains on assets transferred at death, and a portion of Social Security and railroad retirement benefits; deductions including some taxes paid to state and local governments, mortgage interest payment and charitable contributions; and two tax credits, the EITC and the CTC. *Id.*

[25] For a more detailed discussion of the relative progressivity of US social welfare spending, see Bach, *Poor Support/Rich Support, supra* note 2.

[26] CONG. BUDGET OFFICE, THE DISTRIBUTION OF MAJOR TAX EXPENDITURES IN THE INDIVIDUAL INCOME TAX SYSTEM 1 (2013).

FEDERALISM AND LEGAL AND ADMINISTRATIVE
VARIATIONS ACROSS CLASS

To lay bare the structural differences along class lines, this section focuses on two
basic areas of social support: cash assistance for households with dependent children
and health insurance. In the first category fall three major programs: Temporary
Assistance Benefits, the Earned Income Tax Credit (EITC) and the Child Tax
Credit (CTC). The second category includes a whole range of programs, two of
which are the focus of this discussion: Medicaid for pregnant women and the
exclusion of employer-paid health insurance premiums from taxable income. As
one moves from the bottom to the top of the income scale, programs generally
transition from joint federal and state administration to federal administration, from
low to high participation rates, from a focus on fraud to a focus on enrolling those
who are eligible, and from the presence to the absence of additional eligibility
restrictions (mechanisms to scrutinize behavior and designed to share information).
These examples clearly demonstrate that we have a wide variety of punitive or
supportive administrative mechanisms; arguments over what rules and to impose
(work requirements, for example) have everything to do with how we view the
beneficiaries of a particular program and the true goals we have for it.

Cash Assistance for Households with Dependent Children

The United States provides significant income assistance to households with
dependent children. For those in poverty, TANF provides the primary benefit.
For those slightly higher on the income scale, the EITC provides support and for
those both in the middle and at the top, the CTC plays this role. Before comparing
the programs, it is important to know some basic facts about each.

   The TANF program was established in 1996 to replace AFDC. In terms of
income quintile, TANF serves households in the bottom quintile (the bottom fifth
of the income scale). As of July 2017, families of three with no other income than
TANF benefits will remain below 60 percent of the federal poverty line in every
state.[27] This amounts to $12,252 in annual income. The program is authorized by
federal law but administered by states through block grant funding. Participating
states receive the block grant to meet loosely defined program objectives. Restrictions in federal law focus not on ensuring that poor households are supported but
instead on banning assistance for certain categories of lawfully residing immigrants,
forcing recipients to engage in work activities, and forbidding recipients from using
certain education and training activities as a means of complying with these work

---

[27] CTR. FOR BUDGET AND POL'Y PRIORITIES, Policy Brief, *TANF Benefits Are Too Low to Help
Families Meet Basic Needs* (Oct. 13, 2017), www.cbpp.org/research/family-income-support/
policy-brief-tanf-cash-benefits-are-too-low-to-help-families-meet.

requirements. In addition, at this point, TANF is quite small, with projected 2018 expenditures totaling just more than $17 billion.[28]

The EITC is a federal tax credit that can both reduce income tax liability and, in some cases, provide a benefit in excess of the tax liability.[29] In contrast to TANF, it is wholly federally administered. Like TANF, the EITC is restricted to households with earned income.[30] Thus, it does not provide any benefits to those in poverty who have not and/or cannot obtain work. Unlike the majority of tax expenditures, the EITC is targeted to low-income households. It phases in as earned income increases above zero and phases out as earned income/adjusted gross income increases above set thresholds. For example, for calendar year 2018 a single parent household with three or more qualifying children will not receive any EITC benefits if adjusted gross or earned income amounts exceed $49,194 (for a married couple filing jointly with three or more dependent children the limit is $54,884).[31] These maximums are misleading, however, because households just below these income levels receive modest EITC benefits. EITC benefits begin to "phase out" or are reduced pro rata when adjusted gross incomes reach far lower levels. So, for example, for a single parent household with three or more children, the family will receive the maximum EITC (in 2018 $6,431) when earned income is at least $14,290 and both adjusted gross income and earned income are less than $18,660 annually.[32] The EITC maximum benefit of $6,431 plateaus between $14,290 and $18,660 for these families. With higher earned and adjusted gross incomes, between $18,660 and $49,194, the amount of the EITC phases out to zero.[33] Thus the EITC provides the most benefits to lower-income households with children. The maximum childless EITC is only $519 in 2018.[34] Nevertheless, aggregate EITC benefits are quite significant in comparison to TANF. In 2017 the Internal Revenue Service (IRS) delivered $65 billion in EITC benefits to 27 million workers and their families.[35]

The CTC is, like the EITC, a federal tax credit that focuses on the presence of dependent children in the taxpayer's household and, for lower-income families,

---

[28] OFFICE OF MGMT. & BUDGET, *Fiscal Year 2017 Analytical Perspectives of the U.S. Government*, at Table 25–12 (2015), https://obamawhitehouse.archives.gov/sites/default/files/omb/budget/fy2017/assets/25_12.pdf.

[29] I.R.C. § 32.

[30] The relevant statutory provision, I.R.C. § 32, provides the credit for those with "earned income." Earned income includes all taxable income and wages received from working as well as a limited number of disability benefits received prior to retirement age. *What Is Earned Income?*, INTERNAL REV. SERV. (Dec. 16, 2016) www.irs.gov/credits-deductions/individuals/earned-income-tax-credit/earned-income.

[31] I.R.C. § 32; Rev. Proc. 2018–18, 2018–10 I.R.B. 392.

[32] Rev. Proc. 2018–18, 2018–10 I.R.B. 392.

[33] *Id.* For married filing jointly, the phase-out starts at $24,350 and ends at $54,884.

[34] Internal Rev. Ser., Statistics for Tax Returns with EITC, www.eitc.irs.gov/eitc-central/statistics-for-tax-returns-with-eitc/statistics-for-tax-returns-with-eitc.

[35] Internal Rev. Ser., Statistics for Tax Returns with EITC, www.eitc.irs.gov/eitc-central/statistics-for-tax-returns-with-eitc/statistics-for-tax-returns-with-eitc.

requires work. As of 2018, for most families in receipt of the credit, the CTC will provide a credit of $2,000 per child. While the CTC does play some role in alleviating poverty, as of 2018 the credit has been changed substantially. The recent changes double the amount of the credit from $1,000 to $2,000 (but notably only increase the refundable portion to $1,400); require a Social Security number for qualifying children; and significantly increase the phase-out thresholds for eligible households. The CTC, which previously subsidized families predominantly in the first three quintiles,[36] will now benefit families with modified adjusted gross income up to and above $400,000, well into the top quintile of earners.[37] While families with incomes of $400,000 previously would not have received any CTC benefit, as of 2018 they will receive $2,000 per qualifying child. Many low-income families will not similarly benefit because the credit is only refundable up to $1,400 per qualifying child and is further limited to 15 percent of earned income more than $2,500.[38] As the Center on Budget and Policy Priorities, explains, because of a complicated combination of limited refundability and dependence on earned income, "[t]en million children under age 17 in low-income working families will receive nothing or a token increase of $75 or less from the law's CTC expansion. Another 14 million children will get more than $75 but less than the full $1,000-per-child increase that families with higher incomes will receive."[39]

These three programs vary administratively in crucial ways. As noted in the preceding text, only TANF has joint state and federal administration. In fact, the block grant nature of the program has resulted in a degree of state discretion far broader than even other benefit programs that target the poor. As Michele Gilman makes clear in her chapter in this volume, this form of federalism has not been good for poor people. The other two programs, the EITC and the CTC, are entirely federal. They are created through federal legislation and administered by the Internal Revenue Service.

One of the primary features of benefits at the bottom is the failure of these programs to reach all those who are income eligible. TANF is particularly egregious in this respect. In 1996, when the program was created, TANF served 68 percent of families with children in poverty. But over the last two decades this has fallen precipitously. In 2017, TANF served only 23 percent of those families.[40] This decline is due in large part to the use of restrictive eligibility rules and processes.[41] Moving slightly up the income scale, the EITC is far more effective, reaching 79 percent of

---

[36] Rev. Proc. 2018–18, 2018–10 I.R.B. 392.

[37] *Id.*

[38] I.R.C. § 24.

[39] *New Tax Law Tilted to the Wealthy and Corporations* (Apr. 9, 2018), www.cbpp.org/research/federal-tax/new-tax-law-tilted-toward-wealthy-and-corporations.

[40] CTR. FOR BUDGET AND POL'Y PRIORITIES, Policy Brief, *TANF Reaching Very Few Poor Families* (Dec. 13, 2017), www.cbpp.org/research/family-income-support/policy-brief-tanf-reaching-few-poor-families.

[41] *Id.*

eligible households.[42] Finally, while there is no available data clearly indicating participation rates for the CTC, it is fairly easy to claim on tax returns and likely has participation rates as high or higher than the EITC.

Variability in participation rates seems to arise from several factors including the definition of error used by the administering agency, the resources spent on policing error, and the application and participation rules. When discussing error rates in public assistance programs, programs diverge not on whether they are concerned with errors but on the kinds of error they are trying to avert.

Driven by the imagery of extensive "welfare fraud," agencies administering TANF focus on preventing fraud and punishing those who engage in fraud. In contrast, in more favored benefit programs, the emphasis is not on fraud but on ensuring receipt by eligible households. To accomplish these ends, agencies use diametrically opposed eligibility and error detection processes. For TANF and similar benefits, one must prove eligibility prior to receipt, not only by establishing income and resource eligibility, but also by complying with a wide swath of pre-receipt require-ments. In general, no benefits are received until all requirements are met and any failure to comply (by, for example, missing one of many appointments or failing to provide documentation) can result in rejection of the application. In addition, a household found to have committed fraud faces swift and harsh punishment. In New York, for example, intentional program violations can result in denial of benefits for up to five years as well as a misdemeanor prosecution.

Tax benefits are administered quite differently. When applying for the EITC or the CTC, you simply assert eligibility by checking a box or filling out a form. Benefits are provided on the basis of that assertion. Other errors are pursued through the audit process after receipt. But even within the IRS, one can trace differences in the pursuit of fraud in the EITC versus other tax provisions. While it is true that the EITC is similar to other tax provisions in the use of the postreceipt audit process, the IRS has consistently pursued error in the EITC program more aggressively than other arguably more lucrative errors. While there is no question that the EITC erroneous payment rate is significant, "with estimates ranging from the low to high 20% range" of returns claiming the EITC,[43] there is also no question that the audit rates for the EITC are very high. As Susannah Tahk explains, "[C]laiming the EITC doubles a taxpayer's chances of an audit."[44] The rationale for dedicating IRS resources to these errors, over potentially more significant sources of revenue collection, is unclear. As Nina Olsen, the National Taxpayer Advocate, points out, the cost of EITC errors is dwarfed by the cost of error in other portions of the tax code. Citing IRS data, she notes that, "EITC overclaims account for just seven

[42] Natalie Holmes & Alan Berube, THE BROOKINGS INSTITUTE, *The Earned Income Tax Credit and Community Economic Stability* (Nov. 20, 2015), www.brookings.edu/articles/the-earned-income-tax-credit-and-community-economic-stability/.

[43] Francine J. Lipman, *Access to Tax Injustice*, 40 PEPP. L. REV. 1173, 1193–94 (2013).

[44] Susannah Tahk, *The Tax War on Poverty*, 56 ARIZ. L. REV. 791, 844–45 (2014).

percent of gross individual income tax compliance, while business income under-
reported by individuals accounts for $51.9%," or $122 billion in lost revenue.[45]
Similarly, the US Government Accountability Office has noted' that the focus on
the EITC is misplaced given the far larger sources of revenue potentially available if
audit and collection resources were directed toward other sources of error.[46] Finally,
pursuing tax errors by higher-income households also yields significantly higher
revenues. As Francine Lipman points out, "While less than one-quarter as many
examinations were conducted of tax returns with income from $200,000 to $1
million, those examinations generated more tax revenue than examinations of EITC
filers."[47] In light of such data, it is fair to suggest that the dedication of IRS resources
to the EITC, over other sources of error, represents at least in part, value judgments
on the moral status of different taxpayers.

The EITC, like TANF, is characterized by severe sanctions. Taxpayers
who fraudulently claim the EITC cannot receive EITC benefits for 10 years.[48]
Because the EITC depends on the presence of qualifying children in a taxpayer's
household, the 10-year ban may effectively be a lifetime ban for a family.[49] A claim
made with "reckless or intentional disregard of rules" results in a two-year ban.[50]
Although beginning in 2016 parallel sanctions applied to the CTC,[51] sanctions like
this are virtually unheard of in the tax code. In fact, "[t]here are no analogous
sanctions applicable to other improper positions taken on federal income tax
returns."[52]

Moving to other aspects of administration reveals additional significant differences along the income scale. In a clear feature of benefits at the bottom, applying
for and receiving TANF exposes recipients to scrutiny, punitive rules, and significant
risk of exposure to additional punishment. Applying for TANF involves a series of
face-to-face appointments with various agency personnel. During the application
process, applicants are required to disclose a wide range of personal information and

---

[45] *The National Taxpayer Advocate's 2014 Annual Report to Congress: Hearing before the Sub-
comm. on Gov't Operations, H. Comm. on Oversight and Gov't Reform*, 114th Cong. 25 & n. 83
(2015) (written statement of Nina E. Olson, National Taxpayer Advocate).

[46] US Gov't Accountability Office, GAO-13–151, Tax Gap: IRS Could Significantly
Increase Revenues by Better Targeting Enforcement Resources 8 (2012) ("[E]xams
(both correspondence and field) of taxpayers with positive incomes of at least $200,000
produced significantly more direct revenue per dollar of cost than exams of lower income
taxpayers.").

[47] Francine J. Lipman, *Access to Tax Injustice*, 40 Pepp. L. Rev. 1173, 1193–94 (2013).

[48] I.R.C. § 32(k)(1)(B)(i). A similar rule was added to the CTC by the Protecting Americans from
Tax Hikes Act of 2015 (PATH Act), Pub. L. No. 114–113, Div. Q, § 208(a)(1), 129 Stat. 3040, 3083
(codified at I.R.C. § 24(g)).

[49] I.R.C. §§ 32(c)(3), 152(c).

[50] I.R.C. §32(k)(1)(B)(ii). A parallel rule was added to the CTC for taxable years beginning in
2016. I.R.C. § 24(g); PATH Act, § 208(c).

[51] PATH Act, § 208(a)–(c).

[52] Lawrence Zelenak, *Tax or Welfare? The Administration of the Earned Income Tax Credit*, 52
UCLA L. Rev. 1867, 1894 (2005); *see also* Lipman, *supra* note 36, at 1196 (quoting Zelenak).

are subjected to extensive information-verification procedures. Failure to provide this information or documentation can result in a denial of benefits. Applicants do not receive the benefit by merely proving income eligibility. Instead, during the application process and beyond, they are subject to a wide range of nonincome- and nonasset-related criteria. Just to give a few examples, applicants are often drug tested and or required to participate in prebenefit receipt work programs. Failure to comply with any of these requirements results in denial of the application.

The process is also deeply stigmatizing. As Kaaryn Gustafson has persuasively demonstrated, "Welfare rules assume the criminality of the poor . . . [and] the logics of crime control now reign supreme over efforts to reduce poverty or to ameliorate its effects."[53] Practices like these are a large part of the reason that so many families in poverty do not receive help.

Benefits at the bottom are also characterized by rules limiting increases in benefits as families grow. Although as a general matter, TANF households receive higher benefits when there are more children present in the household, in many jurisdictions, this is not the case. Many states currently have "child exclusion" or "family cap" policies. These policies exclude families from receiving additional assistance if their household size increases as the result of the birth of a child. Like TANF, the EITC has both a family cap and work requirements. Prior to 1996, a family's AFDC benefit was determined by, among other factors, the size of the household.[54] Each child in the household added a very small additional amount to the family's AFDC allotment. After 1996, with repeal of AFDC and enactment of TANF, states were no longer required to provide additional benefits when the household size increased.[55] Since then, many states have implemented caps on budget size that do not rise upon the arrival of additional household members.[56]

Another central feature of TANF is its unrelenting emphasis on work. Although state and local programs had been experimenting with work programs before 1996, the TANF program instituted an aggressive national set of work requirements, requiring nearly every adult on welfare to engage in significant work activities and

---

[53] GUSTAFSON, *supra* note 4, at 1.
[54] Rebekah J. Smith, *Family Caps in Welfare Reform: Their Coercive Effects and Damaging Consequences*, 29 HARV. J. L. & GENDER 151, 152–53 (2006) (noting that under AFDC, "states were required to obtain waivers from the federal government to implement policies such as family caps because they violated the Social Security Act by incorporating eligibility criteria based on behavior").
[55] *Id.* at 153–54 ("The final version of TANF . . . did not require states to implement caps, but instead, by remaining silent, allowed states to continue utilizing existing family cap policies or enact new caps without federal oversight."). In fact, states were not even required to have individual benefit programs. They were merely required, as a condition of receipt of federal TANF funds, to institute programs that met the overall purposes of the federal program. Despite this latitude in federal law, all states retained some kind of cash or cash-equivalent benefit program for households with dependent children.
[56] *See* Erika Huber et al., *Welfare Rules Databook: State TANF Policies as of July 2014: OPRE Report 2015–81*, at 238–39 (2015) (Table L10: Family Cap Policies, 1996–2014).

allowing states to mete out harsh penalties for the failure to comply with these requirements.[57] While there is very little evidence to suggest that these programs successfully linked TANF recipients to employment that would lift their families out of poverty, there is extensive evidence that work requirements, like other nonincome-related program criteria, resulted in widespread application denials and case closings.

Like TANF, the federal EITC contains both a family cap and a work requirement. Although the EITC increases for households with between zero and three children, it is capped at that point. Like the TANF family cap, the maximum benefit is provided to households with three "or more" children.[58] Also like TANF, the EITC contains a work requirement. One can only receive the EITC if one receives work income. Families receiving equivalent incomes from other sources – for example, Social Security Disability – are not eligible for the benefit. As discussed in the following text and as noted by Dorothy Brown,[59] these features are not present in the CTC, a tax expenditure program that benefits higher-income families.

Finally, applying for and participating in TANF exposes applicants to severe potential consequences. Consider Florida's drug-testing law. When implementing that law, the Florida Department of Children and Families instituted procedures that included the sharing of positive drug tests with the Florida Abuse Hotline. As described by the District Court in its decision enjoining the Florida program:

> DCF shares all positive drug tests for controlled substances with the Florida Abuse Hotline. . . . After receiving a positive drug test, a hotline counselor enters a Parent Needs Assistance referral into a child welfare database known as the Florida Safe Families Network. . . . [A] referral is then prepared . . . so that "other appropriate response to the referral in the particular county of residence of the applicant" may be taken. . . . [T]he statute governing the Florida Abuse Hotline authorizes the disclosure of records from the abuse hotline to "[c]riminal justice agencies of appropriate jurisdiction," as well as "[t]he state attorney of the judicial circuit in which the child resides or in which the alleged abuse or neglect occurred." Law enforcement officials may access the Florida Safe Families Network and make such use of the data as they see fit.[60]

---

[57] 42 U.S.C. § 607 (2017) (last amended 2012); *see also* Personal Responsibility and Work Opportunity Reconciliation Act, Pub. L. 104–193, § 103(a)(1), 110 Stat. 2105, 2129 (1996).

[58] I.R.C. § 32(b)(1).

[59] Dorothy A. Brown, *The Tax Treatment of Children: Separate but Unequal*, 54 EMORY L. J. 755, 757–58 (2005).

[60] Compl. at 10, *Lebron v. Wilkins*, 820 F. Supp. 2d 1273 (M.D. Fla. 2011) (No. 6:11 Civ. 01473) (stating that applicants are required to sign a "Drug Testing Information Acknowledgement and Consent Release," which includes, among other provisions, that applicants consent that information on a failed test will be shared with the Florida Abuse Hotline "for review to initiate an assessment or an offer of services.").

Moreover, in many cases, these punitive harms associated with information sharing across agencies are imposed disproportionately on African American women and their children.[61]

Health Insurance

The US system of health insurance includes, of course, a wide range of publicly supported programs including Medicare, Medicaid, programs created and funded through the Affordable Care Act (ACA), and various tax expenditures. This section focuses on two pieces of this puzzle: Medicaid for pregnant women as it is administered in one state and the tax exclusion for employer-provided health insurance.

New York's Prenatal Care Assistance Program (PCAP) is funded through the state's Medicaid program. Like many other poverty-targeted programs, Medicaid for pregnant mothers is enabled through federal law, jointly administered by federal and state agencies, and paid for through a combination of federal and state funds. This arrangement allows for significant flexibility for the states. For example, states have significant discretion in choosing the population of those covered, and states vary widely in the choices they make. So Oklahoma and South Dakota cover pregnant women up to 133 percent of the poverty line[62] while New York covers pregnant women up to 218 percent of the poverty line.[63] States also have considerable discretion in structuring their application process.[64]

Contrary to popular perception, even before the ACA, Medicaid and Medicare were not the only significant means through which the United States provided families with economic support for health insurance. In fact, the United States provides extensive economic support to individuals who receive their health insurance through their employers. This benefit comes in the form of the largest US tax expenditure: the exclusion of employer contributions for health care, health insurance premiums, and long-term care insurance. The way this works is fairly simple. Generally, when employers provide economic benefits to workers, those benefits must be included as earned income. Under this tax provision, employer-provided health care coverage is excluded from taxable income. So, even though the employer is providing something with economic value, that income transfer is not

---

[61] These arguments are presented in significantly more detail in Bach, *The Hyperregulatory State*, *supra* note 3.

[62] CTR. FOR MEDICARE & MEDICAID SERVICES, *Medicaid and Chip Eligibility Levels*, www.medicaid.gov/medicaid/program-information/medicaid-and-chip-eligibility-levels/index.html#footnote4.

[63] *Id.*

[64] Matthew Diller, *The Revolution in Welfare Administration: Rules, Discretion, and Entrepreneurial Government*, 75 N.Y.U. L. REV. 1121 (2000) (noting, in part, the ways in which discretion has shifted to states to manipulate the culture and organization of welfare offices).

taxed, resulting in a net transfer of income from the federal government to the individual. In 2018, these benefits will confer almost $228 billion in economic support to these households of employed individuals.[65]

While Medicaid traditionally focused on families in the lower-income quintiles, the tax exclusion of employer contributions for health care benefits higher-income families at higher rates as you move up the income scale. This is due to two primary factors: the type of employers that offer employer-sponsored health insurance and the way that tax brackets affect the value of the benefit. First, employers at the low end of the economy are simply far less likely to offer health insurance. Second, because income tax rates are progressive, that is they are higher as taxable income increases, the value of an exclusion raises as your income raises. As explained by the Tax Policy Center at the Brookings Institution, this benefit "is worth more to the higher-income families who would be more likely to purchase insurance in the first place. In 2015, less than 30 percent of families in the bottom income quintile were offered [employer-sponsored insurance, or ESI]; for them, the average benefit of the ESI exclusion was less than $10. In contrast, nearly 90 percent of families in the top quintile have ESI offers and the average benefit is almost $3,200."[66]

Like many other benefits at the bottom, the PCAP program is characterized by highly intrusive administrative structures. Khiara Bridges's ethnographic study of the PCAP program provides a detailed description of these requirements.[67] As she documents, a PCAP client must provide extensive personal information to a wide variety of professionals about subjects ranging from her diet, income, history with child-welfare agencies, immigration status, mental health history, relationship history, any history of violence, use of contraception, and parenting plans – all well before she has access to this support. In a striking example of how this plays out, Bridges describes an invasive interview that took place as a part of one woman's application for prenatal assistance:

> What is remarkable about this exchange is that Erica was led into a conversation about a romantic relationship that tragically involved severe, homelessness-inducing violence, the healthiness of her relationship with the father of her children, her earnings capacity, the earnings capacity of the father of her children, and any previous contact that she had had with the welfare state (in addition to answering questions about her history, if any, with tobacco and alcohol products, controlled substances, mental illness, and a host of other issues that I have not

---

[65] U.S. Dep't of Treasury, Office of Tax Analysis, Table 3 (Oct. 16, 2017), www.treasury .gov/resource-center/tax-policy/Documents/Tax-Expenditures-FY2019.pdf (estimating the bene-fit at $227.880 billion for 2018 and $242.880 billion for 2019).

[66] *Tax Policy Center Briefing Book: Key Elements of the U.S. Tax System*, www.taxpolicycenter .org/briefing-book/how-does-employer-sponsored-insurance-exclusion-affect-health-insurance-coverage.

[67] Khiara M. Bridges, *Privacy Rights and Public Families*, 34 Harv. J. L. & Gender 113 (2011).

included in this excerpted portion of the interview) because she was pregnant and had presented herself to a public hospital with the hope of receiving state-assisted prenatal care.[68]

Through these mechanisms, "[P]oor women's private lives are made available for state surveillance... and they are exposed to the possibility of punitive state responses." [69]

The contrast between this application process and the administrative mechanisms of the employer-provided health cost exclusion is stark. The exclusion is "applied for," in the broadest sense, not by the employee who benefits but by the employer who fills out the forms. They are invisible to the beneficiaries. There are no invasive questions, no more hurdles, and no possibility of further punitive intervention. Instead there is only financial support.

VISIBILITY, INVISIBILITY, AND ENTITLEMENT

Clearly, the United States provides government benefits to individuals along the entire income spectrum. This chapter has highlighted this phenomenon in the realms of cash assistance to households with dependent children and health insurance, but the observation holds true across the US social welfare state. While benefits for the poor are visible, stigmatizing, and punitive, benefits for those with means are largely invisible. This invisibility is embedded in the structure of those programs. As Suzanne Mettler explains, the "[H]allmark [of submerged state benefits] is the way they obscure government's role from the view of the general public, including those who number among their beneficiaries. Even when people stare directly at these policies, many perceive a freely functioning market system at work."[70]

If one accepts the premise that these are all social welfare benefits, given by the state to individuals for similar needs (medical care or support of dependent children), then the differences in administration cannot have anything to do with the best or the most efficient administrative mechanism to provide support for dependent children or for health care. Instead, it must have something to do with the recipients. The message is clear: benefits for the nonpoor are not a handout. Recipients of benefits like the CTC and the health insurance premium exemption are entitled to those benefits. There is nothing wrong with these beneficiaries and nothing we need to change about them connected to receipt of the benefit. Unlike the women applying for PCAP, there is no need to ask about their life circumstances, relationships, or plans. For the PCAP recipient, we seem to assume that she needs more than just the prenatal care that she is seeking. Perhaps she has a problem

---

[68] *Id.* at 116.
[69] *Id.* at 131.
[70] METTLER, *supra* note 10, at 5.

with her relationships or her finances. Read in the most generous light, the invasive questions indicate a desire to help with the problems that we assume she has. Read less generously, and perhaps more accurately, we mean instead to shame and deter her. If this is generosity, it is at best generosity inextricable from bias. What is crucial is that we assume she has those problems and is in need of help when we make no such assumptions for recipients of the CTC or the health insurance premium exemption. Unlike the poor and stereotypically black recipients of PCAP or TANF, recipients of those tax benefits are not dependent and therefore do not need to be taught independence. They are not likely drug users. They are not likely frauds. They are not likely criminals. But that is not the case for our image of the poor. Despite the fact that the vast majority of support for the poor goes to white families, our image remains that of the welfare queen. It is only if one accepts these assumptions that the structural differences highlighted in this chapter make sense.

MEDICAID WAIVER REQUESTS

In 2017, the Trump administration, while failing to lead their party to the repeal of the ACA, turned some of its energy to wielding an administrative mechanism to make significant changes to the Medicaid program. The administration used a provision in federal law allowing them to grant waiver requests (called 1115 waivers) to states to do demonstration projects that test new approaches to meeting program-matic aims. Several states proposed changes that sought to align the Medicaid program more closely, as a matter of administration, with programs like TANF and SNAP. States sought waivers to include work requirements, drug screening, and eligibility time limits on the program, all hallmarks of the 1996 welfare reform.

While similar requests had been pending for some time with the Department of Health and Human Service's Centers for Medicare and Medicaid Services (CMS), a letter from Tom Price and Seema Verma, quoted at the opening of this chapter, gave significant cause for hope to those states seeking these waivers. At the start of the letter, Price and Verma provided their justification for this new willingness to consider waiver requests, "The expansion of Medicaid through the Affordable Care Act (ACA) to non-disabled, working age adults without dependent children was a clear departure from the core, historical mission of the program." The ACA – which provided, for the first time, Medicaid coverage for individuals below 133 percent of the poverty level who were not pregnant, disabled, or the parent or caretaker of a dependent child – had changed the rules of the game. For Price and Verma, these recipients were not the "truly vulnerable." Instead, their presence called, by this line of thinking, for a different kind of Medicaid program. The letter went on to encourage states to experiment with work requirements that would "build on the human dignity that comes with training, employment and independence." What is interesting about this framing is the focus on dignity. Although states have certainly sought waivers not just for this population, these new recipients lacked human dignity; to obtain it, they needed a set of administrative rules that provide human dignity for them. The stereotype that poor Medicaid recipients are people not worthy of being treated as already possessing dignity justified the policy.

Several months later, in a letter to State Medicaid Directors from CMS, the agency counseled states that, in implementing work requirements, "CMS supports states' efforts to align SNAP or TANF work or work-related requirements with the Medicaid program as a part of a demonstration authorized under section 1115."[71] While there is an ostensibly benign reason for this suggestion (an individual receiving multiple benefits should be subject to just one uniform work requirement), another clear message comes through. The attempt embodied in the ACA to create an entitlement to health care for all, including nondisabled poor individuals without dependents, sent the wrong message. Work requirements, like drug testing, and time limits are hallmarks of benefits for the poor and are heavily racially coded. They assume that the poor, unlike the wealthy, are in need of behavioral control. They assume that poor people are in need of our teaching. And we know this because we have other administrative mechanisms at our disposal that we choose not to use. When we provide the CTC or the exemption for health care expenses or a whole list of other benefits for the wealthy, nothing about how we provide those benefits suggests the same set of assumptions. Instead, we signal through our means of administration that wealthy recipients are worthy and entitled to benefits.

CONCLUSION

At the end of the day as advocates, we must continue to make arguments on the merits that respond to proposals presented by those who deem the poor unworthy. In the Medicaid example, we must continue to demonstrate that the vast majority of Medicaid recipients already work and that – if the TANF experience is a guide – the impact of these changes will not be to transition families to work that sustains their families, but instead will simply diminish the number of those in receipt of the benefit. Beyond this, we cannot stop reminding the public of two essential facts. First, that the poor, like those of means, do not need a program to give them dignity. What they need and deserve instead are programs that provide support and that treat them with dignity. Second, for those who suggest that these programmatic elements are the best or most efficient way to run support programs, we must lay bare their assumptions and remind them that we already have the tools at our disposal to treat the poor with dignity. We do so for the rich every day.

---

[71] Dep't of Health & Human Services, State Medicaid Director Advisory Letter, *Opportunities to Promote Work and Community Engagement among Medicaid Beneficiaries* (Jan. 11, 2018), www.medicaid.gov/federal-policy-guidance/downloads/smd18002.pdf.

2

Laboratories of Suffering

Toward Democratic Welfare Governance

Monica Bell, Andrea Taverna, Dhruv Aggarwal, and Isra Syed

"What was it like receiving TANF?," I asked Yolanda.[1] She had been living in her small, spotless subsidized apartment in southwest Washington, DC, for five years. Several years earlier, Yolanda had been relying on Temporary Assistance for Needy Families (TANF), the current iteration of federal cash assistance to the poor, to help make ends meet. After her family was evicted multiple times during her teens, Yolanda wound up homeless and pregnant and living in DC General, the District's largest shelter for unhoused adults.

"The worst. The worst," Yolanda replied. "It was the worst living." "Why?" I asked. "Having a child and stretching money, and being homeless. I was giving them more than I was receiving," she explained. To stay in the shelter, Yolanda had to pay $150 a month, but she only received $298 per month from TANF, leaving her with $148 per month for every other expense. I asked Yolanda how she was able to make these payments. "Cut back on my stuff," she sensibly replied. "I couldn't get a cell phone. If I had a cell phone I couldn't pay the bill." To get by, Yolanda engaged in a common form of black women's entrepreneurship – hair braiding.[2] Because Yolanda did not report the cash income she earned from braiding hair a few times a week, she was technically violating TANF rules. She confided, "I braided and stuff like that. That helped. Just having that TANF was hard."

Yolanda is far from unique in her assessment of life as a TANF recipient. Regina called her more recent experience using TANF "horrible." "I was receiving TANF and they sent us to this workshop. I can't even describe it. I don't have words to say how I felt at that moment. I just knew I had to get out of there." As reflected in other research, these women repeatedly highlighted the indignities of receiving welfare,

---

[1] "I" refers to the first author. We use pseudonyms to protect interviewees' identities.
[2] *See, e.g.,* Monica C. Bell, *The Braiding Cases, Cultural Deference, and the Inadequate Protection of Black Women Consumers,* 19 Yale J. L. & Feminism 125, 133–36 (2007).

such as the interminable welfare office wait times. They often characterize these experiences as status-based disregard, not standard-issue bureaucratic inefficiency.[3]

Andrica had been in an abusive relationship, and she left her former partner three years ago after he attacked their infant daughter. Andrica is still haunted by the sight of a man she thought she loved picking up their child and then dropping her onto the floor of their cramped apartment. Andrica worries that her daughter has been seriously harmed, and she wants to tell someone what happened – a nurse, a doctor, a therapist. Yet she worries that child welfare officials will disbelieve her, will accuse her of abuse and potentially take her children, because she is a TANF recipient.

"They would misinterpret," she predicted, "and then I'd have cops at my house for something that happened when she was five months old. I'm trying to convince them that it happened at blah-blah-blah, and they're not listening. They probably wouldn't listen to me because of the situation that I'm in." "The situation that you're in?" I asked. "Welfare, public housing," Andrica replied. "I don't think they would believe me if I said it just happened when she was five months. They would look at me in disbelief. I don't think they would believe me." Surprised that she attributed a potential lack of credibility to welfare as opposed to, for example, race or gender,[4] I sought further clarification. "So, you think that because of the public housing and the TANF, they wouldn't believe you?" "Yes, they wouldn't believe me," Andrica confirmed. TANF receipt, even in a relatively generous jurisdiction like DC, has far-reaching and often unanticipated repercussions.

In policy discussions about TANF, the voices and life experiences of those who rely on welfare cash assistance are often lost or flattened. Yet, their policy assessments and ideas are critical for understanding the stakes of TANF policies and structures. State officials are completely free to decide the amount of subsidies, to select the vendors who provide various programs and services, to organize how officials understand and respond to TANF recipients, and even to route TANF funds into programs that are only tangentially related to cash assistance or its recipients. In some jurisdictions, families must be utterly destitute, as Yolanda was, to receive a small subsidy, while others allow minimal assets and a vehicle. In some jurisdictions, advocates and officials propose destigmatizing welfare receipt partly to avoid situations like Andrica's;[5] in many others, stigma is a freely wielded

---

[3] *E.g.*, Sharon Hays, Flat Broke with Children: Women in the Age of Welfare Reform 109–12 (2003); Carter M. Koppelman, *"For Now, We Are in Waiting": Negotiating Time in Chile's Social Housing System*, City & Comm'ty 504 (2018); Vicki Lens, *RESPECT: The Missing Policy Tool of Welfare Reform*, 55 Soc. Work 281 (2010); Linsey Edwards, "Poor Timing: Neighborhoods and the Temporal Constraints of Poverty" (July 5, 2018) (unpublished manuscript) (on file with authors).

[4] *See, e.g.*, I. Bennett Capers, *Evidence without Rules*, 94 Notre Dame L. Rev. 867(2019); Julia Simon-Kerr, *Credibility by Proxy*, 85 Geo. Wash. L. Rev. 152 (2017).

[5] *See, e.g.*, Kate Giammarise, *Pittsburgh Nonprofits Work to Remove Stigma Attached to State "Welfare" Agency*, Pittsburgh Post-Gazette, Apr. 15, 2013. For a broader perspective on the importance of destigmatizing welfare receipt and other group statuses for reducing social

tool for cutting benefits rolls. Without meaningful incorporation of poor people into poverty governance as voters, powerbrokers, and decision makers, the welfare federalist experiment will continue to fall short.[6]

The veneration of American federalism relies on its construction of the states as "laboratories of democracy," the notion that "a single courageous State may, if its citizens choose, serve as a laboratory; and try novel social and economic experiments without risk to the rest of the country."[7] Lawyers, judges, scholars, and policy makers celebrate the democratic experimentalism brought to us through "Our Federalism."[8] After the revival of federalist logic by the Rehnquist Court[9] and especially given the rise of progressive federalism in the early 2000s – exemplified by local adoption of policies such as "sanctuary cities," the Kyoto environmental protocols, and others[10] – strong federalism has seemingly overcome its tragic association with ethnoracial subjugation[11] and has come to occupy a morally neutral space that emphasizes the elegance of the system over its implications for substantive policy. Some scholars even suggest that stronger federalism can better protect dissenters and minorities and can, under some circumstances, improve the efficacy of federal statutes.[12]

In this chapter, we provide background on federal cash assistance to poor families, explain current TANF policy, and propose that antipoverty scholars turn their attention to a fundamental precondition of democratic experimentalism: the

inequality, see Michèle Lamont, *Addressing Recognition Gaps: Destigmatization and the Reduction of Inequality*, 83 AM. SOC. REV. 419 (2018).

[6] Critically, we propose meaningful incorporation of poor people as equal participants in our democratic discourse, not the use of poor people's voices as "entertainment" or mere backdrop. See Ezra Rosser, *Getting to Know the Poor*, 14 YALE HUM. RTS. & DEV. L. J. 66, 69 (2011).

[7] *New State Ice Co. v. Liebmann*, 285 U.S. 262, 311 (1932).

[8] *Younger* v. *Harris*, 401 U.S. 37, 44 (1971).

[9] *See, e.g., Lopez v. United States*, 514 U.S. 549, 583 (1995); *Seminole Tribe v. Florida*, 517 U.S. 44 (2006); *City of Boerne v. Flores*, 521 U.S. 507 (1997); *United States v. Morrison*, 529 U.S. 598 (2000); *see also* Norman W. Spaulding, *Constitution as Countermonument: Federalism, Reconstruction, and the Problem of Collective Memory*, 103 COLUM. L. REV. 1992, 2006–14 (2003).

[10] Spencer E. Amdur, *The Right of Refusal: Immigration Enforcement and the New Cooperative Federalism*, 35 YALE L. & POL'Y REV. 87 (2016); Stella Burch Elias, *The New Immigration Federalism*, 74 OHIO ST. L. J. 703 (2013); Pratheepan Gulasekaram & Rose Cuison Villazor, *Sanctuary Policies & Immigration Federalism: A Dialectic Analysis*, 55 WAYNE L. REV. 1683 (2009); Judith Resnik, Joshua Civin & Joseph Frueh, *Ratifying Kyoto at the Local Level: Sovereigntism, Federalism, and Translocal Organizations of Government Actors (TOGAs)*, 50 ARIZ. L. REV. 709 (2008).

[11] Spaulding, *supra* note 9, at 2014–26; *see also* Robert C. Lieberman & John S. Lipinski, *American Federalism, Race, and the Administration of Welfare*, 31 BRIT. J. POL. SCI. 303, 303 (2001) (characterizing African Americans as "the principal victims of American federalism"); Fred O. Smith Jr., *Abstention in the Time of Ferguson*, 131 HARV. L. REV. 2283 (2018).

[12] *See, e.g.,* Heather K. Gerken, *Dissenting by Deciding*, 57 STAN. L. REV. 1745 (2005); Abbe R. Gluck, *Intrastatutory Federalism and Statutory Interpretation: State Implementation of Federal Law in Health Reform and Beyond*, 121 YALE L. J. 534, 538, 569, 572–74 (2011); Cristina M. Rodríguez, *Negotiating Conflict through Federalism: Institutional and Popular Perspectives*, 123 YALE L. J. 2094 (2014).

presence of meaningful and well-functioning democracy that includes the poor.[13] A democratic structure that operates nondemocratically by weakening the political voices of poor people is an insufficient environment for a just approach to welfare. Instead of laboratories of democracy, states in this domain often function as laboratories of suffering[14] – political entities that experiment upon poor people without robust informed consent. While some democratic deficits are likely inevitable in any system, in welfare, we see a governance structure in which the sole direct beneficiaries of the regime are largely shut out of the democratic processes that structure that regime. This arrangement virtually guarantees inefficacious policy.

THE TRAJECTORY OF FEDERAL CASH ASSISTANCE TO THE POOR

An extensive body of scholarship has documented the history and trajectory of the American welfare state and "welfare reform." Recent work has often focused on the Personal Responsibility and Work Opportunity Reconciliation Act of 1996 (PRWORA) which, among other things, eliminated Aid to Families with Dependent Children (AFDC) and replaced it with TANF. AFDC was a flexible but federally administered program, while TANF is a federal block-grant program that gives money to states to do virtually whatever their officials choose. The implementation of TANF led to a massive decline in welfare rolls, from an annual average of 4.73 million families receiving AFDC in 1995 (4.8 percent of all US households), to 1.37 million families receiving TANF in 2016 (1.1 percent of all US households).[15] Leading poverty policy scholars Kathryn Edin and Luke Schaefer argue that TANF brought about the "virtual extinction" of cash welfare assistance to families in America.[16] Other scholars and commentators claim that PRWORA ended welfare altogether.[17]

---

[13] JAVIER AUYERO, PATIENTS OF THE STATE: THE POLITICS OF WAITING IN ARGENTINA (2012); PIERRE BOURDIEU, PASCALIAN MEDITATIONS (2000); KATHRYN J. EDIN & H. LUKE SCHAEFER, $2.00 A DAY: LIVING ON ALMOST NOTHING IN AMERICA 2 (2015); Edwards, *supra* note 3.

[14] To some audiences, the word *suffering* will at first seem biased, perhaps even melodramatic. We draw from sociological and anthropological theory to understand social suffering as enduring collective pain. See JAVIER AUYERO & DÉBORA ALEJANDRA SWISTUN, FLAMMABLE: ENVIRONMENTAL SUFFERING IN AN ARGENTINE SHANTYTOWN 16 (2009); PIERRE BOURDIEU ET AL., THE WEIGHT OF THE WORLD: SOCIAL SUFFERING IN CONTEMPORARY SOCIETY (1993); VEENA DAS, CRITICAL EVENTS: AN ANTHROPOLOGICAL PERSPECTIVE ON CONTEMPORARY INDIA 154 (1996); IAIN WILKINSON & ARTHUR KLEINMAN, A PASSION FOR SOCIETY: HOW WE THINK ABOUT HUMAN SUFFERING (2016). We center suffering to emphasize that welfare's substance and structure have human costs often omitted from econometric approaches to policy making.

[15] Ife Floyd, LaDonna Pavetti & Liz Schott, *TANF Reaching Few Poor Families*, CTR. BUDGET & POL'Y PRIORITIES, Dec. 13, 2017, www.cbpp.org/research/family-income-support/tanf-reaching-few-poor-families.

[16] EDIN & SCHAEFER, *supra* note 13, at 8.

[17] *E.g.*, JASON DEPARLE, AMERICAN DREAM: THREE WOMEN, TEN KIDS, AND A NATION'S DRIVE TO END WELFARE 101–54 (2004); MICHAEL B. KATZ, THE PRICE OF CITIZENSHIP: REDEFINING

Understanding how the United States decided to nearly shutter the federal welfare program requires integrating the social history of welfare, particularly demographic shifts in who receives it; its cultural history, or the shifting social meaning of cash assistance for the poor among bureaucrats, politicians, and the larger public; its intellectual history, or how thought leaders theorized the best ways to address the problem of poverty; its political history, or how power dynamics between and within political parties allowed particular party factions to determine policy approaches to poverty; and its legal history, the oft-overlooked ways courts have sometimes checked and sometimes facilitated state and local discretion with regard to cash welfare assistance, as well as how the administrative state first streamlined and then lost control of the welfare state. A complete history of American welfare would require not only examination of the period from the New Deal forward but also a more detailed explication of the imposition of British Poor Laws in the American colonies, local social work, private charity, poorhouses, indentured servitude, emergency relief, pensions for veterans, and more. Capturing these interlocking histories is beyond the scope of this chapter, but we provide some background here, drawing primarily upon existing historical work.

National Welfare's Early Years

After the Great Depression, the federal government initiated several systems of cash relief designed to reach various categories of poor people. Prior to the Great Depression, localized systems of welfare support prevailed, sometimes through institutions ("poorhouses"), but often through "outdoor relief," such as in-kind provision of food, shoes, clothing, and sometimes cash.[18] Much of the federal government's approach between the onset of the Great Depression and 1935 centered around emergency relief, in recognition that there was little opportunity for family heads to achieve sustainable livelihoods in a vast sea of unemployment that was mostly expanding, and seemingly envisioned the problem of joblessness as a short-term crisis rather than a persistent social problem.[19] This vision of joblessness as a crisis rather than a durable social problem likely stemmed from the federal government's narrow vision of who would benefit from New Deal programs – mostly whites, many of whom outside the rural South were newly thrust

THE AMERICAN WELFARE STATE 317 (2001); GWENDOLYN MINK, WELFARE'S END (1998); *see also* Peter Germanis, Did a Flexible Block Grant for Welfare Spur State Innovation? Absolutely – But That "Innovation" Didn't Help Poor Families (Jan. 14, 2017), https://mlwiseman .com/wp-content/uploads/2016/05/Block-grants-and-innovation.pdf.

[18] CYBELLE FOX, THREE WORLDS OF RELIEF: RACE, IMMIGRATION, AND THE AMERICAN WELFARE STATE FROM THE PROGRESSIVE ERA TO THE NEW DEAL 53–61 (2012), KAREN M. TANI, STATES OF DEPENDENCY: WELFARE, RIGHTS, AND AMERICAN GOVERNANCE, 1935–1972, at 30–33 (2016).

[19] MICHELE LANDIS DAUBER, THE SYMPATHETIC STATE: DISASTER RELIEF AND THE ORIGINS OF THE AMERICAN WELFARE STATE (2012); TANI, *supra* note 18, at 34–38.

into economic vulnerability, not blacks, whose widespread economic vulnerability was long-standing and purposely orchestrated.[20]

In 1935, in response to political unrest following the Great Depression and as part of the New Deal, Congress passed the Social Security Act (SSA).[21] The SSA included a number of new policies designed to relieve the conditions of poverty, such as old-age assistance, unemployment compensation, grants to ensure the health of mothers and children, aid to the blind, and Aid to Dependent Children (ADC), which sought to support children who lacked "parental support or care by reason of the death, continued absence from the home, or physical or mental incapacity of a parent."[22] ADC functioned through matching grants for states supervised by federal agencies, with varying oversight over its decades of existence.

The oft-told story about PRWORA is that it represented a full-throated embrace of federalism as a means of governing the welfare system. This story is true in some sense, but it gives short shrift to long-standing state and local control over federal cash assistance dollars, especially in its first few decades. Even ADC was emblematic of "intrastatutory federalism," or federalism that emerges from state implementation of federal statutes.[23] As political scientists Robert Lieberman and John Lapinski have explained, ADC's passage produced "a motley collection of federalist arrangements" rather than a standardized, national welfare system.[24] Crucial matters of implementation and planning were left to the states, which further relied on devolved municipal government power. Caseworkers, for example, had extraordinary discretion to deny benefits to recipients, with little guaranteed process, for decades. The SSA did wrest some control from state and local entities by requiring that state officials submit their welfare plans for federal oversight to receive matching funds, and the nature of federal control increased over the program's life.[25] But in reality, states were usually the main arbiters of individuals' entitlements. There were many highly visible efforts by state officials to resist federal welfare requirements and to

---

[20] E.g., RICHARD ROTHSTEIN, THE COLOR OF LAW: A FORGOTTEN HISTORY OF HOW OUR GOVERNMENT SEGREGATED AMERICA 63 (2017). On the movement for racial justice and a more democratic New Deal, see PATRICIA SULLIVAN, RACE AND DEMOCRACY DURING THE NEW DEAL ERA 41–68 (1996). On the complex experiences of blacks, Mexican Americans, and white immigrants in New Deal programs, see FOX, *supra* note 18, at 188–280.

[21] See, e.g., FRANCES FOX PIVEN & RICHARD A. CLOWARD, REGULATING THE POOR: THE FUNCTIONS OF PUBLIC WELFARE 45–77 (1971).

[22] Social Security Act of 1935, Pub. L. No. 74–271, tit. IV, § 406, 49 Stat. 627.

[23] Gluck, *supra* note 12, at 547–50. There is a scholarly debate over whether statutory federalism is properly understood as true federalism or mere decentralization. See, e.g., Edward L. Rubin & Malcolm Feeley, *Federalism: Some Notes on a National Neurosis*, 41 UCLA L. REV. 903 (1994); Vicki C. Jackson, *Federalism and the Uses and Limits of Law: Printz and Principle?*, 111 HARV. L. REV. 2180, 2216–23 (1998). This debate is beyond our scope, but we call the current welfare structure "federalist" for our purposes.

[24] Lieberman & Lipinski, *supra* note 11, at 304–5.

[25] TANI, *supra* note 18, at 227.

limit the scope of the program; welfare's "uncooperative federalism" started early.[26] These challenges arose not only in the Deep South states such as Alabama, Mississippi, and Florida, but also in states like New York, Indiana, and Arizona.[27]

Welfare Growth, Welfare Rights

During the 1960s, the welfare rolls underwent an "explosion," more than doubling across the nation.[28] Due in part to movement organizing, nearly 90 percent of eligible poor Americans were receiving AFDC support by the end of the 1960s.[29] Moreover, the demographic profile of the typical ADC recipient changed. In the program's early decades, nearly half of ADC's beneficiaries were children whose fathers had died. But through revisions to the SSA in 1939, survivors of parental death were shifted to receive Old-Age, Survivors and Disability Insurance, which had previously served only the elderly poor. Thus, by the 1960s, less than 10 percent of child beneficiaries had lost their fathers through death, while roughly 65 percent were children of absentee fathers. Before 1940, less than 20 percent of children receiving ADC were black despite deep black poverty, given that states had almost complete control over program eligibility and often excluded African Americans. By the 1960s, however, more than 40 percent of AFDC's child beneficiaries were black, partly because the parallel civil rights and welfare rights movements made it harder to deny African Americans and other minorities access to AFDC.[30]

Although welfare rolls have never been majority black or Latinx, "controlling images"[31] of unmarried black and Puerto Rican women as welfare recipients began to guide political frames and political action on welfare. Before the mid-to-late 1960s, political discourse surrounding welfare focused on its white female recipients. Yet, the changing demographics of the program, along with conservative concern about the civil rights movement, shifted that lens to one that is now overwhelmingly

[26] On uncooperative federalism – state resistance to federal government mandates while carrying out federal policies – see Jessica Bulman-Pozen & Heather K. Gerken, Essay, *Uncooperative Federalism*, 118 YALE L. J. 1256 (2009).
[27] JULILLY KOHLER-HAUSMANN, GETTING TOUGH: WELFARE AND IMPRISONMENT IN 1970S AMERICA 130–31 (2017); TANI, *supra* note 18, at 155–270.
[28] FRANCES FOX PIVEN & RICHARD A. CLOWARD, REGULATING THE POOR: THE FUNCTIONS OF PUBLIC WELFARE 183–84 (1971).
[29] CHARLES NOBLE, WELFARE AS WE KNEW IT: A POLITICAL HISTORY OF THE AMERICAN WELFARE STATE 98 (1997); Rebecca M. Blank, *What Causes Public Assistance Caseloads to Grow?*, 36 J. HUM. RES. 85, 87 (2001).
[30] Lieberman & Lipinski, *supra* note 11; Sarah A. Soule & Yvonne Zylan, *Runaway Train? The Diffusion of State-Level Reform in ADC/AFDC Eligibility*, 103 AM. J. SOC. 733, 736 (1997).
[31] PATRICIA HILL COLLINS, BLACK FEMINIST THOUGHT 69–73 (2d ed. 2000); *see also* ANGE-MARIE HANCOCK, THE POLITICS OF DISGUST: THE PUBLIC IDENTITY OF THE WELFARE QUEEN (2004); HAYS, *supra* note 3; KOHLER-HAUSMANN, *supra* note 27, at 131.

racialized.[32] In addition to race and family structure, concerns about the place of the federal government in juxtaposition to the states and shifting social meaning of work post–World War II also contributed to ambient discontent with federal cash assistance to poor families.[33]

Social spending as a percentage of gross national product had also doubled between the early 1960s and the mid-1970s. Professor Charles Reich declared governmental redistribution including ADC as "the new property," predicting that, "[a]s we move toward a welfare state, [government] largess will be an ever more important form of wealth."[34] It was during these years that the grassroots welfare rights movement, led largely by black mothers who received welfare, gained mainstream power and recognition. Perhaps the leading welfare advocacy organization during this period, with tens of thousands of members, was the National Welfare Rights Organization (NWRO). NWRO saw itself as the architect of a "poor people's movement."[35] From its birth in the mid-1960s through its shuttering in 1975, NWRO collaborated with various organizations, including Legal Services attorneys, to pursue at least three goals: ensuring that qualified poor families received the benefits to which they were entitled, pushing back against sustained efforts to curtail or eliminate government benefits to poor families, and advancing a rights-based framework for welfare.

Congress and federal bureaucrats tried to shield ADC from the ire of its detractors through both substantive policy and more cosmetic reforms. For example, SSA amendments passed in 1962 renamed the program AFDC in an attempt to increase its palatability, along with other modifications intended to quiet the fever-pitch criticism.[36] One of the most substantively important 1962 amendments allowed states to seek waivers of certain AFDC requirements from the Department of Health, Education, and Welfare (HEW) to experiment with new welfare programs, so long as the department believed their experiment would likely promote AFDC's broad goals.[37] In 1967, Congress amended the SSA to add a work incentive, administered by the Department of Labor, that allowed states to refer certain people in their caseload to work and training programs. To slightly ease the potential burden of this policy change on families, Congress included a provision that would exempt a small portion of earnings in calculating AFDC eligibility. Congress also limited federal funding for benefits that would accrue to children of unemployed parents and absent parents.[38]

---

[32] MARTIN GILENS, WHY AMERICANS HATE WELFARE: RACE, MEDIA AND THE POLITICS OF ANTIPOVERTY POLICY 67–79 (1999); Scott J. Spitzer, *The Emergence of Race in National Welfare Politics: The 1962 and 1967 Amendments to AFDC*, 5 THE SIXTIES 75 (2012).

[33] TANI, *supra* note 18, at 152.

[34] Charles A. Reich, *The New Property*, 73 YALE L. J. 733, 778 (1964).

[35] HANCOCK, *supra* note 31, at 44.

[36] Public Welfare Amendments of 1962, Pub. L. No. 87–543, § 104, 76 Stat. 172, 185.

[37] 42 U.S.C. § 1315; *see also* Irene Lurie, *Major Changes in the Structure of the AFDC Program Since 1935*, 59 CORNELL L. REV. 825 (1974).

[38] *E.g.*, Wilbur J. Cohen & Robert M. Ball, *Social Security Amendments of 1967: Summary and Legislative History*, SSA BULLETIN (Feb. 1968), www.ssa.gov/policy/docs/ssb/v31n2/v31n2p3.pdf.

Despite these legislative changes to AFDC, which decisively gave states more leeway to cut their welfare rolls, the Supreme Court provided tentative support for a somewhat more nationally standardized approach to AFDC during the 1960s and 1970s.[39] For example, in *King v. Smith* (1968), the Supreme Court struck down an Alabama regulation denying a child AFDC benefits if the child had a "substitute father" – that is, if the child's mother had a consistent male sexual partner. The Court struck down the regulation on statutory grounds, concluding that Alabama's broad definition of "parent" was out of step with Section 406 of the SSA.[40] In *Shapiro v. Thompson* (1969), the Court struck down statutory provisions in Connecticut, Pennsylvania, and the District of Columbia that required welfare applicants to have resided in their state for at least a year before applying for benefits. The Court concluded that these provisions unconstitutionally discriminated against welfare recipients, violating their right to interstate travel.[41] *Goldberg v. Kelly* (1970) was perhaps the most foundational piece of the Supreme Court's welfare jurisprudence during this period, declaring that welfare was a statutory entitlement. Thus, states could not arbitrarily terminate welfare recipients' benefits. State officials had to provide due process, including notice and an opportunity to be heard, before cutting off cash assistance to a family.[42]

Yet the Court stopped short of declaring welfare a constitutional right and declined to see poverty as a suspect classification. Only two weeks after announcing its ruling in *Goldberg*, the Court issued its decision in *Dandridge v. Williams* (1970),[43] upholding a Maryland family cap provision that set a $250 monthly maximum for AFDC grants irrespective of the size of the family. The plaintiffs, poor parents who each had eight children, argued that the provision violated both the SSA and the Equal Protection Clause. Plaintiffs' constitutional claim was that the cap discriminated against large families in deprivation of their fundamental right to welfare, thereby violating the Fourteenth Amendment's Equal Protection Clause.

---

[39] *E.g.*, Elizabeth Bussiere, (Dis)Entitling the Poor: The Warren Court, Welfare Rights, and the American Political Tradition 84–98 (1997).

[40] 392 U.S. 309 (1968). Although the language of the Alabama law targeted "cohabitation," the state defined cohabitation as a consistent sexual relationship (perhaps once a week, perhaps once every six months) – regardless of the man's actual residency. *Id.* at 314.

[41] 394 U.S. 618 (1969); *see also Dunn v. Rivera*, 404 U.S. 1054 (1972), affg mem. 329 F. Supp. 554 (D. Conn. 1971) (declaring unconstitutional "emergency" residency requirements implemented after *Shapiro*); *Saenz v. Roe*, 526 U.S. 489 (1999) (holding that giving lower benefit amounts to welfare recipients because of the short duration of their state residency violates their right to interstate travel). In *Shapiro*, the Court had originally written a majority opinion ruling for the state, concluding that wealth is not a suspect classification. The Court reheard the case the next term and reached this statutory conclusion. Bussiere, *supra* note 39, at 102–4.

[42] *Goldberg v. Kelly*, 397 U.S. 254 (1970).

[43] 397 U.S. 471 (1970). On the constitutional theory underlying a Fourteenth Amendment welfare right, see Frank I. Michelman, *Foreword: On Protecting the Poor through the Fourteenth Amendment*, 83 Harv. L. Rev. 7 (1969).

However, while acknowledging that the case involved "the most basic economic needs of impoverished human beings,"[44] the majority applied rational basis review, declining to see welfare as a fundamental right that would trigger heightened scrutiny of the family cap law. In reaching its decision, the Court reaffirmed the centrality of state control over the welfare system, noting that "the federal law gives each State great latitude in dispensing its available funds."[45] Nonetheless, these cases taken together set a minimal baseline of standardization across states, thereby shifting welfare policy realities somewhat further in a nationalist direction. At the same time, *Dandridge* – especially coupled with *Wyman v. James* (1971), which held that requiring welfare recipients to subject themselves to home searches did not violate the Fourth Amendment – signaled the apparent end of expanded constitutional welfare protections.[46]

"New Federalism"

The 1970s brought still more changes to welfare, motivated by widespread unease with the program and its beneficiaries. For example, in 1971, HEW mandated that states establish procedures to detect and punish welfare fraud, creating and expanding specialized welfare fraud units, "midnight raids" on welfare recipients' homes, and more.[47] In his first term, President Nixon proposed eliminating ADC and replacing it with an expansive universal basic income for families, again hoping to alleviate backlash against welfare programs targeted toward the poor.[48]

Yet, attacks on AFDC landed most squarely during the 1980s. Charles Murray, a conservative public intellectual, gained notoriety by lamenting the moral hazard associated with welfare, arguing that AFDC promoted nonmarital childbirth and undermined the work ethic of poor people.[49] President Ronald Reagan took up Murray's argument and constructed his central domestic policy agenda against black "welfare queens," while championing a "New Federalism" that would result in a sharp

---

[44] *Id.* at 485.

[45] *Id.* at 478.

[46] *Wyman v. James*, 400 U.S. 309 (1971); TANI, *supra* note 18, at 268–69.

[47] KOHLER-HAUSMANN, *supra* note 27, at 131–33, 184–205; Spencer Headworth, "Policing Welfare: From Provision to Punishment in Public Assistance 42" (May 4, 2018) (unpublished manuscript) (on file with authors).

[48] KOHLER-HAUSMANN, *supra* note 27, at 134–40; Scott J. Spitzer, *Nixon's New Deal: Welfare Reform for the Silent Majority*, 43 PRESIDENTIAL STUD. Q. 455, 456 (2012). The question of whether income-support policy should be explicitly targeted by race and/or by class motivated much intellectual debate during the 1970s and 1980s. *See, e.g.,* DAVID ELLWOOD, POOR SUPPORT (1989); WILLIAM JULIUS WILSON, THE TRULY DISADVANTAGED 109–24 (1985); Theda Skocpol, *Targeting within Universalism: Politically Viable Policies to Combat Poverty in the United States, in* THE URBAN UNDERCLASS 411, 414 (Christopher Jencks & Paul E. Peterson eds., 1991).

[49] *See* CHARLES MURRAY, LOSING GROUND 218 (1984).

devolution of poverty governance to states and territories.[50] Amid hysteria over the crack cocaine "epidemic," those "welfare queens" were routinely portrayed as crack addicts who used government assistance to subsidize unsavory and unspeakable activities.[51] And, unlike in the 1960s and early 1970s, there was no longer a democratically engaged, grassroots social movement to disrupt prevailing images of welfare recipients., Even though they often represented or governed some of the highest-poverty areas, the rising number of black elected officials were unreliable allies of the poor.[52]

Reagan initially set out to shift responsibility for welfare governance – and welfare's funding burden – to the states. But his proposal unsurprisingly encountered resistance from state and local officials. Shifting power to the states also meant imposing costs upon the states.[53] The National Governors Association called Reagan's initial welfare plan "unacceptable"; its spokesperson explained, "The Governors view welfare as a national, or Federal, responsibility because national economic policy largely determines how many people need welfare and what level of assistance should be provided."[54] The organization favored shifting some responsibilities to the states, but wanted to limit the shift to policy areas it argued were more firmly within state control, such as education and transportation.[55] Later, Reagan backed away from his proposal to *fully* shift funding responsibility and instead proposed a more gradual shift toward revenue sharing.[56] When introducing the proposal during his 1983 State of the Union Address, President Reagan labeled it a "comprehensive federalism proposal that will continue our efforts to restore to States and local governments their roles as dynamic laboratories of change in a creative society."[57]

Yet, even as the Reagan administration embraced federalism with its right hand, its left hand sought and implemented policies that usurped welfare governance power from states and localities. It is important to note, first, that curtailing welfare had been one of Reagan's signature agendas as governor of California.[58] As president, Reagan was willing to expand federal control to cut welfare and other aid to the poor. For example, Reagan's first budget, the Omnibus Reconciliation Act of 1981 (OBRA), set a $1,000 asset limit for AFDC eligibility across all states and territories. This change stripped subnational governmental power to determine their

---

[50] *See, e.g.,* KATZ, *supra* note 17, at 317–25; Soule & Zylan, *supra* note 30.

[51] *See, e.g.,* CRAIG REINARMAN & HARRY G. LEVINE, *Crack in Context: America's Latest Demon Drug, in* CRACK IN AMERICA: DEMON DRUGS AND SOCIAL JUSTICE 1 (1997).

[52] On the complex relationship between black elected officials and the black poor during this period, see, for example, JAMES FORMAN JR., LOCKING UP OUR OWN: CRIME AND PUNISHMENT IN BLACK AMERICA 13 (2017).

[53] For more on this fiscal federalism problem, see David A. Super, *Rethinking Fiscal Federalism,* 118 HARV. L. REV. 2544 (2005).

[54] B. Drummond Ayres Jr., *Reagan Plans Welfare Shift to States,* N.Y. TIMES, Aug. 14, 1981, at A8.

[55] *Id.*

[56] Robert Pear, *Reagan Modifies "New Federalism" Plan,* N.Y. TIMES, Jan. 26, 1983, at A17.

[57] Ronald Reagan, President of the United States, Address before a Joint Session of the Congress on the State of the Union (Jan. 25, 1983).

[58] KOHLER-HAUSMANN, *supra* note 27, at 142.

own limits, as they had been doing since 1935.[59] This and 21 other changes to AFDC under OBRA made about 15 percent of the caseload no longer eligible for the program.[60] OBRA also cut funding for food stamps and Medicaid.[61]

The Family Support Act of 1988 (FSA) – an unhappy compromise bill between conservatives, progressives, and moderates – mandated that every state and territory adopt a new work and training program. That program, Job Opportunities and Basic Skills (JOBS), was generally flexible but still set numerous work participation guidelines that states were expected to implement. The FSA also set guidelines for other major changes to state welfare programs, which in turn affected municipal governments.[62] As the executive director of the US Conference of Mayors said in 1983 in response to Reagan's welfare reform proposals (to the *New York Times*), "Why is it … that this Administration, which says it wants to make things easier for local governments, keeps telling us what we want or need?"[63] The answer, perhaps, was that strong federalism was a mere instrument; ending welfare was the goal.[64]

Welfare (b. 1935, d. 1996?)

As the 1990s began, conservative and moderate discontent with AFDC was still at fever pitch. A recession in the late 1980s produced a slight increase in the welfare rolls, and states had difficulty contributing funds to the JOBS program. Official statistics suggested that less than 8 percent of welfare recipients had a full-time or part-time job.[65] To be sure, research suggests that many AFDC recipients *did* work, but often off the books, finding it virtually impossible to meet their families' basic needs with either welfare alone or low-wage work alone.[66] (Yolanda's strategy was

---

[59] *See* Leah Hamilton, Ben Alexander-Eitzman & Whitney Royal, *Shelter from the Storm: TANF, Assets, and the Great Recession*, SAGE OPEN (2015), https://doi.org/10.1177/2158244015572487.

[60] *E.g.*, U.S. GEN. ACCOUNTING OFF., AN EVALUATION OF THE 1981 AFDC CHANGES: FINAL REPORT 10–11 (1985); Blank, *supra* note 29, at 87.

[61] Headworth, *supra* note 47, at 15.

[62] *See, e.g.*, John O'Connor, *US Social Welfare Policy: The Reagan Record and Legacy*, 27 J. SOC. POL'Y 37, 46–47 (1998). For example, states were directed to adopt AFDC-UP, an offshoot of AFDC that allowed unemployed fathers to live with their dependent children without disqualifying them from receiving welfare benefits.

[63] Pear, *supra* note 56.

[64] *See* Sheryll D. Cashin, *Federalism, Welfare Reform and the Minority Poor: Accounting for the Tyranny of State Majorities*, 99 COLUM. L. REV. 552, 568 (1999) ("That federalism is often used as a stalking-horse for other substantive ends is at least suggested by the lack of consistency among many would-be federalists"). Some conservatives reject this instrumentalist mode of federalism. *See, e.g.*, Ernest A. Young, *The Conservative Case for Federalism*, 74 GEO. WASH. L. REV. 874 (2006) (making a Burkean argument for federalism).

[65] *E.g.*, Gary Burtless, *Employment Prospects of Welfare Recipients*, *in* THE WORK ALTERNATIVE: WELFARE REFORM AND THE REALITIES OF THE JOB MARKET 71, 76 (Demetra Smith Nightingale & Robert H. Haveman eds., 1994).

[66] KATHRYN EDIN & LAURA LEIN, MAKING ENDS MEET: HOW SINGLE MOTHERS SURVIVE WELFARE AND LOW-WAGE WORK 42–44, 218–21 (1997).

not new.) In addition, AFDC also covered a considerable number of parents with serious disabilities who did not qualify for federal low-income disability benefits (SSI), suggesting that many welfare recipients were unable to work.[67] Yet, the political portrayal of welfare recipients as hapless (black or Latina) women living on the dole for no reason held considerable power, and the counterargument could not be that many welfare recipients were working – but perhaps fraudulently collecting welfare as well. There was no good way to unsettle the perception that welfare recipients did not work, and it was politically infeasible to oppose work.

Bill Clinton pushed to end welfare long before he became president. As a leader in the National Governors' Association, Clinton had helped build support for the FSA.[68] A former president of the moderate Democratic Leadership Council, Clinton saw the Democratic Party's image – prowelfare, protax, weak on crime and "traditional family values" – as a serious weakness.[69] In *Putting People First*, Clinton-Gore campaign's official campaign book, the candidate called for welfare to be available for just *two* years to poor families, after which they would find a traditional job or be expected to do a community service job.[70] Yet the original proposal was part of a bundle of antipoverty measures, such as guaranteed work and, most prominently, health care. Expanding health care coverage was the centerpiece of Clinton's domestic agenda during his first two years as president, and it was intended to alleviate one of the major hardships associated with employment – losing guaranteed health care coverage from Medicaid.[71] The Clinton administration hoped health care legislation would assuage the concerns of progressive Democrats and set the stage for bipartisan welfare reform. However, the plan, spearheaded by First Lady Hillary Clinton, failed and set the stage for a resounding defeat for House Democrats in 1994.[72]

During the 1994 campaign, GOP congressional leaders promoted a "Contract with America" that proposed, among other changes, a "Personal Responsibility Act" that would "[d]iscourage illegitimacy and teen pregnancy by prohibiting welfare to minor mothers and denying increased AFDC for additional children while on welfare, cut spending for welfare programs, and enact a tough two-years-and-out provision with work requirements to promote individual responsibility."[73] The GOP

---

[67] *See, e.g.,* Pamela J. Loprest & Gregory Acs, *Profile of Disability among Families on AFDC,* URBAN INSTITUTE: ELEVATE THE DEBATE (Aug. 1, 1996).

[68] Diana M. Zuckerman, *Welfare Reform in America: A Clash of Politics and Research,* 56 J. SOC. ISSUES 587, 588–89 (2000).

[69] *See* Jon F. Hale, *The Making of the New Democrats,* 110 POL. SCI. Q. 207, 222 (1995).

[70] BILL CLINTON & AL GORE, PUTTING PEOPLE FIRST: HOW WE CAN ALL CHANGE AMERICA 165 (1992).

[71] Zuckerman, *supra* note 68, at 589–91.

[72] *See* Susan Cornwell, *From "Hillarycare" Debacle in 1990s, Clinton Emerged More Cautious,* REUTERS, June 6, 2016, www.reuters.com/article/us-usa-election-hillarycare/from-hillarycare-debacle-in-1990s-clinton-emerged-more-cautious-idUSKCN0YS0WZ.

[73] Contract with America, http://global.oup.com/us/companion.websites/9780195385168/resources/chapter6/contract/america.pdf.

supported none of the additional safety-net provisions that Clinton administration officials had proposed. Antipoverty organizations expressed consternation over the bill that became PRWORA. For example, Marian Wright Edelman of the Children's Defense Fund called PRWORA "a crucial moral litmus test."[74] Several Clinton administration officials resigned in protest of the legislation, citing its failure to deliver comprehensive reform that encouraged work while protecting vulnerable families.[75] Although relatively few politicians came out strongly against welfare reform, some progressives and members of the Congressional Black Caucus did. Rep. John Lewis (D-GA) paraphrased a passage from the Christian gospels, rhetorically inquiring, "What does it profit a great nation to conquer the world, only to lose its soul?"[76]

PRWORA instituted fundamental changes to America's cash safety net. It limited the amount of time federal funding would cover a welfare recipient to five years; if states wanted to cover people for longer, they had to pay for it themselves. It demanded that beneficiaries work or participate in authorized "work-promoting activities" (usually administered by private contractors and extremely variable in quality) for at least 30 hours per week, or be sanctioned through benefit reduction. PRWORA also increased state standards for child support enforcement.[77] Most importantly, it ended welfare's status as a statutory right and instituted a system of block grants to states, which they were not required to spend on cash assistance or even on work programs. States vigorously cut their TANF rolls, which allowed them to redirect some of the block grant to their general coffers.[78]

PRWORA authorized the exclusion of many of society's most vulnerable from receiving welfare benefits. For example, several groups of immigrants, including but not exclusively the undocumented, were barred from TANF eligibility.[79] PRWORA also created collateral consequences for criminal justice involvement. For example, by default, those who had been convicted of drug felonies were barred from

---

[74] Alison Mitchell, *Two Clinton Aides Resign to Protest New Welfare Law*, N.Y. TIMES, Sept. 12, 1996, www.nytimes.com/1996/09/12/us/two-clinton-aides-resign-to-protest-new-welfare-law .html.

[75] *See, e.g.*, Jason DeParle, *Mugged by Reality*, N.Y. TIMES, Dec. 8, 1996 (on David Ellwood); Barbara Vobejda & Judith Havemann, *2 HHS Officials Quit Over Welfare Changes*, WASH. POST, Sept. 12, 1996, at A01 (on Mary Jo Bane and Peter Edelman).

[76] Robert Pear, *Clinton to Sign Welfare Bill that Ends U.S. Aid Guarantee and Gives States Broad Power*, N.Y. TIMES (Aug. 1, 1996), www.nytimes.com/1996/08/01/us/clinton-sign-welfare-bill-that-ends-us-aid-guarantee-gives-states-broad-power.html. *Cf. Mark* 8:36 (King James) ("For what shall it profit a man, if he shall gain the whole world, and lose his own soul?").

[77] *E.g.*, Sarah K. Bruch, Marcia K. Meyers & Janet C. Gornick, *The Consequences of Decentralization: Inequality in Safety Net Provision in the Post-Welfare Reform Era*, 92 SOC. SERV. REV. 3 (2018).

[78] *See, e.g.*, Andrew Hammond, *Welfare and Federalism's Peril*, 92 WASH. L. REV. 1721, 1732 (2017).

[79] *See, e.g.*, Philip Kretsedemas, *Reconsidering Immigrant Welfare Restrictions*, 16 STAN. L. & POL'Y REV. 463 (2005); Michael J. Wishnie, *Laboratories of Bigotry? Devolution of the Immigration Power, Equal Protection, and Federalism*, 76 N.Y.U. L. REV. 493 (2001).

receiving TANF. The legislation also barred "fugitive felons" – people with out-standing felony warrants – from TANF receipt.[80] These exclusions are alarming when examined through the lens of criminal justice inequality: because government has long used the criminal justice system to respond to race-class marginalization in urban space, warrants and drug arrests are often just as much a product of race, disadvantage, and geography as of criminality.[81] Importantly, states *can* opt out of many provisions: most states, for example, have opted out of the drug felon ban.[82] But to opt out, state officials must expend energy and political capital to affirmatively pass legislation. Instead, many states made TANF even more stringent than PRWORA required.[83]

As noted previously, the claim that PRWORA was a watershed moment for federalist *governance* is a bit misplaced. Federalism and localism have always been core to American poverty alleviation, even in the ADC/AFDC era. There was extensive state and local discretion under AFDC, especially given HHS's willingness to freely grant state experimentation waivers in the late 1980s and early 1990s.[84] The text of PRWORA lays bare its mission to advance a strong *national* agenda for welfare reduction and conservative perspectives on family, with strong federalism as its tool. The legislation opens with "findings" that celebrate marriage, which it deems "the foundation of a successful society."[85] It laments the "crisis" of "out-of-wedlock" pregnancy and childbirth, speculating that nonmarital birth causes poor education, school discipline, violent crime, and incarceration.

Thus, PRWORA was a watershed moment for conservative policy making using federalist rhetoric. Despite Bill Clinton's role, PRWORA is better understood as the full realization of President Reagan's "new," politically motivated federalism, with a home outside the courts. Professor Jessica Bulman-Pozen helpfully describes Republican governors' advocacy for welfare reform as "partisan federalism," recognizing that their advocacy "was at once a push to devolve power to the states and a push to move the substantive commitments of welfare policy in a Republican

---

[80] *E.g.*, KAARYN GUSTAFSON, CHEATING WELFARE: PUBLIC ASSISTANCE AND THE CRIMINALIZATION OF POVERTY 51–70 (2011).

[81] *See, e.g.*, ELIZABETH HINTON, FROM THE WAR ON POVERTY TO THE WAR ON CRIME 278–81 (2016); ISSA KOHLER-HAUSMANN, MISDEMEANORLAND: CRIMINAL COURTS AND SOCIAL CONTROL IN AN AGE OF BROKEN WINDOWS POLICING 51–58 (2018).

[82] Maggie McCarty et al., *Drug Testing and Crime-Related Restrictions in TANF, SNAP, and Housing Assistance*, Cong. Res. Serv., Nov. 28, 2016, https://fas.org/sgp/crs/misc/R42394.pdf.

[83] *E.g.*, Sheryll D. Cashin, *Federalism, Welfare Reform and the Minority Poor: Accounting for the Tyranny of State Majorities*, 99 COLUM. L. REV. 552, 556–57 (1999); Wishnie, *supra* note 79, at 495 n. 9. Because state governments cannot go into debt in the way that the federal government can, states struggle to support robust welfare spending over the long term and face constant pressures to cut.

[84] *See, e.g.*, Susan Kellam, *Welfare Experiments: Are States Leading the Way Toward National Reform?*, 4 CQ RES. 793 (1994).

[85] Personal Responsibility and Work Opportunity Reconciliation Act, Pub. L. No. 104–193, 110 Stat. 2105, Sec. 101.

direction."[86] Perhaps the governors' views were as balanced as this phrasing suggests, but at the federal level, the scales were tipped more strongly toward the latter push than the former. Welfare reform was not just run-of-the-mill partisan jockeying. Republicans' (and "New Democrats'") advocacy was designed to achieve a *specific* partisan goal of shrinking the welfare state.

WELFARE TODAY

Under current TANF policy, the federal government provides a block grant, or fixed amount of funding, to each state to provide cash welfare and antipoverty services to needy families with children.[87] States must contribute some of their own funds to these programs and abide by federal program requirements, including, for example, limits on the length of time that families can receive aid and a requirement that a minimum share of recipients engage in work.[88] As noted previously, TANF cash assistance is now a miniscule program, covering only about 1 percent of American families even though 12.7 percent of all Americans, and 18 percent of American children, were living in poverty in 2016.[89] Instead of TANF cash assistance, the main source of federal income support for poor families – poor *working* families – is the Earned Income Tax Credit (EITC).[90]

Although states were not completely disempowered in the ADC/AFDC era, states today almost completely determine core aspects of the program, like eligibility criteria and benefit levels, and may exercise substantial discretion in how to implement the program's federal requirements. This flexibility results in wide policy variation across states and introduces state political economy dynamics into all program decisions.[91] Intense system variation raises questions about the goals of

---

[86] Jessica Bulman-Pozen, *Partisan Federalism*, 127 HARV. L. REV. 1077, 1105–6 (2014).

[87] Gene Falk, *The Temporary Assistance for Needy Families (TANF) Block Grant: A Primer on TANF Financing and Federal Requirement*, U.S. CONG. RES. SERV. (Dec. 14, 2017).

[88] *Id.*

[89] Jessica L. Semega, Kayla R. Fontenot & Melissa A. Kollar, *Income and Poverty in the United States: 2016*, U.S. CENSUS BUREAU (Sept. 12, 2017), www.census.gov/library/publications/2017/demo/p60-259.html.

[90] *See, e.g.*, SARAH HALPERN-MEEKIN ET AL., IT'S NOT LIKE I'M POOR: HOW WORKING FAMILIES MAKE ENDS MEET IN A POST-WELFARE WORLD 100–25 (2015); Sara Sternberg Greene, *The Broken Safety Net: A Study of Earned Income Tax Credit Recipients and a Proposal for Repair*, 88 NYU L. REV. 515 (2013). Notably, the EITC is administered at the federal level, with most states offering their own versions of the EITC. Many of the states with the lowest median and per capita incomes (e.g., Alabama, Kentucky, Mississippi, West Virginia) do not have their own EITC.

[91] *E.g.*, Bruch et al., *supra* note 77. Professor Jonah Gelbach has argued that the "crazy-quilt collection of state programs" makes it difficult from an empirical perspective to identify causes of particular outcomes, thus undermining states as efficacious welfare laboratories. Jonah B. Gelbach, *Uncontrolled Experiments from the Laboratories of Democracy: Traditional Cash Welfare, Federalism, and Welfare Reform*, in THE LAW AND ECONOMICS OF FEDERALISM 110, 182 (Jonathan Klick ed. 2017). To be sure, causal inference from field experimentation is a

the new welfare system, whether current federal requirements are sufficient to ensure that states meet those goals, and the proper role of state policy making in determining which families should receive antipoverty assistance.

This section outlines the federal requirements in TANF and the broad areas of state policy making. It then contrasts two state programs, Illinois and Kentucky, to demonstrate the breadth of state difference and the unanticipated outcomes resulting from the primary role of state political economy dynamics in program decisions.

Federal TANF Requirements

States operate their TANF cash assistance programs under minimal federal policy requirements. Several of these federal requirements formed the most salient aspects of the 1996 welfare reform, appearing to create a strict, punitive federal structure within which states were constrained. For example, the 1996 reform imposed a lifetime limit on receipt of federal TANF cash assistance, required that a minimum share of recipients engage in work, and required that states contribute their own funds (termed "maintenance of effort" funding) alongside federal funding.[92]

However, even the highest-profile federal requirements contain space for substantial state policy choices. For example, while the lifetime limit of 60 months of federally funded cash assistance appears categorical, states may exempt up to 20 percent of the caseload for "hardship," which each state individually defines.[93] States may also use their own funding to provide benefits past 60 months and determine which individuals are barred from receiving aid after reaching the limit (i.e., only one individual or the entire family unit).[94] States may also choose a shorter time limit than the federal maximum.[95] While some of this state discretion entails explicit policy choices, much of the discretion is exercised through subtle, implicit means, by defining certain categories or determining how to measure data points.

The federally required work participation rate allows similar flexibility in measurement and definition that ultimately amounts to wide state discretion. States must

---

challenge across many social policy interventions, not just TANF. *See, e.g.,* Robert J. Sampson, *Moving to Inequality: Neighborhood Effects and Experiments Meet Social Structure,* 114 Am. J. Soc. 189, 224–28 (2008). Yet Gelbach helpfully reminds us of why extreme state policy variation in welfare is detrimental for empirical research: Measuring how a particular intervention led to a particular outcome is almost futile in this policy space, which means states can learn little from each other about what works.

[92] Falk, *supra* note 87.

[93] Linda Giannarelli et al., U.S. Dep't Health & Hum. Servs., Welfare Rules Databook: State TANF Policies as of July 2016 (2017); Megan Thompson et al., U.S. Dep't Health & Hum. Servs., State TANF Policies: A Graphical Overview of State TANF Policies as of July 2016 (May 2018).

[94] Giannarelli et al., *supra* note 93.

[95] *Id.*

achieve a work participation rate of at least 50 percent of all families and 90 percent of two-parent families or face reductions in their federal funding, but states may, within some limits, determine which activities count toward being "engaged in work" and which work-related services to offer.[96] States may receive a "credit" to lower the required work participation rate based on decreases in the caseload, a key and often-utilized alternative for achieving stipulated outcomes.[97]

Some states have also altered their program to boost their work participation rate through changes in recipient population rather than program outcomes. For example, some states have created programs to provide very low benefits, as little as $8 to $10 per month, to working poor families, who are then counted toward the work requirement.[98] Others have shifted nonworking families into assistance programs funded only by the state, which are not subject to TANF guidelines, thus removing them from the population measured by TANF's work participation rate.[99] Ultimately, TANF imposes relatively few federal program requirements on states, and the existing requirements include space for significant state discretion.

Areas of State Policy-Making Discretion

Setting aside the flexibility permitted within federal requirements, many other core policy decisions in TANF are entirely and explicitly within state discretion. States are largely able to choose which families receive cash support, the generosity of that assistance, and the share of TANF funding devoted to cash assistance. This scope of policy-making choice offers nearly a blank slate to design any program related to alleviating poverty.

For individual TANF cash assistance recipients, states determine eligibility for the program, benefit levels, and sanctions for noncompliance with program requirements.[100] These choices vary widely and include a significant number of discrete policy decisions. Eligibility determinations include income thresholds, limitations on assets, which members of the household are included in these calculations, special rules around families without children, and whether families must complete job searches prior to benefit receipt.[101] Income thresholds, or the maximum net income with which a family can remain eligible, vary considerably, from $269 per month for a family of three in Alabama (roughly 15 percent of the 2018 federal poverty line) to $2,243 per month for a family of three in Minnesota (a bit less than 130 percent of the 2018 federal poverty line).[102] Many states have also begun to offer

[96] Falk, *supra* note 87.
[97] *Id.*
[98] Floyd et al., *supra* note 15.
[99] *Id.*
[100] GIANNARELLI ET AL., *supra* note 93.
[101] *Id.*
[102] *Id.*

or require potential recipients to participate in formal diversion programs prior to receiving TANF cash assistance.[103] These programs provide a lump sum cash payment in place of monthly benefits and aim to defuse an immediate economic crisis without ongoing TANF enrollment.

Once a family has been found eligible, states also develop the formula for determining the level of benefits received, including any safe harbor under which earnings from employment do not decrease TANF cash assistance.[104] Benefit levels vary greatly, from $170 in Mississippi to $923 in Alaska per month for a family of three with no other income.[105] States may require ongoing activities for a family to remain eligible, such as school attendance by minor children and work activities for adults.[106] Finally, states choose the penalties for failure to comply, from full benefit termination to a written warning.[107]

At the program level, states determine which services to provide from a broad array of potential policies. The only requirement is that services meet one of TANF's four stated broad goals: (1) "provide assistance to needy families so that children may be cared for in their own homes or in the homes of relatives"; (2) "end the dependence of needy parents on government benefits by promoting job preparation, work, and marriage"; (3) "prevent and reduce the incidence of out-of-wedlock pregnancies"; and (4) "encourage the formation and maintenance of two-parent families."[108]

States spend an average of 24 percent of TANF funds on basic cash assistance (i.e., cash payments to needy families).[109] Other common uses of TANF funds include refundable tax credits for low-income families, child care and early education, child welfare, job training, nonmarital pregnancy prevention, and programs "grandfathered in" under TANF's predecessor.[110] Many states spend a substantial portion of their funding to support investigating recipients for fraud, sometimes through dedicated welfare fraud units.[111] In some states, more than half of TANF block grant funds are used to fund other, entirely separate systems (e.g., child welfare), raising the prospect that TANF block grant funds may have displaced funding for other required services that previously came solely from the state.[112]

Finally, states' administration of TANF cash assistance also varies dramatically, with several states devolving substantial responsibility to local governments for

---

[103] *Id.*
[104] *Id.*
[105] *Id.*
[106] *Id.*
[107] *Id.*
[108] 42 U.S.C. §§ 601, 604 (2018).
[109] U.S. Dep't Health & Hum. Servs., *TANF and MOE Spending and Transfers by Activity, FY 2016* (Feb. 1, 2018), www.acf.hhs.gov/ofa/resource/tanf-and-moe-spending-and-transfers-by-activity-fy-2016-contains-national-state-pie-charts.
[110] *Id.* States may fund some programs not otherwise eligible for funding under TANF if these programs were in place prior to the 1996 reform.
[111] *See* GUSTAFSON, *supra* note 80, at 63–69; Headworth, *supra* note 47, at 38–47.
[112] GIANNARELLI ET AL., *supra* note 93.

administrative implementation, policy-making responsibility, or both. As of 2010, 14 states granted policy-making authority to counties or other local governments.[113] Their discretion ranges from designing specific aspects of the program (e.g., hours needed to meet work requirements) to receiving a block grant from the state with the ability to design core program elements (e.g., eligibility, benefit levels, require-ments). Some states have gone so far as to argue, in lawsuits alleging noncompliance with federal welfare law, that local governments, not states, bear responsibility for compliance.[114]

This second-order devolution raises further questions about the theory of federal-ism at work in TANF policy. Proponents of local devolution make many of the same arguments as proponents of federalism: local governments, which have the closest contact with individual recipients, better understand the needs of the population and can most effectively translate that understanding into policy choices. Opponents argue that that devolution could lead to a race to the bottom.

Empirical work provides complex results. Professors Byungkyu Kim and Richard Fording find that states with devolution have greater caseload declines and are more likely to use punitive tools like sanctions but have marginally better employment outcomes, which could suggest greater familiarity with the local population and economy.[115] Fording, along with Professors Joe Soss and Sanford Schram, has also found that under first- and second-order devolution, there is sharp heterogeneity in how the racial composition of state and local jurisdictions interacts with the puni-tiveness of cash assistance policy. Generally, states and counties with a larger proportion of black residents tend to be most willing to sanction cash welfare recipients for various infractions, suggesting that devolution produces greater sensi-tivity to prevailing racial attitudes.[116] Studying the attitudes of county-level bureau-crats implementing TANF cash assistance, Professors Celeste Watkins-Hayes and Norma Riccucci find that caseworkers' views of recipients and perceptions of local expectations play a substantial role in their decisions in individual cases.[117] Interest-ingly, Riccucci finds significant county-level variation in TANF implementation and caseworker understanding of program priorities even in a highly centralized

---

[113] *Id.*

[114] Justin Weinstein-Tull, *Abdication and Federalism*, 117 COLUM. L. REV. 839, 847–68 (2017).

[115] Byungkyu Kim & Richard C. Fording, *Second-Order Devolution and the Implementation of TANF in the U.S. States*, 10 STATE POL. & POL'Y Q. 341, 361 (2010).

[116] Richard C. Fording, Joe Soss & Sanford F. Schram, *Race and the Local Politics of Punishment in the New World of Welfare*, 116 AM. J. SOC. 1610 (2011).

[117] CELESTE WATKINS-HAYES, THE NEW WELFARE BUREAUCRATS: ENTANGLEMENTS OF RACE, CLASS, AND POLICY REFORM 186–90 (2009); Norma Riccucci, *Street-Level Bureaucrats and Intrastate Variation in the Implementation of Temporary Assistance for Needy Families Policies*, 15 J. PUB. ADMIN. RES. & THEORY 89 (2005); *see also* Matthew Diller, *The Revolution in Welfare Administration: Rules, Discretion, and Entrepreneurial Government*, 75 N.Y.U. L. REV. 1121, 1130–45 (2000).

state TANF system, indicating that implementation likely varies meaningfully across localities within a state regardless of the level of responsibility formally devolved.[118]

TANF federalism has, in some cases, allowed states to be more generous than the federal government would be. For example, in recent years, at least nine states and the District of Columbia have increased their subsidy amounts. Yet, even the increased subsidy amounts leave families in deep poverty.[119] The suffering, even in "generous" states, persists.

TANF Federalism in Action: Illinois and Kentucky

A closer examination of programs in two states, Illinois and Kentucky, demonstrates the wide range of state policies enacted, the interaction between various policy choices within a state program, and the roles of federal environment-setting and state-level political economy in shaping these choices. Perhaps most importantly, these states show the complexity of where cash welfare assistance now sits in the safety net and the difficulty of defining what constitutes a successful cash welfare program.

Illinois's TANF program spends only 5 percent of total funding on cash assistance to needy families – among the lowest percentage in the nation.[120] More than 80 percent of TANF funding goes to other services for children: 57 percent to child care subsidies, 20 percent to the child welfare system, and 4 percent to early education programs.[121] For every 100 families in poverty in Illinois, only 16 receive TANF. This number is lower than the national average of 23, and it is less than half of the number in other states with traditionally liberal state-level politics (e.g., California, New York, Massachusetts).[122] Illinois provides monthly benefits of $432 to a family of three with no other income, exactly the same as the national median.[123] These families may qualify for the program with up to $840 in monthly income, slightly above the national median, and face no limit on their assets.[124] The initial picture is that Illinois might be one of the tougher places to be a TANF recipient, especially if relying on benefits in a relatively high-cost-of-living place, like Chicago.

However, a more complex picture emerges when examining Illinois's broader ecosystem of cash welfare assistance to poor families. TANF provides only a portion of Illinois's cash safety net for families. Illinois also has an array of solely state-funded

[118] Riccucci, *supra* note 117.
[119] Ife Floyd, *TANF Cash Benefits Have Fallen by More Than 20 Percent in Most States and Continue to Erode*, Center on Budget and Policy Priorities Brief, Oct. 13, 2017.
[120] U.S. Dep't Health & Hum. Servs., *supra* note 109.
[121] *Id.*
[122] Floyd et al., *supra* note 15.
[123] GIANNARELLI ET AL., *supra* note 93.
[124] *Id.*

welfare programs that do not use federal TANF funding and thus are not subject to TANF's stringent federal standards.[125] Beneficiaries of these solely state-funded programs also do not count toward TANF's work participation requirements. Several states have used this type of program to shift certain families – typically those who have a tough time getting or keeping employment because they lack basic skills, struggle to keep housing, have children with behavioral problems, are survivors of intimate partner violence, or have physical or mental health challenges that are not of a type or severity to qualify for disability-based subsidies but that nonetheless make traditional work difficult[126] – off TANF. That way, the state can meet its work participation requirement while still providing cash assistance to destitute families. Illinois's state-funded welfare program serves more Illinois families than the TANF program does, averaging 21,600 monthly cases compared to 18,600 in TANF.[127]

Illinois's policy decisions around TANF highlight a few broader trends. First, many states approach TANF strategically, shifting funding and recipients between various programs to attempt to meet federal requirements and maximize funding, without necessarily changing the services provided to recipients. They try to minimize suffering while heeding the federal call to minimize welfare. Second, assessing how well welfare reduces human suffering within states requires examining not only TANF policies but also total welfare ecosystems, including noncash benefits. Illinois's welfare ecosystem likely alleviates poverty more effectively than its TANF statistics would suggest, even though access to assistance among families in poverty likely remains low. Finally, even in states that traditionally favor liberal policies, the fungibility of TANF funding and other fiscal or political challenges within the state can create strong incentivizes to shift TANF funds away from basic assistance to families and instead use them to displace state spending on other programs.

Kentucky's TANF program provides a useful comparison case. Kentucky devotes 62 percent of funding to basic assistance, the highest share in the nation.[128] Other significant funding shares include job training and education activities (13 percent) and child care (12 percent).[129] In terms of family access to TANF, 20 of every 100 families in poverty receive TANF, slightly below the national average but largely in line with neighboring states (e.g., Tennessee, Ohio).[130] Kentucky's program

---

[125] *See* Ill. Dep't Hum. Serv., TANF Caseload Reduction Report for Fiscal Year 2016 (Dec. 9, 2015), www.dhs.state.il.us/OneNetLibrary/27897/documents/HCD%20Reports/TANF%20Reports/TANFCaseloadReductionReportFY2016.pdf.

[126] *See, e.g.,* Hays, *supra* note 3, at 103; Sandra Susan Smith, Lone Pursuit 141–44 (2007).

[127] *See* U.S. Dep't Health & Hum. Servs., Temporary Assistance to Needy Families: 12th Report to Congress for Fiscal Years 2014 and 2015 (Jan. 25, 2015), www.acf.hhs.gov/sites/default/files/ofa/12th_annual_tanf_report_to_congress_final.pdf; Peter Germanis, The Failure of TANF Work Requirements in 2015: The Need for a Much Better Way (Dec. 18, 2016), http://mlwiseman .com/wp-content/uploads/2016/05/The-Failure-of-TANF-Work-Requirements.2015.pdf

[128] *Id.*

[129] *Id.*

[130] Floyd et al., *supra* note 15.

seems to fare better when examining the number served, without comparison to the poverty rate: Kentucky served an average of 25,300 families per month in 2015, approximately the same number as Virginia or New Jersey, whose populations are much larger.[131]

Examining individual-level policies, Kentucky remains close to the national median on eligibility, permitting eligibility for a family of three with up to $908 in monthly income and assets up to $2,000, with an exemption for all vehicles.[132] Monthly benefit levels, though, fall well below the national median and Illinois: a family of three with no other income receives a maximum benefit of $262.[133] Even in a state that generally has a low cost-of-living, this is a very small subsidy and has remained the same since 1996, despite substantial inflation during that time.[134] (To be sure, the federal TANF block grant to states has remained the same in nominal terms since 1996, at $16.5 billion. The block grant has fallen in real value by one-third during that time due to inflation.[135] Thus, it is not surprising that Kentucky has followed the federal government's lead in its stagnant TANF budget.)

Kentucky's program adds two nuances to our understanding of TANF variation across states. First, the adequacy of a state TANF program varies according to its economic needs and poverty levels. Though serving a high number of families numerically, Kentucky still falls below average when examining the number served compared to the poverty rate. Second, the adequacy of state programs varies over time, and not solely due to policy changes: inflation, economic changes, and other factors can alter the impact of the state's safety net on its citizens.

Potential Contributors to Divergent State Policy Choices

The complexity of state politics and policy decisions make it difficult to delineate a single set of reasons for how specific states make TANF policy. TANF policy sits within complex ecosystems of welfare, criminal justice, child protection, and other aspects of policy environments that are challenging if not impossible to consider in isolation.[136] However, research has suggested several potential contributing factors. First, research suggests that the amount of TANF benefits provided to recipients is substantially impacted by benefit levels in neighboring states, potentially reflecting

---

[131] U.S. Dep't Health & Hum. Servs., *supra* note 127.

[132] GIANNARELLI ET AL., *supra* note 93.

[133] *Id.*

[134] U.S. Dep't of Health & Hum. Servs., *supra* note 127.

[135] Liz Schott, Ife Floyd & LaDonna Pavetti, *How States Use Federal and State Funds under the TANF Block Grant*, Ctr. on Budget and Policy Priorities, Apr. 2, 2018, www.cbpp.org/research/family-income-support/how-states-use-funds-under-the-tanf-block-grant.

[136] *See* Frank Edwards, *Saving Children, Controlling Families: Punishment, Redistribution, and Child Protection*, 81 AM. SOC. REV. 575 (2016).

state fears that generous welfare benefits will encourage in-migration of low-income families.[137] The stringency of state requirements for recipients does not appear impacted by neighboring states, though.[138]

Second, political ideology also appears predictive, with conservative jurisdictions enacting more stringent policies, particularly regarding sanctions on recipients for noncompliance with requirements.[139] Research suggests that this effect occurs at both the state and local level. States with more liberal voters tend to have higher benefit levels and more lenient policies,[140] but even within states, counties with more liberal voters employ sanctions against recipients at lower rates than those with more conservative voters.[141]

Third, the racial composition of beneficiaries appears correlated with TANF policy decisions. Researchers have found that states with higher proportions of African Americans on their caseloads enact more stringent policies than those with lower proportions, and that African American recipients are more likely to face sanctions than white recipients.[142] Policies that place shorter limits on benefit receipt and deny additional TANF benefits to children born while the family is on welfare are also correlated with the racial composition of recipients.[143]

While none of these factors is dispositive, or potentially even causal rather than correlative, they provide some insight into the ideological, political, social, and economic considerations at play in state TANF policy decisions. They also raise questions around whether TANF's current structure achieves the goals of federalism, or even whether safety-net spending is an appropriate forum in which to apply federalist principles.

WELFARE'S FUTURE: TOWARD LABORATORIES OF DEMOCRACY?

Even postwelfare reform, the debate over how much to constrain state welfare governance rages on. The federal government only slightly tweaked the program through a protracted reauthorization process in the early 2000s: Congress directed HHS to limit which activities states could allow for meeting the work participation rate.[144] Most recently, a 2018 bill to reauthorize (and rename) TANF seeks to check

---

[137] Matthew Fellowes & Gretchen Rowe, *Politics and the New American Welfare States*, 48 AM. J. POL. SCI. 362 (2004).
[138] *Id.*
[139] Joe Soss, Sanford F. Schram, Thomas P. Vartanian & Erin O'Brien, *Setting the Terms of Relief: Explaining State Policy Choices in the Devolution Revolution*, 45 AM. J. POL. SCI. 378 (2001).
[140] Fellowes & Rowe, *supra* note 137.
[141] Richard Fording, Joe Soss & Sanford F. Schram, *Devolution, Discretion, and the Effect of Local Political Values on TANF Sanctioning*, 81 SOC. SERV. REV. 285 (2007).
[142] Amanda Sheely, *Devolution and Welfare Reform: Re-evaluating "Success,"* 57 SOC. WORK 321 (2012).
[143] Soss et al., *supra* note 139.
[144] *See* Deficit Reduction Act of 2005, Pub. L. No. 109–171, 7101(c)(1), 120 Stat. 4, 136 (2006); *see also* Noah Zatz, *Welfare to What?*, 57 HASTINGS L. J. 1131, 1140–43 (2006).

states' nearly unbridled freedom to spend TANF funds. The bill requires that at least 25 percent of welfare block grant funds go toward cash assistance.[145] Some critics argue that this threshold is too low to be meaningful, pointing out that only five states (Illinois, Indiana, Kansas, North Carolina, and Texas) are not currently meeting this threshold.[146] Conservative critics, seeing TANF as "something of a mess," are concerned that the proposal will not fix TANF's structural problems.[147] Peter Germanis, an architect of Reagan's welfare agenda, argues that the House bill would fail to cure "the root cause of TANF's problems – the block grant structure and excessive state flexibility."[148] As we illustrate in the Illinois example, diverting TANF funds from cash assistance to other state programs can sometimes allow more generous state-funded cash assistance programs: federal oversight does not imply greater state generosity. Many national commentators across the political spectrum would like to see increased federal control over states' TANF spending.

Given the perpetual debate over welfare's substance and structure, we do not expect major change in the block grant design in the near future. The devolution of cash welfare assistance is now entrenched, and the likelihood of creating a robust national welfare state is virtually nonexistent in the status quo. Indeed, the Left antipoverty movement is now fighting to protect Medicaid and Supplemental Nutrition Assistance (food stamps) from meeting the same fate as cash welfare.[149] Some welfare opponents have even criticized the EITC – a subsidy many conservatives favor because it only goes to workers – claiming that the tax credit is too costly and vulnerable to fraud.[150]

Because strong welfare federalism is with us to stay, the question welfare supporters have been facing is, how can federalism be marshaled to achieve better outcomes for poor families? A full answer to this question is beyond the scope of this chapter.

---

[145] Jobs and Opportunity with Benefits and Services for Success Act, H.R. 5861, 115th Cong. (2018).

[146] LaDonna Pavetti & Liz Schott, *House Bill to Reauthorize TANF Makes Improvements But Doesn't Go Far Enough*, CTR. ON BUDGET & POL'Y PRIORITIES, May 23, 2018, www.cbpp.org/research/family-income-support/house-bill-to-reauthorize-tanf-makes-improvements-but-doesnt-go-far.

[147] Robert VerBruggen, *House Republicans Are Trying to Re-Reform Welfare: Their Bill Is Ambitious – and Risky*, NAT'L REV., May 25, 2018.

[148] Peter Germanis, The House Ways and Means TANF Reauthorization Bill: Fixing the Problems or Just Treating the Symptoms? (June 17, 2018), https://mlwiseman.com/wp-content/uploads/2016/05/VerBruggen.pdf.

[149] *See, e.g.*, Glenn Thrush, *Trump Signs Order to Require Recipients of Federal Aid Programs to Work*, N.Y. TIMES, Apr. 10, 2018, www.nytimes.com/2018/04/10/us/trump-work-requirements-assistance-programs.html.

[150] *See, e.g.*, Shai Akabas & Matt Graham, *The Earned Income Tax Credit: Facts, Statistics and Context*, BIPARTISAN POL'Y CTR., June 12, 2013, https://bipartisanpolicy.org/blog/earned-income-tax-credit-facts-statistics-and-context/. To be sure, the EITC is not without its detractors. More usual criticisms focus on the insufficiency of the EITC to truly root out poverty, given that it has largely replaced welfare. *See, e.g.*, HALPERN-MEEKIN ET AL., *supra* note 90, at 100–25 (2015); Anne L. Alstott, *Why the EITC Doesn't Make Work Pay*, 73 LAW & CONTEMP. PROBS. 285 (2009); Greene, *supra* note 90, at 530–36.

But as a starting point, we return to two key points from the beginning of this chapter. First, democratic experimentalism is widely viewed as a positive aspect of federalism across most of the ideological spectrum and, to some, the essence of our republican government. This is one reason the current structure is unlikely to change soon: it deeply resonates with the American zeitgeist.

Second, to alleviate suffering, policy makers and scholars must take a holistic view of poor people's lives to best design welfare policy. Viewing democratic experimentalism from a grounded perspective, we see that one of the major crises that has plagued welfare since its inception is that poor people have had *so little say* in its content and structure. That is, it has been undemocratic.[151] For roughly one decade in welfare's 73-year history, welfare recipients were part of a movement that shaped the national agenda and pushed against the dehumanization of welfare recipients. Since the demise of the welfare rights movement, families who rely on welfare have become faceless, nameless and, too often, mired in shame. As Regina and Andrica remind us, instead of a survival tool around which poor people rally, TANF receipt is viewed even by its beneficiaries as a hardship and a deeply discrediting status. In lieu of welfare, the penal system has risen to become the central mode of managing the nonworking poor.[152]

One of the long-standing central arguments for federalism has been that it elicits greater democratic participation than centralized governance does.[153] Yet our republic of welfare, despite its federalist moorings, has not functioned well on this measure. It has denied voice, deliberation, and meaningful participation to America's poor, especially the ethnoracially marginal and/or immigrant poor, thus violating their right to meaningful democratic participation[154] and failing to be sufficiently responsive to their concerns.[155] While this failure is not specific to

---

[151] *See, e.g.,* David A. Super, *Laboratories of Destitution: Democratic Experimentalism and the Failure of Antipoverty Law*, 157 U. PA. L. REV. 541 (2008). For an explanation of the importance of democracy with respect to another federal antipoverty program, Medicaid, see JAMILA MICHENER, FRAGMENTED DEMOCRACY: MEDICAID, FEDERALISM AND UNEQUAL POLITICS 11–13 (2018).

[152] *See, e.g.,* BRUCE WESTERN, HOMEWARD: LIFE IN THE YEAR AFTER PRISON 61 (2018).

[153] *See, e.g.,* Franita Tolson, *Election Law "Federalism" and the Limits of the Antidiscrimination Framework*, 58 WM. & MARY L. REV. 2211, 2244–45 (2018) (quoting *Gregory v. Ashcroft*, 501 U.S. 452, 458 (1991)). Newer perspectives see both nationalism and federalism as mere "means to the same end: a well-functioning democracy." Heather K. Gerken, *Federalism as the New Nationalism: An Overview*, 123 YALE L. J. 1889, 1891 (2014). Either way, assessments of democratic participation are central to assessing the value of federalism.

[154] *See, e.g.,* K. SABEEL RAHMAN, DEMOCRACY AGAINST DOMINATION 3 (2016) (explaining that democracy "connotes a constructive, positive commitment to expanding agency, investing in the institutions, civil society associations, and practices that make possible collective political action"); Guy-Uriel E. Charles, *Racial Identity, Electoral Structures, and the First Amendment Right of Association*, 91 CALIF. L. REV. 1209 (2003). For a parallel discussion of incarcerated citizens, see AMY E. LERMAN & VESLA M. WEAVER, ARRESTING CITIZENSHIP: THE DEMOCRATIC CONSEQUENCES OF AMERICAN CRIME CONTROL 229–30 (2014).

[155] Bertrall L. Ross II & Terry Smith, *Minimum Responsiveness and the Political Exclusion of the Poor*, 72 LAW & CONTEMP. PROBS. 197, 212–20 (2009).

welfare, one might find its implication most troubling in this domain: welfare policy most directly affects the poorest Americans, yet poor Americans have long had virtually no power over the institutions and actors that make decisions about welfare policy.

Consider the influence of money in politics, protected under a dubiously expansive First Amendment theory that envisions wealth as a facilitator of speech, such that all but the most local races are financed through corporate largess – a harm to nonaffluent voters that Professor Daniel Tokaji has labeled "vote dissociation."[156] Consider disenfranchisement on the basis of former felony incarceration, a phenomenon that falls heavily on the same subjugated communities that would benefit most directly from a stronger welfare state.[157] Consider *Shelby County* v. *Holder* (2013), where the Supreme Court, in a 5–4 decision, struck down Section 4(b) of the Voting Rights Act of 1965, effectively gutting the provision that required states with a history of race-based disenfranchisement to submit changes to their election policies and practices to the federal government for "preclearance." Race and poverty intersect in several of the affected states; they simultaneously have large racial minority populations and some of the nation's highest poverty rates (e.g., Alabama, Arizona, Georgia, Louisiana, Mississippi).[158] Congress could modify the Voting Rights Act to reinvigorate this provision, but this is unlikely to occur.

Other recent Supreme Court decisions have permitted state curtailment of the right to vote. For example, the Court has rejected a facial challenge to a law that requires voters to show official state ID and has upheld a law that permit state officials to purge registered voters from the rolls if they do not response to a mailed notice.[159] A contextual, sociological view of poor people's lives reveals that these laws seriously imperil their voting rights, given the costs and difficulty of interfacing with street-level bureaucracies, the grind of housing instability, and more.[160] Professor

---

[156] *See, e.g., Buckley* v. *Valeo*, 424 U.S. 1 (1976); *Citizens United* v. *Federal Election Commission*, 558 U.S. 310 (2010); Daniel P. Tokaji, *Vote Dissociation*, 127 YALE L. J. F. 761 (2018).

[157] *See, e.g.,* LERMAN & WEAVER, *supra* note 154; JEFF MANZA & CHRISTOPHER UGGEN, LOCKED OUT: FELON DISENFRANCHISEMENT AND AMERICAN DEMOCRACY (2006); Naomi F. Sugie, *Chilling Effects: Diminished Political Participation among Partners of Formerly Incarcerated Men*, 62 SOC. PROBS. 550 (2015).

[158] 570 U.S. 2 (2013). *Shelby County* struck down Section 4(b), the provision that identifies the jurisdictions that were required to undergo Section 5 preclearance. On the federalist thrust of *Shelby County*, see, for example, Guy-Uriel E. Charles & Luis Fuentes-Rohwer, *State's Rights, Last Rites, and Voting Rights*, 47 CONN. L. REV. 481 (2014); Joshua S. Sellers, Shelby County *as a Sanction for States' Rights in Elections*, 34 ST. LOUIS U. PUB. L. REV. 367 (2015). On the race-poverty nexus in Section 5 preclearance, see Janai S. Nelson, *The Causal Context of Disparate Vote Denial*, 54 B.C. L. REV. 579, 603–4 (2013).

[159] *Crawford* v. *Marion County Election Bd.*, 553 U.S. 181 (2008) (upholding voter ID law); *Husted* v. *A. Philip Randolph Institute*, No. 16–980 (June 11, 2018) (upholding voter purge law).

[160] *See, e.g.,* MATTHEW DESMOND, EVICTED 296–99 (2016); Eva Rosen, *Horizontal Immobility: How Narratives of Neighborhood Violence Shape Housing Decisions*, 82 AM. SOC. REV. 270 (2017); Edwards, *supra* note 3; *see also* Sari Horwitz, *Getting a Photo ID So You Can Vote Is Easy. Unless You're Poor, Black, Latino or Elderly*, WASH. POST, May 23, 2016.

Atiba Ellis has called the collective effect of the Court's voting rights jurisprudence "tiered personhood," an exclusion of "voters of lowest political castes from full participation in the political community based upon assumptions of unworthiness."[161]

Voting is only one means of democratic participation. Yet other means, such as participating in forums, providing comments on new rules that state and local agencies might implement, and taking to the streets are also illusory for many of the most destitute poor, who have the scarcest time and money for organizing. The problem of legal estrangement – a process by which institutions signal to poor people that they are outsiders within their own nation – also chills their democratic participation.[162] Movement building and power sharing will be essential to any successful effort to democratize welfare. Truly heeding the concerns of poor Americans as political equals will be critical to developing more efficacious welfare policy, with a set of goals around which there is consensus. In the status quo, federalist democratic welfare experimentation is generally something done *to* poor people, not with their consent or meaningful choice.

CONCLUSION

When scholars conduct research on human subjects, they are required by law to adhere to a strict ethical code to procure informed consent. When the population studied is a "vulnerable population," including the "economically or educationally disadvantaged," they must meet higher-than-usual standards to minimize risk of harm.[163] We could hold our laboratories of democracy to analogous standards. While scientific laboratories must affirmatively show that they have sufficient processes in place to protect vulnerable populations, federalism norms mean that states-as-laboratories are presumed protective, and members of vulnerable populations bear the burden of showing when state processes fall short.[164] As cash welfare continues its moribund existence, scholars, policy makers, and activists should renew their ethical commitment to democratically engage poor people, especially in welfare governance. This approach, we propose, will make welfare – be it federalist or nationalist – work better for all.

---

[161] Atiba R. Ellis, *Tiered Personhood and the Excluded Voter*, 90 CHI.-KENT L. REV. 463, 466 (2015).

[162] Monica C. Bell, *Police Reform & the Dismantling of Legal Estrangement*, 126 YALE L. J. 2054 (2017).

[163] 45 CFR § 46.111(b); James M. DuBois et al., *Restoring Balance: A Consensus Statement on the Protection of Vulnerable Research Participants*, 102 AM. J. PUB. HEALTH 2220 (2012).

[164] *See, e.g., Younger v. Harris*, 401 U.S. 37, 48–54 (1971); Smith, *supra* note 11, at 2296–2305.

3

The Difference in Being Poor in Red States versus Blue States

Michele Gilman

Pundits tell us that our nation is divided between red and blue states, generally defined by their citizens' support for Republican or Democratic presidential candidates. In the popular imagination, red states are inhabited by pick-up truck driving, church-going, beer-swilling, country music lovers who are politically conservative. By contrast, in blue states, people drive electric cars, sip wine and eat arugula, listen to NPR, and are bleeding heart, godless liberals. Although these dueling stereotypes assume that blue state residents are more affluent, neither considers the lives of low-income people. Nevertheless, a person's experience at the bottom of the economic ladder differs widely depending on where they live, and red state versus blue state policy differences are driving part of that geographic divergence.

These disparities in poverty support have nothing to do with one's beverage or music preferences. Instead, red states generally have more punitive public benefits policies than blue states. This division is likely to widen in coming years as Republican politicians at the federal and state levels increasingly attach "behavior modification" requirements to governmental assistance, using federalism tools such as waivers to do so. For instance, in January 2018, the Trump administration approved the first waivers to states that want to impose work requirements on Medicaid recipients. In the first wave of applications, 10 states applied for waivers; all have Republican governors; eight are Republican controlled in both the executive and legislative branches. A majority of these states are also among the stingiest when it comes to cash assistance benefits under the Temporary Assistance to Needy Families (TANF) (or welfare) program. Meanwhile, the Trump administration is currently floating the idea of allowing states to impose lifetime limits on Medicaid coverage.

Work requirements and lifetime caps are brand new to Medicaid, but they are not new to low-income Americans. In 1996, Congress passed, and President Clinton signed, welfare reform, known as the TANF program, which changed welfare funding from an open-ended federal entitlement to a block grant system. TANF requires that program recipients work within two years of receiving benefits, and it limits lifetime receipt of benefits at five years, although states can – and many do – choose shorter time limits. TANF also permits states to cap benefits at a certain family size (known as family caps), to drug test beneficiaries, and to adopt other methods of attempted behavioral control, such as denying benefits to mothers who do not identify the paternity of their children and cutting benefits to families with truant children.

Upon signing TANF into law, President Clinton announced, "After I sign my name to this bill, welfare will no longer be a political issue. The two parties cannot attack each other over it. Politicians cannot attack poor people over it. There are no encrusted habits, systems, and failures that can be laid at the foot of someone else." Clinton's prediction fell flat, as low-income people continue to be attacked as lazy "takers" and "welfare queens," even though the economy fails to provide a stepping-stone out of poverty for many workers. After 22 years of experience with TANF, the evidence establishes that it fails to meet the needs of poor families. Indeed, the withering of TANF as a safety-net program has increased extreme poverty (or earnings of less than $2 a day), even as the country has climbed out of recession.[1] Nevertheless, Republicans at the federal and state levels are methodically expanding behavior control mechanisms into other public benefits programs, a phenomenon I call "welfare creep." This threatens to worsen poverty overall, but its impacts will likely be harsher in red states. We can expect that poor residents living in red states will face additional layers of disadvantage in coming years, and that behavior modification laws will help propel this divergence. This chapter traces the extent of welfare creep, identifies its causes, and examines its impacts.

WELFARE CREEP

In 1992, Lucie A. Williams wrote about emerging behavior modification proposals, such as Learnfare (conditioning welfare eligibility on regular school attendance) and family caps (denying additional benefits to families that have children while on assistance), that the Bush-era federal government permitted states to adopt under a welfare waiver program. As she wrote, "The idea behind all of these projects is the same: only those women and children who conform to middle class majoritarian values deserve government subsistence benefits."[2] Congress later codified these behavior modification options in TANF, giving states the decision whether to implement them. Today, welfare creep is resulting in "patchwork federalism," in which poor people receive vastly different levels of support depending solely on

---

[1] H. Luke Shaefer & Kathryn Edin, *Welfare Reform and the Families It Left Behind*, PATHWAYS, Winter 2018, https://inequality.stanford.edu/sites/default/files/Pathways_Winter2018_Families-Left-Behind.pdf.

[2] Lucie A. Williams, *The Ideology of Division: Behavior Modification Welfare Reform Proposals*, 102 YALE L. J. 719, 720–21 (1992).

where they live. This part examines the expanding scope of three behavior control mechanisms: work requirements, family caps, and drug tests.

Work Requirements

Work requirements do not work. They neither increase work rates nor reduce poverty for three main reasons: (1) large swaths of the poor are children, the elderly, or disabled, and are not expected to work; (2) many people who want to work either cannot find work or face significant personal barriers to work; and (3) many workers do not earn enough to lift themselves out of poverty. Nevertheless, Republicans are expanding work requirements throughout the safety net.

TANF: TANF imposes work obligations on both recipients and the states, and failure to comply results in sanctions (for individuals) or fiscal penalties (for states). The rules are complex. In brief, and with some exceptions, states must engage half of all single-parent TANF families in work activities for at least 30 hours a week, with higher requirements for two-parent families.[3] A family faces sanctions if a parent fails to meet the work requirements; sanctions can include termination of benefits for the entire family.

TANF supporters tout its success by pointing a 75 percent drop in the welfare rolls since 1996. To be sure, in the immediate aftermath of TANF's enactment, work rates among TANF recipients rose due to the new work requirements and a strong economy, as well as expansions of the Earned Income Tax Credit and child care funding. However, work rates subsequently fell during the recession as welfare leavers struggled to find and keep jobs.[4] Indeed, studies have shown that mandatory work requirements do not lead to higher work participation rates or stable employment over time.[5] Moreover, states removed many families from TANF through stringent eligibility requirements, sanctions, and diversionary tactics.[6] States also used the bulk of their TANF funds for purposes other than cash assistance, such as child care and job training programs, and even to fill state budgetary gaps.[7] All these reasons contributed to the precipitous drop in the number of TANF recipients.

---

[3] For an overview of work requirements, see Heather Hahn et al., Urban Institute, *Work Requirements in Social Safety Net Programs*, Dec. 2017, at 4–6, www.urban.org/sites/default/files/publication/95566/work-requirements-in-social-safety-net-programs.pdf

[4] *Id.* at 5; *see also* Gene Falk et al., Congressional Research Service, *Work Requirements, Time Limits, and Work Incentives in TANF, SNAP, and Housing Assistance*, Feb. 12, 2014, https://greenbook-waysandmeans.house.gov/sites/greenbook.waysandmeans.house.gov/files/R43400_gb.pdf.

[5] MaryBeth Musumeci and Julia Zur, Kaiser Family Foundation, *Medicaid Enrollees and Work Requirements: Lessons from the TANF Experience*, Aug. 18, 2017, www.kff.org/medicaid/issue-brief/medicaid-enrollees-and-work-requirements-lessons-from-the-tanf-experience/.

[6] Falk et al., *supra* note 4, at 19–20.

[7] Liz Schott, Ladonna Pavetti, and Ife Floyd, Center on Budget and Policy Priorities, *How States Use Federal and State Funds under the TANF Block Grant*, Oct. 15, 2015, www.cbpp.org/research/family-income-support/how-states-use-federal-and-state-funds-under-the-tanf-block-grant.

Despite TANF's underlying premise, work is not necessarily a pathway out of poverty because low-wage workers earn very little money (the federal minimum wage has been $7.25 since 2009) and often have unpredictable hours, while also bearing the costs of working, such as child care, transportation, and uniforms. Meanwhile, some people have severe barriers to work, such as limited education, criminal histories, domestic violence, mental and physical disabilities, or addiction issues.[8] Imposing work requirements on these people pushes them deeper in poverty and homelessness.

Housing: The federal government subsidizes housing for low-income people through a variety of programs, including public housing and housing choice vouchers, which pay a portion of rent in the private housing market. Yet only 25 percent of eligible families receive housing assistance due to limited funding.[9] Currently, the law governing subsidized housing programs does not contain work requirements, although most residents of public housing must meet an eight-hour monthly community service or self-sufficiency requirement.

Since 1999, HUD has granted permission to nine public housing authorities (PHAs) and seven housing choice voucher programs to impose work requirements, with the goal of moving residents to self-sufficiency.[10] While the programs vary in terms of the definition of work, hour requirements, and enforcement, residents can face eviction for failure to comply. Trump's 2019 budget included work requirements for all public housing residents.[11] Under his budget, which is being codified in proposed legislation, housing agencies and owners of property that accept subsidized funding could evict or terminate subsidies for households with able-bodied, working-age adults who do not work or participate in training or education programs. Notably, Trump's budget does not include money for services to assist people in obtaining or maintaining work, such as job training, child care, or transportation.

As with TANF, work requirements in housing have not been shown to have a meaningful impact on either work or poverty rates. To begin with, only 6 percent of subsidized households contain working-age, nondisabled members who are unemployed.[12] More than half these households are headed by elderly or disabled residents; these are populations that either cannot or should not be required to work.[13]

---

[8] Musumeci & Zur, *supra* note 5.

[9] Hahn et al., *supra* note 3, at 14 (describing work requirements in subsidized housing programs).

[10] Diane K. Levy, Leiha Edmonds & Jasmine Simington, Urban Institute, *Work Requirements in Public Housing Authorities: Experiences to Date and Knowledge Gaps*, Jan. 2018, www.urban .org/sites/default/files/publication/95821/work-requirements-in-public-housing-authorities.pdf.

[11] Office of Management and Budget, Budget of the U.S. Government, *Efficient, Effective, Accountable: An American Budget, Fiscal Year 2019*, at 64, www.whitehouse.gov/wp-content/ uploads/2018/02/budget-fy2019.pdf.

[12] Alicia Mazzara & Barbara Sard, Center on Budget and Policy Priorities, *Chart Book: Employment and Earnings for Households Receiving Federal Rental Assistance*, Feb. 5, 2018, www .cbpp.org/research/housing/chart-book-employment-and-earnings-for-households-receiving-federal-rental.

[13] *Id.*

A study of work requirements within Charlotte, North Carolina's PHA found modest impacts on work rates and negligible impacts on income. By contrast, numerous studies show that *voluntary* work programs that provide support and services to job seekers and workers are more effective at improving work rates and reducing poverty than mandatory requirements.[14]

Medicaid: Work requirements are expanding into Medicaid, which is the nation's health insurance program for the needy and disabled that covers 74 million Americans. Under the Medicaid program, states can seek demonstration waivers under Section 1115 of the Medicaid statute to experiment with new policies. The Trump administration has advised states that it will approve waivers so that states can require Medicaid recipients to work. By July 2018, the Centers for Medicare and Medicaid Services granted waivers to Kentucky, New Hampshire, Indiana, and Arkansas and was considering seven other similar state requests.[15] A federal judge halted implementation of the Kentucky waiver and sent it back to the Department of Health and Human Services (HHS) for further review.

Experts have long debated the wisdom of work requirements in Medicaid: would they provide a pathway out of poverty or hurt vulnerable people given that health is a precondition to work?[16] A survey of low-income adults in Kentucky found that participants "thought it was unrealistic to assume that requiring people to work as a condition for receiving health insurance would enable them to rise out of poverty and smoothly transition to employer-based coverage."[17] Among the focus group participants, one-third said they were working but earning such low wages that they still qualified for Medicaid. Other participants reported that they struggled to find work due to prior convictions, lack of access to public transportation, or difficulty passing a credit check. Still others were either mentally or physically disabled or homeless.

This survey mirrors nationwide research. Six in ten adults on Medicaid are already working; of those who do not work, 35 percent are disabled, 28 percent are family caregivers, 18 percent are in school, 8 percent are retired, and 8 percent

---

[14] *See* James A. Riccio, MDRC, *Sustained Earnings Gains for Residents in a Public Housing Jobs Program,* Jan. 2019, www.mdrc.org/publication/sustained-earnings-gains-residents-public-housing-jobs-program; Abt Associates, *Evaluation of the Compass Family Self-Sufficiency (FSS) Programs Administered in Partnership with Public Housing Agencies in Lynn and Cambridge, Massachusetts,* Sept. 2017, http://abtassociates.com/AbtAssociates/files/3c/3c791568–51a4–4934-9d99–0c9cef7fdbb9.pdf.

[15] *See* Kaiser Family Foundation, *Medicaid Waiver Tracker: Which States Have Approved and Pending Section 115 Medicaid Waivers?,* May 8, 2018, www.kff.org/medicaid/issue-brief/which-states-have-approved-and-pending-section-1115-medicaid-waivers/.

[16] Jessica Greene, *What Medicaid Recipients and Other Low-Income Adults Think about Medicaid Work Requirements,* HEALTH AFFAIRS, Aug. 30, 2017, www.healthaffairs.org/do/10.1377/hblog20170830.061699/full/.

[17] *Id.*

cannot find jobs.[18] Moreover, a Medicaid work requirement does little to shift people toward employer-based health coverage because the jobs that low-income people obtain, such as in agriculture or food service, typically do not offer health benefits.

SNAP: States are also enforcing work requirements for Supplemental Nutrition Assistance Benefits (SNAP), commonly known as food stamps. Currently, about 40 million people receive SNAP, and the average income of SNAP households is less than $10,000 per year. The average benefit is $126 per person per month (or $1.40 per person per meal); amounts hinge on family size and income.[19] Work requirements are not new to SNAP; Congress authorized them in the 1996 welfare reform law that also created TANF. [20] SNAP requires that able-bodied adults between the ages of 18 and 49 without dependents (known as ABAWD) work 80 hours per month unless they fall within an exception, otherwise they cannot receive benefits for more than three months within three years.[21] States can get waivers from this SNAP time limit if their unemployment rate hits 10 percent. In 2009, during the economic recession, the Obama administration suspended SNAP work requirements nationwide. As the economy improves, however, states are reimposing time limits and work requirements with federal permission.

Republicans are proposing to tighten SNAP's work requirements and time limits further. In February 2018, the US Department of Agriculture (USDA) began soliciting public comment on a proposal to eliminate the remaining time limit waivers, which still exist in five states and parts of 28 other states.[22] President Trump's 2019 budget proposal goes even further. It limits waivers to counties where unemployment is at least 10 percent for more than a year, imposes work requirements on adults between the ages of 50 and 62, and limits work exemptions.[23]

---

[18] Rachel Garfield, Robin Rudowitz & Anthony Damico, Kaiser Family Foundation, *Understanding the Intersection of Medicaid and Work*, Dec. 7, 2017, www.kff.org/medicaid/issue-brief/understanding-the-intersection-of-medicaid-and-work/.

[19] Center on Budget and Policy Priorities, *A Quick Guide to SNAP Eligibility and Benefits*, Feb. 7, 2018, www.cbpp.org/research/food-assistance/a-quick-guide-to-snap-eligibility-and-benefits.

[20] *See* Hahn et al., *supra* note 3.

[21] USDA, Supplemental Nutrition Assistance Program: Able-Bodied Adults without Dependents, www.fns.usda.gov/snap/able-bodied-adults-without-dependents-abawds.

[22] Supplemental Nutrition Assistance Program: Requirements and Services for Able-Bodied Adults without Dependents: Advance Notice of Proposed Rulemaking, 83 Fed. Reg. 8013 (Feb. 23, 2018), www.federalregister.gov/documents/2018/02/23/2018-03752/supplemental-nutrition-assistance-program-requirements-and-services-for-able-bodied-adults-without.

[23] Caitlin Dewey, The Trump Administration Takes Its First Big Step toward Stricter Work Requirements for Food Stamps, WASH. POST (Feb. 22, 2018), www.washingtonpost.com/news/wonk/wp/2018/02/22/the-trump-administration-takes-its-first-big-step-toward-stricter-work-requirements-for-food-stamps/.

Overall, the budget aims to cut SNAP funding by $213.5 billion over 10 years. In support of the budget, Agriculture Secretary Sonny Perdue said, "Too many states have asked to waive work requirements, abdicating their responsibility to move participants to self-sufficiency."[24]

However, his rhetoric does not match the reality. To begin with, SNAP benefits decrease incrementally with income, so there is no disincentive to work. Moreover, according to the USDA, 43 percent of SNAP participants live in a household with earnings.[25] At the same time, 68 percent of recipients are children, elderly, disabled, or caretakers.[26] Unemployed ABAWDs are only about 6.8 percent of SNAP recipients, and this population includes people with serious barriers to work, such as people with criminal convictions, individuals suffering undiagnosed mental illness, veterans, and teenagers aging out of foster care.

Under the leadership of former Republican Governor Scott Walker, Wisconsin has been particularly aggressive in toughening work requirements for SNAP recipients. In 2018, the Wisconsin legislature passed a bill raising the amount of time an ABAWD has to spend job searching, and the state also added parents of children between the ages of 6 and 19 to the list of people who must meet work requirements (although this change will require a federally approved waiver).[27] Since work requirements went into effect in Wisconsin in 2013, 25,000 of 700,000 SNAP recipients have found work; the state does not know what happened to the 86,000 people who lost their SNAP eligibility under these rules.[28] In Michigan, the State Senate passed a bill in April 2018 to require Medicaid recipients to work – but the bill exempts rural, predominantly white districts with high unemployment rates from the requirement. This has led to charges that the proposed legislation is racially discriminatory.[29] As two commentators opined, "If work requirements were a good idea, conservative Michigan legislators wouldn't need to exempt their rural constituents."[30]

---

[24] Press Release, USDA, USDA Seeks Ideas to Help SNAP Participants Become Independent, Feb. 22, 2018, www.usda.gov/media/press-releases/2018/02/22/usda-seeks-ideas-help-snap-participants-become-independent.

[25] USDA, Characteristics of Supplemental Nutrition Assistance Program Households: Fiscal Year 2015, Jan. 17, 2018, www.fns.usda.gov/snap/characteristics-supplemental-nutrition-assistance-households-fiscal-year-2015.

[26] See Hahn et al., *supra* note 3.

[27] See Robert Samuels, *Wisconsin Is the GOP Model for "Welfare Reform": But as Work Requirements Grow, So Does One Family's Desperation*, WASH. POST, Apr. 22, 2018, www.washingtonpost.com/politics/you-ever-think-the-government-just-dont-want-to-help-as-requirements-for-welfare-grow-so-does-one-familys-desperation/2018/04/22/351cb27a-2315-11e8-badd-7c9f29a55815_story.html?utm_term=.a57ad38786a7.

[28] Id.

[29] Nicholas Bagley & Eli Savit, *Michigan's Discriminatory Work Requirements*, N.Y TIMES, May 8, 2018, www.nytimes.com/2018/05/08/opinion/michigan-medicaid-work-requirement.html.

[30] Id.

Family Caps

TANF permits states to impose family caps, or limits on the amount of benefits to families who have another child while on welfare. The idea behind family caps is to reduce the birth rate among unmarried, poor women, thereby assuming that poor women are irresponsible. In truth, however, the average number of children for welfare mothers is 1.8,[31] which is lower than the national average of 2.1.

Nevertheless, at peak, 24 states had TANF family caps.[32] Seven states have since rescinded these policies, including California in 2016.[33] These states experienced what study after study confirms – family caps have no impact on birth rates.[34] This is because most welfare recipients are not aware of family cap policies, thus making it a nonfactor in their decision making. Moreover, additional welfare payments are too paltry to justify having a child. As one study concluded, "It appears that women do not make decisions about the birth of their children based on the addition of $42 per month in ... benefits."[35] Not only are family caps unjustified, but, by cutting support to families, the caps are also "harmful to children, cause lifelong damage to their learning and development, and increase the 'deep poverty rate' of children by 13 percent."[36]

Nevertheless, the proposed Trump 2019 budget would extend family caps into the SNAP program, capping benefits at six persons per household. This would impact 80,000 SNAP households; the cap would max SNAP benefits at $925 per month. This means, for example, that a family of nine would see their benefits decrease from $4.87 per day per person to $3.43 per day per person. This is "significantly lower than even the most conservative amount the USDA says is needed to feed a family."[37] The cap may intend to reduce birth rates, but it would instead reduce benefits for multi-generational families who live together for financial and child care support.

---

[31] Office of Family Assistance, U.S. Dep't of Health & Human Svcs., Characteristics and Financial Circumstances of TANF Recipients, Fiscal Year 2010, www.acf.hhs.gov/ofa/resource/character/fy2010/fy2010-chap10-ys-final.
[32] Berkeley Law Center on Reproductive Rights and Justice, *Bringing Families Out of "Cap"tivity: The Path toward Abolishing Welfare Family Caps*, Aug. 2016, www.law.berkeley.edu/wp-content/uploads/2015/04/2016-Caps_FA2.pdf.
[33] *Id.*
[34] Diana Romero & Madina Agénor, *US Fertility Prevention as Poverty Prevention: An Empirical Question and Social Justice Issue*, 19 WOMEN'S HEALTH ISSUES, 355 (Nov.–Dec. 2009), www.ncbi.nlm.nih.gov/pmc/articles/PMC2775139/.
[35] Patricia Donovan, *Does the Family Cap Influence Birthrates? Two New Studies Say "No,"* 1 The Guttmacher Report 10–11 (Feb. 1998), www.guttmacher.org/gpr/1998/02/does-family-cap-influence-birthrates-two-new-studies-say-no.
[36] Teresa Wiltz, The Pew Charitable Trusts, *Welfare Caps: More Harm Than Good?*, Stateline, July 13, 2016, www.pewtrusts.org/en/research-and-analysis/blogs/stateline/2016/07/13/welfare-caps-more-harm-than-good
[37] Caitlin Dewey, *Trump's Budget Would Cut Off Food for Poor People if They Have Too Many Kids*, WASH. POST, May 24, 2017, www.washingtonpost.com/news/wonk/wp/2017/05/23/trumps-budget-would-penalize-poor-people-for-having-too-many-kids/?utm_term=.6fec558cb787.

Drug Tests

TANF gives states the authority to require drug testing as a condition of welfare receipt. For its supporters, welfare drug testing is a means to combat drug abuse and reduce drug crimes, while also ensuring that government funds are not used to pay for illegal substances. Today, 15 states mandate drug testing under TANF, and 17 other states are currently considering it.[38] Federal courts have already struck down drug testing laws in Michigan and Florida as unconstitutional under the Fourth Amendment because they constituted suspicionless government searches.[39] In response to this litigation, several states have retooled their drug testing laws to require reasonable suspicion, which, depending on the state, can arise from applicant job histories, criminal backgrounds, personal observations, or questionnaires.[40]

As with other behavior modification tools, drug testing in the TANF program has proved costly and ineffective, thus raising doubts that it should be expanded into other government programs. For example, under TANF in 2014, seven states spent more than $1 million on drug testing, but in six of them fewer than 1 percent of persons tested positive (as compared to estimates of 9.4 percent of the general population).[41] Drug testing is also arbitrary given the weak correlation between poverty and drug addiction.[42] Kaaryn Gustafson describes drug testing as a "degradation ceremony," in which politicians "engage in the dramaturgy of poverty, producing stories, meanings, and symbols that then shape the lives of poor parents and their children."[43]

Nevertheless, drug testing is now creeping into other forms of government assistance. Republicans in Congress have introduced bills to require drug tests for SNAP, TANF, rental assistance, and unemployment insurance.[44] In addition, President Trump has signaled that his administration will approve program waivers to permit drug testing in a variety of safety-net programs. Some states are also eager to

---

[38] National Conference of State Legislatures (NCSL), Drug Testing for Welfare Recipients and Public Assistance, Mar. 24, 2017, www.ncsl.org/research/human-services/drug-testing-and-public-assistance.aspx.

[39] *Marchwinski v. Howard*, 60 Fed. App'x 601 (6th Cir. 2003) (in this case, the en banc court was evenly split, thus the district court decision was affirmed per 6th Circuit rules); *Lebron v. Sec. of the Fla. Dep't of Children and Families*, 772 F.3d 1352 (11th Cir. 2014).

[40] *See* NCSL, *supra* note 37.

[41] Bryce Covert & Josh Israel, *What 7 States Discovered after Spending More Than $1 Million Drug Testing Welfare Recipients*, THINK PROGRESS, Feb. 26, 2015, https://thinkprogress.org/what-7-states-discovered-after-spending-more-than-1-million-drug-testing-welfare-recipients-c346e0b4305d/.

[42] Jordan C. Budd, *Pledge Your Body for Your Bread: Welfare, Drug Testing, and the Inferior Fourth Amendment*, 19 WM. & MARY BILL RTS. J. 751, 776–77 (2011).

[43] Kaaryn Gustafson, *Degradation Ceremonies and the Criminalization of Low-Income Women*, 3 U.C. IRVINE L REV. 297, 321 (2013).

[44] *See, e.g.*, H.R. 2179, Drug Testing for Welfare Recipients Act (2017) (introduced by Rep. Rouzer R-NC).

jump on this bandwagon. Consider the SNAP program. Currently, SNAP allows drug testing only in two circumstances. First, there are five states that take advantage of a federal statutory option and permit people convicted of drug felonies to remain eligible for SNAP – but only if they submit to a drug test. Second, an individual disqualified from TANF for failing or refusing to take a drug test can be simultaneously disqualified from SNAP.[45]

Several Republican politicians are pushing for more. In December 2017, Governor Walker of Wisconsin ordered implementation of the state's drug testing law for SNAP benefits, despite the absence of a required waiver from the USDA,[46] and he also rallied 12 other governors to sign a letter asking the USDA to approve drug testing waivers. His optimism that the waiver will eventually be granted appears sound given that the USDA, which oversees the SNAP program, issued a press release in December 2017 stating "how important it is for states to be given flexibility to achieve the desired goal of self-sufficiency for people." [47]

With regard to Unemployment Insurance (UI), states have not historically conducted drug tests on applicants because the Social Security Act, which governs the federal-state UI program, only allows states to add qualifying requirements that relate to the "fact or cause" of a worker's unemployment.[48] Nevertheless, as unemployment ballooned during the recession, some states wanted to conduct drug testing, assuming that it would cut down their eligible UI population and, thus, costs.[49] In 2012, Congress passed a compromise bill that allows states to test UI claimants under two conditions: (1) when the worker loses their job due to illegal drug use; and (2) when the worker applies for jobs in an occupation that regularly conducts drug testing.[50] Under the Obama administration, the Department of Labor (DOL) then issued regulations defining the latter category of jobs to mean occupations involving transportation, guns, or positions where testing is legally required. Three states subsequently passed laws permitting drug testing pursuant to these regulations.[51]

---

[45] Maggie McCarty et al., Congressional Research Service, *Drug Testing and Crime-Related Restrictions in TANF, SNAP, and Housing Assistance*, Nov. 28, 2016, at 11, https://fas.org/sgp/crs/misc/R42394.pdf.

[46] *See* Vann R. Newkirk II, *Wisconsin's Welfare Overhaul Is Almost Complete*, THE ATLANTIC, Dec. 12, 2017, www.theatlantic.com/politics/archive/2017/12/wisconsin-drug-testing-food-stamp-program-walker/547997/.

[47] Press Release, USDA, *USDA Seeks Ideas to Help SNAP Participants Become Independent*, Feb. 22, 2018, www.usda.gov/media/press-releases/2018/02/22/usda-seeks-ideas-help-snap-participants-become-independent.

[48] Rontel Batie & George Wentworth, *Drug Testing Unemployment Insurance Applicants: An Unconstitutional Solution in Search of a Problem*, National Employment Law Project Policy Brief, Feb. 2017, www.nelp.org/content/uploads/Drug-Testing-Unemployment-Insurance-Applicants.pdf.

[49] *Id.*

[50] *Id.*

[51] *Id.*

However, congressional Republicans[52] and several Republican governors[53] were unhappy with what they viewed as an unduly narrow interpretation by DOL, and Congress thus repealed the Obama-era regulation pursuant to the Congressional Review Act. Then, in January 2018, DOL announced that it would seek public comment on a broader rule that allows drug testing in a wider array of occupations, and the rulemaking is moving forward.[54]

The relationship between subsidized housing and drug testing is a bit more complex. There are no federal policies permitting or prohibiting drug testing as a condition of moving into public housing.[55] Instead, federal housing law requires that local PHAs deny admission to households that include tenants determined to be engaging in illegal drug use or alcohol use that interferes with other residents' ability to enjoy the premises.[56] In addition, PHAs may enforce a "One Strike" policy, under which a household faces eviction if one of its members engages in drug-related criminal activity – even if the leaseholder has no knowledge of or control over the activity.[57] Congress enacted this policy as part of the War on Drugs in the 1980s as a way to reduce drug abuse and drug-related crime and to make subsidized housing safer.[58] Yet policies and enforcement vary widely by jurisdiction, and thus, "similar households in different locations may encounter radically different rules when attempting to access or retain housing assistance."[59]

A few PHAs have proposed or adopted drug testing for their public housing residents, such as the Norwalk Housing Authority in Connecticut. Similar proposals by PHAs in Chicago and Flint were dropped after legal opposition.[60] For their part, private landlords can mandate drug testing for tenants who receive federally subsidized vouchers, and some landlords have done so.[61] As private actors, they do not face

---

[52] Human Resources Subcommittee Staff, Chairman Kevin Brady, Ways and Means, *CRA: UI Drug Testing Overreach*, https://waysandmeans.house.gov/wp-content/uploads/2017/02/CRA-UI-Drug-Testing-Background.pdf.

[53] J. B. Wogan, *What the Unemployment Drug-Testing Bill That Trump Just Signed Means for States*, Governing, Mar. 28, 2107, www.governing.com/topics/health-human-services/gov-congress-drug-testing-unemployment-states-trump.html.

[54] *See* Lydia Wheeler, *Labor Department Eyes Drug Test Rule for Unemployment Pay*, The Hill, Jan. 3, 2018, http://thehill.com/business-a-lobbying/367154-labor-department-eyes-drug-test-rule-for-unemployment-pay.

[55] Marah A. Curtis, Sarah Garlington & Lisa S. Schottenfeld, *Alcohol, Drug, and Criminal History Restrictions in Public Housing*, 15 Cityscape 37 (2013) (summarizing range of approaches used nationwide), www.huduser.gov/portal/periodicals/cityscpe/vol15num3/ch2.pdf.

[56] *See* McCarty et al., *supra* note 45, at 19–20 (describing the complexities of crime-related restrictions in housing assistance).

[57] The Supreme Court upheld this One Strike policy in *U.S. Dept. of Housing and Urban Development v. Rucker*, 535 U.S. 125 (2002).

[58] Lahny R. Silva, *Collateral Damage: A Public Housing Consequence of the "War on Drugs,"* 5 U.C. Irvine L. Rev. 783, 789–92 (2015), www.law.uci.edu/lawreview/vol5/no4/Silva.pdf.

[59] Curtis et al., *supra* note 55, at 38.

[60] *See* McCarty et al., *supra* note 45, at 17.

[61] *Id.*

the same constitutional constraints as government entities. Meanwhile, congressional Republicans have introduced a variety of bills to mandate drug testing in housing programs nationwide.[62] At the state level, Wisconsin will soon begin drug screening for its public housing residents;[63] this will likely spur other states to follow given Wisconsin's role as a leader in public benefits reform.

Moreover, Wisconsin has also sought a waiver from HHS to drug test Medicaid recipients and to mandate treatment for anyone with positive test results.[64] If granted, it would be the first state with mandatory drug screening for Medicaid recipients. And, whither goes Wisconsin, so do other – mostly Republican – states.

PUNISHING THE POOR

We have much more data today about the effectiveness of behavior control mechanisms than we did when welfare reform went into effect in 1997. As discussed previously, the evidence shows that they are counterproductive and harmful, particularly to children. These tools are also unnecessary because poor Americans share the same values and work ethic as mainstream Americans.[65] The question thus arises why Republicans are pushing to expand these tools into additional social welfare programs. To be sure, there are some economic similarities between the early 1990s and today – both eras are marked by low unemployment and a booming economy, making it easier to fault nonworkers than during recessionary times. The highly polarized political climate is also similar. In 1992, as welfare reform proposals were gathering steam, Lucie Williams explained that they were driven by "an ideology of division," which "sought to divert workers' justified anger from the wealthy and to focus it on welfare recipients."[66] This explanation holds particular resonance today.

The three main figures behind welfare creep are all white, male, Republican politicians. First, former Speaker of the House Paul Ryan, a Republican from Wisconsin, burnished a reputation throughout his career as a policy wonk with poverty expertise. (He joined Congress in 1999; ran for Vice President in 2012; and served as Speaker from 2015 to 2018, before retiring from Congress). He regularly hyped the supposed success of welfare reform and advocated for block grants across the safety net. He cautioned that the safety net was becoming a "hammock that lulls able-bodied people to lives of dependency and complacency, that drains them of

---

[62] *See e.g.,* H.R. 2179, Drug Testing for Welfare Recipients Act (2017) (Rep. Rouzer R-NC).
[63] Laurel White, *Assembly Approves Walker Welfare Package*, WIS. PUBLIC RADIO, Feb. 15, 2018, www.wpr.org/assembly-takes-walker-welfare-package.
[64] Paige Winfield Cunningham, *Want Medicaid Coverage? A Drug Test Should Come First, Wisconsin Governor Says*, WASH. POST, Apr. 2, 2017, www.washingtonpost.com/powerpost/ want-medicaid-coverage-a-drug-test-should-come-first-wisconsin-governor-says/2017/04/02/ 190068f0-160c-11e7-ada0-1489b735b3a3_story.html?utm_term=.3cb38513144b.
[65] William Julius Wilson, WHEN WORK DISAPPEARS 181 (1997).
[66] Williams, *supra* note 2, at 741–42.

their will and their incentive to make the most of their lives."[67] Although he later walked back these comments, he issued lengthy antipoverty plans to great fanfare in 2014 and 2016 that identified harms of poverty, but centered on cutting expenditures while expanding work requirements, public-private partnerships, and state flexibility.[68] The emphasis on federalism is a key component of welfare creep.

Second, former Governor Scott Walker of Wisconsin, elected in 2010 and defeated in 2018, focused early in his tenure on (successfully) weakening organized labor in his state and then turned his attention to behavior modification proposals. In early 2018, he steered the Republican-controlled Wisconsin legislature to pass a slew of public assistance reform bills that, among other things, expand work requirements for food stamps; require Medicaid recipients to maintain health savings accounts; cut Medicaid benefits for parents behind in child support payments; and require drug testing and employment for people in subsidized housing.[69] These bills passed with nary a Democratic vote. Under his leadership, Wisconsin was also seeking a federal waiver to adopt work requirements within Medicaid. Conservative activists are touting Wisconsin's approach as a blueprint for the Republican Party, and a conservative advocacy group, the Foundation for Government Accountability, has staff in 14 states pushing for similar reforms.[70] Notably, Walker was self-consciously following in the footsteps of former Wisconsin Governor Tommy Thompson who, in the mid-1990s, implemented many of the welfare reform ideas that Congress later expanded nationally in TANF.[71] The state-level push for welfare creep will exacerbate red and blue state differences.

Third, President Trump is actively peddling behavior modification proposals. Experts attribute the ascendance of President Trump to his appeal to white, working-class voters who have faced decades of wage stagnation and job losses due to globalization and technological displacement.[72] Trump was able to channel their discontent and funnel it toward minority groups, immigrants, and the poor, who he

[67] Greg Sargent, *Scott Walker and the Hammock Theory of Poverty*, WASH. POST, Feb. 3, 2015, www.washingtonpost.com/blogs/plum-line/wp/2015/02/03/scott-walker-and-the-hammock-theory-of-poverty/?utm_term=.ddf26ee6c382.

[68] Chairman Paul Ryan, House Budget Committee Majority Staff, *Expanding Opportunity in America* (2014), http://budget.house.gov/uploadedfiles/expanding_opportunity_in_america.pdf; Paul Ryan, *A Better Way* (2016), https://abetterway.speaker.gov/.

[69] Scott Bauer, *Walker Signs 9 Bills Limiting Wisconsin Welfare into Law*, U.S. NEWS & WORLD REP., Apr. 10, 2018, www.usnews.com/news/best-states/wisconsin/articles/2018-04-10/walker-to-sign-9-welfare-overhaul-bills-into-law.

[70] Reid Wilson, *Wisconsin Welfare Reform Could Be Model for GOP*, THE HILL, Feb. 21, 2018, http://thehill.com/homenews/state-watch/374781-wisconsin-welfare-reform-could-be-model-for-gop; Jen Fifield, *Where the Work-for-Welfare Movement Is Heading*, The Pew Charitable Trusts, STATELINE, Jan. 25, 2018, www.pewtrusts.org/en/research-and-analysis/blogs/stateline/2018/01/25/where-the-work-for-welfare-movement-is-heading.

[71] *See* Williams, *supra* note 2, at 726.

[72] See Andrew Gelman & Julia Azar, *19 Things We Learned from the 2016 Election*, 9–10 (Sep. 19, 2017), www.stat.columbia.edu/~gelman/research/published/what_learned_in_2016_5.pdf; Brian F. Schaffner, Matthew MacWilliams & Tatishe Nteta, *Understanding White*

painted as undeserving interlopers. In turn, these working-class individuals see themselves as "victimized by the poor."[73] Katherine Cramer calls this strategy a "politics of resentment," in which "[p]eople understand their circumstances as the fault of guilty and less deserving social groups, not as the product of broad social, economic, and political forces."[74]

In December 2017, after Trump signed a massive tax cut package whose benefits flow to the wealthiest Americans and corporations, Trump and his Republican counterparts in the House and Senate immediately began proposing cuts to public benefits programs, along with behavior modification requirements. In his 2018 State of the Union address, Trump threatened to cut off public assistance to recipients unwilling to do a "hard day's work."[75] He followed up this rhetoric in April 2018, signing an executive order directing federal agencies to strengthen and introduce new work requirements for recipients of Medicaid, food stamps, housing benefits, and TANF.[76] As a result, federal agencies are expected give states much more leeway in adopting work requirements and other behavior control mechanisms and, in turn, this will likely fuel a red and blue state policy divergence.

These Republican attacks on the poor weaken societal responsibility for aiding the needy and divert the nation's attention from the fortunes the wealthy are amassing. Currently, the top 1 percent of the wealthy hold one-third of the nation's assets, while the top 1 percent of earners take home one-fifth of the nation's total income. Although states vary in their degrees of economic inequality, inequality has risen in each and every state since the mid-1970s.[77] This widening economic inequality shows no signs of slowing down. Moreover, higher levels of economic inequality at the state level are associated with a corresponding safety-net retrenchment.[78]

In advocating for welfare creep, Republicans are seizing advantage of several dynamics within the American polity. Since the founding of America, the poor have been categorized as either deserving – meaning they cannot be blamed for the poverty, such as children, widows, and the disabled, or undeserving – meaning they should be self-sufficient, such as able-bodied adults. The modern welfare state,

---

Polarization in the 2016 Vote for President: The Sobering Role of Racism and Sexism, 133 POL. SCI. QUART. 9 (2018).

[73] Gustafson, *supra* note 43, at 354–55.

[74] Katherine J. Cramer, THE POLITICS OF RESENTMENT: RURAL CONSCIOUSNESS IN WISCONSIN AND THE RISE OF SCOTT WALKER 9 (2017).

[75] President Donald J. Trump's State of the Union Address, Jan. 30, 2018, www.whitehouse.gov/briefings-statements/president-donald-j-trumps-state-union-address/.

[76] Executive Order Reducing Poverty in America by Promoting Opportunity and Economic Mobility, Apr. 10, 2018, www.whitehouse.gov/presidential-actions/executive-order-reducing-poverty-america-promoting-opportunity-economic-mobility/.

[77] Lyle Scruggs & Thomas Hayes, *The Influence of Inequality on Welfare Generosity: Evidence from the US States*, 45 POL. & SOC. 35, 38–39 (2017).

[78] *Id.* at 51.

created during the New Deal, reinforced this dichotomy.[79] Social insurance programs designed for white working men, such as social security and unemployment
insurance, have carried no stigma, provided generous benefits pursuant to objective
criteria, and been federally administered. By contrast, cash assistance programs for
the undeserving, such as single mothers, became stingy, stigmatized, and state
administered. The relentless blame targeted at the "undeserving" makes them easy
political targets. Meanwhile, it ignores structural determinants of poverty such as
globalization, the weakening of unions, and economic shifts from a manufacturing
to service economy, as well as the lack of living wage, affordable housing, or child
care for American workers.

The stigma around poverty is the flipside of the American conception of our
nation as a meritocracy, where the most talented and hard-working rise to the top. In
this view, failure to thrive in a capitalist economy is equated with moral failings.[80]
However, Americans are not as upwardly mobile as we like to think.[81] In fact, we are
less mobile than other developed countries.[82] Forty percent of children born in the
bottom quintile of the income distribution will stay there. The same "stickiness" is
present at the top quintile. In short, one's economic standing in life is largely
determined by the "birth lottery," that is, who your parents are.[83] Indeed, intergenerational wealth transfers, or inheritance, is a major determinant of economic
stability.[84] While individual merit certainly plays a role in one's life outcomes, it is
blunted by the effects of discrimination and growing up poor.[85] Meanwhile, rich
people get ample government benefits, such as tax deductions for home mortgages
and employer-provided health care worth thousands of dollars, but these are viewed
as earned, rather than as government charity. As Wendy Bach explains, these
programs are designed to incentivize behavior, but their inclusion in the tax code
submerges their nature as social support.[86]

Race underlies these political dynamics. Martin Gilens concludes that Americans
"hate" welfare because they associate it with African Americans, who they stereotype
as lazy.[87] Although African Americans are disproportionately poor, the majority of
public assistance recipients are white. Still, the media relentlessly portrays poor
people as black in its stories and images, and this has a large impact on public

---

[79] *See* Michele Gilman, *The Return of the Welfare Queen*, 22 J. OF GENDER, SOC. POL'Y & THE
L., 247, 257–59 (2014).
[80] Gustafson, *supra* note 43, at 343.
[81] Stephen J. McNamee & Robert K. Miller Jr., THE MERITOCRACY MYTH 61 (2d ed. 2009).
[82] Raj Chetty et al., *Economic Mobility*, in PATHWAYS: STATE OF THE STATES 2015 55 (2015).
[83] McNamee & Miller, *supra* note 79, at 60. *See also* David B. Grusky, Marybeth J. Mattingly &
Charles Varner, *Executive Summary*, PATHWAYS, STATE OF THE STATES: THE POVERTY AND
INEQUALITY REPORT 2015 6 (2015) (discussing state variations in social mobility).
[84] McNamee & Miller, *supra* note 81, at 61.
[85] *Id.* at 221.
[86] Wendy Bach, *Poor Support/Rich Support: (Re)Viewing the American Social Welfare State*, FLA.
TAX REV.13–14 (2017).
[87] Martin Gilens, WHY AMERICANS HATE WELFARE (1999).

opinion.[88] The very word *welfare* evokes an emotional response that "exploit[s] racial animus" – and that is the very point.[89] Racial animus toward the poor is crystallized in the trope of the welfare queen, who is portrayed as a lazy, black mother of too many children who refuses to work while living off government largesse. President Reagan introduced this stock character, and she remains a part of political theater. The truth is that most TANF recipients are not African American; they stay in the program for short-term spells; they marry at the same rates of other women; and they have long worked to meet basic expenses.[90] "The overriding myth continues to be that welfare persists because of the characteristics of the families, not because of larger, structural conditions of society," such as discrimination, wage stagnation, and lack of work-related benefits.[91] Despite the rhetoric, the political salience of the welfare queen far outstrips her budgetary impact – TANF is a meager 0.47 percent of annual federal expenditures.

In 1996, President Clinton signed welfare reform to position himself as a centrist; he and other Democrats also said that they hoped linking welfare with work would ultimately increase public support for safety-net programs.[92] Yet this never happened. As Joe Soss and Sanford Schram explain, "[W]elfare reform did not alter the way Americans distinguish the deserving from the undeserving or think about policies for the disadvantaged" because welfare does not touch the lives of most Americans, thus leaving "elite rhetoric, media frames, and widely held cultural beliefs" firmly in place.[93] Today's Democrats appear to have recognized the folly of championing the poor by making their lives harsher. Thus, behavior modification proposals no longer garner significant bipartisan support. Instead, Republicans are making welfare creep a central part of their domestic policy prescriptions. In turn, this is driving a red and blue state divide for poor Americans.

PATCHWORK FEDERALISM FOR THE POOR

The Constitution allocates power between the federal and state levels of government, making the core question of federalism about where to set the boundaries. Supporters of increased federalism – that is, greater power to the states – argue that it moves decision making closer to the people, pushes states to serve as laboratories of innovation, and increases efficiencies resulting from more localized service

---

[88] *Id.* at 134–35.

[89] Kenneth J. Neubeck & Noel A. Cazenave: WELFARE RACISM: PLAYING THE RACE CARD AGAINST AMERICA'S POOR 3 (2001).

[90] Gilman, *supra* note 79, at 263–64.

[91] Joel F. Handler & Yeheskel Hasenfeld, BLAME WELFARE, IGNORE POVERTY AND INEQUALITY 158 (2009).

[92] *See* Jason DeParle, AMERICAN DREAM: THREE WOMEN, TEN KIDS, AND A NATION'S DRIVE TO END WELFARE 138–54 (2005).

[93] Joe Soss & Sanford F. Schram, *Welfare Reform as a Failed Political Strategy: Evidence and Explanations for the Stability of Public Opinion*, 24 FOCUS 17, 21 (2006).

provision.[94] Federalism rhetoric was potent and effective during the debates that lead to enactment of TANF.[95] While federalism is neither inherently progressive nor conservative,[96] devolution to states on issues of redistribution is generally bad for poor people.[97] As compared to the federal government, states tend to adopt more punitive redistribution policies and are less responsive to the needs of the poor. In addition, federalism makes it harder for antipoverty advocates to lobby because they must advocate in 50, rather than one, jurisdiction.[98] Devolution of social welfare policy also drives massive disparities between states that make one's ability to weather or even overcome poverty partly dependent on the state where they live.[99]

Today, public assistance in the United States is a shared federal and state undertaking. By contrast, in early American history, states and localities carried all the burdens of poor relief. The federal government began to play a role after the Civil War, by establishing pensions for veterans and their widows. Still, the federal role remained small until the Great Depression of the 1930s, when states were overwhelmed by massive need. The New Deal, spearheaded by President Roosevelt, made the federal government central to poor relief through the implementation of social security, unemployment insurance, aid to families with children, jobs programs, and other social welfare measures. The New Deal carried out these programs through a system of cooperative federalism, in which the federal government funded the bulk of public assistance programs and set program parameters, while states administered funds to beneficiaries and sometimes contributed a share to program expenditures. Lyndon Johnson's Great Society programs, such as Medicaid, continued this model.

By contrast, TANF represented a shift to New Federalism, in which the federal government provides a set level of funding in the form of a block grant and gives the states wider discretion to set eligibility and enforcement standards. Yet as Andrew Hammond has explained, the TANF block grants not only resulted in massive disparities among states but also in an overall reduction in spending on poverty alleviation and a concurrent inability of the federal government to respond to economic and natural emergencies.[100] For this reason, he cautions progressive federalists – those who see states as a bulwark against the current conservative,

---

[94] *See, e.g., Gregory v. Ashcroft*, 501 U.S. 452, 458 (1991) (setting forth federalism justifications).

[95] *See* Sheryll D. Cashin, *Federalism, Welfare Reform and the Minority Poor: Accounting for the Tyranny of State Majorities*, 99 COLUM. L. REV. 552, 553 (1999).

[96] *See* Heather K. Gerken, *Federalism and Nationalism: Time for a Détente?*, 59 ST. LOUIS L. 997 (2015).

[97] David A. Super, *Laboratories of Destitution: Democratic Experimentalism and the Failure of Antipoverty Law*, 157 U. PA. L. REV. 541 (2008).

[98] *See* Stephen D. Sugarman, *Welfare Reform and the Cooperative Federalism of America's Public Income Transfer Programs*, 14 YALE L. & POL'Y REV. 123, 136 (1996).

[99] Sarah K. Bruch, Marcia K. Meyers & Janet C. Gornick, *The Consequences of Decentralization: Inequality in Safety Net Provision in the Post-Welfare Reform Era*, 92 Soc. Svc. Rev. 3, 23 (2018).

[100] Andrew Hammond, *Welfare and Federalism's Peril*, 92 WASH. L. REV. 1721 (2017).

Trumpian federal regime – against advocating for federalism when it comes to redistributive programs. Power to the states is usually disempowering for the poor.

Hammond's warning with regard to block grant funding holds true in connection with regard to welfare creep. Welfare creep is occurring primarily through federally granted waivers, which are permitted under various statutes. These statutes give federal agencies the selective authority to allow states to deviate from statutory requirements under certain circumstances. In short, they involve "the delegation of the power to unmake Congress's law."[101] Waivers are an increasingly popular governance tool because, in theory, they give states flexibility while ensuring federal oversight and adherence to core statutory purposes.[102] In addition, in an era of extreme partisanship, they provide a way around statutory gridlock because they shift some specific policy-making decisions down the line and off the front pages.[103]

While waivers may have regulatory merits, Edward Stiglitz argues that in safety-net programs, waivers inevitably lead to state retrenchment.[104] This is because states, unlike the federal government, must balance their budgets. They cannot issue money, and they are restricted in their spending and revenue-raising ability.[105] As a result, "[T]hey face the strongest budget pressure to control spending and decrease services at precisely the time that safety nets have the most value in blunting poverty and inequality."[106] States thus tend to seek waivers that allow them to reduce costs and services – waivers for Medicaid work requirements are a prime example of this phenomenon.

At the same time, as Thad Cousser explains, when safety-net financial responsibility shifts from the federal to state governments, such as through block grants, low-income taxpayers pick up a greater share of the tab.[107] This is because moderate- and low-income people pay a larger share of state tax burdens due to their regressive nature compared to federal taxes, which are generally more progressive.[108] Thus, devolution means that low-income people pay a larger share of their income in return for less services. This impact is greater in red states, which are comparatively more regressive than blue states.[109]

---

[101] David J. Barron & Todd D. Rakoff, *In Defense of Big Waiver*, 113 COLUM. L. REV. 265, 269 (2013).

[102] Brietta Clark, Safeguarding *Federalism by Saving Health Reform: Implications of National Federation of Independent Business v. Sebelius*, 46 LOY. L.A. L. REV. 541 (2013); Bruce Frohnen, *Waivers, Federalism, and the Rule of Law*, 45 PERSP. ON POL. SCI. 59 (2016) (criticizing waivers for lack of rule of law norms)

[103] *See* Barron & Rakoff, *supra* note 98, at 270; Jessica Bulman-Pozen, *From Sovereignty and Process to Administration and Politics: The Afterlife of American Federalism*, 123 YALE L. J. 1920, 1944–46 (2014).

[104] Edward H. Stiglitz, *Forces of Federalism, Safety Nets, and Waivers*, 18 THEORETICAL INQUIRIES L. 125 (2017).

[105] David A. Super, *Rethinking Fiscal Federalism*, 118 HARV. L. REV. 2544 (2005).

[106] Stiglitz, *supra* note 104, at 138.

[107] Thad Kousser, *How America's "Devolution Revolution" Reshaped Its Federalism*, 64 REV. FRANCAISE DE SCIENCE POLITIQUE 65, 76–77 (2014).

[108] *Id.* at 79.

[109] INSTITUTE OF TAXATION AND ECONOMIC POLICY, WHO PAYS? (5th ed. 2015).

Meanwhile, waivers in safety-net programs have failed to provide the innovations promised by federalism. For instance, more than one-third of all federal Medicaid spending is through waiver programs. Yet as the General Accountability Office reported in 2018, state Medicaid waiver programs have not been rigorously evaluated, making it difficult to draw meaningful lessons from state policy variations.[110] Likewise, in the context of TANF, states as "[l]aboratories have produced very little innovation … it is hard to link observed variation in benefits or other program components to anything other than race, political culture, ill-informed choice, and the lingering influence of AFDC funding."[111]

As each state goes it alone, safety-net waivers have resulted in a patchwork of policies across the country. For instance, under the TANF program, "where a family lives helps determine whether it receives cash assistance, the amount and types of assistance, and the requirements to maintain eligibility."[112] Postrecession, the national poverty rate has fallen by 3 percent, while the TANF caseload has nevertheless plunged 28 percent – indicating that many people are not getting the help they need to make ends meet.[113] Indeed, TANF serves only 23 out of 100 poor families, which is a sharp drop from 68 out of 100 when TANF was enacted.[114] Yet states vary widely in this TANF-to-poverty ratio; Louisiana's TANF program reaches 4 out of 100 poor families, while California's reaches 66 out of 100.[115] There are 15 states in which TANF reaches 10 percent or lower of the poor population. Not surprisingly then, rates of extreme poverty – or families living on less than $2 a day – are highest where TANF is least accessible, particularly in Appalachia and the Deep South.[116]

Poverty rates also vary by state. While the national poverty rate is around 12 percent, that number masks huge differences among states. The poorest regions are the South and West; while poverty rates are lowest in New England, the Mid-Atlantic, and the Upper Midwest.[117] Poverty rates only tell part of the story, however, because they do not capture the scope or scale of relief efforts. The effectiveness of the overall safety net

[110] U.S. Government Accountability Office, Medicaid Demonstrations: Evaluations Yielded Limited Results, Underscoring Need for Changes to Federal Policies and Procedures (Jan. 2018), www.gao.gov/assets/690/689506.pdf. *See also* Frank Thompson & Courtney Burke, *Executive Federalism and Medicaid Demonstration Waivers: Implications for Policy and Democratic Process*, 32 J. of Health Pol. 971, 982 (2007):
[111] Michael Wiseman, *Why Haven't the States Become Authentic "Laboratories of Democracy"?* Pathways: State Policy Choices (2018).
[112] Hahn et al., *supra* note 3, at 7.
[113] *See* Ife Floyd, Ladonna Pavetti & Liz Schott, Center on Budget and Policy Priorities, *TANF Reaching Few Poor Families*, Dec. 13, 2017, www.cbpp.org/research/family-income-support/tanf-reaching-few-poor-families.
[114] *Id.*; Hahn et al., *supra* note 3, at 30.
[115] Schott, Pavetti & Floyd, *supra* note 7.
[116] Shaefer & Edin, *supra* note 1.
[117] Marybeth J. Mattingly & Charles Varner, *Poverty*, Pathways: State of the States, The Poverty and Inequality Report 2015 18 (2015).

varies widely by state, as shown by the "poverty relief ratio," which "reports the amount of income support provided, relative to the amount required to provide for all low-income households' basic needs."[118] This metric shows that some states meet only about 26 percent of need, while others meet as much as 40 percent of need. The states with the highest relief ratios tend to be in the West and Northeast, while the lowest ratios are in the South and some interior states.[119] "It follows that, when one's market income falls short, much rides on whether one lives in a state with an effective safety net."[120] States with weak safety nets tend also to score lower in other domains related to economic security, such as labor markets, poverty, inequality, education, health, and economic mobility. In other words, disadvantages tend to be concentrated in certain states.[121] These layers of disadvantage also operate regionally, particularly in the South, making it hard for individuals to escape their effects simply by moving across state lines.[122]

Race explains part of the state variation in the poverty relief ratio. Consider the geographic differences in TANF policies across the country. Over the last two decades, scholars have consistently found that TANF policies are more punitive and less generous in states with higher proportions of minority populations.[123] The Urban Institute recently reaffirmed these findings after studying multiple TANF policy choices in every state and concluding that states with harsher sanction policies, higher asset limits, and shorter time limits are states where African American people are disproportionately concentrated.[124] Not surprisingly then, "States with TANF-to-poverty ratios in the bottom half nationally are home to the majority (56 percent) of African American people but only 46 percent of non-Hispanic white people."[125]

By contrast, as Brown and Best explain, race is not correlated with variations in SNAP policies (food assistance) or Children's Health Insurance Program (CHIP) policies (heath care for low-income children). With regard to CHIP, state policy variations are driven by economic need (states tend to be more generous where need is greater), as well as by politics (Republican legislative control at the state level is associated with higher-income eligibility levels). In comparison, SNAP policies are tied most closely with political variables; states with Republican governors generally have much stricter

---

[118] Karen Long Jusko & Katherine Weisshaar, *Are We Providing Enough to Those Who Have Too Little? Measuring Poverty Relief*, POL. SCI. RSCH. & METHODS 1 (2017), https://people.stanford.edu/kljusko/sites/default/files/20170222_jusko_weisshaar.pdf.

[119] Karen Jusko & Kate Weisshaar, *Safety Net*, PATHWAYS: THE POVERTY AND INEQUALITY REPORT 19 (2014), https://inequality.stanford.edu/sites/default/files/media/_media/pdf/pathways/special_sotu_2014/Pathways_SOTU_2014_Safety_net.pdf.

[120] Karen Long Jusko, *Safety Net*, PATHWAYS: STATE OF THE STATES, THE POVERTY AND INEQUALITY REPORT 41 (2015).

[121] Grusky et al., *supra* note 83, at 6.

[122] *Id.* at 8.

[123] Gustafson, *supra* note 43, at 306.

[124] Hahn et al., *supra* note 3, at 18, 23.

[125] *Id.* at 7.

eligibility requirements. Notably, in 2018, Republicans dominate states with unified control of government; Republicans hold twenty-six, while Democrats hold eight.[126]

Early indicators of welfare creep seem to be bringing these three dynamics – economic, racial, and political – into play. First, an improving economy is making it politically more palatable to blame the poor for their plight, even though wages remain stubbornly stagnant. Second, Trump and his fellow Republicans are aggressively terming all safety-net programs as "welfare," in a ploy to reduce public support for public assistance. By turning *welfare* into a dirty word, they are rhetorically pushing all needy people into the "undeserving" category and extending racist tropes about the needy. Whereas CHIP was long considered a bipartisan program to assist innocent (i.e., deserving) children, Trump is now proposing $7 billion in budget cuts to the program to reduce the deficit – which is ballooning due to the 2017 tax cuts for the wealthy. This follows a four-month funding gap for CHIP in late 2017 after the program became a bargaining chip in a government shutdown over the budget. This new politicized dynamic around CHIP suggests that even the most bipartisan safety-net programs are no longer secure. Third and finally, welfare creep is almost exclusively a Republican project.

The convergence of these economic, racial, and political factors will fall most harshly on red states, as early signs suggest. Of the 10 states that first applied for Medicaid work waivers, seven are in the bottom half of states in terms of the TANF-to-poverty ratios, and six of the ten have TANF-to-poverty ratios of less than 10 (meaning fewer than 10 out of 100 eligible families are receiving TANF). Five of the ten states are in the bottom half of states when considering their poverty relief ratio. Four of the states are among the most regressive in terms of tax policies (states in which the bottom 20 percent pay up to seven times as much of their income in taxes as the wealthy). All 10 of these waiver-seeking states are led by Republican governors, and eight of the states are entirely Republican controlled in both the executive and legislative branches.

Being poor in America is difficult wherever you live – but there tends to be more generous support in blue states. In addition, postrecession labor force participation in blue states is outpacing red states, likely due to the variations in industrial structure (manufacturing and retail are concentrated in red states, while blue states have growth in technology and life sciences).[127] At the same time, red states are increasingly adopting behavior modification requirements as a condition of receiving public assistance. The red state/blue state divide is a real one for poor Americans. It can mean the difference between being able to pay rent, put food on the table, or obtain necessary medical care.

---

[126] *See* National Conference of State Legislatures, *State Partisan Composition*, Apr. 11, 2018, www.ncsl.org/Portals/1/Documents/Elections/Legis_Control_071018_26973.pdf.

[127] Robin Brooks, Jonathan Fortun & Greg Basile, *Global Macro Views – The Red-Blue Labor Market Split*, Institute of International Finance, Mar. 8, 2018.

PART II

States, Federalism, and Antipoverty Efforts

4

States' Rights and State Wrongs

Supplemental Nutritional Assistance Program Work Requirements in Rural America

Rebecca H. Williams and Lisa R. Pruitt

A resurgence in work requirements for safety-net programs, including the Supplemental Nutrition Assistance Program (SNAP), has marked the early years of the Trump administration. While work requirements have long been a feature of SNAP, some lawmakers at both the federal and state levels are moving to revive and expand these work requirements, further limiting the availability of this critical benefit to those in need.[1] These proposals to constrain SNAP access are problematic for several reasons. While work requirements theoretically create incentives for employment and increase self-sufficiency, evidence shows that simply mandating work does little to improve employment outcomes.[2] Even when jobs can be found, those jobs do not necessarily lift people out of poverty or eliminate the need for food assistance.[3]

Work requirements are particularly ill-fitting for rural communities, where the need for safety-net programs and food system supports is acute for a variety of reasons. Nonmetropolitan counties comprise 76 percent of the US counties with the highest rates of food insecurity.[4] As a result, people in these rural areas rely on

---

[1] Caitlin Dewey, *GOP Proposes Stricter Work Requirements for Food Stamp Recipients, A Step toward a Major Overhaul of the Social Safety Net*, WASH. POST (Apr. 12, 2018); Olivia Paschal, *The Farm Bill and the Assault on Poor Families*, THE ATLANTIC (Aug. 24, 2018). We thank Jaclyn Feenstra, Jon P. Ivy, and Jackie Nguyen for research assistance.

[2] *See* HEATHER HAHN, WORK REQUIREMENTS IN SAFETY NET PROGRAMS: LESSONS FOR MEDICAID FROM TANF AND SNAP 3–6 (Apr. 2018), www.urban.org/research/publication/work-requirements-safety-net-programs; LADONNA PAVETTI, CTR. ON BUDGET AND POLICY PRIORITIES, WORK REQUIREMENTS DON'T CUT POVERTY, EVIDENCE SHOWS 1–7 (June 7, 2016), www.cbpp.org/sites/default/files/atoms/files/6-6-16pov3.pdf.

[3] *See* HAHN, *supra* note 2, at 3–4; PAVETTI, *supra* note 2, at 9–11; Matthew Desmond, *Americans Want to Believe Jobs Are the Solution to Poverty: They're Not*, N.Y. TIMES (Sept. 11, 2018). *See generally* Lisa R. Pruitt, *Missing the Mark: Welfare Reform and Rural Poverty*, 10 J. GENDER, RACE & JUST. 439 (2007) (discussing impact of welfare reform's work requirements on rural poverty).

[4] Jessica Leigh Hester, *Rural America Is Hungry*, CITYLAB (May 8, 2017). For Office and Management standards defining "nonmetropolitan" counties, see OFFICE OF MANAGEMENT

SNAP benefits more heavily than their urban counterparts; indeed, rural households are about 25 percent more likely to receive SNAP benefits than urban households.[5] At the same time, rural places tend to have weaker labor markets and a general lack of economic opportunity. Structural factors such as geographic isolation, lack of access to transportation, and insufficient child care also complicate the work lives of rural residents. Such structural deficits undermine the ability of would-be SNAP beneficiaries to meet work requirements.

This chapter takes up the issue of SNAP work requirements in the context of rural America. We begin with a brief overview of SNAP and examine the recent push to strengthen SNAP work requirements. We then turn to an overview of the social safety net in rural America. We next examine employment data and information on safety-net use across the rural-urban axis; for work requirements to be effective – and, indeed, appropriate – jobs must be available in the first place. Finally, we present a case study about the results of early efforts to impose work requirements on SNAP receipt in Maine.

This chapter's connection to federalism is the sometimes-dramatic state variation in work requirements. A quick glance at the list of states with work requirements suggests that many also feature the greatest percentages of rural population. The unfortunate upshot is that states with work requirements are also the states where it is arguably most structurally difficult to find and keep a job, especially within a given state's rural reaches. We acknowledge that structural obstacles to employment also operate within certain parts of metropolitan areas, including those areas with more depressed job markets and poor public transportation. We are also sensitive to the conflation, in the national imaginary, of whiteness with rurality and blackness with urbanicity, though we resist that conflation as inaccurate with respect to many states and regions. Our aim is not to establish that rural people always have a more difficult time than urban people finding and keeping employment. Rather, we aim to highlight particular structural challenges associated with rural poverty and rural employment, issues often overlooked in our urbanormative society.

SNAP WORK REQUIREMENTS: HISTORY AND EVOLUTION

Work requirements are not new to SNAP. Originally called the Food Stamp Program, SNAP went into effect in 1964 as part of Johnson's so-called War on Poverty. By 1977, the program had been amended to add many of the general work

---

AND BUDGET, STANDARDS FOR DEFINING METROPOLITAN AND MICROPOLITAN STATISTICAL AREAS, www.census.gov/programs-surveys/metro-micro/about.html.

[5] *See SNAP Matters in Every Community – Metros, Small Towns, and Rural Communities*, FOOD RESEARCH & ACTION CENTER, www.frac.org/snap-county-map/snap-counties.html; *see also* Vann R. Newkirk II, *A Republican Plan Could Worsen Rural America's Food Crisis*, THE ATLANTIC (May 2, 2018).

requirements still in place today; namely that nonexempt[6] individuals register for work, accept a job if offered, and not quit a job without good cause.[7] In 1996, the Personal Responsibility and Work Opportunity Reconciliation Act (PRWORA) imposed additional SNAP work requirements for able-bodied adults without dependents (ABAWDs),[8] setting a three-month time limit on benefits for ABAWDs who failed to work or participate in a qualifying Education and Training (E&T) Program for at least 80 hours per month.[9]

In implementing ABAWD work requirements, the federal government gave states the option to request a waiver of the three-month ABAWD time limit.[10] Under current law, states with high unemployment rates or a lack of available jobs are eligible to apply to the US Department of Agriculture (USDA) for temporary waivers to the ABAWD time limit for all or part of the state.[11] States have broad discretion over whether to request a waiver; indeed, almost every state has voluntarily implemented a waiver during difficult economic times.[12] Such waivers were especially critical for states during and after the Great Recession. In 2009, the American Recovery and Reinvestment Act (ARRA) temporarily suspended SNAP's ABAWD time limit, from April 2009 to October 2010, which resulted in a rise in SNAP access across the United States.[13] Thereafter, between 2011 and 2014, a majority of states had or qualified for a state waiver due to ongoing postrecession economic difficulties.[14]

---

[6] For a list of exemptions, see HEATHER HAHN ET AL., URBAN INST., WORK REQUIREMENTS IN SOCIAL SAFETY NET PROGRAMS: A STATUS REPORT OF WORK REQUIREMENTS IN TANF, SNAP, HOUSING ASSISTANCE, AND MEDICAID 10 (2017), www.urban.org/sites/default/files/publication/95566/work-requirements-in-social-safety-net-programs.pdf.

[7] Amendments to the Food Stamp Act of 1964, Pub. L. No. 91–671, § 5, 84 Stat. 2048, 2050 (1971) (adding work registration and job acceptance requirements); Food Stamp Act of 1977, Pub L. 95–113, § 6, 91 Stat. 913, 965 (1977) (penalizing recipients who quit a job without good cause). In addition to these requirements, SNAP's general requirements were also amended in 1985 to mandate participation in E&T programs as required by the states. Food Security Act of 1985 Pub. L. 99–198, § 1517, 99 Stat 1354, 1573 (1985).

[8] An ABAWD is a person between the ages of 18 and 49 who has no dependents and is not disabled. USDA FOOD AND NUTRITION SERVICE, *Supplemental Nutrition Assistance Program (SNAP): Able-Bodied Adults without Dependents (ABAWDs)*, www.fns.usda.gov/snap/able-bodied-adults-without-dependents-abawds.

[9] Personal Responsibility and Work Opportunity Reconciliation Act of 1996, Pub. L. No. 104–193, §824, 110 Stat. 2105, 2323 (1996).

[10] USDA FOOD AND NUTRITION SERVICE, *supra* note 8.

[11] *Id.*

[12] *See* ED BOLEN & STACY DEAN, CTR. ON BUDGET AND POL'Y PRIORITIES, WAIVERS ADD KEY STATE FLEXIBILITY TO SNAP's THREE-MONTH TIME LIMIT 1 (Feb. 6, 2018), www.cbpp.org/sites/default/files/atoms/files/3-24-17fa.pdf.

[13] *Id.* at 5; Lori Robertson, *Romney's Food Stamp Stretch*, FACTCHECK, Sep. 27, 2012, www.factcheck.org/2012/09/romneys-food-stamp-stretch/.

[14] CONG. RESEARCH SERV., R42505, SUPPLEMENTAL NUTRITION ASSISTANCE PROGRAM (SNAP): A PRIMER ON ELIGIBILITY AND BENEFITS 11 (2018).

TABLE 4.1 *2018 SNAP ABAWD Waivers by State*
(Rural Pop. Indicated by Percentage)[*]

No Waiver		Partial Waiver		Statewide Waiver
Alabama (23%)	Texas (11%)	Arizona (5%)	New Jersey (0%)	Alaska (32%)
Arkansas (38%)	Wisconsin (26%)	Colorado (13%)	New York (7%)	California (2%)
Delaware (0%)	Wyoming (69%)	Connecticut (5%)	North Dakota (50%)	Louisiana (16%)
Florida (3%)		Georgia (17%)	Ohio (20%)	Nevada (9%)
Indiana (22%)		Hawaii (19%)	Oregon (16%)	New Mexico (33%)
Iowa (40%)		Idaho (33%)	Pennsylvania (11%)	
Kansas (32%)		Illinois (11%)	Rhode Island (0%)	
Maine (41%)		Kentucky (41%)	South Dakota (52%)	
Mississippi (54%)		Maryland (2%)	Tennessee (22%)	
Missouri (25%)		Massachusetts (1%)	Utah (10%)	
Nebraska (35%)		Michigan (18%)	Vermont (65%)	
North Carolina (22%)		Minnesota (22%)	Virginia (12%)	
Oklahoma (34%)		Montana (65%)	Washington (10%)	
South Carolina (15%)		New Hampshire (37%)	West Virginia (38%)	

[*] Rounded to the nearest percentage.
Source: Data from 2017 USDA ERS State Profiles, www.ers.usda.gov/data-products/state-fact-sheets/. The terms "rural" and "urban" here refer to data for nonmetro and metro areas, the county-wide classification used by the U.S. Office of Management and Budget.

Since 2015, however, the number of state waivers has dwindled dramatically. In 2015, 31 states had statewide ABAWD waivers, and 13 states had partial waivers.[15] As of 2018, only five states – Alaska, California, Louisiana, Nevada, and New Mexico – have statewide waivers of the time limit.[16] Twenty-eight states are approved for partial waivers, while 17 states have no waiver at all.[17] These are listed in the Table 4.1, which also indicates the percentage of each state's population that is rural.

[15] *ABAWD Waivers*, USDA FOOD AND NUTRITION SERVICE, www.fns.usda.gov/snap/abawd-waivers (select "FY15 Quarter 4 ABAWD Waiver Status").

[16] *Id.*

[17] *Id.*

Many states no longer qualify for waivers due to improved economic circumstances. Among states that do qualify, many have chosen to forego waivers and impose work requirements, despite continued high unemployment in all or part of the state.[18]

Reinstatement of the ABAWD work requirements and time limits has had a significant impact on unemployed SNAP recipients. In 2016 alone, at least a half-million unemployed or underemployed individuals lost SNAP benefits due to reinstatement of the federal ABAWD provisions.[19] This trend has continued into 2018, with the number of Americans participating in SNAP falling to its lowest level in eight years.[20]

Despite the decrease in state waivers of work requirements and a corresponding decline in the number of SNAP recipients, lawmakers and administrative officials continue to search for ways to tighten the program's work requirements and further reduce program enrollment. In early 2018, the Trump administration proposed a budget that would cut SNAP funding by nearly 30 percent over the next decade.[21] More recently, House Republicans passed Farm Bill legislation seeking to advance this and other Trump administration goals.[22] The legislation greatly expands the population required to work 20 hours or more per week for SNAP benefits, including individuals with children over six years old and all able-bodied adults under 60.[23] The bill also mandates monthly reporting of work hours and penalizes those who fail to comply by making them program ineligible for one year (or three years if it is the individual's second "violation").[24] Finally, the bill limits states' ability to qualify for waivers, greatly reducing states' ability to respond to economic downturns when SNAP access is especially critical for struggling individuals and families.[25]

[18] *See, e.g.,* Sue Berkowitz, *Thousands in SC Will Lose Food Aid in July,* THE STATE (Apr. 24, 2016), www.thestate.com/opinion/op-ed/article73362857.html (describing former South Carolina governor Nikki Haley's decision not to seek ABAWD waivers); Desare Frazier, *Thousands of Single Mississippians Off Food Stamp Rolls,* MISS. PUB. BROADCASTING (Apr. 11, 2016), www .mpbonline.org/blogs/news/2016/04/11/thousands-of-single-mississippians-without-children-off-food-stamp-rolls/ (detailing Mississippi governor Phil Bryant's decision not to seek ABAWD waivers); Alana Semuels, *The End of Welfare as We Know It,* THE ATLANTIC (Apr. 1, 2016) (describing Arkansas governor Asa Hutchinson's decision not to seek ABAWD waivers).

[19] ED BOLEN ET AL., CTR. ON BUDGET AND POL'Y PRIORITIES, MORE THAN 500,000 ADULTS WILL LOSE SNAP BENEFITS IN 2016 AS WAIVERS EXPIRE 1 (Mar. 18, 2016), www.cbpp.org/research/food-assistance/more-than-500000-adults-will-lose-snap-benefits-in-2016-as-waivers-expire.

[20] In 2010, roughly 40.3 million people were enrolled in SNAP. As of 2018, 40 million individuals are enrolled. *See* USDA FOOD AND NUTRITION SERVICE, SUPPLEMENTAL NUTRITION ASSISTANCE PROGRAM PARTICIPATION AND COSTS, 1969–2017, www.fns.usda.gov/pd/supplemental-nutrition-assistance-program-snap (hereinafter SNAP PARTICIPATION AND COSTS).

[21] *See* OFFICE OF MGMT. & BUDGET, EXEC. OFFICE OF THE PRESIDENT, AN AMERICAN BUDGET: MAJOR SAVINGS AND REFORMS 128 (2018); Caitlin Dewey et al., *Trump's Budget Hits Poor Americans the Hardest,* WASH. POST (Feb. 12, 2018).

[22] Agriculture and Nutrition Act of 2018, H.R. 2, 115th Cong (2018).

[23] *Id.* at §4015.

[24] *Id.*

[25] *See id.; see also* ED BOLEN ET AL., CTR. ON BUDGET AND POL'Y PRIORITIES, HOUSE AGRICULTURE COMMITTEE'S FARM BILL WOULD INCREASE FOOD INSECURITY AND HARDSHIP 15 (2018), www .cbpp.org/sites/default/files/atoms/files/4-16-18fa.pdf (hereinafter BOLEN ET AL., FARM BILL).

While the Senate has yet to approve the House's Farm Bill and its attendant work requirement provisions, the proposal is emblematic of the current push by some federal and state lawmakers to tighten SNAP work requirements. Should this movement be successful, previous research on safety-net work requirements suggests that such reforms would have negative impacts on rural Americans.[26]

THE ECONOMIC LANDSCAPE AND BARRIERS TO WORK IN RURAL AMERICA

America's population is 14 percent rural, and more than 46 million people reside in nonmetropolitan counties.[27] Rural economies fall along a broad spectrum, ranging from chronically poor communities to wealthier exurban areas, and they include college towns and other areas experiencing rural gentrification.[28] Even with this diversity, an economic divide has long existed between rural and urban America.[29] Nonmetro poverty rates have exceeded metropolitan poverty rates every year since 1959.[30] The most recent American Community Survey data indicate that the 2016 nonmetropolitan poverty rate was 16.9 percent, while the metropolitan poverty rate was 13.6 percent.[31] High-poverty counties (those with poverty rates of 20 percent or more) are disproportionately rural; fully one-third of nonmetro counties were labeled "high-poverty" from 2009 to 2013, whereas just one-sixth of metropolitan counties were so designated.[32] The vast majority of "persistent poverty" counties – those where the poverty rate has been higher than 20 percent for each of the last four decennial censuses – are nonmetropolitan.[33] Many factors contribute to this rural-

---

[26] *See generally* BRUCE A. WEBER ET AL., RURAL DIMENSIONS OF WELFARE REFORM (2001); KATHLEEN PICKERING ET AL., WELFARE REFORM IN PERSISTENT RURAL POVERTY (2006); Leif Jensen & Yoshimi Chitose, *Will Workfare Work? Job Availability for Welfare Recipients in Rural and Urban America*, 16 POP. RES. & POL'Y REV. 383 (1997); Leonard E. Bloomquist et al., *Too Few Jobs for Workfare to Put Many to Work*, RURAL DEVELOPMENT PERSPECTIVES (1988).

[27] USDA ECON. RESEARCH SERVICE, RURAL AMERICA AT A GLANCE 1 (2017), www.ers.usda.gov/webdocs/publications/85740/eib-182.pdf?v=43054 (hereinafter RURAL AMERICA AT A GLANCE).

[28] *See* LAWRENCE C. HAMILTON ET AL., CARSEY INSTITUTE, PLACE MATTERS: CHALLENGES AND OPPORTUNITIES IN FOUR RURAL AMERICAS (2008), https://scholars.unh.edu/cgi/viewcontent.cgi?article=1040&context=carsey

[29] This has been observed since the 1960s, when official poverty rates were first recorded. *Rural Poverty & Well-Being: Poverty Overview*, USDA ECONOMIC RESEARCH SERVICE, www.ers.usda.gov/topics/rural-economy-population/rural-poverty-well-being/poverty-overview/ (hereinafter *Poverty Overview*). *See also* EDWARD T. BREATHITT, THE PEOPLE LEFT BEHIND: A REPORT BY THE PRESIDENT'S NATIONAL ADVISORY COMMISSION ON RURAL POVERTY (1967), https://files.eric.ed.gov/fulltext/ED016543.pdf.

[30] Bruce Weber & Kathleen Miller, *Rural Poverty Then and Now*, in RURAL POVERTY IN THE UNITED STATES 28, 40 (Ann. R. Tickmayer et al. eds., 2017).

[31] *Poverty Overview, supra* note 29.

[32] Weber & Miller, *supra* note 30 at 51.

[33] "Over 300 rural counties (15.2 percent of all rural counties) are persistently poor, compared with just 50 urban counties (4.3 percent of all urban counties)." RURAL AMERICA AT A GLANCE, *supra* note 27 at 5. These counties are largely concentrated in four regions that reflect different races and nationalities: the Mississippi Delta and Black Belt; the Texas border counties; Indian

urban poverty gap, including industrial and economic restructuring, lower wages, and higher unemployment within rural communities.[34]

For work requirements to lift individuals out of poverty, labor markets must be robust and offer jobs that pay a living wage. But many rural economies lack these types of jobs. For example, economic diversification is less common in rural economies because new industries are deterred by certain characteristics of the rural economy such as physical isolation, low population density, and low-skill workers.[35]

Globalization, which transformed the US economy from goods based to services based, has only compounded the difficulties faced by rural economies.[36] Many industries that experienced the greatest economic growth – financial markets[37] and producer services [38] – are located in urban areas. In contrast, extractive industries, manufacturing, and construction, all which make up disproportionate parts of rural economies, are in decline.[39] Meanwhile, low-skill jobs in personal and consumer services have increasingly come to dominate many rural economies.[40]

Not only are rural job markets limited, available jobs tend to pay poorly. College-educated rural workers experience much lower returns on their human capital investments than do urban workers.[41] At the other end of the skills gap, the expansion of the low-skill service sector has led to a proportional increase in jobs that tend to pay less, provide irregular work schedules, feature less security, and lack advancement opportunities.[42] These economic shifts have hit workers with a high school education or less the hardest,[43] and such workers comprise a higher proportion of rural work forces than urban ones.[44] The effects of these trends are evident when one looks at median household income in rural areas, which has been about 25 percent lower than the median urban income since 2007.[45]

country in the West and Southwest; and Appalachia and the Ozark highlands. *See* PICKERING ET AL., *supra* note 26 at 11–18.

[34] *See* Jennifer Sherman, *Rural Poverty: The Great Recession, Rising Unemployment, and the Underutilized Safety Net, in* RURAL AMERICA IN A GLOBALIZING WORLD 523–24 (Conner Bailey et al. eds., 2014).

[35] Tim Slack, *Work in Rural America in the Era of Globalization, in* RURAL AMERICA IN A GLOBALIZING WORLD 573, 574–75 (Conner Bailey et al. eds., 2014).

[36] *Id.* at 578.

[37] Linda Lobao, *Economic Change, Structural Forces, and Rural America: Shifting Fortunes across Communities, in* RURAL AMERICA IN A GLOBALIZING WORLD 543, 549 (Conner Bailey et al. eds., 2014).

[38] DAVID LOUIS BROWN & KAI A. SCHAFFT, RURAL PEOPLE & COMMUNITIES IN THE 21ST CENTURY 150–51 (2011).

[39] Slack, *supra* note 35, at 578.

[40] BROWN & SCHAFFT, *supra* note 38, at 150–51.

[41] James P. Ziliak, "Economic Change and the Social Safety Net: Are Rural Americans Still Behind?" 12 (Mar. 21, 2018) (unpublished manuscript on file with author).

[42] BROWN & SCHAFFT, *supra* note 38, at 150–51.

[43] Slack, *supra* note 35, at 576.

[44] Ziliak, *supra* note 41, at 8.

[45] RURAL AMERICA AT A GLANCE, *supra* note 27, at 4. Government data calculates household income using all cash inflows, including those from social safety-net programs, but excluding noncash benefits (such as food stamps and housing subsidies), tax credits, and capital gains or

Unemployment

Unemployment and underemployment also contribute to rural economic difficulties. While employment levels in urban areas[46] have recovered from the Great Recession and surpassed 2008 levels, as of 2015, rural employment levels were still far below prerecession benchmarks.[47] Both rural and urban areas experienced a 2 percent per year drop in employment between 2007 and 2010, but urban areas rebounded 1.9 percent per year from 2010 to 2015, while rural areas saw less than half that amount of employment growth (+0.8 percent annually).[48] By 2015, rural employment was still 400,000 jobs shy of its 2007 level, while urban employment had experienced a net gain of 3.6 million jobs over the same period.[49]

In the past, the rural poor were more likely to work than the urban poor. For example, 32.7 percent of rural poor heads of household (aged 16+) were working in 1989, compared to 24.8 percent of similarly situated urban householders.[50] While numbers of working poor remain high, the percent of the rural poor who are not working increased drastically from 1980 to 2015.[51] By 2013, only 23.6 percent of rural poor householders worked, while 28 percent of urban ones did.[52] This reversal was not driven by improving conditions in urban areas, but rather by a shift away from employment among the rural poor.[53] This increase in nonworking rural poor suggests that rural residents are struggling not only because jobs pay poorly but also with finding jobs at all.

Underemployment

Underemployment remains a significant problem in many rural areas. Underemployment is a broad category that includes those who are unemployed, those who are discouraged (that is, they would like to work but have not looked for work in the past four weeks), those who are employed at low or inadequate hours

---

losses. *How the Census Bureau Measures Poverty*, U.S. CENSUS BUREAU, www.census.gov/topics/income-poverty/poverty/guidance/poverty-measures.html.
[46] Unless noted otherwise, we use "rural" and "urban" interchangeably with "nonmetro" and "metro," the former being US Census Bureau terms and the latter being Office of Management and Budget terms.
[47] RURAL AMERICA AT A GLANCE, *supra* note 27, at 3–4.
[48] *Id.*
[49] *Id.*
[50] Brian C. Thiede et al., *Working, but Poor: The Good Life in Rural America?*, 59 J. OF RURAL STUD. 183, 185 (2018) (citing Daniel T. Lichter et al., *Changing Linkages between Work and Poverty in Rural America*, 59 RURAL SOC. 395 (1994)).
[51] Brian C. Thiede, "Economic Disadvantage, Employment, and Policy in Rural America," presented at The Geography of Opportunity Annual Poverty Research and Policy Forum, Washington, DC, Sept. 26, 2017, Slide 13 (on file with author).
[52] Thiede et al., *supra* note 50, at 187.
[53] *Id.*

(involuntary part time), and those who are low income.[54] Underemployment was generally higher in rural areas for all years 1999 to 2009.[55] One specific type of underemployment, working poverty,[56] was higher in rural areas than in urban areas for all years during the period 2000–2013.[57] Historically disadvantaged groups in rural areas, including female-headed households and racial minorities, had especially high rates of working poverty.[58]

Even for those rural residents able to find jobs that would satisfy SNAP work requirements, challenges common to rural areas, such as geographic isolation and infrastructure deficits, can cause the costs of going to work to outweigh the benefits. Barriers of this type make it difficult for rural residents to maintain steady employment.

The spatial dispersion of rural workers and employers forces rural workers to commute longer distances to work.[59] On average, rural workers travel 38 percent more miles to work than urban workers.[60] Lower-income residents travel the farthest distances, commuting 59 percent more miles than urban residents.[61] The costs of commuting are significant for rural workers, who spend a greater portion of their budgets (20 percent) on transportation than do urban workers (13 percent).[62] Furthermore, public transportation is simply unavailable in many rural communities – 38 percent of rural residents live in areas with no public transportation at all.[63]

A lack of sufficient child care creates an additional hurdle for rural workers. A 2016 report by the Center for American Progress introduced the term "child care deserts" to describe the severe deficit of child care resources in America's rural communities.[64] The report, which analyzed county data in eight states, found that the majority of rural zip codes are "child care deserts," and that 55 percent of rural

---

[54] Slack, *supra* note 35, at 579.

[55] *Id.* at 579–81.

[56] Definitions of working poverty vary. The federal government defines the working poor as individuals who spent at least 27 weeks in the labor force (working or looking for work), but who still earned less than the official household poverty threshold. U.S. Bureau of Labor Statistics, BLS Reports No. 1068, A Profile of the Working Poor, 2015 (Apr. 2017), www.bls.gov/opub/reports/working-poor/2015/home.htm.

[57] Thiede et al., *supra* note 50, at 187.

[58] *Id.* at 188.

[59] Brown & Schafft, *supra* note 38, at 199.

[60] *Id.*

[61] *Id.*

[62] Todd Litman, Cmty. Transp. Ass'n of America, Public Transportation's Impact on Rural and Small Towns 15 (2017), www.apta.com/resources/reportsandpublications/Documents/APTA-Rural-Transit-2017.pdf.

[63] Brian Dabson et al., Rural Policy Research Inst., Rethinking Federal Investments in Rural Transportation 7 (Apr. 2011), www.rupri.org/Forms/RUPRI_Transportation_April2011.pdf.

[64] Rashid Malik et al., Ctr. for American Progress, Child Care Deserts (Oct. 2016), https://cdn.americanprogress.org/content/uploads/2016/10/01070626/ChildcareDeserts-report3.pdf. "A child care desert is defined as a ZIP code with at least 30 children under the age of 5 and either no child care centers or so few centers that there are more than three times as many children under age 5 as there are spaces in centers." *Id.* at 1.

children under the age of five live in such deserts.[65] Inability to access child care has significant implications for working parents with children over six years old who would be subject to expanded work requirements under the proposed Farm Bill legislation. If these parents are required to miss work when their children are sick or out of school, they likely would struggle to meet their work requirements.

For those who are unemployed and underemployed in rural America, SNAP serves as a lifeline. Should new and stricter work requirements be implemented, the effects will be disproportionately felt in rural areas where steady, full-time employment may be scarce or unavailable, or where rural infrastructure deficits make it more difficult or costly to get and keep a job. This will occur even though many residents are willing to work. Finally, work requirements will penalize rural residents who do work but nevertheless struggle to fulfill the 20 hour-per-week requirement,[66] even if the failure to meet that threshold results from an employer's inability or unwillingness to schedule an employee for the requisite number of hours.

THE IMPORTANCE OF SAFETY-NET PROGRAMS IN RURAL AMERICA

Empirical studies suggest that the social safety net plays a critical role in ameliorating the impacts of rural poverty. The work of rural economist James Ziliak, for example, suggests that the social safety net is differentially effective at poverty alleviation along the rural-urban continuum.[67] Ziliak found that for most years from 1979 to 2015, and for most families (disaggregated by education level and gender of head of household), social safety-net programs lifted a higher percentage of people and households out of poverty in rural areas than in urban areas.[68] Ziliak also concluded that rural households rely on social safety-net programs more than urban households; rural residents receive 20 percent more of their income from government transfers than do urban residents.[69]

Recent analysis by another rural economist, Jennifer Warlick, provides further evidence of the efficacy of SNAP in rural areas.[70] Warlick found that in 2013, SNAP

[65] *Id.* at 3.
[66] See BOLEN ET AL., FARM BILL, *supra* note 25, at 14.
[67] Ziliak, *supra* note 41, at 22, Figure 15.
[68] *Id.* Ziliak compares the percentage of households whose income falls below the poverty line based on net income, which includes government cash transfers, food stamps, and tax credits, with the percentage of households that fall below the poverty line when social safety-net sources of income are excluded from the calculation (market income). Those households that fall below the poverty line based on market income but not on net income are those lifted out of poverty by social safety-net programs.
[69] Here, income includes Social Security, Aid to Families with Dependent Children (AFDC)/ TANF, Supplemental Security Income (SSI), SNAP, EITC, general assistance, unemployment compensation, veteran's benefits, and education assistance. It does not include in-kind transfers from Medicare, Medicaid, or military health insurance. *Id.* at 17.
[70] Jennifer Warlick, *The Safety Net in Rural America, in* RURAL POVERTY IN THE UNITED STATES 389 (Ann R. Tickamyer et al. eds., 2017). The programs she analyzed were Social Security,

reduced child poverty in rural places by 15.4 percent, compared to 14.6 percent in urban places.[71] Among all social safety-net programs, SNAP is second only to Social Security in reducing poverty for rural children.[72] Further, "research shows that SNAP participation leads to healthier children who are more likely to graduate from high school and become self-sufficient earners in adulthood."[73] Indeed, Warlick found that eight of the ten safety-net programs were more effective in rural areas than in urban ones.[74]

Safety-net programs in rural areas are more effective despite spatial and social barriers to enrollment in many such programs. For programs that require in-person enrollment, as eight states do for SNAP, the distance required to travel to the program office may be prohibitive for rural residents.[75] This problem is particularly acute for the 4.2 percent of rural households without access to a vehicle.[76] Further, only 24–27 percent of rural residents are able to use public transit to access necessary amenities, including grocery stores[77] and health care services, compared to 71–74

---

refundable tax credits, SNAP, SSI, housing subsidies, unemployment insurance, child support, school lunch, TANF/General Assistance (GA) (means-tested cash transfers), and Women, Infants, and Children (WIC). *Id.* at 396–97. For each program, Warlick compared the Supplemental Poverty Measure (SPM) poverty rate in 2013 to what that poverty rate would have been without the cash value of the safety-net program. The difference was then divided by the SPM poverty rate without the program to yield the proportion of families the program had lifted out of poverty. *Id.* at 391.

    Instead of using the Official Poverty Measure (OPM), Warlick used the Supplemental Poverty Measure (SPM), an alternative metric developed by the Census Bureau in the 1990s. One of the main differences is that the SPM includes an adjustment for cost of living. Because this varies geographically, the SPM may overreport the effectiveness of safety-net programs in rural areas and underreport their effectiveness in urban areas. However, "The SPM is preferred when measuring the impact of safety net programs on the level of poverty because it has more comprehensive definitions of the resources available to families and their monetary needs than does the [OPM]." *Id* at 389.

[71] Warlick, *supra* note 70, at 394.

[72] *Id.* SNAP reduces poverty among rural children by one-third. *Id.*

[73] *Id.* at 398, Table 14.2.

[74] *Id.* at 398–99.

[75] *Id.* at 404.

[76] Jeremy Mattson, Upper Great Plains Transportation Inst., Rural Transit Fact Book 13 (Oct. 2017), www.surtc.org/transitfactbook/downloads/2017-rural-transit-fact-book.pdf

[77] Lack of public transportation to grocery stores only exacerbates the difficulties many rural residents face in accessing and affording food. Due to a decline in rural population, many rural grocery stores are closing permanently. As a result, 98 percent of America's food deserts – defined as living 10 or more miles from a grocery store – are in rural America. Lengthy trips to the grocery stores and higher markup on perishable items increase the costs associated with grocery shopping in rural areas, making SNAP an even more important resource for defraying food costs. *See* Lois Wright Morton & Troy C. Blanchard, Rural Sociological Society, Rural Realities, Starved for Access: Life in Rural America's Food Deserts (2007), www.iatp.org/sites/default/files/258_2_98043.pdf; Jon M. Bailey, Center for Rural Affairs, Rural Grocery Stores: Importance and Challenges (Oct. 2010), http://files.cfra .org/pdf/rural-grocery-stores.pdf; *see also* Ryan Schuessler, *Food Deserts in America's Breadbasket*, Al Jazeera (June 10, 2018).

percent of urban residents and 44–47 percent of those living in suburbs.[78] Even programs that allow enrollment (or reporting of work hours) online are often less accessible in rural places given the lower rates of broadband access.[79]

Furthermore, rural residents often feel community pressure not to enroll in government programs, which rural communities are more likely to view as "handouts."[80] Yet they often have no choice, in part because charitable support is far less available in rural areas. Median nonprofit human service expenditures per low-income resident[81] in 2010 were nearly 23 times higher in urban counties than in rural ones.[82]

MAINE AS A CASE STUDY FOR SNAP WORK REQUIREMENTS

Among Maine's 1.3 million residents, about 540,000 live in rural areas[83] and 11 of the state's 16 counties are nonmetro.[84] With 41 percent of the state's population living in rural areas, Maine is the sixth most rural state in the nation, tied with Kentucky. Rural poverty in Maine hit a 40-year low in 1999, at 12.8 percent,[85] with Maine's urban residents nevertheless faring slightly better, at 9.6 percent.[86] SNAP is credited with keeping an average of 47,000 Maine residents – including 16,000 children – out of poverty each year between 2009 and 2012.[87]

Against this backdrop, Governor Paul LePage moved to impose work requirements on Maine's SNAP recipients in 2014.[88] SNAP receipt in Maine had peaked at

---

[78] Mattson, *supra* note 76, at 17.

[79] Warlick, *supra* note 70, at 404.

[80] *See* Alisha Coleman-Jensen & Barry Steffen, *Food Insecurity and Housing Insecurity, in* Rural Poverty in the United States 257, 268–69 (Ann R. Tickamyer et al. eds., 2017); *see also* Sarah Whiteley, *Case Study: Food Insecurity and Hunger in the Rural West, in* Rural Poverty in the United States 288–90 (Ann R. Tickamyer et al. eds., 2017).

[81] "Low-income resident" here means a person with an income at or below 150 percent of the Federal Poverty Line. Scott Allard, "Geography and Opportunity in America," presented at Annual IRP Forum Sept. 26, 2017, Slide 29.

[82] The figure was $884/low-income person in urban counties but just $39/low-income person in rural counties. *Id.*

[83] USDA Econ. Res. Serv., State Fact Sheets: Maine (May 24, 2018), https://data.ers.usda .gov/reports.aspx?StateFIPS=23&StateName=Maine&ID=17854 (hereinafter State Fact Sheets: Maine).

[84] *Id.*

[85] *Id.*

[86] *Id.*

[87] Ctr. on Budget and Pol'y Priorities, Maine Food Supplement Program (Mar. 14, 2018), www.cbpp.org/sites/default/files/atoms/files/snap_factsheet_maine.pdf (hereinafter Maine Food Supplement Program).

[88] Jennifer Levitz, After Linking Work to Food Stamps, Maine Seeks Same with Medicaid, Wall St. J (Apr. 14, 2017); Niraj Chokshi, Need Food? Maine's Governor Wants You to Work for It, Wash. Post (July 24, 2017).

252,000 in 2012, and by 2016 it had fallen by nearly a quarter, to less than 190,000.[89] That same year, 16.4 percent of Maine households suffered from food insecurity.[90]

Also by 2016, Maine's overall poverty rate had risen to 12.5 percent.[91] The rural poverty rate was 15.1 percent and the urban poverty rate was significantly lower, at 10.7 percent, with the disparity between the two having increased between 1999 and 2016, from a gap of 3.2 percent to 4.4 percent.[92] Maine's three most urban counties are Cumberland, Sagadahoc, and York,[93] with 2016 poverty rates between 8 percent and 10 percent in those places.[94] Maine's most rural counties fall into two categories: (1) coastal and experiencing rural gentrification: Lincoln and Knox, with a poverty rate of 11 percent; and (2) inland and experiencing socioeconomic distress: Piscataquis, Washington, and Aroostook, with poverty rates ranging from 16 percent to 19 percent. The county with the highest rate of poverty – 20 percent in 2016 – is Somerset County.[95] The poverty and rurality data for all Maine counties are depicted in Table 4.2.

Consistent with national trends, unemployment rates tend to be higher in Maine's rural areas. Unemployment is very low, 2.5 percent in 2017, in Cumberland, Maine's most populous county.[96] Cumberland's unemployment rate peaked at 6.5 percent in 2010.[97] Cumberland's economic recovery and current low unemployment rate contrasts with the state's more rural counties, including Somerset, where unemployment peaked at 11.1 percent in 2010, and had fallen to about 5 percent by 2017.[98] The unemployment rates of nonmetropolitan Washington and Aroostook counties similarly hovered around 5 percent in 2017, far below their 2010 rates but well above the rates for urban parts of Maine.

[89] USDA Food and Nutrition Service, Supplemental Nutrition Assistance Program State Activity Report Fiscal Year 2012 (Oct. 2013), www.fns.usda.gov/pd/snap-state-activity-reports (hereinafter SNAP State Report FY 2012); USDA Food and Nutrition Service, Supplemental Nutrition Assistance Program State Activity Report Fiscal Year 2016 (Sept. 2017), www.fns.usda.gov/pd/snap-state-activity-reports.
[90] Maine Food Supplement Program, *supra* note 87.
[91] State Fact Sheets: Maine, *supra* note 83.
[92] *Id.*
[93] USDA Economic Research Service, Population estimates for the U.S., States, and Counties, 2010–17, www.ers.usda.gov/data-products/county-level-data-sets/download-data/.
[94] USDA Economic Research Service, Poverty estimates for the U.S., States, and Counties, 2016, www.ers.usda.gov/data-products/county-level-data-sets/download-data/.
[95] *See* USDA Economic Research Service, 2013 Rural-Urban Continuum Codes, www.ers.usda.gov/data-products/rural-urban-continuum-codes.aspx; *see also* Sarah Kahn-Troster et al., Maine Rural Health Profiles: Somerset County 6 (Sept. 2016), www.mehaf.org/content/uploaded/images/reports-research/maine%20rural%20health%20profiles_somerset_september%202016_hyperlinksfixed.pdf.
[96] USDA Economic Research Service, Unemployment and median household income for the U.S., States, and counties, 2007–17, www.ers.usda.gov/data-products/county-level-data-sets/download-data/.
[97] *Id.*
[98] *Id.*

TABLE 4.2 *Poverty, Unemployment, and Density of Maine Counties*

County Name	Number on Rural-Urban Continuum Code**	Population of County (2010)*	Poverty Rate (2016)*	Unemployment Rate (2010)*	Unemployment Rate (2017)*	Population Density per sq. mi (2016)*
Piscataquis	8	17,535	17.88%	10.7%	4.0%	4.4
Lincoln	8	34,457	11.08%	7.6%	3.2%	75.6
Washington	7	32,856	17.09%	10.8%	4.9%	12.8
Knox	7	39,736	11.01%	7.4%	3.1%	108.8
Aroostook	7	71,870	15.03%	9.7%	4.8%	10.8
Franklin	6	30,768	13.36%	9.2%	4.0%	18.1
Waldo	6	38,786	14.22%	8.5%	3.6%	53.1
Somerset	6	52,228	18.67%	11.1%	4.8%	13.3
Hancock	6	54,418	10.80%	8.8%	3.8%	34.3
Oxford	6	57,833	13.08%	10.7%	3.8%	27.8
Kennebec	4	122,151	13.49%	7.6%	3.2%	140.8
Androscoggin	3	107,702	12.27%	8.6%	3.1%	230.2
Penobscot	3	153,923	13.94%	8.5%	3.7%	45.3
Sagadahoc	2	35,293	9.19%	6.7%	2.7%	139.1
York	2	197,131	8.18%	8.0%	2.9%	199
Cumberland	2	281,674	10.09%	6.5%	2.5%	337.2

Source: *https://factfinder.census.gov/faces/nav/jsf/pages/index.xhtml
** http://www.ers.usda.gov/data-products/rural-urban-continuum-codes.aspx; code range is from 1 to 9 with 9 being the most rural

Work Requirements in Maine

Soon after his 2010 election as governor, [99] Republican Paul LePage targeted the state's safety-net programs for reduction.[100] Until LePage's election, Maine had been a leader in providing social services,[101] but LePage's administration tightened eligibility for SNAP, Medicaid, and cash assistance.[102] The press criticized LePage for "hoarding" federal block-grant funds that were previously going to antipoverty programs.[103] LePage nevertheless also announced plans to add work requirements to Medicaid, to remove young adults from public health coverage, and to eliminate the state's general-assistance funds for the indigent.[104]

Maine's SNAP Participation

As noted earlier, about 190,000 Maine residents – some 14 percent of the state's population – participated in the SNAP program in 2016,[105] down from about 250,000 in 2012.[106] Part of this drop is attributable to an improving economy, but part is attributable to the greater strictures on SNAP access under Governor LePage. Among those 62,000 removed from the rolls, about 7,000 are ABAWDs.

Nearly 46 percent of current SNAP recipients are in families with elderly or disabled members, and more than 62 percent of current SNAP recipients are in families with children.[107] More telling, regarding the purported goals of work requirements, is the fact that some 42 percent of Maine's SNAP recipients are in working families.[108] In other words, the fact that adult(s) are employed does not alleviate these families' food insecurity and need for SNAP.

Maine's Experience with Work Requirements

In late 2014, Maine did not reapply for its waiver from the SNAP work requirements. It began mandating that, to receive federal food assistance, ABAWDs must work, undergo training, or volunteer 20 hours each week.[109] At that time, Maine estimated that 11,953

[99] Abby Goodnough, *Medicaid Cuts Are Part of a Larger Battle in Maine*, N.Y. TIMES (Dec. 24, 2011).
[100] *See* Annie Lowrey, *The People Left Behind When Only the "Deserving" Poor Get Help*, THE ATLANTIC (May 25, 2017).
[101] Jamie Neikrie, *Op-Ed: If at First You Don't Succeed*, THE TUFTS DAILY (Feb. 15, 2018).
[102] Lowrey, *supra* note 100.
[103] Eric Russell, *Maine Sits on Millions in Federal Welfare Dollars, Yet Poverty Rises*, PORTLAND PRESS HERALD (Oct. 23, 2016).
[104] Lowrey, *supra* note 100.
[105] SNAP Participation and Costs, *supra* note 20.
[106] SNAP State Report FY 2012, *supra* note 89.
[107] MAINE FOOD SUPPLEMENT PROGRAM, *supra* note 87.
[108] *Id.*
[109] Levitz, *supra* note 88.

ABAWD residents were receiving SNAP benefits.[110] In the first round of removals from the program in December 2014, just three months after the program started, more than half (6,866) of ABAWD recipients were dropped from the SNAP rolls.[111]

Food Supplement Employment and Training

Aside from employment or community service, an ABAWD can satisfy the work requirement by completing training for 20 hours/week. Under a federal grant, Maine runs a training program geared toward providing job training to its ABAWD population.[112] Unfortunately for many rural residents, the state provides only four locations where ABAWDs can participate in training and education under the Food Supplement Employment and Training (FSET) program.[113] All FSET sites are located in urban areas along the Interstate 95 corridor.[114] While this decision maximizes the number of users, it does not serve rural residents who are not within driving distance of a center or do not have access to public transportation to get there.[115]

Additionally, the state budgeted for only 1,000 training participants in the first year of the work requirements,[116] with only 150 spots in long-term educational programs.[117] Beyond the educational spots, the remaining services largely are confined to job search assistance and training.[118] The job search components alone do not qualify as training that meets the work requirement. Maine's FSET program, then, was designed to provide job-skills training to only about 1 percent of the nearly 12,000 potential ABAWDs in the system.

Additional Asset Restrictions

Maine began imposing an asset test for its food assistance program in November 2015.[119] Childless households with more than $5,000 in assets are no longer eligible

---

[110] Paul Leparulo et al., *Memo: Preliminary Analysis of Work Requirement Policy on the Wage and Employment Experiences of ABAWDs in Maine* (Apr. 19, 2016), https://web.archive.org/web/20161101061909/ and www.maine.gov/economist/econdemo/ABAWD%20analysis_final.pdf.

[111] *Id.*

[112] Dep't of Health and Human Servs., State of Maine, Food Supplement Employment and Training Plan (E&T) FFY 2015 (Oct. 1, 2014), www.maine.gov/dhhs/ofi/services/snap/documents/FSET-CSSP-Approved-by-FNS.pdf.

[113] *Id.* at 2.

[114] *Id.* at 8.

[115] *Id.* at 2.

[116] *Id.* at 5.

[117] *Id.* at 6.

[118] *Id.* at 7 ("Maine estimates that 92.5% of the 1,000 ABAWDs served will go directly to job search.").

[119] See Noel K. Gallagher, *Maine Plans to Deny Food Stamps When Applicant's Assets Top $5,000*, Portland Press Herald (Sep. 16, 2015).

for SNAP benefits in Maine.[120] The asset test Maine uses includes liquid assets like cash, checking and savings accounts, stocks, bonds, and shares, as well as nonliquid assets like personal property, licensed and unlicensed vehicles, buildings, and land.[121] The state does, however, exclude many types of property from the asset limit, including houses, pensions, household goods, personal effects, life insurance, some vehicles, tools and equipment for employment, livestock, certain government benefits such as the Earned Income Credit (EITC), and certain educational savings accounts.[122]

If a household has more than one vehicle, the value of the vehicles are included, minus a $4,650 deduction for each vehicle.[123] Thus, for example, if a Maine household with two adults owned two cars valued at $7,200 each, then – without taking into account any other assets – the household asset total would be $5,100, leaving them ineligible for SNAP. Yet people need vehicles – especially in the absence of public transportation – to seek work, job training, and educational opportunities. This asset limitation, then, is counterproductive because each adult typically needs a reliable vehicle to maintain employment and, therefore, SNAP eligibility.

Negative Effects on Food Security and Strain on the Nonprofit Sector

A 2016 survey of Maine food pantry users revealed the negative impacts of the work requirements and asset limits for SNAP recipients.[124] A quarter of those surveyed indicated that they lost SNAP benefits in the last year.[125] Twenty-four percent of those who lost benefits cited the three-month time limit and work requirement.[126] Another 7 percent cited the asset test.[127] The remaining two-thirds who lost benefits were dropped from the program for a variety of reasons, including increased earnings, marriage, lost application paperwork, or being unable to schedule a required interview with a caseworker.[128] As a consequence, many Maine residents were forced to turn to food banks for "more than just emergency assistance, but as a means of long term survival."[129] This has put a strain on the state's nonprofit sector, including the more limited agencies serving rural communities.

---

[120] OFFICE FOR FAMILY INDEPENDENCE FOOD SUPPLEMENT PROGRAM, MAINE DEPARTMENT OF HEALTH AND HUMAN SERVICES, ASSET ELIGIBILITY STANDARDS 1, www.maine.gov/sos/cec/rules/10/ch301.htm.

[121] *Id.* at 2.

[122] *Id.* at 3–9.

[123] *Id.* at 10–11.

[124] GOOD SHEPHERD FOOD BANK, HUNGER PAINS: WIDESPREAD FOOD INSECURITY THREATENS MAINE'S FUTURE 14 (Feb. 2, 2017), https://gsfb.org/wp-content/uploads/2017/02/Food-Pantry-Report-2–6-171.pdf.

[125] *Id.*

[126] *Id.*

[127] *Id.*

[128] *Id.*

[129] Levitz, *supra* note 88 (quoting Jan Bindas-Tinney, advocacy director for Preble Street, a Portland, Maine group that distributes food to the needy).

Conflicting Studies of Consequences of SNAP Work Requirements

Maine's Office of Policy and Management released a 2016 report claiming that the work requirements were a success.[130] They supported their claim with data showing a positive growth in wages for those subject to the work requirement, including those who were dropped from the program.[131] Their report lacked any counterfactual examples, however, and did not evaluate other possible causes for wage growth. Since 2016, conservative "think tanks" have released related reports reaching conclusions similar to those of Maine's Office of Policy and Management.[132]

The Center on Budget and Policy Priorities (CBPP) laid out a clear rebuke of these conservative reports in December 2016.[133] The CBPP analysis took the conservative groups to task for failing to take into account that many SNAP recipients already work or would soon be working, even absent the time limit. The conservative reports claimed the work requirements succeeded by pointing to the better economic circumstances of the affected individuals. However, nothing in their approach isolated the impact of the work requirements. The conservative reports also did not consider the potentially severe impact of the time limit on those cut off from SNAP, nor did they address why ABAWDs are out of work in the first place.

A close look at what has happened in Maine since SNAP work requirements were reinstated in 2014 suggests that the push to reduce SNAP rolls achieved only modest reductions and therefore modest savings. What remains unknown is how many former SNAP recipients have sought work and been unable to find it, as well as how many have found work to which they could not feasibly commute because of prohibitive distances or lack of reliable transportation. We also do not know how many rural residents have been unable to satisfy alternative requirements – as for job training – because of spatial limits on training opportunities. Answers to these questions (and others like them) are necessary before the efficacy of the work requirements – as well as their human toll – can be fully evaluated.

[130] Leparulo & Rector, *supra* note 110.
[131] Id.
[132] *See, e.g.,* Robert Rector et al., Heritage Foundation, Maine Food Stamp Work Requirement Cuts Non-Parent Caseload by 80 Percent (Feb. 8, 2016), www.heritage.org/sites/default/files/2018-04/BG3091.pdf; Jonathan Ingrim et al., Foundation for Government Accountability, "The Case for Expanding Food Stamp Work Requirements to Parents" (Feb. 15, 2018), https://thefga .org/wp-content/uploads/2018/02/The-case-for-expanding-food-stamp-work-requirements-to-parents.pdf.
[133] DOTTIE ROSENBAUM & ED BOLEN, CTR. ON BUDGET AND POLICY PRIORITIES, SNAP REPORTS PRESENT MISLEADING FINDINGS ON IMPACT OF THREE-MONTH TIME LIMIT (Dec. 14, 2016), https://cbpp.org/research/food-assistance/snap-reports-present-misleading-findings-on-impact-of-three-month-time.

CONCLUSION

While safety-net work requirements have political appeal, in practice they often fail to achieve their stated goal of promoting self-sufficiency. Work requirements are particularly ineffective when jobs that pay a living wage are unavailable or effectively out of reach – due to weak and undiversified job markets, lack of transportation, prohibitive travel distances, or the need to take care of elderly, disabled, or dependent family members. These challenges are especially acute in many rural areas, where the safety net is critical to residents' survival and historically more effective at poverty alleviation than in urban areas. Further, rising percentages of nonworking poor (presumably because jobs are unavailable) compared to working poor in rural areas should be a cautionary signal to those who see work requirements as a straightforward antidote to safety-net reliance.

5

State and Local Tax Takeaways

Francine J. Lipman

There is nothing new about poverty. What is new, however, is that we have the resources to get rid of it.

Dr. Rev. Martin Luther King Jr.[1]

INTRODUCTION

Taxes are the price we pay for a civilized society.

Oliver Wendell Holmes[2]

What federal tax structures giveth to low- and middle-income families, state and local tax structures take away. This is the story of our unjust American tax system. While the overall federal tax structure is generally progressive, state and local tax systems are notably regressive.[3] When analyzed as a whole, the combined tax system imposed on Americans today is mildly progressive.[4] The share of all taxes paid by the

---

[1] Dr. Martin Luther King Jr., *The Quest for Peace and Justice*, Nobel Peace Prize Lecture, Oslo, Norway (Dec. 11, 1964) (juxtaposing extreme wealth against extreme poverty in America more than 50 years ago "the poor in America know that they live in the richest nation in the world, and that even though they are perishing on a lonely island of poverty they are surrounded by a vast ocean of material prosperity"). *Id.*

[2] "Taxes are what we pay for civilized society," *Compania General De Tabacos De Filipinas v. Collector of Internal Revenue*, 275 U.S. 87, 100, dissenting; opinion (Nov. 21, 1927). This quote is engraved in the stone on the entrance to the national office of the Internal Revenue Service at 1111 Constitution Avenue, Washington, DC.

[3] Inst. on Tax'n & Econ. Pol'y, *Who Pays Taxes in America in 2017?*, Apr. 2017.

[4] Davis et al., Inst. on Tax'n & Econ. Pol'y, *Who Pays? A Distributional Analysis of the Tax Systems in All Fifty States* (5th ed. Jan. 2015) (analyzing all 50 state and local tax structures plus the District of Columbia to measure the effective tax rates and distribution among nonelderly residents focusing on income levels) (hereinafter *Who Pays?*). The report excludes individuals who are 65 and older because the federal and state governments taxation of these individuals is very favorable with age-based exclusions and deductions. "Because so many states offer special

richest Americans only slightly exceeds their share of the nation's income. Similarly, the share of all taxes paid by the poorest Americans is only slightly less than their share of the nation's income. Our current tax systems have not stalled rising income and wealth inequality. The lowest 20 percent of all income families ($14,000 average annual income) cannot afford any tax liability yet they currently pay 15.9 percent, while the richest 1 percent of all income households ($1,827,000 average annual income) can afford to pay more than their current rate of only 30.4 percent to support government systems that provide and protect their enormous income levels and accumulated wealth.[5]

In a seemingly prosperous America with low unemployment rates and exploding capital markets, there is record income and wealth inequality,[6] with almost 45 million people living in poverty.[7] The highest 1 percent of income households receive more income than the entire lower half of all income households.[8] The wealth disparity is even more egregious as the top 1 percent own more wealth than the combined household wealth of the lower 90 percent.[9] Our aggregate federal and state tax systems have not done much to offset America's many decades old increasing income and wealth inequality.[10]

Aggregate taxes paid across all income groups is roughly proportional to their aggregate share of income. The highest-income 1 percent of all households receive 20.3 percent of the nation's aggregate income and pay a commensurate percent, 22.9 percent, of all taxes.[11] The bottom 20 percent of income earners receive only a small fraction of the nation's income, or 3.5 percent, and pay a similar percent of all taxes, 1.9 percent.[12] While proportionality of aggregate tax liability to aggregate income might seem fair on its face, given the diminishing marginal value of income and wealth it is not. A more progressive aggregate tax system would be a more just and effective remedy for these debilitating economic trends.

---

consideration for elderly taxpayers, including elderly families in the *Who Pays* analysis would not give an accurate depiction of how the tax structure treats the majority of taxpayers." *Id.*

[5] Inst. on Tax'n & Econ. Pol'y, *Who Pays Taxes in America in 2018?*, Apr. 2018.

[6] Edward N. Wolff, Nat'l Bureau of Econ. Research, *Household Wealth Trends in the United States, 1962 to 2016: Has Middle Class Wealth Recovered?* (Nov. 2017) (noting that the racial and ethnic wealth gap has widened considerably).

[7] Liana Fox, U.S. Census Bureau, *The Supplemental Poverty Measure: 2016* (Sept. 2017) (describing a 14 percent poverty rate for 2016).

[8] Inst. on Tax'n & Econ. Pol'y, *Fairness Matters: A Chart Book on Who Pays State and Local Taxes* (Jan. 2017) at Chart 2.

[9] *Id.*

[10] "The bottom line is that before-tax income inequality has risen since the 1970s, despite an increase in government transfer payments. Because high-income people pay higher average tax rates than others, *federal* taxes reduce inequality. But the mitigating effect of taxes is about the same today as before 1980. Thus, after-tax income inequality has increased about as much as before-tax inequality." Frank Sammartino, Center on Budget & Pol'y Priorities, *Taxes and Income Inequality* (June 15, 2017) (emphasis added).

[11] Inst. on Tax'n & Econ. Pol'y, *Who Pays Taxes in America in 2018?*, Apr. 2018.

[12] *Id.*

The current aggregate tax structure hurts our most vulnerable families living in or on the brink of poverty because they do not have the capacity to pay any amount of their limited financial resources to the government. After the sweeping 2017 tax reform, the lowest 20 percent of all income groups pays an effective aggregate tax rate of 16 percent, the next income quartile pays 21 percent, the third quartile pays 25 percent, and the fourth income quartile pays 29 percent, while the highest-income households pay an aggregate effective tax rate of only 30 percent.[13] This tax structure pushes the most vulnerable Americans into – and deeper into – the abyss of poverty. Moreover, the current structure has not stalled rising income and wealth inequity. America is a low-tax country at less than 26 percent of gross domestic product, well below most developed countries including Canada, France, the United Kingdom, Spain, Israel and Germany.[14] The United States could increase its effective tax rate by 30 percent and still be below the Organisation for Economic Co-operation and Development average of more than 34 percent.

While the aggregate tax system is mildly progressive, state and local tax systems are notably regressive. The lowest 95 percent of all income earners pay on average a higher percent of their income in state and local taxes than their share of aggregate income.[15] By comparison, the top 5 percent of all income earners pay a lower percent of their income in state and local taxes than their aggregate share of household income.[16] As a result, the lowest quartile of income earners pays a higher effective state and local tax rate than the highest 1 percent of all income earners. The ratio of effective state and local tax rates for lowest-income to highest-income taxpayers is as high as seven times in Wyoming, Washington, and Florida. None of these states has an income tax so they rely heavily on regressive consumption tax revenues. For state and local governments, this is a no-win race to the bottom because as income becomes increasingly concentrated among the wealthy, consumption, as well as state and local tax revenues decrease.

This chapter will review the basic components of state and local tax systems focusing on their many regressive attributes and make suggestions on how states might improve them. America has 50 state tax laboratories, plus the District of Columbia, that offer a myriad of dynamic time-tested tax structures. Nearly every state currently taxes lower-income families at a higher effective tax rate than higher-income families.[17] On average, the lowest-income families are paying state and local taxes at an effective rate that is twice as high as the rate that the top 1 percent of income households enjoy. "Identifying state tax trends serves a dual purpose: first, as a leading indicator providing a sense of what we can expect in the coming months

---

[13] Inst. on Tax'n & Econ. Pol'y, *Fairness Matters: A Chart Book on Who Pays State and Local Taxes* (Jan. 2017).

[14] *Id.*

[15] *Id.*

[16] *Id.*

[17] *Who Pays, supra* note 4, at 1.

and years, and second, as a set of case studies, placing ideas into greater circulation and allowing empirical consideration of what has and has not worked."[18] As state and local governments continue to confront tax reform in these challenging times, this chapter serves as a guide for front line progressive tax innovations, justice, and equity for all.

STATE AND LOCAL TAX SYSTEM BASICS

Every state and local tax system in America is regressive, costing low- and middle-income households a greater percentage of their income than wealthy households. This results from an overreliance on consumption taxes versus progressive income taxes to raise revenue. Given this reliance, disproportional distribution is a rational result given that low- and middle-income households necessarily must spend a significant percentage of their income to sustain themselves, as compared to wealthy families who enjoy the luxury of saving and investing. Given wage stagnation and rising costs of living, including sky-rocketing housing and health care rates, some low-income households are forced to spend more than their household income by borrowing or using other outside resources to cover their basic living expenses.

While many states supplement regressive consumption taxes with more progressive income taxes, state and local governments rely much less on progressive income tax structures than the federal government. As a result, contrary to fundamental tax theories such as wherewithal to pay and tax equity, the lower your household income the higher your overall state and local effective tax rates. The Institute on Taxation and Economic Policy has recently determined that the nationwide average state and local effective tax rates by income group were 10.9 percent for the poorest 20 percent of households, 9.7 percent for the middle 20 percent, and 7.0 percent for the top 1 percent.[19] The lowest-income households had an average effective tax rate that was more than 50 percent higher than the highest-income households.

Taking the most from those who have the least is neither sustainable nor moral. This structure is not only unjust, it is not practicable given diminishing revenues and real income levels. As a result, state and local governments are having to rethink how they can better raise revenues. The next sections detail common state and local tax structures, including property, consumption, and income taxes. Each section describes the current regressive and progressive characteristics of these state structures and explains how they might be restructured to better serve all Americans.

---

[18] Jarad Walczak, Tax Found., *Trends in State Tax Policy, 2018*, at 2 (Dec. 14, 2017).
[19] *Who Pays, supra* note 4, at 3.

Property Taxes

Taxes on property are a significant revenue source for state governments, comprising about 22 percent of total revenues in 2015.[20] Property taxes, which are typically determined by the current fair market value of the taxed real and personal property multiplied by a fixed flat rate, are generally regressive in their overall effect. Most states and local governments assess property taxes on real property, including residences, rental properties, office buildings, and other commercial properties, as well as personal property such as automobiles, motorcycles, boats, and, in some cases, business furniture, fixtures, and equipment.

For most homeowners, their principal residence represents a significant percentage of their net worth. This is less true for higher-income homeowners who also hold nonproperty taxed assets, such as cash, stocks, and bonds. Because their "property-taxed assets" represent a smaller percentage of their wealth, higher-income households have an effective property tax rate that is lower than low- and middle-income homeowners. Lower-income households, who do not own their own home, but rent, effectively pay property taxes through higher rental payments made to their landlord, the property owners. As a result of these factors, property taxes are regressive.[21]

States that also assess property taxes on real and personal business property, like buildings, furniture, fixtures, and equipment, reduce the regressivity because business property taxes are generally paid by higher-income earners. While these business owners may pass the tax costs to customers, the customers may or may not reside in the tax assessing state. Researchers have determined that about 40 percent of typical state property taxes fall on businesses (excluding rental property taxes that economists have determined are borne by tenants), thereby mitigating the overall regressivity of property taxes to some extent.[22]

Forty-six states and Washington, DC have some type of limit on the amount of property taxes they can assess. The only states without any current state-imposed property tax limits are Hawaii, New Hampshire, Tennessee, and Vermont.[23] Eight states and Washington, DC impose three different types of property tax limits, including Arizona, Arkansas, Colorado, Illinois, Michigan, Montana, New Mexico, and Texas.[24] The three basic types of property tax limitations include ceilings imposed on assessments, revenues, and rates. Assessment limits impose a ceiling on how much the assessed value of taxed property can increase over time. California imposed this form of limitation in 1978 through its passage of Proposition 13, which limited increases in assessed values of taxed property to 2 percent a year until owners

[20] *Id.* at 26.
[21] *Id.* at 13.
[22] *Id.*
[23] Jarad Walczak, Tax Found., *Property Tax Limitation Regimes: A Primer* (Apr. 23, 2018).
[24] *Id.*

transfer the property in an arm's-length transaction.[25] This limitation has resulted in dramatically unequal property tax burdens among similar neighboring properties in California and discourages certain property transfers. This lock-in effect undermines homeownership and mobility for low- and middle-income households.[26] To somewhat mitigate these constraints, California property tax laws exempt certain transfers of principal residences to family members from reassessment, while homeowners who are 55 or older can transfer their home's "assessed value" to a new home of equal or lesser value in most California counties.[27]

Rate limits cap property tax rates that governments may impose. Rate limits may cap the amount of annual rate increases, establish a maximum ceiling rate, or require affirmative voter authorization for certain rate increases. Revenue limits constrain any increases in aggregate tax revenue, permitting governments to determine the design of a tax system (e.g., rates or assessments) up to a maximum amount of revenue. Rate and revenue limits impose significant constraints on state and local government spending, including for necessary resources such as public education, police, and other health and safety personnel. While across the board limits may or may not be more equitable among property owners, they do not protect low- and fixed-income homeowners from increased property tax burdens due to rising home values. Each of these types of property tax limits has advantages and disadvantages. Because none of these structures are flawless, more narrowly targeted taxpayer remedies may provide more effective relief. Two potential remedies for lower-income families are inflation-adjusted homestead exemptions and annual property tax relief based upon household income.

A homestead exemption reduces regressivity. States that allow a generous homestead exemption that is regularly inflation adjusted for increases in housing values mitigate some of the hardship of tax regressivity. As housing values increase over time due to inflation as well as appreciation, states concerned about tax incidence on lower-income households have correspondingly increased the value of their homestead exemptions. States that are less concerned about tax incidence have allowed their annual homestead exemption amounts to shrink to a less meaningful offset. The presence of an inflation adjusted homestead exemption reduces state and local tax regressivity.

Another approach to reduce the regressivity of property taxes is to provide some type of targeted property tax reduction for low-income households. States may provide a property tax offset or reduction triggered when a property owner's tax bill exceeds a certain percentage of their household income. The most effective and targeted property tax credits are made available to low-income homeowners and

---

[25] *See generally,* William H. Oakland, *Proposition 13 – Genesis and Consequences,* 32 NAT'L TAX J. 387–409 (June 1979).
[26] Jarad Walczak, Tax Found., *Property Tax Limitation Regimes: A Primer* (Apr. 23, 2018).
[27] *Id.*

renters regardless of age. Unfortunately, most states only provide property tax reductions to senior citizens. Only nine states and Washington, DC currently offer broad-based property tax reductions for all low-income property owners regardless of age or disability.[28] Property tax reductions can be administered through the state's income tax system through a refundable income tax credit. However, with this system, property owners have to file annual income tax returns to receive reimbursements of property taxes paid. While this adds administrative burdens and potentially additional tax preparation and filing fees, it does allow governments to simultaneously verify reported incomes. This approach also requires state residents to pay the full amount of property tax liabilities first, then seek reimbursements, which may create cash flow hardships for taxpayers. Nevertheless, these property tax reductions do mitigate to some extent the regressive imposition of state and local property taxes. Another novel alternative for less regressive property taxes is Vermont's assessment of certain property taxes targeted for schools based upon household incomes rather than property values.[29]

Consumption (Sales and Excise) Taxes

Consumption (sales and excise) taxes are among the most regressive taxes governments assess. The bottom 40 percent of households based upon income in all states, except the no sales tax state of Oregon, pay more in state and local consumption taxes than in income taxes.[30] Even worse, the bottom 80 percent of households based upon income pay more in state and local consumption taxes than on income taxes in *most* states.[31] Alaska, Delaware, Montana, New Hampshire, and Oregon currently have no statewide general sales taxes. But Delaware and Montana collect more in excise taxes than in income taxes from low- and middle-income households.[32] Alaska and New Hampshire, also with no income tax systems, impose excise taxes on the lowest-income households of 3.4 and 2.9 percent, respectively. These high effective state tax rates on low-income households are more than 11 times the low effective rates of only 0.3 and 0.2 percent enjoyed by the highest-income households in Alaska and New Hampshire, respectively.[33] Despite the extreme regressivity of consumption taxes, in 2012, consumption taxes comprised more than any other state revenue resource, or about 23 percent.[34]

---

[28] Maine, Maryland, Michigan, Minnesota, Montana, New Jersey, Vermont, West Virginia, and Wisconsin. *Id.* at 28–139.
[29] *Who Pays, supra* note 4, at 120.
[30] Inst. on Tax'n & Econ. Pol'y, *Fairness Matters: A Chart Book on Who Pays State and Local Taxes* (Jan. 2017), at Chart 14.
[31] *Id.*
[32] *Id.*
[33] *Who Pays, supra* note 4, at 23.
[34] *Id.* at 25.

States that rely heavily on consumption taxes with no income taxes often hold themselves out as "low tax" states. However, for low-income households, many of these states, including Washington, Florida, and Texas, have among the highest effective state tax rates. Washington has the highest effective tax rate on the first quintile of income earners of any state at 16.8 percent.[35] By comparison, the highest-income households in Washington enjoy an effective tax rate of only 2.8 percent.[36] Florida and Texas are also among the top three most regressive tax states, with effective tax rates on these same low-income households of 12.9 percent and 12.5 percent, respectively. High-income households in Florida and Texas enjoy effective tax rates of only 2.5 percent and 3.2 percent, respectively. South Dakota is another state that relies heavily on consumption taxes, as it does not have any individual or corporate income tax system. Nevertheless, South Dakota has one of the most regressive tax structures, assessing an 11.3 percent rate on the lowest-income households and a 2.2 percent rate on the highest-income households.[37]

While consumption tax rates are typically flat, unlike the federal and many state income tax structures, these taxes only apply to certain consumption. Income that is invested or saved is not subject to these taxes. Because lower-income and increasingly middle-income families are forced to consume most of their income for food, shelter, and other necessities, they have little or nothing left over for saving or investments. In sharp contrast, high-income households are able to save and invest so their consumption is significantly less than their household income. Moreover, as the wealthy increase their income and wealth at a disproportionate rate, their increased income is added to savings and investments, creating more wealth, not more consumption and, therefore, not subject to consumption taxes. Low-income households suffer almost eight times the effective consumption tax rate as high-income households, and middle-income households suffer a tax rate that is five times the rate enjoyed by their wealthy counterparts.[38] Current state and local consumption tax structures are highly regressive, with an average 7 percent rate for the lowest-income households, a 4.7 percent rate for middle-income households, and a 0.8 percent rate for the highest-income households.[39]

Sales taxes are usually calculated as a percentage of the consumers' price of a broad base of taxable goods. Taxing basic necessities such as food, medications, clothing, toiletries, and women's hygiene products[40] exacerbates consumption tax regressivity because low-income households necessarily spend most, if not all, of

---

[35] *Id.* at 23.
[36] *Id.*
[37] *Id.*
[38] *Id.* at 12.
[39] *Id.*
[40] Ema Sagner, Nat'n Pub. Radio, *More States Move to End "Tampon Tax" That's Seen As Discriminating Against Women* (Mar. 25, 2018) (describing excluding women's menstrual products from sales tax exclusions as compared to dandruff shampoo, lip moistures, and erectile dysfunction medications is discriminatory).

their income on these required living expenses. Because sales taxes are based upon product prices, they generate larger amounts for more expensive goods and are automatically inflation adjusted as prices rise. Moreover, more expensive, luxury goods generate a larger dollar amount of tax, albeit assessed at the same fixed rate (e.g., sales tax on a Ford Fiesta versus on a Porsche 911 Carrera).

Excise taxes, by contrast, are imposed on narrow categories of goods, typically items for which consumption is measured and taxed based upon the amount of volume consumed (for example, gasoline, tires, alcohol, tobacco, marijuana). Excise taxes are typically based on volume of consumption (per gallon, ounce, pint, pack, cigarette, joint, etc.). Thus, the same excise tax is assessed on the buyer of the most expensive, top-of-the-line exotic imported beer as on the buyer of the generic store brand no-name beer. Accordingly, excise taxes are structurally the most regressive taxes. Overall, state and local excise taxes on items such as gasoline, cigarettes, and alcohol cost about 1.6 percent of the household income of the lowest-income families, 0.8 percent of the income of middle-income families, and 0.1 percent of the income of the highest-income families.[41] Current excise taxes are sixteen times greater on low-income households and eight times greater on middle-income households as compared to the highest-income households. Moreover, because excise taxes are tied to units and volume as compared to price or current market value, they are not price adjusted for inflation and erode in real dollar value over time. State and local governments have to affirmatively adjust rates upward on a regular basis to maintain steady revenue flows. This will often require state and local legislation, which even if politically possible, takes time and resources before implementation.

States that exclude groceries and other necessities from state and local sales taxes can meaningfully reduce tax regressivity. Because low-income families spend about 75 percent of their income on sales-taxable items, compared to only 16 percent for high-income households, eliminating state and local sales taxes on items that are required for a basic standard of living can significantly reduce the sales tax burden on lower-income households.[42] However, because these exclusions apply to all consumers, they can be expensive for state coffers. For example, excluding groceries from sales taxes may reduce aggregate sales tax revenue from 5 to 30 percent.[43] Even under a moderately progressive exemption for grocery purchases, the bottom 40 percent of households (measured by income) receive only about 25 percent of the benefit.[44] Presently, only three states subject groceries to full state and local sales

[41] Who Pays, supra note 4, at 25.
[42] Inst. on Tax'n & Econ. Pol'y, Policy Brief, Options for a Less Regressive Sales Tax in 2017 (Sept. 2017).
[43] Nicolas Johnson & Iris J. Lav, Center on Budget & Pol'y Priorities, Should States Tax Food? Examining the Policy Issues and Options (Apr. 1998).
[44] Inst. on Tax'n & Econ. Pol'y, Policy Brief, Options for a Less Regressive Sales Tax in 2017 (Sept. 2017).

taxes, including Alabama (4 percent), Mississippi (7 percent), and South Dakota (4.5 percent).[45] Although South Dakota does provide a limited taxpayer refund of either sales or property taxes to certain seniors and disabled residents,[46] most South Dakotans pay the full sales tax on food due to narrow refund limitations. Six states (Arkansas, Illinois, Missouri, Tennessee, Utah, and Virginia) tax food at lower rates than other sales taxed goods at rates ranging from 1 percent to 5 percent.[47] Alternatively, Hawaii, Idaho, Kansas, and Oklahoma tax groceries in full, but offer limited tax credits or rebates to reimburse certain taxpayers.[48] These credits or rebates are typically a flat amount for certain family members and may not fully reimburse annual sales taxes paid on grocery purchases. These reimbursements often require the burden and expense of an income tax return or other filing and may not generate a tax benefit for lower-income households if the credit is not refundable. There are state administrative costs for these offsets as well. On the whole, however, these strategies are better targeted to lower-income families reducing regressivity and state tax revenue losses.

Unlike groceries, clothing purchases, including shoes, are not typically subsidized for financially challenged families. However, regular clothing and shoe purchases are especially necessary for families with young children. These families spend a higher percentage of their income on clothing than higher-income families. Eight states exclude certain clothing purchases from state sales tax.[49] Minnesota, New Jersey, Pennsylvania, and Vermont exempt all clothing from any sales tax. In four states, clothing up to a certain amount per item is exempt (the cap is $175 in Massachusetts, $110 in New York, $250 in Rhode Island, and $50 in Connecticut).[50] Notably, Connecticut imposes a luxury goods tax on clothing and footwear that costs more than $1,000.[51] These exclusions or luxury taxes mitigate the inherent regressivity in state sales taxes.

Other necessary items that are often excluded from state sales tax include health and safety items like car seats, bicycle helmets, safety wear, prescription medicines, and prosthetics. College textbooks are additional items that are sometimes exempt from state consumption taxes. Nine states specifically exempt feminine hygiene products from sales taxes (Connecticut, Florida, Illinois, Maryland, Massachusetts, Minnesota, New Jersey, New York, and Pennsylvania) and seven more states have

---

[45] Eric Figueroa & Samantha Waxman, Center on Budget & Pol'y Priorities, *Which States Tax the Sale of Food for Home Consumption in 2017?* (Mar. 1, 2017).

[46] *Id.*

[47] *Id.*

[48] *Id.*

[49] Richard Borean & Liz Malm, Tax Found., *Map State Sales Taxes and Clothing Exemptions* (Nov. 19, 2013).

[50] *Id.*

[51] State of Conn. Dep't of Rev. Servs., *Exemptions from Sales and Use Taxes*, setting forth a 7 percent luxury tax on clothing and footwear greater than $1,000, www.ct.gov/drs/cwp/view .asp?a=1477&q=269920.

recently introduced state tax feminine hygiene exemption legislation.[52] These exclusions, for items that low-income households often must acquire by necessity, can meaningfully reduce consumption tax burdens and regressivity for these households.

Additionally, sales tax holidays can reduce the impact of certain consumption taxes. Sales tax holidays are a limited period when a state waives or reduces sales tax on certain items and quantities. These holidays are typically short in duration. More than a dozen states have annual sales tax holidays before school starts in the fall, covering back-to-school items including clothing, computers, and school supplies.[53] A limited number of states have annual holidays for severe weather preparedness items; Louisiana and Mississippi have an annual sales tax exemption for "2nd Amendment" related items.[54] To the extent that low-income families are able to take advantage of these scheduled holidays, their aggregate sales tax burden is reduced. However, sales tax holidays, like general sales tax exclusions for groceries, utilities, or prescription medicines, benefit all taxpayers regardless of their household income and wealth levels. Because of this limitation as well as increased complexity for businesses and tax administrators, the benefits from sales tax holidays for low-income households likely are not as effective or efficient as targeted tax credits for sales tax burdens.[55] Tax policy experts agree that sales tax holidays should not be an alternative for more comprehensive state tax reform.[56]

State Income Taxes

State and local individual and corporate income tax systems are typically the most progressive elements of state and local taxation. Forty-one states and the District of Columbia have broad-based individual income tax systems that partially offset the regressivity of consumption and property taxes.[57] The nine states without broad-based individual income tax systems are Alaska, Florida, Nevada, New Hampshire, South Dakota, Tennessee, Texas, Washington, and Wyoming. These states necessarily rely more heavily on consumption and property taxes that disproportionately burden lower-income households.

States without income tax systems tend to be high tax rate states for many low-income families and low tax rate states for the highest-income households. Five of

[52] For an excellent discussion of the pink tax, see JENNIFER WEISS-WOLF, PERIODS GONE PUBLIC: TAKING A STAND FOR MENSTRUAL EQUALITY (2017).
[53] See Fed'n of Tax Administrators, 2018 State Sales Tax Holidays, www.taxadmin.org/sales-tax-holidays.
[54] Id.
[55] Joseph Bishop-Henchman & Scott Drenkard, Tax Found., Sales Tax Holidays: Politically Expedient, but Poor Tax Policy (July 25, 2017), Inst. on Tax'n & Econ. Pol'y, Sales Tax Holidays: An Ineffective Alternative to Real Sales Tax Reform (July 2017).
[56] Id.
[57] Inst. on Tax'n & Econ. Pol'y, Fairness Matters: A Chart Book on Who Pays State and Local Taxes (Jan. 2017), at Chart 5.

the nine states without individual income tax structures require their low- and middle-income residents (those in the bottom 40 percent of the income distribution) to pay more than 10 percent of their annual income in state taxes.[58] The effective state tax rates for low-income households are 14.2 percent in Washington, more than 11 percent for residents of Texas and Florida, and more than 10 percent for residents of Tennessee and South Dakota.[59] Three of the four states with lower tax rates on low- and middle-income households (Alaska, Nevada, and Wyoming) have sizeable mining and tourism industries that provide significant tax revenues from out of state taxpayers. In sharp contrast, the top 1 percent of income households enjoy shockingly low effective state tax rates; less than 2 percent in Florida, Nevada, South Dakota, and Wyoming, and less than or equal to 3 percent in Alaska, New Hampshire, Texas, Tennessee, and Washington.[60]

States with income tax structures vary in their progressivity. Income tax systems can be progressive or even regressive due to differences in state and local tax rates, deductions, exclusions, exemptions, credits, and other tax benefits and burdens. Of the three major taxes used by states to raise revenues, the individual income tax is the only system with effective tax rates that generally rise with income levels. Progressive individual income tax systems can mitigate the burden of regressive state and local consumption and property taxes. On average, low-income American households pay one-tenth of the effective income tax rate applicable to the highest-income households, and middle-income households pay about half of the same effective tax rate. The differences in the extent of the progressivity of state and local income taxes depend on broad policy choices including tax rate structure, use of deductions, exemptions, exclusions, tax preferences, and tax credits that benefit low-income taxpayers, as well as use or avoidance of regressive tax provisions that benefit higher-income taxpayers.

States with individual income tax systems typically assess tax liabilities with one tax rate across all income levels (flat tax structure) or with a graduated tax rate structure comprised of increasing tax rates as income levels increase (progressive tax rates). Of the 41 states with individual income tax systems, eight have flat tax rate structures and thirty-three (plus the District of Columbia) use graduated tax rate structures. The eight states with flat tax rates are Colorado (4.63), Illinois (4.95), Indiana (3.3), Massachusetts (5.1), Michigan (4.25), North Carolina (5.75), Pennsylvania (3.07), and Utah (4.7).[61] Graduated rate income tax structures tend to be more progressive than flat rate tax systems. However, graduated brackets that have narrow income ranges at the bottom may cause most taxpayers to be subject to high or even the highest marginal income tax rates. In states with flat tax rate income structures,

[58] *Id.*
[59] *Id.*
[60] *Id.* at Chart 6.
[61] *Id.* at Chart 8.

low-income households pay average effective tax rates of 1.0 percent of household income, and the highest-income households pay 4.5 percent, compared to –0.1 percent of household income for low-income households, and 3.3 percent for the highest-income households in states with graduated tax rate structures.[62] However, other important features can inhibit or enhance the progressivity of tax rate structures.

Over time, the real dollar value of tax brackets, deductions, and credits decrease due to inflation. To mitigate these changes, tax systems should be indexed for inflation to ensure that nominal amounts are automatically increased over time so that real values are not modified. For example, progressive tax rate systems generally subject certain ranges of income to predetermined fixed rates. Each higher income range on top of the first range is subject to a higher tax rate and this pattern is repeated until the last range of income subject to the highest marginal tax rate has no ceiling. To ensure that the ranges of income do not effectively decrease over time due to inflation and create unintended bracket creep, that is, nominal income amounts increasing and being subjected to a higher marginal tax rate than the real dollar amounts warrant, the dollar amount for the ranges or tax brackets should be indexed for inflation. This is also true for the dollar amounts of tax deductions, thresholds, and credits, so that these benefits do not lose their real values over time. All aspects of an income tax system should be indexed for inflation so they retain their original values. Tax system indexing can reduce inadvertent tax increases for lower-income taxpayers who are predominantly wage earners and suffer wage stagnation despite real inflation.

Progressive income tax systems are typically designed so that they exempt from taxation a modest amount of income through standard deductions and personal and dependency exemptions. This creates a zero-bracket tax rate range beginning at $1 of taxable income, up to some predetermined amount. The predetermined amount may be modeled on poverty thresholds or some other basic living standard. Given how dated poverty thresholds are under the official poverty measure, states are well advised to use the geographically relevant and up-to-date poverty thresholds now determined by the US government and used in the Supplemental Poverty Measure.[63] Ten states provide income tax credits to ensure that low-income and poverty-level families do not pay state income tax.[64] For example, Ohio has a nonrefundable income tax credit that ensures that families with incomes at or below $10,000 can offset in full any state income tax liability. Kentucky has a similar tax credit that ensures that families at or below the poverty threshold are not subject to

---

[62] *Id.* at Chart 7.
[63] For a detailed description of the poverty thresholds, *see* Francine J. Lipman, *(Anti)Poverty Measures Exposed*, 21 FLA. TAX REV. 389–532 (2017).
[64] *See Who Pays, supra* note 4, at 10.

state income tax. However, these credits likely do not offset other state, local, and federal taxes.

Tax systems can be structured to subsidize families with children or other dependents. Some tax systems use a different standard deduction or zero bracket amount based upon family composition, including whether taxpayers are married, unmarried, or single parents with dependents (head of household). State tax systems often increase the excluded amount of household income if it includes additional family members, including children and other related dependents. The exclusion of additional income based upon the number of qualifying dependents in the household can be achieved through increased deductions, exemptions (another term for deductions), or even tax credits. As long as these amounts are indexed for inflation, they meaningfully mitigate regressivity, especially in flat tax rate structures. Because of these exclusions and other deductions, none of the state flat tax systems have effective tax rates equal to the nominal tax rate because some amount of income is excluded, which decreases the effective tax rate and can mitigate regressivity.

STATE TAX CREDITS: EARNED INCOME TAX CREDITS AND CHILD CARE CREDITS

Many states provide their residents with state income tax credits. As discussed previously, some states have income tax credits intended to reimburse certain taxpayers for sales taxes paid on groceries, or for property taxes paid by eligible seniors and other qualifying targeted taxpayers. A number of states have child and dependent care tax credits to reimburse working parents for some amount of their out-of-pocket child care expenses. These credits reimburse taxpayers for some or all their relevant out-of-pocket expenses made during the calendar year. Income tax credits are more valuable than income tax deductions because they reduce income tax liabilities, dollar for dollar, down to zero, and in certain cases (refundable tax credits) below zero, generating a negative tax or a cash refund equal to the negative tax.

Earned Income Tax Credits (EITCs) are typically refundable tax credits targeted to low- and middle-income working parents.[65] The amount of the credit increases based upon the amount of earned income up to certain amounts (before it starts phasing out) and the number of qualifying children in the household. The federal EITC was enacted in the 1970s to incentivize work by offsetting regressive Social Security and Medicare taxes. The EITC has been enhanced over time and, at certain lower earned-income levels, it not only offsets regressive federal payroll taxes but also delivers a wage subsidy. In 2017, 27 million taxpayers received $65 billion in

---

[65] For an overview on the EITC, *see* Francine J. Lipman & Dawn Davis, *Heal the Suffering Children: Fifty Years after the Declaration of War on Poverty*, 34 B.C. J. L. & Soc. Just. 311, 323–24 (2014) (recounting the antipoverty benefits of the EITC).

federal EITC, averaging $2,445 per household.[66] The refundable EITC and Child Tax Credit lifted more than 8.1 million people out of poverty, including more than 4.4 million children in 2016.[67] Moreover, scholarly research has determined that the addition of these financial resources in low-income households generates rich current and future dividends resulting in better health for the family, improved academic performance in school, increased current household earnings, and future earnings from the adult children.[68]

By 2019, at least 29 states and the District of Columbia are scheduled to have EITCs that should mitigate income tax system regressivity, poverty, and inequality by reducing effective income tax rates and tax burdens for low- and middle-income households. State EITCs have added $4 billion to low-income working families' households annually.[69] State EITCs increase proven antipoverty benefits of the federal EITC in at least two ways. First, state EITCs can increase the amount of EITC cash refunds low-income households receive, which enhances the already proven benefits of the federal EITC. Second, scholars have demonstrated that state EITCs increase taxpayer participation rates for the federal EITC, further increasing EITC household dollars due to state promotional efforts as well as the enriched incentive of higher aggregate tax refunds.[70]

While 24 of these nonfederal jurisdictions' EITCs are refundable, mirroring the federal EITC, the balance, including Delaware, Hawaii, Ohio, Oklahoma, South Carolina, and Virginia, have nonrefundable EITCs.[71] These states only allow their EITCs to reduce taxpayers' income tax liability down to zero (and not below). In these states, a taxpayer can only receive the tax dollars she paid into the government coffers as state withholding or estimated tax payments refunded. Ohio's EITC is even more limited and targeted to higher-income earners as it cannot exceed

[66] Internal Revenue Service, *EITC Tax Return Statistics*, www.eitc.irs.gov/eitc-central/statistics-for-tax-returns-with-eitc/statistics-for-tax-returns-with-eitc.

[67] Liana Fox, U.S. Census Bureau, *The Supplemental Poverty Measure: 2016 Current Population Reports* (Sept. 2017) at Appendix A-7.

[68] Chuck Marr, Chye-Ching Huang, Arloc Sherman & Brandon Debot, Center on Budget & Pol'y Priorities, *EITC and Child Tax Credit Promote Work, Reduce Poverty, and Support Children's Development, Research Finds* (Oct. 1, 2015), www.cbpp.org/cms/?fa=view&id=3793.

[69] Erica Williams & Samantha Waxman, Center on Budget & Pol'y Priorities, *States Can Adopt or Expand Earned Income Tax Credits to Build a Stronger Future Economy* (Feb. 7, 2018).

[70] *See generally* David Neumark & Katherine E. Williams, Econ. Self-Sufficiency Pol'y Research Inst. Working Paper Series, *Do State Earned Income Tax Credits Increase Participation in the Federal EITC?* (Nov. 29, 2016).

[71] The states with refundable EITCs include California, Colorado, Connecticut, Illinois, Indiana, Iowa, Kansas, Louisiana, Maine, Massachusetts, Maryland, Michigan, Minnesota, Nebraska, New Jersey, New Mexico, New York, Oklahoma, Oregon, Rhode Island, Wisconsin, Vermont, and the District of Columbia. Washington state has a refundable EITC, but with no current state income tax it has not been funded to date. Center on Budget & Pol'y Priorities, *State Earned Income Tax Credits* (Aug. 23, 2017); Erica Williams & Samantha Waxman, Center on Budget & Pol'y Priorities, *States Can Adopt or Expand Earned Income Tax Credits to Build a Stronger Future Economy* (Feb. 7, 2018).

50 percent of Ohio income taxes owed on taxable income above $20,000.[72] These attributes limit the ability of these states' EITCs to reduce the tax burden on low-income households and, under certain circumstances, a low-income family might not receive any benefit from a nonrefundable state EITC.

State EITCs can be simple to administer and implement because they most commonly are derived directly from the federal EITC. State EITCs are often structured as a percentage of the federal EITC ranging from 3 percent in Montana (when it goes into effect in 2019) to 40 percent in the District of Columbia (for families). California's relatively new refundable EITC is 85 percent of the federal EITC on up to 50 percent of the federal income ranges. Fortunately, the federal EITC is indexed for inflation so it increases annually. Sweeping tax reform in 2017 modified inflation indexing for the entire federal tax system, including for the EITC. As a result, future EITC amounts will not likely increase due to inflation as much as they have in the past.[73] For calendar year 2018 the maximum federal EITC for a qualifying family with three or more children is $6,431.[74]

State EITCs have been dynamic and ever-evolving, with many states adding EITCs and making a variety of rate and other changes to the EITC requirements. Some states have implemented their own unique EITC structures and rules. Minnesota's EITC relies on state-specific qualifying income phase-in and phase-out schedules and allows 21- to 24-year-old wage earners without qualifying children to claim EITC credits. Indiana does not integrate recent federal EITC enhancements, but rather relies on prior federal EITC guidelines.[75] California initially did not allow self-employed individuals (or sole proprietorships) to qualify for the EITC, but they eliminated this "employee only" limitation in 2017, adding another one million California EITC beneficiaries.[76] District of Columbia representatives have proposed an EITC enhancement bill that provides a 50 percent "savings match" for EITC recipients who save a portion of their refund for at least six months.[77] Legislators supporting the DC Rainy Day Refund Act argue that this proposal is an "evidence-based approach that lifts more taxpayers out of poverty by encouraging savings and helping families weather unpredictable fluctuations in income."[78] Although incremental state improvements to EITCs may make sense, frequently

---

[72] *Id.*
[73] *Id.* (estimating that by 2027 the difference for a family of three or more children will be $343).
[74] Internal Revenue Service, 2018 EITC Income Limits, Maximum Credit Amounts and Tax Law Updates, www.irs.gov/credits-deductions/individuals/earned-income-tax-credit/eitc-income-limits-maximum-credit-amounts-next-year.
[75] Erica Williams & Samantha Waxman, Center on Budget & Pol'y Priorities, *States Can Adopt or Expand Earned Income Tax Credits to Build a Stronger Future Economy* (Feb. 7, 2018).
[76] *Id.*
[77] The DC Line, Nadeau Bill Increases Tax Refund for Low-Income DC Taxpayers (June 26, 2018).
[78] *Id.*

changing rates and requirements can add to taxpayer confusion as well as potentially higher annual tax preparation fees.

Because state EITCs are targeted to low- and middle-income working families, the aggregate cost to a state can be modest. Current refundable state EITCs cost less than 1 percent of annual state tax revenues.[79] State EITCs are low cost because low-income households account for a low aggregate share of state tax revenues despite embodying a large number of taxpayers.[80] A few hundred dollars per family can make a critical difference to a family's ability to cover basic living expenses without seriously affecting state budgets. Scholars have determined that EITC refunds are spent quickly and locally and therefore have a $1.5 – $2 multiplier effect, serving as an economic stimulant for low-income neighborhoods generating tax revenues and potentially creating jobs.[81] States may proactively increase an EITC to offset an increase in sales or excise taxes to mitigate any increased regressivity and household tax burden. Federal laws allow states to use Temporary Assistance to Needy Families (TANF) grants to finance the refundable component of EITCs going to families with children. Unfortunately, many states do not have sufficient federal TANF funds because TANF block grants are not adjusted for inflation and have thus been reduced meaningfully over time. In 2016, only five states used meaningful federal TANF funds for tax credits. However, 9 percent of total federal and required state TANF funds were spent on tax credits for low-income working families, most commonly state EITCs.[82]

State refundable EITCs can be particularly helpful in states without individual income tax systems because these states typically rely heavily on sales, excise, and property taxes. Because of this reliance, low- and middle-income families in these states pay a higher share of their income in taxes than higher-income families. Washington is the only current state without an income tax system with an EITC. The Washington Working Families Tax Rebate is designed to use Internal Revenue Service data on federal EITC recipients to determine state credit eligibility.[83] Officials estimate that administration costs for states without a state income tax system are only 4 percent of the cost of the EITC.[84] Administrative costs in states that

---

[79] Erica Williams & Samantha Waxman, Center on Budget & Pol'y Priorities, *States Can Adopt or Expand Earned Income Tax Credits to Build a Stronger Future Economy* (Feb. 7, 2018).

[80] To determine the costs for various levels of state refundable EITCs, *see* Erica Williams & Samantha Waxman, Center on Budget & Pol'y Priorities, How Much Would a State Earned Income Tax Credit Cost in Fiscal Year 2019? (June 8, 2018).

[81] The United States Conference of Mayors, *Dollar Wise Best Practices: Earned Income Tax Credit* (2008), http://usmayors.org/dollarwise/resources/eitc08.pdf.

[82] Liz Schott, Ife Floyd & Ashley Burnside, Center on Budget & Pol'y Priorities, *How States Use Funds under the TANF Grant* (Apr. 2, 2018).

[83] Erica Williams & Samantha Waxman, Center on Budget & Pol'y Priorities, *States Can Adopt or Expand Earned Income Tax Credits to Build a Stronger Future Economy* (Feb. 7, 2018).

[84] *Id.*

already have an income tax are typically well below 1 percent of the cost of the EITC.[85] While Washington has not funded its state EITC to date, it could become an effective offset to remedy Washington's current ranking as the state with the highest average tax rate on low-income residents in America in 2015 (16.8 percent).[86]

ABSENCE (OR PRESENCE) OF TAX BREAKS FOR WEALTHY HOUSEHOLDS

While state income tax systems can mitigate regressivity by focusing on tax burden reductions or tax benefits for low- and middle-income families, they can also reduce or exacerbate tax regressivity by the absence or presence of tax breaks for higher-income households. For example, the federal income tax system provides tax-preferred income tax rates for dividends and long-term capital gain income. These reduced tax rates overwhelmingly benefit higher-income and wealthy households, who are more likely to own and trade in stocks, bonds, and other capital investments. Some states, such as California, mitigate these tax benefits by not providing tax preferences for this category of income. While Tennessee does not have a broad-based income tax, it subjects capital gains, dividends, and interest income to an income tax. By comparison, Arizona, Arkansas, Hawaii, Iowa, Montana, New Mexico, North Dakota, South Carolina, Vermont, and Wisconsin exclude certain capital gains from taxation,[87] while Kansas excludes all pass-through business income from state taxation.[88] These business and investment income tax preferences undermine progressivity and exacerbate regressivity.

Another tax provision that exacerbates regressivity is a state income tax deduction for federal income taxes paid. This deduction effectively subsidizes taxpayers' federal income tax liability through a reduction of their state tax liability. Because federal income taxes are progressive, higher-income individuals pay a greater percentage of their income in federal income taxes than lower-income households and, therefore, enjoy a greater relative state income tax benefit and subsidy. Lower-income taxpayers who pay relatively little in federal income taxes, but relatively more in other federal taxes like Social Security and Medicare payroll taxes and excise taxes, do not receive much, if any, benefit from a state income tax deduction for federal income tax expenses. Six states provide all or partial deductions for federal income taxes paid, including Alabama, Iowa, Louisiana, Missouri, Montana, and Oregon. These deductions decrease the effective federal and state tax rates for higher-income taxpayers in these states. Alternatively, Washington, DC, Hawaii, and Maine limit

---

[85] *Id.*

[86] See *Who Pays, supra* note 4, at 4 (describing Washington as the state with the most regressive tax system).

[87] *Id.* at 10, 60.

[88] *Id.* at 62.

certain allowable tax deductions for higher-income individuals.[89] These deduction limitations mitigate tax system regressivity and bolster progressivity.[90]

CONCLUSION

This chapter has exposed many of the best and worst practices of state and local tax systems in an effort to show how tax structures impact different income groups of taxpayers differently. In America today, the lower the household income, the higher the effective state and local tax rate. The average effective state and local tax rates by household income are 10.9 percent for the bottom 20 percent, 9.4 percent for the middle 20 percent, and 5.4 percent for the top 1 percent. This allocation of tax burden is inconsistent with fundamental tax policies including the ability to pay, tax fairness, and vertical equity principles.

As this chapter has described the basic problem is that state and local governments rely on regressive taxes for most of their revenue. The reliance on property and consumption taxes that burden low- and middle-income families at a higher rate than higher-income households is neither fair nor sustainable. As income and wealth are increasingly concentrated in smaller and smaller subsets of the population, it becomes less viable to rely on broad-based regressive taxes to fund government systems. As state and local governments face decreasing revenue streams, there are innovative tax structures they can implement to shift their systems into more workable, equitable, and principled regimes. The 50 state and District of Columbia tax systems provide a wide range of detailed examples, data, and resources for legislators, taxpayers, and scholars to study to better evaluate what strategies might better serve our common goal of tax justice for all Americans, regardless of income level.

In each of the broad categories of state and local taxes there are a variety of strategies that can mitigate inherent overall regressivity. This chapter has explained that broad-based exclusions, exemptions, and holidays from taxation can help, but are expensive and benefit the richest as well as the poorest households. A better design is to target low-income households by offsetting their tax burden with refundable tax credits. While this approach most often requires the administrative burdens of filing and processing tax returns, a delayed lump sum reimbursement rather than an immediate abatement, and more complexity in an all-ready complicated system, refundable tax credits can mitigate regressivity. With about 30 state and the District of Columbia EITCs in place, many state and local governments are piggybacking on federal EITCs to expand and, in some cases, improve upon and complement the federal EITC, a long-standing, successful antipoverty tax program.

---

[89] *Id.* at 46, 52, 68 (describing state income tax phase-outs and limits on itemized deductions for higher-income taxpayers in Washington, DC, Hawaii, and Maine).

[90] *Id.* at 42, 56, 68.

Tax and poverty advocates and scholars should continue to follow the successes and failures of these state and local initiatives as they evolve.

Most importantly, this chapter brings into sharp focus how critical it is to consider the details of state and local tax systems in addition to the federal tax system when considering tax burdens and benefits. When tax policy discourse is focused narrowly on federal income tax distribution, we exclude the most regressive aspects of US tax systems. If state and local tax systems are excluded from tax policy analysis, tax distribution appears much more progressive than it is for most Americans. By excluding state and local taxes, the most significant tax burdens for many low- and middle-income families are not even considered. This all too common oversight distorts the analysis by understating the tax burden suffered by many low- and middle-income families. US tax policy discussions must include state and local tax systems so that their regressive impact is properly assessed and incorporated. Comprehensive tax system analyses should result in better policies, procedures, and structures that accurately account for and more justly allocate all tax burdens and benefits.

6

Early Childhood Development and the Replication of Poverty

Clare Huntington

INTRODUCTION

Traditional understandings of federalism – especially around experimentalism – suggest that states are likely to take varying approaches to important policy questions, particularly in areas as sensitive as family law. And indeed, there are patterns of convergence and divergence in state approaches to supporting early childhood development. Surprisingly, however, the divergences do not always follow predictable political lines. These similarities and differences raise a puzzle that deserves attention by scholars and advocates.

In the United States, differences in early childhood play a key role in replicating poverty. Clear evidence establishes that child development in the first five years of life lays essential groundwork for future learning and the acquisition of life skills. In today's economy, educational achievement is strongly correlated with adult earnings, but children from low-income families begin school at a significant disadvantage. Differences in early childhood explain much of the income-based achievement gap in education. And disadvantage during early childhood has a particularly pernicious effect on boys' academic achievement. Early interventions can make a difference for all children, but these interventions must start early. And they must involve both parents and children because one of the central insights of the literature on early childhood development is that children do not develop in a vacuum. Instead, child development is dependent on the relationship between a parent or other long-term caregiver and a child.

As compared with other wealthy countries, the United States makes limited investments in families with young children. Indeed, the level of public investment in children from birth to age three is inversely related to the importance of this period for child development. Public investments are highest for school-age children and lowest for children from birth to age three.[1] Investments for children from three to five fall in between. Many wealthy countries mediate the impact of poverty on child development by providing universal health care, including prenatal care, home visiting for new parents, heavily subsidized child care and preschool, and, most fundamentally, a child allowance, which ensures families have money to care for children. The United States does offer prenatal care and health care to virtually all low- and moderate-income citizens, as well as some food assistance and income support, largely through the Earned Income Tax Credit (EITC). But in most other areas, including housing, child care, preschool, and basic income guarantees, government support for families falls far short of the need.[2] Additionally, the support available to noncitizen families, especially undocumented individuals, is far more limited.

Numerous scholars and advocates have called for greater investments in families – and early childhood in particular – but rather than revisiting these arguments, this chapter takes a different tack, exploring the investments that *are* made and focusing in particular on the web of funding across levels of government. As this chapter describes, the bulk of money available to support child development from the prenatal period until age three comes from the federal government, and there is fairly limited variation in how this money is spent across the states. For the period from age three until entrance to kindergarten, the federal government and states largely share the cost of supporting early childhood development, leading to significant differences among the states, particularly in access to preschool for three- and four-year-olds. This chapter explores these funding differences, emphasizing the political economy of state choices and noting that, perhaps surprisingly, some red states are making a substantial effort to invest in early childhood education, especially for four-year-olds. The chapter closes with insights for both advocates and scholars.

EARLY CHILDHOOD DEVELOPMENT

Since the beginning of the twentieth century, scholars have identified and explored the importance of early childhood development. In the 1920s, the psychologist Jean

---

[1] Sara Edelstein et al., *How Do Public Investments in Children Vary with Age? A Kids' Share Analysis of Expenditures in 2008 and 2011 by Age Group*, URBAN INSTITUTE at 5 (Oct. 2012), www.urban.org/sites/default/files/publication/25911/412676-How-Do-Public-Investments-in-Children-Vary-with-Age-A-Kids-Share-Analysis-of-Expenditures-in-and-by-Age-Group.PDF (estimating investments from outlays and tax expenditures).

[2] The underlying assumption in the United States is that families can and should care for themselves with limited governmental support. For a description of this neoliberal approach to family policies and its historical roots, see Maxine Eichner, *The Privatized American Family*, 93 NOTRE DAME L. REV. 213, 252–59 (2017). For an argument about why the state should support families, see MAXINE EICHNER, THE SUPPORTIVE STATE (2010).

Piaget posited a theory of cognitive development that recognized various stages, beginning at birth.[3] In the 1950s, the psychoanalyst Erik Erikson followed this model, also positing a theory of development beginning at birth and extending through the life course with distinct phases, each requiring the resolution of a particular crisis or tension.[4] By the 1960s, psychologists began studying the impact of early experiences on intelligence, challenging the belief that cognitive differences are innate.[5] The findings of these researchers led to the creation of early childhood development programs, including a pilot program that ultimately inspired Head Start.[6] These programs, in turn, led to more studies establishing the benefits of early childhood education.[7] In the 1970s, scholars began to look broadly at a child's environment. One of the most influential scholars, Urie Bronfenbrenner, posited that child development occurs in nested, interacting systems, including psychological, social, cultural, economic, and political systems, all which interact to shape child development.[8] More recently, neuroscientists have added an important layer of understanding to child development, documenting the neuroscientific basis for many of the insights first articulated by psychologists.[9]

This research has generated two key insights about early childhood development. First, child development begins early – during the prenatal period – and is critical for future learning, as illustrated by the neuroscientific evidence on brain development.[10] Beginning in the prenatal period and lasting for several years, brain cells form circuits. The neural circuits that are used repeatedly grow stronger, but those that are not used regularly die off. These neural circuits are critical to language, emotions, logic, memory, motor skills, and behavioral control. The basic neural circuitry for vision and hearing develops shortly before and soon after birth, and the circuits used for language and speech production peak before age one. The higher level circuits used for cognitive functions develop throughout the first several years

---

[3] ROBERT SIEGLER ET AL., HOW CHILDREN DEVELOP 130–31 (3d ed. 2011) (describing Piaget's theories).

[4] ERIK H. ERIKSON, CHILDHOOD AND SOCIETY 219–34 (1950); ERIK H. ERIKSON, GROWTH AND CRISES OF THE HEALTHY PERSONALITY, *in* IDENTITY AND THE LIFE CYCLE: SELECTED PAPERS, 1 PSYCHOL. ISSUES 50, 50–88 (George S. Klein ed., 1959).

[5] *See e.g.*, BENJAMIN S. BLOOM, STABILITY AND CHANGE IN HUMAN CHARACTERISTICS 68–76, 88–89 (1964); J. McVICKER HUNT, INTELLIGENCE AND EXPERIENCE 3–4, 6–7, 10, 65–66, 362–63 (1961).

[6] *See generally* Bettye M. Caldwell & Julius B. Richmond, *Programmed Day Care for the Very Young Child – A Preliminary Report*, 26 J. MARRIAGE & FAM. 481, 482–85 (1964) (describing work on developing an early childhood development program focused on education).

[7] *See* SIEGLER ET AL., *supra* note 3, at 318–19 (describing these studies); L. ALAN SROUFE ET AL., THE DEVELOPMENT OF THE PERSON: THE MINNESOTA STUDY OF RISK AND ADAPTATION FROM BIRTH TO ADULTHOOD (2005) (describing a longitudinal study that also began in the 1970s).

[8] *See* URIE BRONFENBRENNER, THE ECOLOGY OF HUMAN DEVELOPMENT: EXPERIMENTS BY NATURE AND DESIGN 3–4, 21–22 (1979).

[9] For an accessible summary of this research, see CENTER ON THE DEVELOPING CHILD AT HARVARD UNIVERSITY, https://developingchild.harvard.edu/.

[10] For the basis for this summary, *see id.*

of life. Executive functions – generally understood as the ability to hold information in the short term, ignore distractions, and switch gears between contexts and priorities – are developed from birth through late adolescence, with a particular emphasis on development from age three to five.

Second, early childhood development is relational, turning on the interaction between a child and a parent or other caregiver. The neural circuits for communication, language, and social skills are developed through repeated exchanges between a parent and child, with the child babbling, for example, and the adult responding in kind. When a child begins speaking, this, too, turns on a child speaking and interacting with parents and other caregivers. A child's psychosocial development also occurs through the adult-child relationship. Very young children attach to their primary caregiver, looking to this person when in danger or need. A secure attachment encourages a child to explore the child's surroundings. It also helps a child develop a sense of self-efficacy, with the child confident that the child can turn to the parent for needed help. Securely attached children thus learn to regulate their own emotions and solve problems. Finally, through responsive interactions, a child develops basic social intelligence, learning how to read the emotions of another person.

The evidence on maternal depression illustrates the relational nature of early childhood development. Instead of engaging in repeated, responsive exchanges with her baby, a clinically depressed mother typically is either hostile and aggressive to her children or withdrawn and disengaged.[11] Both forms of parent-infant interaction have a negative impact on the child's brain development, with brain scans showing that infants and toddlers with depressed mothers have similar patterns of brain activity as depressed adults.[12] Further, maternal depression is both widespread and strongly correlated with poverty. One study of mothers with nine-month-old children found that 10 percent of the women with income levels over 200 percent of the poverty level were severely depressed as compared with 25 percent of the women living below the poverty level.[13]

Despite this widespread and growing knowledge about early childhood development, much remains unknown and the evidence is still developing.[14] Moreover, the precise relationship between early experiences and later outcomes is complex and

---

[11] See NAT'L SCI. COUNCIL ON THE DEVELOPING CHILD, *Maternal Depression Can Undermine the Development of Young Children* 3 (Ctr. on the Developing Child at Harv. Univ, Working Paper No. 8, 2009), http://developingchild. harvard.edu/index.php/resources/reports_and_working_papers/working_papers/wp8/.

[12] See *id.* at 3–4.

[13] See *id.* at 1–2 (citing calculations using the Early Childhood Longitudinal Study, Birth Cohort 9-month restricted use data).

[14] See Jay Belsky, Opinion, *The Downside of Resilience*, N.Y. TIMES (Nov. 28, 2014), www .nytimes.com/2014/11/30/opinion/sunday/the-downside-of-resilience.html (explaining that "some children are more affected by their developmental experiences – from harsh punishment to high-quality day care – than others" but noting that the reasons are not well known).

not fully understood.[15] Indeed, child development is a dynamic process, with a child influenced by numerous, often interacting, forces. Some factors, such as exposure to lead paint, directly influence a child; other factors, such as parental education, indirectly influence a child by affecting parenting; and still other factors, such as poverty, have both a direct and an indirect influence.[16] Without overly simplifying the literature, it is possible to draw broad conclusions about the impact of early childhood experiences on life outcomes, as the next section describes.

RELATIONSHIP BETWEEN EARLY CHILDHOOD
DEVELOPMENT AND POVERTY

Given the importance of early childhood development to learning and the acquisition of skills, it is unsurprising that disadvantages during early childhood have lifelong ramifications.[17] Numerous factors help explain why children from low-income families tend to be low-income adults. These factors include living in racially and economically segregated neighborhoods,[18] attending inadequate schools,[19] and growing up in poor neighborhoods with few resources,[20] but a critical factor is disadvantage during early childhood. Infants from different socioeconomic backgrounds display, on average, similar levels of cognitive ability, but as early as 18

[15] See L. Alan Sroufe et al., *Implications of Attachment Theory for Developmental Psychopathology*, 11 DEV. & PSYCHOPATHOLOGY 1, 2–6 (1999) (describing the now dominant understanding of child development – that genetics, early experiences, environment, and relationships all interact in a highly complex and mutually influencing fashion and that all the causal pathways are not fully understood). For a particularly accessible summary, see Jeanne Brooks-Gunn & Lisa B. Markman, *The Contribution of Parenting to Ethnic and Racial Gaps in School Readiness*, 15 FUTURE CHILD. 139, 143–47 (2005).
[16] See Sroufe et al., *supra* note 15.
[17] See NAT'L RESEARCH COUNCIL & INST. OF MED., COMM. ON INTEGRATING THE SCI. OF EARLY CHILDHOOD DEV., FROM NEURONS TO NEIGHBORHOODS: THE SCIENCE OF EARLY CHILDHOOD DEVELOPMENT 125 (Jack P. Shonkoff & Deborah A. Phillips eds., 2000) (citations omitted) (surveying the literature and concluding that "[o]ne of the most significant insights about educational attainment in recent years is that educational outcomes in adolescence and even beyond can be traced back to academic skills at school entry. Academic skills at school entry can, in turn, be traced to capabilities seen during the preschool years and the experiences in and out of the home that foster their development."). Julia B. Isaacs, Brookings Inst., *Starting School at a Disadvantage: The School Readiness of Poor Children*, SOC. GENOME PROJECT, Mar. 2012, at 1 (discussing reasons why children from low-income families start school at a disadvantage as well as programs to combat this problem).
[18] Raj Chetty et al., *Where Is the Land of Opportunity? The Geography of Intergenerational Mobility in the United States*, 129 Q. J. ECON. 1553, 1557, 1608–11 (2014).
[19] See Joseph G. Altonji & Richard K. Mansfield, *The Role of Family, School, and Community Characteristics in Inequality in Education and Labor-Market Outcomes*, in WHITHER OPPORTUNITY? RISING INEQUALITY, SCHOOLS, AND CHILDREN'S LIFE CHANCES, 339, 339–40 (Greg J. Duncan & Richard J. Murnane eds., 2011).
[20] Raj Chetty et al., *Childhood Environment and Gender Gaps in Adulthood*, 106 AM. ECON. REV. (PAPERS & PROC.) 282, 282, 284, 287 (2016); Chetty et al., *Where Is the Land of Opportunity?*, *supra* note 18, at 1610–11.

months, researchers can detect a divergence.[21] By the start of kindergarten, children from lower socioeconomic backgrounds, as compared with their peers in more economically advantaged homes, score much lower on tests of cognitive ability and on measures of noncognitive abilities, such as the capacity to self-regulate, get along with peers, listen, and focus.[22] The differences can be significant, with some children entering kindergarten using the vocabulary of a 21-month-old and others using the vocabulary of a 10-year-old.[23] This gap in school readiness predicts much of a child's subsequent school achievement.[24]

A significant portion of the difference in school readiness is attributable to the home environment.[25] One review of parenting studies found that approximately one-third to one-half of the gap in school readiness can be attributed to parenting differences.[26] The underlying studies measured various aspects of parenting during early childhood, including nurturance and discipline, but the most salient factor affecting school readiness was language use – whether parents spoke and read to their children.[27] Other factors, particularly economic resources, also influence school readiness, but again, the salient window is early childhood. Studies have found that low socioeconomic status during early childhood predicts educational achievement more than low socioeconomic status during the school-age years.[28] Further, the impact of early disadvantage is particularly acute for boys: comparing different-sex children with the same mother, boys show significantly lower rates of kindergarten readiness than girls.[29] When a child begins school, it is possible to

---

[21] *See* Nat'l Research Council & Inst. of Med., *supra* note 17, at 137.

[22] *See* Emma García, Econ. Policy Inst., Inequalities at the Starting Gate: Cognitive and Noncognitive Skills Gaps between 2010–2011 Kindergarten Classmates 15–17, 20 (2015); Nat'l Research Council & Inst. of Med., *supra* note 17, at 149.

[23] *See* Nat'l Research Council & Inst. of Med., *supra* note 17, at 138–39.

[24] *See id.* at 125, 138–39, 149 (discussing multiple studies making this finding as it relates to both cognitive abilities and skills such as self-regulation). *See generally* Greg J. Duncan & Katherine A. Magnuson, *Can Family Socioeconomic Resources Account for Racial and Ethnic Test Score Gaps?*, 15 Future Child. 35 (2005) (discussing the aspects of parental socioeconomic status that appear to account for racial and ethnic school readiness gaps).

[25] *See* Nat'l Research Council & Inst. of Med., *supra* note 17, at 157 ("[T]he home environment accounts for the lion's share of the variation in what young children know and are ready to learn when they enter kindergarten.").

[26] *See* Brooks-Gunn & Markman, *supra* note 15, at 139, 150–51. For an extended exploration of the relationship between parenting during early childhood and life outcomes, see Clare Huntington, Failure to Flourish: How Law Undermines Family Relationships 7–10, 15–22, 145–46, 149–52, 159–64 (2014).

[27] *See* Brooks-Gunn & Markman, *supra* note 15, at 139, 147–50.

[28] *See* Nat'l Research Council & Inst. of Med., *supra* note 17, at 159.

[29] One study tracked a million children born in Florida between 1992 and 2002. *See* David Autor et al., *Family Disadvantage and the Gender Gap in Behavioral and Educational Outcomes*, Institute for Policy Research Northwestern University Working Papers Series 8–10 (2015), www .ipr.northwestern.edu/publications/docs/workingpapers/2015/IPR-WP-15-16.pdf. The study examined family disadvantage, as defined by income, maternal education, and family structure. Contrasting different-sex children born to the same mother, the study found that boys, as compared with their female siblings, had similar birth outcomes (birth weight, APGAR scores,

remediate some of the school readiness gap, and school readiness does not predict all later achievement,[30] but there is no question that early childhood has a profound and lasting effect on learning and the acquisition of skills.

Educational achievement matters because of the strong correlation between education and higher earnings. This relationship reflects the bifurcation of the American economy into high-skill occupations and low-skill service jobs, with a sharp reduction in manufacturing and operative jobs that pay a decent wage.[31] Income differences based on educational achievement are significant: in 2016, the median earnings for young adults (aged 25–34) working full-time were $50,000 for those with a bachelor's degree, $31,800 for those with a high school diploma or the equivalent, and $25,400 for those who did not complete high school.[32] Additionally, with each level of educational attainment, young people are more likely to work full-time.[33]

In sum, differences in early childhood affect school readiness and success in school, and academic achievement, in turn, affects adult earnings. As the next section describes, it is possible to promote early childhood development with targeted public investments and supports, leading to lifelong benefits for both children and society.

EFFECTIVE INTERVENTIONS

The first attempts to foster early childhood development focused on preschool programs, and for good reason. There is clear evidence that quality early childhood education programs, which typically start at age three or four, have a lasting, positive

and so on), but over time, a gender gap appeared. The boys were less ready to begin kindergarten, had lower test scores, lower high school graduation rates, and higher rates of committing serious crimes as a minor, among other differences. *See id.* at 13–28. Moreover, the greater the family disadvantage, the greater the gender gap in boy-girl outcomes. *See id.* at 18. The study considered whether neighborhood and school environments might differentially affect boys and girls and thus explain the gender gap, but the study concluded that these factors explained only part of the gap and that family influence appears to be the primary factor. *See id.* at 31–32. The study did not track whether mothers spend more time with female children than male children, or whether boys are more sensitive to father absence. For a study documenting the effects of high-poverty, disadvantaged neighborhoods on boys relative to girls, and finding a significant difference, see Chetty et al., *Childhood Environment and Gender Gaps in Adulthood*, supra note 20, at 282, 287.

[30] *See id.* at 125. New research is showing that late adolescence is another sensitive period of brain development, offering an opportunity to correct earlier deficits. *See* LAURENCE STEINBERG, AGE OF OPPORTUNITY: LESSONS FROM THE NEW SCIENCE OF ADOLESCENCE 8–45 (2014); *see also* CAROL S. DWECK, MINDSET: THE NEW PSYCHOLOGY OF SUCCESS 7 (2007) (explaining that cognitive ability is not fixed, and in the "growth mindset," people believe that their "basic qualities are things [they] can cultivate through [their] efforts").

[31] *See* DAVID AUTOR, CTR. FOR AM. PROGRESS, THE POLARIZATION OF JOB OPPORTUNITIES IN THE U.S. LABOR MARKET 5–6 (2010).

[32] *See* NAT'L CTR. EDUC. STATISTICS, ANNUAL EARNINGS OF YOUNG ADULTS, https://nces.ed.gov/programs/coe/indicator_cba.asp.

[33] *See id.*

impact on both educational achievement and adult outcomes.[34] Numerous studies have established that these programs reduce the use of special education and grade repetition and improve educational outcomes, including an increased likelihood that the participants will attend a four-year college.[35] Beyond educational achievement, the programs foster social-emotional development, reduce rates of teen and adult incarceration, reduce rates of teen pregnancy, improve skilled-employment rates, and improve earnings as adults.[36] Critics of these programs contend that cognitive benefits fade over time, but there is solid evidence that even if some academic achievement benefits do weaken, the programs have a long-lasting positive impact on educational progress and attainment overall as well as positive adult outcomes.[37] These long-term benefits are not limited to small, demonstration programs but are also found in large-scale programs run in multiple locations.[38]

More recently, research has shown the importance of fostering early childhood development long before a child reaches preschool and focusing on the relationship between parents and children.[39] Beginning with pregnancy, prenatal care lays the basic foundation for child development because it reduces the risks of preterm delivery and low-birthweight infants.[40] Low birthweight, in turn, is associated with long-term health consequences and intellectual and developmental disabilities.[41]

---

[34] *See* LYNN A. KAROLY, M. REBECCA KILBURN & JILL S. CANNON, EARLY CHILDHOOD INTERVENTIONS: PROVEN RESULTS, FUTURE PROMISE 55–78, 128–29 (2005); Katherine A. Magnuson & Jane Waldfogel, *Early Childhood Care and Education: Effects on Ethnic and Racial Gaps in School Readiness*, 15 FUTURE CHILD. 169, 171, 173–75 (2005).

[35] *See, e.g.*, KAROLY, KILBURN & CANNON, *supra* note 34, at 55–78, 128–29; MICHAEL PUMA ET AL., U.S. DEP'T HEALTH & HUMAN SERVS., ADMIN. FOR CHILDREN AND FAMILIES, HEAD START IMPACT STUDY FINAL REPORT: EXECUTIVE SUMMARY iv–v, xxv (2010); ECONOMIC OPPORTUNITY INST., THE LINK BETWEEN EARLY CHILDHOOD EDUCATION AND CRIME AND VIOLENCE REDUCTION, www.eoionline.org/early_learning/fact_sheets/ELCLinkCrimeReduction-Jul02 .pdf; Kenneth A. Dodge et al., *Impact of North Carolina's Early Childhood Programs and Policies on Educational Outcomes in Elementary School*, 88 CHILD DEVELOPMENT 996, 1010–11 (2016).

[36] *See* previous note for a discussion of these findings.

[37] *See* KAROLY, KILBURN & CANNON, *supra* note 34, at 128.

[38] *See id.* at 114–15.

[39] *See* James Heckman et al., *The Life-Cycle Benefits of an Influential Early Childhood Program* 1–6 (Nat'l Bureau of Econ. Research, Working Paper No. 22993, 2016), http://heckmanequation .org/ content/resource/lifecycle-benefits-influential-early-childhoodprogram. Policy makers have begun to embrace the critical importance of working with both parents and children. Often called the 2Gen approach, this model is designed to work with both children and their parents to address the entire family's educational and economic needs. *See also* US Dept. of Education, *2Gen Tools to Help Children & Families Thrive, A Resource for Staff Implementing Federal, State, and Local Programs Serving Children and Families* (2017), www2.ed.gov/about/inits/ed/earlylearning/files/2017/2gen-toolkit-resource-for-staff-and-families.pdf.

[40] *See Pregnancy and Prenatal Care*, THE CENTERS FOR DISEASE CONTROL AND PREVENTION (Sept. 15, 2017), www.cdc.gov/healthcommunication/toolstemplates/entertainmented/tips/ PregnancyPrenatalCare.html.

[41] *See Low Birthweight*, MARCH OF DIMES (Mar. 2018), www.marchofdimes.org/complications/ low-birthweight.aspx.

In the first two years of life, home-visiting programs improve child health, decrease the rate of maternal depression, and help parents learn the skills needed to care for their children. These home visits focus on both children and parents, helping parents achieve economic stability and fostering attentive parenting and beneficial practices, such as reading with a child.[42] Research shows that home visiting leads to numerous and significant benefits, including improved school readiness of children, a reduction in behavioral problems and cognitive deficits for children, lower rates of maternal depression, and higher rates of paternal involvement and maternal employment.[43]

A slew of other interventions – again, starting early and focusing on the parent-child interaction – have been shown to improve child outcomes. There is considerable research on the use of text messaging, for example, to encourage positive and enriching interactions between parents and preschool children. These interventions have led to considerable gains in school readiness and parental engagement.[44]

Although generally not undertaken in the United States, a truly robust effort to foster early childhood development would focus on the multiple forces influencing the parent-child relationship. When a parent works multiple jobs, has to commute by unreliable and inefficient public transportation, has to move multiple times because of unaffordable and low-quality housing, and earns a meager wage with limited benefits, it is much harder to provide children with the responsive relationships needed for early childhood development. Thus, a truly comprehensive effort to foster early childhood development would address income and employment, housing stability, and transportation, among other critical factors that shape family life.

Given the high stakes of early childhood development, as well as the clear benefits of interventions during this period, the question is how federalism influences these kinds of investments. As the next section describes, the federal government provides the bulk of funding for children from the prenatal period until age three, and thus there are fewer state-level differences in these investments, although some certainly exist. By contrast, where states are making significant investments in early childhood development, particularly with preschool, there is considerable variation around the country, but not always along predictable political lines.

---

[42] *See* NATIONAL HOME VISITING RESOURCE CENTER, 2017 HOME VISITING YEARBOOK 9–11 (James Bell Associates & Urban Institute, 2017), www.jbassoc.com/wp-content/uploads/2018/03/2017-Home-Visiting-Yearbook.pdf.

[43] *See* Harriet J. Kitzman et al., *Enduring Effects of Prenatal and Infancy Home Visiting by Nurses on Children: Age-12 Follow-Up of a Randomized Trial*, 164 ARCHIVES PEDIATRIC ADOLESCENT MED. 412 (2010); David L. Olds et al., *Effects of Home Visits by Paraprofessionals and by Nurses: Age-Four Follow-Up of a Randomized Trial*, 114 PEDIATRICS 1560 (2004). For an overview of the research on the model program, *see Proven Effective through Extensive Research*, NURSE FAMILY PARTNERSHIP, www.nursefamilypartnership.org/about/proven-results/.

[44] *See* Benjamin N. York et al., *One Step at a Time: The Effects of an Early Literacy Text Messaging Program for Parents of Preschoolers*, 53 J. HUM. RESOURCES 3 (2018).

FUNDING FOR EARLY CHILDHOOD DEVELOPMENT

Public investments in children are highest during the period from kindergarten through 12th grade and lowest from birth to age three.[45] Combining a wide range of public expenditures – on education, income security, health care, nutrition, housing, and social services – one calculation shows that for every public dollar spent supporting the development and education of children from birth to age 18, only seven cents is spent on children from birth to age three, and twenty-five cents is spent on children aged three to five.[46] These differences can also be captured in calculations of annual, per-child spending: the public invests $720 per child aged zero to two, $2,689 per child aged three to five, and $10,799 per child aged six to eighteen.[47]

Further, the source of funds varies greatly depending on the age of the child. The federal government provides the bulk of funds for children from birth to age three, primarily in form of health care, income supports, food assistance, and housing subsidies.[48] These supports continue as the child ages, but education becomes the primary investment in children, with the federal and state governments roughly splitting the cost of educating children aged three to five,[49] and state and local governments shouldering most of the cost of educating children from kindergarten through 12th grade.[50]

Beyond this basic overview, the web of funding for early childhood development is a complex mix of federal, state, and local investments. And there is a wide variation among states and localities for some kinds of public investments, particularly preschool, but not for others, notably health care for pregnant women and young children.[51] To understand the degree of public investment in early childhood development, appreciate the breakdown among federal, state, and local

[45] *See* Edelstein et al., *supra* note 1, at 5 (noting that the "federal estimates include tax expenditures – that is, reductions in taxes as a result of child-oriented tax provisions – in addition to direct spending from federal programs, also known as outlays").
[46] *See* Charles Bruner, *Early Learning Left Out, Building an Early-Learning System to Secure America's Future*, CHILD & FAMILY POLICY CENTER at 5 (Oct. 2013), https://files.eric.ed.gov/fulltext/ED558052.pdf.
[47] *See id.*
[48] *See* Edelstein et al., *supra* note 1, at 5.
[49] *See id.*
[50] States contribute approximately 47 percent of the total funding, localities contribute 40–50 percent, and the federal government contributes only 7–10 percent. *See* Am. Speech-Language-Hearing Ass'n, *Overview of Funding for Pre-K-12 Education* (2018), www.asha.org/Advocacy/schoolfundadv/Overview-of-Funding-For-Pre-K-12-Education/; Wong, Kenneth, *Can the States Address the Equity and Innovation? Rethinking the State's Fiscal Role in Public Education* GOV'T FIN. R. (Oct. 2001). The federal funds are largely from Title I of the Elementary and Secondary Education Act, which provides funding for schools with a high percentage of children from low-income families.
[51] For a good resource tracking state investments in a variety of 0–5 programs and supports, *see* NAT'L CONFERENCE OF STATE LEGISLATURE, EARLY CARE AND EDUCATION STATE BUDGET

governments, and identify the variation among states and localities, it is helpful to describe some of the major investments chronologically, from fetal development until kindergarten.

Beginning with prenatal care, the federal government provides funding to states through Medicaid and the Children's Health Insurance Program (CHIP), which covers pregnant women who exceed the income eligibility requirement for Medicaid.[52] Both programs require state matching funds, although the rate differs depending on numerous state-specific criteria.[53] These programs – particularly Medicaid – are a major source of funding, with Medicaid covering half of all births in the United States.[54] The combination of Medicaid and CHIP ensures that nearly all pregnant women have access to prenatal care.[55]

Moving to the period between birth and entry into preschool, again Medicaid and CHIP are the primary source of funds for health care for low- and moderate-income children. The two programs pay for health care critical to child development, including well-child visits, services to address developmental delays, and screening and treatment for a wide range of disabilities and medical conditions. Combining spending on prenatal care and health care for children from birth to age three, in fiscal year 2016, the federal government spent $34 billion in Medicaid funds and $2 billion in CHIP funds.[56] Medicaid covers 28 million children and CHIP an additional eight million children.[57]

ACTIONS FY 2017 (Apr. 2017), www.ncsl.org/research/human-services/early-care-and-education-state-budget-actions-fy-2017.aspx.

[52] *See* GEORGETOWN UNIV. HEALTH POLICY INST., CENTER FOR CHILDREN AND FAMILIES, CHILDREN'S HEALTH INSURANCE PROGRAM (2017).

[53] For a description of the state matching requirements under Medicaid and CHIP, see *Understanding How States Access the ACA Enhanced Medicaid Match Rates*, KAISER FAMILY FOUND. (Sept. 2014), www.kff.org/medicaid/issue-brief/understanding-how-states-access-the-aca-enhanced-medicaid-match-rates/ (describing the statutory formula for determining state matches under Medicaid, which depends on numerous factors and ranges from a floor of 50 percent to 73 percent, although states that expanded coverage under the Affordable Care Act were given further subsidies; and further describing the state match requirement under CHIP).

[54] *See* Charles Bruner and Kay Johnson, *Federal Spending on Prenatal to Three: Developing a Public Response to Improving Developmental Trajectories and Preventing Inequities*, CENTER FOR THE STUDY OF SOCIAL POLICY at 22 (Mar. 2018), www.cssp.org/publications/documents/Federal-Spending-Prenatal-to-Three.pdf.

[55] *See id.* at 4. For a discussion of prenatal care for undocumented immigrants, who are not eligible for Medicaid, *see Health Coverage of Immigrants*, KAISER FAMILY FOUND. (Dec. 13, 2017), www.kff.org/disparities-policy/fact-sheet/health-coverage-of-immigrants/ ("Since 2002, states have had the option to provide prenatal care to women regardless of immigration status by extending CHIP coverage to the unborn child. In addition, some states have state-funded health programs that provide coverage to some groups of immigrants regardless of immigration status. There are also some locally-funded programs that provide coverage or assistance without regard to immigration status.").

[56] *See* Bruner & Johnson, *supra* note 54, at 22.

[57] *See id.*

Another major source of funding for services for children in the first three years of life is Title V Maternal and Child Health block grants, enacted in 1935 as part of the Social Security Act. Title V block grants provide funds to state public health agencies for a broad range of activities, such as increased access to services to prevent, assess, diagnose, and treat a range of conditions in children, with a particular emphasis on children with special needs. States are required to match every $4 in federal funds with $3 in state funds, but most states allocate more funding than the minimum and also draw on local and private funds. As might be expected, blue states invest heavily in this program, but many red states do as well, including Alabama, Arkansas, Kentucky, Georgia, South Carolina, Tennessee, and Utah.[58] In a recent year, the Title V program served 2.6 million pregnant women, 3.8 million infants, and 3.5 million toddlers, although these numbers include those who do not receive direct services.[59]

Other major forms of public investment in children from birth to age three include income supports, food assistance, housing subsidies, and child care subsidies.[60] In fiscal year 2016, the federal government invested $16 billion in the EITC and the refundable Child Tax Credit (CTC), reaching 7.4 million children under age three.[61] Twenty-nine states have a state-level EITC, although the amount varies widely by state.[62] The federal government spent more than $13 billion on food assistance, both through the Supplemental Nutrition Assistance Program (SNAP) and the Women, Infants and Children program.[63] The federal government spent $2 billion on various housing subsidies (excluding low-income housing tax credits, available to developers) serving 540,000 children under age three.[64] And through numerous block grants and programs, as well as the nonrefundable Child and Dependent Care Tax Credit, the federal government provided child care subsidies for 407,000 children under the age of three, with a total investment of $4.2 billion.[65]

---

[58] In fiscal year 2015, the federal government spent $526 million, but the combined expenditures from all levels of government and for all children (not limited to 0–3) was $6.3 billion. See U.S. Dep't Health & Human Servs., Maternal and Child Health, Explore the Title V Federal-State Partnership, https://mchb.tvisdata.hrsa.gov/; see Bruner & Johnson, *supra* note 54, at 23.

[59] See Bruner & Johnson, *supra* note 54, at 23.

[60] This chapter does not describe all of the supports available to families. There are other, smaller programs as well, such as Part C of the Individuals with Disabilities Education Act (IDEA), also known as the Early Disabilities Intervention Program for Infants and Toddlers with Disabilities. This funding provides grants to states for services for infants and toddlers with developmental delays or physical or mental conditions that might lead to developmental delays. *See id.* at 4.

[61] *See id.* at 4. In contrast to these two major programs, cash assistance under the Temporary Assistance to Needy Families Act was only $800 million in 2016 and cash assistance under the Supplemental Security Income program was $849 million. *See id.*

[62] For details on these variations, see *Tax Credits for Working Families: Earned Income Tax Credit*, NATIONAL CONFERENCE OF STATE LEGISLATURES (Apr. 2018), www.ncsl.org/research/labor-and-employment/earned-income-tax-credits-for-working-families.aspx.

[63] *See* Bruner & Johnson, *supra* note 54, at 4.

[64] *See id.* at 22, 50.

[65] *See id.* at 32–33, 48.

Some of these investments serve a high percentage of low-income children, but other investments fall far short. Medicaid and CHIP, for example, are entitlements, with relatively generous eligibility thresholds for children and pregnant women – a national median of 200 percent of the poverty level for pregnant women and higher for children.[66] Similarly, the federal EITC and the refundable CTC, combined, reach 90 percent of all eligible families.[67] Other supports, however, most notably housing assistance and child care subsidies, do not begin to satisfy the demand for these supports. Looking at the US population as a whole, housing supports reach only 5 percent of all families, and child care subsidies are available for only 3.4 percent of all children from birth to age three.[68]

There is relatively limited state-level variation in access to these federal supports. For Medicaid and CHIP, for example, the eligibility thresholds for children are quite similar around the country.[69] Similarly, food assistance through SNAP has some state-level variation, but there is not a wide divergence.[70]

In general, then, when the federal government provides much of the funding, and when children are the direct beneficiaries, there is less variation among the states. By contrast, when states make the investments, there is much more variation. State-level EITCs, for example, vary widely by state. In California, the state pays 85 percent of the amount of the federal tax credit, nearly doubling the total amount for eligible families (although California limits eligibility to lower-income families), whereas Louisiana pays only 3.5 percent of the amount of the federal tax credit.[71] These differences tend to follow predictable political divides, with red states providing either no program or only a very limited state-level EITC.[72]

Even with federal programs, such as Medicaid, when the beneficiaries are adults, there is much greater state-level variation. Eligibility thresholds for adults under Medicaid vary widely by state, with the variation running along political lines, and red states covering fewer adults.[73] This variation affects children. For example, one critical intervention in the period from birth to age three is treatment for parents suffering from depression and other mental health concerns. Medicaid covers behavioral health services including outpatient services, inpatient services,

---

[66] See *Where Are States Today? Medicaid and CHIP Eligibility Levels for Children, Pregnant Women, and Adults*, KAISER FAMILY FOUND. (Mar. 2018), www.kff.org/medicaid/fact-sheet/ where-are-states-today-medicaid-and-chip/; Bruner & Johnson, *supra* note 54, at 23–24.
[67] See Bruner & Johnson, *supra* note 54, at 15.
[68] See *id.* at 4.
[69] See *Where Are States Today?*, KAISER FAMILY FOUND., *supra* note 66.
[70] See *A Closer Look at Who Benefits from SNAP: State-by-State Fact Sheets*, CENTER ON BUDGET AND POLICY PRIORITIES (Mar. 2018), www.cbpp.org/research/a-closer-look-at-who-benefits-from-snap-state-by-state-fact-sheets
[71] See Catlin Nchako & Lexin Cai, *Tax Credits for Working Families: Earned Income Tax Credit*, NAT'L CONFERENCE OF STATE LEGISLATURES (Apr. 2018), www.ncsl.org/research/labor-and-employment/earned-income-tax-credits-for-working-families.aspx.
[72] See *id.*
[73] See *Where Are States Today?*, KAISER FAMILY FOUND., *supra* note 66.

psychiatric medication and substance abuse, and home and community-based services.[74] States also have the option to include nonclinical behavior health services such as peer support and community residential services.[75] In states with greater coverage, then, children benefit because more parents have access to mental health services.

It is worth considering one program – home visiting – in greater detail, partly because of the exceptionally strong evidence base for the intervention and partly because it is one investment in the first three years of life that began with state-level efforts. Beginning in the 1990s, states started home-visiting programs, but in 2010, as part of the Affordable Care Act, Congress created the Maternal, Infant, and Early Childhood Home Visiting Program (MIECHV). This program funds evidence-based, home-visiting programs. States are not required to provide matching funds, but they cannot replace existing state-level investments with federal funds. In 2017, with $342 million in federal funding,[76] the MIECHV reached more than 156,000 families in 27 percent of the counties in the United States, serving predominantly low-income families.[77] Including state funding, 301,000 families were served through home-visiting programs.[78]

Despite this influx of federal funding, home-visiting programs still reach only a tiny fraction of the families who would benefit,[79] although the investments in home visiting do not necessarily run along red-blue lines. With one exception, no state serves more than 5 percent of the families who would benefit from home visiting.[80] On the high end, home-visiting programs serve 5 percent of the targeted families in

---

[74] *See Medicaid's Role in Financing Behavioral Health Services for Low-Income Individuals*, KAISER FAMILY FOUND. (June 2017), www.kff.org/medicaid/issue-brief/medicaids-role-in-financing-behavioral-health-services-for-low-income-individuals/.

[75] *See id.*

[76] *See* U.S. HEALTH RESOURCES & SERVS. ADMIN., MATERNAL, INFANT, AND EARLY CHILDHOOD HOME VISITING PROGRAM FY 2017 FORMULA FUNDING AWARDS (Sept. 2017), https://mchb.hrsa.gov/maternal-child-health-initiatives/home-visiting/fy17-home-visiting-awards.

[77] *See* U.S. HEALTH RESOURCES & SERVS. ADMIN., HOME VISITING (Apr. 2018), https://mchb.hrsa.gov/sites/default/files/mchb/MaternalChildHealthInitiatives/HomeVisiting/pdf/home-visiting-infographic-2017.pdf. States are also permitted to use funds from a variety of other federal sources, such as Title V of the Maternal and Child Health Block Grant Program and Medicaid, to fund home-visiting programs. For a helpful overview of state investments in home-visiting programs, including for some states the breakdown of federal versus state funding, *see id.*

[78] *See* NATIONAL HOME VISITING RESOURCE CENTER, DATA SUPPLEMENT *2017 HOME VISITING YEARBOOK* (2018), www.nhvrc.org/wp-content/uploads/NHVRC_Data-Supplement-Summary_FINAL.pdf (the figure in the text is for visits during 2016).

[79] *See id.* (defining families who would benefit from home visiting as families who meet one or more of the target criteria, including a parent who is low-income, has limited education, or is parenting alone).

[80] The percentages in the text were calculated using National Home Visiting Resource Center, *Home Visiting by State* (2018), www.nhvrc.org/explore-research-and-data/hv-by-state/. For an overview of investments by states, see NATIONAL HOME VISITING RESOURCE CENTER, *supra* note 42, at 193–237.

Kansas, 4.3 percent in Kentucky, and 3.7 percent in Rhode Island; and on the low end, home-visiting programs serve 0.7 percent of the targeted families in California, 0.5 percent of families in Georgia, and 0.3 percent in Nevada. Missouri is the outlier, although that state serves only 9.5 percent of the families who would benefit from home visiting.

Turning to public investments in preschool, there is significant divergence in state spending, but it does not run along a predictable red-blue political divide. The baseline is the federal investment – $9.2 billion in fiscal year 2016, serving 1.1 million children in Head Start programs.[81] With Head Start funding, the federal government pays 80 percent of the cost of running a Head Start program, with the remainder provided by states, localities, or private entities. The federal government also invests in preschool through the Preschool Development Grant – $230 million in fiscal year 2016 – which helps expand access to and improve the quality of prekindergarten programs for low-income children.[82]

Beyond these federal funds, which have not increased recently, many states now make considerable investments in preschool, mostly for four-year-olds. State funding for preschool rose 47 percent between 2012 and 2017,[83] with a total investment of $7.4 billion annually.[84] As a result of the federal funding and increased state funding, 44 percent of all four-year-olds in the 2016–17 academic year were enrolled in preschool.[85]

These national numbers, however, mask significant state variations, and the variations decidedly do not follow the red-blue divide.[86] Consider the 2016–17 enrollment figures. Five states (including the District of Columbia) enrolled more than 80 percent of four-year-olds in a program that receives state or federal funds: DC (88 percent), Florida (87 percent), Oklahoma (84 percent), Vermont (84 percent), and Wisconsin (80 percent).[87] An additional eight states enrolled at least 50 percent of four-year-olds in a program that receives state or federal funds: Iowa (69 percent),

[81] *See* NATIONAL HOME VISITING RESOURCE CENTER, *State Profile- Missouri* (2018), www.nhvrc .org/wp-content/uploads/DS-MO-Profile.pdf.
[82] *See* Emily Parker et al., Educ. Comm'n of the States, *State Pre-K Funding for 2015–16 Fiscal Year: National Trends in State Preschool Funding* 2 (Jan. 2016), www.ecs.org/wp-content/ uploads/01252016_Prek-K_Funding_report-4.pdf.
[83] *See* Louisa Diffey et al., *State Pre-K Funding 2016–17 Fiscal Year: Trends and Opportunities*, EDUC. COMM'N OF THE STATES 1 (Jan. 2017), www.ecs.org/wp-content/uploads/State-Pre-K-Funding-2016-17-Fiscal-Year-Trends-and-opportunities-1.pdf.
[84] *See id.* at 9.
[85] *See* Allison H. Friedman-Krauss et al., *The State of Preschool 2017*, NAT'L INST. FOR EARLY EDUC. RESEARCH at 26 (2018), http://nieer.org/wp-content/uploads/2018/05/State-of-Preschool-2017-Full.5.15.pdf.
[86] States have long diverged in their use of Head Start funds, and thus a variation already existed, *see* W. Steven Barnett & Allison Friedman-Krauss, *State(s) of Head Start*, THE NAT'L INST. FOR EARLY EDUC. RES. 28, 31 (2016), http://nieer.org/wp-content/uploads/2016/12/HS_Full_ Reduced.pdf, but with some states making enormous new investments, the differences are even starker.
[87] *See* Friedman-Krauss et al., *supra* note 85, at 26.

West Virginia (67 percent), Georgia (64 percent), New York (60 percent), Texas (59 percent), New Mexico (55 percent), Arkansas (50 percent), and South Carolina (50 percent). Some of these states have made enormous enrollment increases since 2002. Florida, for example, increased enrollment by 77 percentage points, Vermont by 67 percentage points, and Iowa by 59 percentage points.[88] Some states, however, enrolled very few four-year-olds in a program that receives state or federal funds: Minnesota (20 percent), Washington (19 percent), Massachusetts (18 percent), Missouri (18 percent), Indiana (16 percent), Nevada (15 percent), Hawaii (14 percent), New Hampshire (14 percent), Idaho (13 percent), and Utah (12 percent). And seven states have no dedicated state funding for preschool: Idaho, Montana, New Hampshire, North Dakota, South Dakota, Utah, and Wyoming.[89]

Turning to preschool for three-year-olds, nationally, federal and state investments in preschool programs reached only 16 percent of all three-year-olds in the 2016–17 academic year, but again there is considerable variation at the state level. The District of Columbia and Vermont each enrolled 66 percent of three-year-olds, Arkansas enrolled 35 percent, Illinois enrolled 30 percent, New Jersey enrolled 29 percent, Mississippi enrolled 28 percent, New Mexico enrolled 22 percent, and Kentucky, Louisiana, and West Virginia each enrolled 20 percent.[90] These states stand in contrast to the 38 states that enrolled fewer than 10 percent of their three-year-olds.[91]

Finally, there is also variation in the quality of the programs and the amount states spend per pupil. When it comes to meeting quality standards, the list is mixed politically. The four states that met all the quality benchmarks in 2017 were Alabama, Mississippi, Rhode Island, and West Virginia, followed closely by Arkansas, Kentucky, Maine, Michigan, New Mexico, North Carolina, Oklahoma, Tennessee, Washington, Louisiana, and Oregon.[92] By contrast, the spending variations more closely reflect the traditional red-blue divide. At the top of the list, the District of Columbia spends $17,000 per student, followed by New Jersey ($12,200), Oregon ($9,500), Washington ($8,200), Connecticut ($7,800), Delaware ($7,400), and Pennsylvania ($7,300).[93] Close to the bottom of the list, Florida, which has exceptionally high enrollments, spends only $2,300 per student, Mississippi ($2,400), Nevada ($2,600), and South Carolina ($3,000).[94] But other red states, such as West Virginia, ranked higher, spending $6,500 per student and ranking 10th in the nation.[95]

---

[88] *See id.* at 25.
[89] *See id.* at 9.
[90] *See id.* at 26.
[91] *See id.*
[92] *See id.* at 10.
[93] *See id.* at 29.
[94] *See id.*
[95] *See id.*

At the local level, some cities are adopting universal prekindergarten programs. For example, New York City's universal prekindergarten program, Pre-K for All, was offered for the first time during the 2014–15 school year.[96] The program provides all four-year-olds a full week of full or half days, from September to June. Some locations offer extended hours, dual language programs, and transportation for children with disabilities. The city is making a particular push to enroll low-income children, English language learners, and children from families impacted by incarceration.[97] Chicago is beginning a universal prekindergarten program in the 2018–19 school year, with plans for full implementation by 2021. In the first phase, the city is prioritizing low-income children.[98] And Memphis is in the planning process for a universal prekindergarten program, aiming for full implementation by 2022.[99]

INSIGHTS FOR ADVOCATES AND SCHOLARS, AND QUESTIONS FOR FUTURE RESEARCH

As the preceding description illustrates, the starkest difference among states is the level of support for preschool. As noted, these differences do not track the traditional red-blue political divide. Mississippi enrolls far more three- and four-year-olds in preschool than Massachusetts – 28 percent and 36 percent, as compared with 14 percent and 18 percent, respectively. Some deep red states – notably, Oklahoma and West Virginia – are national leaders in enrollment and also rank high for both quality and per-pupil spending.[100] And other red states, such as Alabama, have both increased enrollment and maintained high-quality standards.

It is worth considering Oklahoma in greater detail. In 1998, Oklahoma adopted a goal of universal access to state-funded preschool for four-year-olds, funding

---

[96] *See* CTR. STUDY CHILD CARE EMPLOYMENT, UNIV. CALIFORNIA, BERKELEY & NAT'L INSTIT. EARLY EDU. RES., *New York Pre-K for All* (2018), http://cscce.berkeley.edu/files/2017/10/Pre-K-Parity_NewYorkCity.pdf

[97] *See* NYC DEP'T EDUC., *Pre-Kindergarten* (2018), http://schools.nyc.gov/ChoicesEnrollment/PreK/default.htm.

[98] *See Mayor Emanuel Announces Plan to Make Full Day Four-Year-Old Pre-Kindergarten Universal*, Office of the Mayor, City of Chicago, Mayor's Press Office (2018), www.cityofchicago.org/content/dam/city/depts/mayor/Press%20Room/Press%20Releases/2018/May/053018_Universal PreK.pdf.

[99] *See Remarks for Pre-K Plan Announcement*, City of Memphis, Office of Mayor Jim Strickland (2018), www.memphistn.gov/UserFiles/Servers/Server_11150732/File/Gov/Executive%20Division/Office%20of%20Communications/031718%20Strickland%20Remarks.pdf; *Ordinance No. 5685: An Ordinance to Create a Pre-K Education Special Fund*, City of Memphis, Office of Mayor Jim Strickland (2018), https://memphistn.gov/UserFiles/Servers/Server_11150732/File/Ordinance%205685.pdf.

[100] *See* Friedman-Krauss et al. *supra* note 85, at 10 (showing that both Oklahoma and West Virginia met nine and ten of the current quality standards, respectively; further West Virginia ranks sixth in the nation for spending on preschool and Oklahoma ranks thirteenth).

prekindergarten as an additional grade of school.[101] Oklahoma's support of early childhood development does not stop with prekindergarten. Among other programs, the state created the Oklahoma Early Childhood Program in 2006, focused on children from birth to age three. This program addresses both quality and access to preschool for the first three years of life; it also adopts a two-generation approach, working with parents to foster economic independence.[102] Further, Oklahoma offers a program called SoonerStart, which serves the needs of developmentally delayed infants and toddlers and is a collaborative program, working with parents and other caregivers.[103] Finally, Oklahoma City has implemented the Educare program, which serves children from birth to age five who are at risk for school failure.[104] Educare provides a range of services, including year-round, full-day care and mental health services for children and families.[105]

These state variations raise a series of questions, outlined here and worthy of considerably more research.

To begin, are the state-level preschool investments part of a broader antipoverty strategy? There are numerous factors to look at, and the answer may differ with each state. In Oklahoma, for example, despite the investments in early childhood development, the state did not expand Medicaid under the Affordable Care Act, and it has only a small, nonrefundable state-level EITC. West Virginia is one of the few red states that did expand Medicaid, enrolling 166,000 people under the expansion,[106] but it does not have a state-level EITC.

What is driving the state-level investments in preschool in states that do not typically provide robust social welfare programs? Mississippi and Massachusetts, for example, offer sharp contrasts. Under Temporary Assistance for Needy Families, the maximum benefit in Mississippi is $170 per month as compared with $618 in Massachusetts.[107] But, as previously noted, Mississippi enrolls 36 percent of all four-year-olds in state- or federally funded preschool as compared with Massachusetts at 18 percent.[108] The differential may be rooted in the child poverty rate in each state

---

[101] *See* Janet Barresi, Okla. State Dept. Educ., *A Look at Oklahoma's Early Childhood Education Programs* (2011), http://ok.gov/sde/sites/ok.gov.sde/files/Early%20Childhood%20Programs.pdf.

[102] *See* Okla. State Dept. of Educ., *Early Childhood Fast Facts 2017*, http://sde.ok.gov/sde/sites/ok .gov.sde/files/documents/files/Early%20Childhood%20Fast%20Facts%202017.pdf.

[103] *See id.*

[104] *See* Okla. City Educare, *Who We Are*, http://okceducare.org/who-we-are/facts-and-figures/.

[105] *See id.*

[106] *See* Louise Norris, *West Virginia and the ACA's Medicaid Expansion*, Healthinsurance.org, Mar. 26, 2018, www.healthinsurance.org/west-virginia-medicaid/. W. Va. Dept. of Health & Human Res. (WV_DHHR). "165,917 West Virginians Are Enrolled in Medicaid Expansion as of Monday, March 26, 2018." 26 Mar. 2018, 6:46 A.M. Tweet.

[107] *See* Gene Falk, Cong. Research Serv., RL 32760, The Temporary Assistance for Needy Families (TANF) Block Grant: Responses to Frequently Asked Questions 10 (2016).

[108] *See* Friedman-Krauss et al. *supra* note 85, at 26.

(the child poverty rate in Mississippi is 31 percent as compared with 13 percent in Massachusetts[109]), but there are surely other explanations as well.[110]

What is the rhetoric of early childhood development and state funding? Some red states frame early childhood development as common sense policy, not as a political issue. In Oklahoma, for example, local leaders say "[t]his isn't a liberal issue. ... This is investing in our kids, in our future. It's a no-brainer."[111] In Florida, which amended its state constitution in 2002 to require prekindergarten access for four-year-olds[112] and now enrolls 87 percent of all four-year-olds, Governor Rick Scott, a Republican, stated that "[f]amilies want their children to have high-quality educational opportunities and research shows a good education begins early. That is why investing $1.1 billion in early childhood education is so important for our state. I am committed to continued support for early learning, and making sure Florida remains number one in the nation for access to prekindergarten."[113]

How can advocates and policy makers in other states learn from these success stories? There is a rational economic argument to be made for investments in early childhood development because interventions during the first several years of life are more cost effective than interventions during the school years and far more cost effective than programs for adults, such as job training initiatives.[114] Similarly, to the extent the greater political support for preschool turns on research showing the importance of early childhood development generally and preschool in particular, this research may have made the issue of government support less contentious. But there is still far more to be understood about how states, especially red states, have overcome partisan opposition to public investments. Alabama, for example, has had sustained political support for both broad access and high-quality preschool, leading to substantial gains in that state on both fronts.[115] The question for further research is what created and sustained this political support.

Relatedly, can this political momentum transfer to other kinds of supportive efforts and programs? Rational arguments about costs and benefits, and research showing profound impacts, often are not enough to win support for effective programs. One insight from the success with preschool is that it may be easier to garner widespread

---

[109] *See Child Poverty Rates Increased during the Great Recession*, NAT'L CONFERENCE OF STATE LEGISLATURES, www.ncsl.org/research/human-services/child-poverty-rates.aspx.

[110] Sometimes investments are a result of a court order. *See* Michael A. Rebell, *Right to Comprehensive Educational Opportunity*, 47 HARV. C.R.-C.L. L. REV. 47, 82–89 (2012).

[111] Nicholas Kristof, *Oklahoma! Where the Kids Learn Early*, N.Y. TIMES (Nov. 9, 2013), www.nytimes.com/2013/11/10/opinion/sunday/kristof-oklahoma-where-the-kids-learn-early.html (quoting Skip Steele, Republican Tulsa City Council member).

[112] FLA. CONST. art. IX, § 1, cl. b (amended 2002).

[113] *Governor Rick Scott Highlights Early Learning Funding in Miami*, RICK SCOTT: 45TH GOVERNOR FLA., www.flgov.com/gov-rick-scott-highlights-early-learning-funding-in-miami.

[114] *See* JAMES J. HECKMAN, GIVING KIDS A FAIR CHANCE 3–41, 125–32 (2013).

[115] *See* Friedman-Krauss et al. *supra* note 85, at 23.

support for programs that do not rely on parents. Given the antipathy for poor adults, it is not surprising that states are investing in programs that help children directly rather than programs that work through parents, although home-visiting programs are a step in the right direction. Similarly, cash transfers are still anathema to much of the country, and thus programs that provide direct services, whether it is health care or preschool, stand to earn far more support than, say, a child allowance. Additionally, preschool may be popular because it is less intrusive, particularly because it is voluntary. In short, there may be limitations to building on the success of preschool.

What are the trade-offs in terms of policy but also politics? Oklahoma may be investing in preschool, but its support of K–12 education is flagging, down nearly 16 percent in the last decade.[116] West Virginia is somewhat better, increasing its state support of K–12 education by nearly 4 percent in the same period,[117] and the public spending per pupil in the state places it 15th in the country, as compared with Oklahoma, which is 45th in the country.[118] But both states pay their teachers a pittance as compared with other states: the average salary for public schools teachers in Oklahoma is $45,300 (50th in the country), and in West Virginia is $45,600 (49th in the country).[119] This is low even as compared with other rural states, such as Kansas, which ranks 4th in the country and Nebraska, which ranks 21st.[120] Thus, just as the support for preschool may not be a foundation for other antipoverty efforts, it would be helpful to know whether the investments in preschool are at the cost of broader investments in education.

Finally, what are the dangers in calling for additional support for early childhood development? The emphasis on this developmental period and, particularly the pre-natal period, can lead to interventions that interfere with autonomy and bodily integrity. As described previously, the neuroscience that underscores the importance of early childhood development also shows that cognitive development begins pre-natally. This could lead to the kinds of interventions that severely limit women's autonomy and privacy. In some states, for example, it is a crime to expose a fetus to a narcotic or a controlled substance,[121] and women who have been using such substances have been put in rehabilitation centers for the duration of their pregnancy (or longer)[122]

---

[116] *See* Michael Leachman et al., *A Punishing Decade for School Funding*, CENTER ON BUDGET AND POLICY PRIORITIES (Nov. 2017), www.cbpp.org/research/state-budget-and-tax/a-punishing-decade-for-school-funding.

[117] *See id.*

[118] *See id.*

[119] *See id.*

[120] *See id.*

[121] *See, e.g.,* TENN. CODE ANN. § 39-13-107(c)(2) (2015).

[122] *See* Stephanie Chen, *Pregnant and Addicted, Mothers Find Hope*, CNN (Oct. 24, 2009, 10:39 AM), www.cnn.com/2009/CRIME/10/24/pregnant.addicts/index.html (describing a rehabilita-tion program for pregnant women and new mothers; some women go voluntarily and some are sent by the state).

or prosecuted after the baby is born.[123] More broadly, supportive programs for low-income families often come with intrusive strings attached,[124] thus, it is critical to track whether the investments in early childhood development follow this trend.

CONCLUSION

Overwhelming evidence establishes the acute importance of the first five years of life for human development. Public investments in this period can have profound and lasting impacts on both individuals and society. As this chapter has shown, when the federal government invests in early childhood, as it does for the prenatal period until age three, there is more convergence at the state level, with most states offering basic support, at least for children, if not their parents. By contrast, when states take the lead in making public investments, there is a much greater divergence in public investments. This divergence, however, does not always follow predictable political lines, and there is a particularly interesting story to understand about the high level of red-state support for preschool.

The investments in preschool are certainly welcome and provide some basis for cautious optimism about a broader antipoverty program aimed at early childhood. As the evidence of the cost-effectiveness of these programs builds, the investments may help persuade the public of the importance of fostering early childhood development, which could lead to ever-earlier supports. This must include investments in the whole family, and especially parents, who are the linchpin in early childhood development.

---

[123] *See Hicks* v. *State*, 153 So. 3d 53, 54 (Ala. 2014) (upholding conviction of a mother charged with chemical endangerment for exposing a fetus to a controlled substance); *State* v. *McKnight*, 576 S.E.2d 168, 171, 174–75 (S.C. 2003) (upholding conviction of a mother charged with homicide by child abuse for exposing a fetus to cocaine in violation of South Carolina law, which the Court interpreted as applying both to born and unborn children).

[124] *See, e.g.*, Wendy A. Bach, *The Hyperregulatory State: Women, Race, Poverty, and Support*, 25 YALE J. L. & FEMINISM 317, 318–20 (2014) (describing this phenomenon); Khiara M. Bridges, *Towards a Theory of State Visibility: Race, Poverty, and Equal Protection*, 19 COLUM. J. GENDER & L. 965, 971–78 (2010) (describing the intrusive conditions attached to a program designed to promote prenatal health).

7

States Diverting Funds from the Poor

Daniel Hatcher

Purpose matters. Government exists to protect and maximize the welfare of its citizens, including the vulnerable. When that purpose is undermined, harm results.

Unfortunately, states are doing just that – prioritizing their short-term financial interests over the public good, and hiring private contractors to help. Partnerships between state agencies and private revenue maximization consultants are using schemes to divert billions in federal aid and other funds from children and the poor to government coffers and private profit.[1]

The practices undermine the purpose of government, destroy the intended benefits of fiscal federalism, and harm the most vulnerable among us. Consider the following examples from Ohio, New Jersey, and Iowa.

Ohio's juvenile courts developed a strategy to maximize revenue by ordering poor children to be removed from their homes. The courts signed "subgrantee" contracts indicating that the state will reroute federal foster care funds it receives to the juvenile courts. Under the agreements, courts can only get paid when ruling that poor children are "unruly" or delinquent and that the children must be removed from their homes. The more child removals ordered by the courts, the more revenue the courts receive. To help maximize the funds, some of the juvenile courts hired a private revenue contractor called Justice Benefits, Inc. (JBI). "JBI works on a contingency basis and assists the Court in identifying, documenting costs and preparing claims – JBI is paid 22% on monies recovered through claims submitted by the Court."[2]

New Jersey forces school districts to work with a private revenue contractor called the Public Consulting Group (PCG) to maximize claims for school-based Medicaid

[1] *See generally*, DANIEL L. HATCHER, THE POVERTY INDUSTRY: THE EXPLOITATION OF AMERICA'S MOST VULNERABLE CITIZENS (2016) (hereinafter POVERTY INDUSTRY) (detailing practices discussed in this chapter).

[2] Miami County, Ohio, Commissioners Meeting Minutes Summary, Dec. 30, 2014, www.co .miami.oh.us/Archive/ViewFile/Item/379.

funds, and punishes the schools with a loss of state funding if they fail to meet quotas. Then, although intended to help schools serve the needs of low-income children with disabilities, the state diverts the majority of the federal aid to its general coffers and PCG receives a cut as its contingency fee.[3] To bolster the claims, PCG advised New Jersey to include $435 million owed to the school employees' pension fund as state expenditures – but a 2017 federal audit determined the state had not made scheduled payments to the fund in nearly 20 years.[4]

The Iowa state foster care agency hired a private revenue contractor called MAXIMUS, Inc. to help increase the number of foster children who are determined to be disabled – not to provide more help in serving the children's disabling conditions, but so the state can take their disability benefits. The company has helped apply for Social Security disability benefits on the children's behalf, and helped the state take control of the children's funds as representative payee. Then, rather than using the funds to help the children, Iowa diverts the children's money to general revenue.[5] MAXIMUS's cost proposal to the Iowa Department of Human Resources considers children as "units" – applying "anticipated units" and "unit costs" to describe costs for services in helping Iowa obtain the children's funds.[6]

These are not isolated practices. As detailed in my book, *The Poverty Industry: The Exploitation of America's Most Vulnerable Citizens*, states and their human service agencies team up with private companies in multiple ways to maximize revenue from the vulnerable: taking Social Security survivor and disability benefits from foster children, using illusory budget shell games to siphon away billions in Medicaid funds intended for children and low-income adults, diverting child support payments for foster children and families on public assistance into government revenue, and using nursing homes to take the facilities' federal aid while the elderly receive poor care.[7] Some states take even more, including confiscating Veteran's Assistance benefits from foster children whose parents died in the military. Nebraska will even take a foster child's burial plot away if she has one.[8]

These examples just scratch the surface of what is taking place across the country, where state and county governments are partnering with private companies to develop countless ways to use the vulnerable as a source of revenue and profit. In seeking to expose the practices, it is difficult to find stopping points – because each revenue scheme will intersect with another, which will intersect with another, and

3   US Dept. of Health and Human Services, Office of Inspector General, *New Jersey Claimed Hundreds of Millions in Unallowable or Unsupported Medicaid School Based Reimbursement*, A-02-15-01010 (Nov. 2017) at 2.
4   *Id* at 8–9.
5   *See* POVERTY INDUSTRY, *supra* note 1, at 80–90.
6   MAXIMUS, Inc., Bid Proposal for Iowa Department of Human Services SSI Advocacy Project, § K Cost Proposal, Feb. 12, 2009, 3 (on file with author).
7   POVERTY INDUSTRY, *supra* note 1.
8   *See generally*, POVERTY INDUSTRY, supra note 1 (detailing practices discussed in this chapter).

so on. Thus, to illustrate the interconnections of just a sampling of the practices, Anna is introduced, a hypothetical foster child who encounters and is impacted by the revenue strategies in different states. Although hypothetical, the vulnerable children Anna represents are very real.

Why is this happening? Both "red" and "blue" states have faced poor economic conditions and a political climate opposed to raising sufficient revenue through general taxation. So states are looking for money elsewhere, including schemes that are largely unknown to the public to divert federal aid and other funds from children and the poor. In doing so, states have lost sight of their purpose – focusing on their own fiscal interests rather than the best interests of their citizens.

The resulting harm to vulnerable populations is intense, lasting, and the reverberations affect us all. When a state foster care agency hires a contractor to help the state take resources away from abused and neglected children, the public's belief in government's commitment to the common good is harmed by such an egregious breach of trust and moral integrity. And the public is also harmed financially. When agencies take resources from foster children, they are less likely to become self-sufficient after leaving care, more likely to need public assistance, more likely to be unemployed, and more likely to become incarcerated – and we all pay the price. When a foster child in Cleveland, Camden, or Des Moines is harmed, we are all harmed.

A fundamental realignment is required so that states are true to their purpose, to exist not for themselves but for the good of the people. To be clear, the diversionary tactics described in this chapter do not result in valid arguments to cut government aid programs. The levels of public assistance are significantly insufficient to meet current needs. If states are misusing federal aid that is intended solely for the vulnerable, then the appropriate response is not to cut the funding but to stop the misuse.

The remainder of this chapter summarizes how state practices diverting aid from the poor are undermining the purpose of government and the intended benefits of fiscal federalism, through the lens of the hypothetical Anna encountering numerous revenue strategies. Although the examples provided here are not exhaustive, they are representative of the expanding strategies using the vulnerable as revenue, now permeating into virtually every type of poverty program and service.

EXAMPLES OF STATE REVENUE SCHEMES

It could be the same foster care child, Anna, 13 years old, from an impoverished neighborhood, mentally disabled, targeted for multiple sources of revenue. She is solitary in her need for care and assistance – but multiple in her role as a source of funds for the state and its revenue contractors.

Anna faces similar experiences as other vulnerable children who end up in foster care. Although still a child, she already suffers from post-traumatic stress disorder

(PTSD), which foster children experience at twice the level of US war veterans. She was taken into foster care from an impoverished home due to allegations of neglect, a home weakened by struggles to overcome poverty and bouts with homelessness. Rather than helping the family stay intact, the state's removal of Anna from her home increased her trauma. Because she is older and disabled, and sometimes responds angrily to the trauma she feels inside, adoption is unlikely. Anna hopes to reunify with her biological parents, but few resources are provided to help their struggle and the state moves forward to terminate their parental rights despite the lack of an adoptive resource. Growing up in foster care, the statistics are lined up against Anna – facing likely future homelessness, struggles to find work, a high probability of making less than $10,000 annually, likely needing to apply for food stamps, lacking health insurance, increased chances of never finishing high school, only a 2 percent chance of getting a college degree, and likely involvement in the criminal justice system.[9]

Anna needs help that is solely focused on her best interests, but she encounters a system that considers her as a source of funds. Once in foster care, she is processed through the agency's revenue maximization unit. Anna has a small trust fund with $1,900 inherited from her deceased uncle. If she lives in Iowa, the state child welfare manual directs the foster care agency (DHS) to first try to take those minimal funds from Anna:

[A]pproach the trustee, seeking to have DHS made payee for the income of the trust. If sufficient funds are not available from the trust to meet the total cost of care, request the trustee to petition the district court to release funds to cover the cost of foster care maintenance (or as much of the cost of maintenance as possible).[10]

If Anna lives in Nebraska, the state would scour her for even more possible resources. In addition to Social Security and Veterans Administration (VA) benefits, a state regulation encourages the agency to consider taking the following assets from foster children – even burial spaces:

1. Cash on hand; 2. Cash in savings or checking accounts; 3. Stocks; 4. Bonds; 5. Certificates of deposit; 6. Investments; 7. Collectable unpaid notes or loans; 8. Promissory notes; 9. Mortgages; 10. Land contracts; 11. Land leases; 12. Revocable burial funds; 13. Trust or guardianship funds; 14. Cash value of insurance policies; 15. Real estate; 16. Trailer houses; 17. Burial spaces; 18. Life estates; 19. Farm and business equipment; 20. Livestock; 21. Poultry and crops; 22. Household goods and other personal effects; and 23. Federal and state tax refunds.[11]

---

[9] Id. at 15.
[10] Iowa Dept. of Human Services, Out-of-Home Placement Policy and Procedures, Employees' Manual, Title 17, Chapter E at 160–61, http://dhs.iowa.gov/sites/default/files/17-E.pdf.
[11] 479 NAC 2–001.08.

After identifying other possible assets to take from Anna, the state refers her for further processing by its revenue contractor, using her to apply for and take her Social Security disability benefits, a process detailed in the following text.

States Taking Foster Children's Benefits

The state's revenue contractor is given access to sift through Anna's medical records. During this process, the state refers Anna to physicians where she is prescribed multiple psychotropic medications. Then, the revenue contractor begins the process of applying for federal aid on her behalf, determining that she may be eligible for disability benefits, called Supplemental Security Income (SSI), if the Social Security Administration determines she came from a poor family and is disabled enough. The contractor also seeks out other children in the state foster care system who have dead parents, to apply for Old-Age, Survivors, and Disability Insurance benefits (OASDI, or "survivor benefits"). Survivor benefits are similar to life insurance, property rights belonging to children after a parent worked and paid payroll tax contributions. The state plugs Anna into a strategy where it seeks to maximize these benefits and then routes the funds to state coffers under the rationale of repaying itself for foster care costs.[12]

Across the country, private contractors often help with the process, identifying children who may be eligible for the benefits, and seeking to have the children determined disabled or locating those who have dead or disabled parents.[13] Contract documents describe procedures where the children are viewed almost like resources to be mined on a conveyor belt – using data analytics, dissection, and algorithms – and ranking the children in terms of how much revenue they can potentially produce and how quickly, rather than prioritizing the children's needs.[14] In Maryland, the state contracted with MAXIMUS, whose assessment report described foster children as a "revenue generating mechanism."[15] MAXIMUS's cost proposal to the Iowa Department of Human Resources described children as "units."[16] If Anna is in Florida, PCG provided an assessment for how the state can obtain more children's Social Security benefits, describing "[p]redictive analytics" and "data mining techniques" to "score" and "triage" the foster children to maximize the revenue.[17]

To carry out the process, a contractor applies for the SSI disability benefits on Anna's behalf, helps with the appeals process when there are questions of whether

[12] POVERTY INDUSTRY, *supra* note 1, at 80–90.
[13] *Id.*
[14] *Id.* at 82–90.
[15] Maryland Department of Human Resources, MAXIMUS *Benefits & Eligibility Advocacy Services*, SSI/SSDI Assessment Report, Feb. 2013 (on file with author).
[16] MAXIMUS, Inc., Bid Proposal for Iowa Department of Human Services SSI Advocacy Project, § K Cost Proposal, Feb. 12, 2009, at 3 (on file with author).
[17] Public Consulting Group, Social Security Advocacy Assessment, State of Florida, Department of Children and Families, Sep. 14, 2012, at 6, 28, 29.

she is disabled enough, and then helps the state apply to become representative payee to gain control over Anna's resulting funds. Although a representative payee is a fiduciary, obligated to only use the beneficiary's funds for her best interests, the state instead diverts Anna's money to state revenue. PCG's assessment report for Florida describes increasing the "penetration rate" of disabled children to convert their benefits into $21 million annual government revenue: "PCG has estimated that increasing the SSI penetration rate to meet the national best practice of 20% would produce approximately 2,538 children newly eligible for SSI benefits," which the report explains would result in $21 million annually in new government revenue.[18] Usually, the state does not even tell children or their advocates that it is applying for the funds or applying to gain access to the money as representative payee.

The state uses Anna through what is essentially a loophole. Instead of adhering to its fiduciary obligation to only serve Anna's best interests, the state relies on another federal regulation that explains it can use a child's funds to pay for unmet current maintenance needs. Thus, the state asserts that it should be able to take Anna's benefits to repay the state cost of her care under the theory that the current maintenance clause allows such self-reimbursement. However, the rationale ignores what should be an absolute legal and moral barrier to the revenue strategy – that the state, not Anna, has the obligation to pay for the foster care costs. In fact, the Supreme Court has recognized that foster children have no legal debt obligation for their own care.[19] As a representative payee, the state is supposed to exercise individualized fiduciary discretion to decide how use Anna's benefits only for her unmet needs or conserving funds in a way that is best for her. The state's revenue strategy of instead taking Anna's funds for itself directly breaches that fiduciary requirement.[20]

If the state used Anna's funds to help her as intended, the money could provide her with extra needed tutoring, possibly a computer, and many other services and items that are not already paid for by the government. For example, Anna loved a presentation she saw about computer-generated artwork, and she wants to learn, but she has never had the chance. She could use her own funds to purchase necessary equipment and classes to learn the skill that could lead to a future career. Also, Anna could save her benefits for the difficult transition to independence as she ages out of care. In fact, the 2014 Achieving a Better Life Experience Act (or Able Act) established 529A savings accounts specifically for children's Social Security disability benefits. The law allows disabled children to conserve their benefits in a way that is exempt from the otherwise existing $2,000 asset limit. A child like Anna can then

---

[18] *Id.* at 5.
[19] *Wash. State Dep't of Soc. & Health Servs. v. Guardianship Estate of Keffeler*, 537 U.S. 371, 382 (2003) (holding that the state was not a creditor and therefore did not violate the Social Security Act's anti-attachment provision, but the court recognized it was not deciding several other possible legal challenges to the practice).
[20] Poverty Industry, *supra* note 1, at 80–82.

use the conserved funds for education costs, or for many other needs including assistive technology, housing, transportation, and employment training.

In 2018, after several years of policy advocacy, litigation, and legislative effort,[21] the Maryland General Assembly passed legislation, which would help Anna if she lived there, that begins to protect foster children's Social Security and Veteran's Assistance benefits. But no other state has done so. Titled "Protecting the Resources of Children in State Custody," the legislation requires that when the state foster care agency acts as representative payee for a child receiving disability or survivor benefits, the state must conserve at least 40 percent of the funds for the child starting at age 14, at least 80 percent of the funds starting at age 16, and 100 percent of the funds starting at age 18.[22] The legislation includes the 529A (ABLE) accounts as an option for the savings, and also requires the state to provide foster children with financial literacy training, which can help inspire the children to become involved in planning for their future. Hopefully, more states will enact similar legislation and make further improvements to protect all foster children's resources.

If Anna doesn't live in Maryland, the state will take her Social Security disability benefits until she ages out of care, and she will be left with nothing. Further, while in foster care, she is also plugged into another revenue strategy, this time one that uses her poverty and her disabilities to take her school-based Medicaid resources.

States Diverting Medicaid Resources from the Vulnerable

The state revenue practices of taking Social Security benefits from foster children are stark and widespread, but are a fraction of the scope of state Medicaid maximization strategies. Each year, states are diverting millions in disability and survivor benefits from foster children – whereas with Medicaid resources taken from vulnerable populations, the amount is in the billions.[23]

---

[21] *See, e.g.*, Daniel L. Hatcher, *Foster Children Paying for Foster Care*, 27 CARDOZO L. REV. 1797 (2006); AP, *States' Use of Foster Kids' Benefits Assailed*, Mar. 16, 2011, http://baltimore.cbslocal .com/2011/03/16/states-use-of-foster-kids-benefits-is-assailed/; Daniel L. Hatcher, *How Maryland Robs Its Most Vulnerable Children*, BALTIMORE SUN, Oct. 14, 2013; Daniel L. Hatcher, *Legislation Needed to Protect Foster Kids' Assets*, BALTIMORE SUN, Mar. 3, 2015; WAMU (NPR in Washington, DC), *The Kojo Nnamdi Show, How Local Foster Care Plays a Role in "The Poverty Industry,"* June 28, 2016; Daniel L. Hatcher, *Maryland Needs to Stop Forcing Foster Children to Pay for Their Own Care*, BALTIMORE SUN, Apr. 2, 2018.

[22] Maryland General Assembly, 2018 Regular Session, House Bill 524 (also indicates that when the department acts as payee for any child it must "use or conserve the benefits in the child's best interest, including using the benefits for services or special needs not otherwise provided by the Department or conserving the benefits for the child's reasonably foreseeable future needs"), http://mgaleg.maryland.gov/2018RS/bills/hb/hb0524E.pdf.

[23] POVERTY INDUSTRY, *supra* note 1, at 114–35.

States again often hire private revenue contractors to help, finding ways to leverage the Medicaid funding structure toward financial self-interest. Resulting strategies are numerous and complex, including terminology such as "bed taxes," "intergovernmental transfers" (IGT), "upper payment limits" (UPL), "random moment time studies" (RMTS), and "school-based Medicaid claiming."[24]

Medicaid is a shared program between the federal government and states, structured around matching grants. For a state to receive a federal Medicaid matching grants, it much first use state funds on eligible health care services for vulnerable children and adults. For example, Maryland has a 50 percent match percentage, so if Maryland spends $50 on eligible services it can claim an additional $50 match from the federal government – for a total of $100 available for the needed services. Some other states benefit from a higher federal match, like in Mississippi, where the federal government pays almost 75 percent.

But states often subvert the intended shared financing through schemes to maximize claims for federal matching funds with no additional state spending. The state part of the match is often illusory. Worse still, once the additional federal Medicaid funding is claimed, many states divert the aid from vulnerable populations to general state use. Rather than raising sufficient state revenue through equitable and general taxation, states are taking aid from the poor to fund themselves.[25] Again, the practices are bipartisan. In Texas, over a five-year period, former Governor Rick Perry "used such illusory schemes to divert more than $1.7 billion in federal Medicaid matching funds to his general coffers."[26] In California, Governor Jerry Brown signed a 2013 bill to use a bed tax revenue strategy that was estimated would result in $3 billion in Medicaid routed to the state general fund over a three-year period.[27]

Which brings us back to Anna, as the state uses her in such a strategy to take Medicaid resources from her and her school.

While taking Anna's Social Security disability benefits, the state may also be diverting her school-based Medicaid resources. When children are poor and disabled, states can claim federal Medicaid matching funds on their behalf for much-needed school-based health services and related administrative costs – including special education, rehabilitative services, physical and speech therapy, and services under Medicaid's Early and Periodic Screening, Diagnostic, and Treatment (EPSDT) program.[28] According to the most recent Government Accountability Office (GAO) investigation into school-based Medicaid claiming, at least 18 states were diverting a portion of Medicaid funding from children into state revenue, with

[24] *Id.*
[25] *Id.*
[26] *Id.* at 118.
[27] *Id.* at 142.
[28] *Id.* at 126.

10 of those states diverting between 40 and 85 percent of the federal aid.[29] Again, revenue maximization consultants are helping.

If Anna lives in New Jersey, the GAO explains that the state's schools have received a small fraction of the Medicaid funds intended for poor schoolchildren, the remainder going to the state and its contractor.[30] Similar to how PCG is helping several states obtain more foster children's Social Security benefits, the company contracts with New Jersey and several other states to help maximize school-based Medicaid. PCG helps New Jersey run the Special Education Medicaid Initiative (SEMI). Tellingly, New Jersey decided to administer the program out of its Department of Treasury. The state program requires school districts to collaborate with the contractor, plugging impoverished disabled schoolchildren like Anna into projections and equations to target increased federal Medicaid funds. All the aid is supposed to help the schools directly serve the children. However, New Jersey takes most of the federal aid, PCG receives a contingency fee, and only a fraction goes to the schools. In a 2017 audit, the US Department of Health and Human Services, Office of Inspector General explains that New Jersey gives only 35 percent of the Medicaid funds to the schools. New Jersey budget documents indicate the fraction provided to schools is even smaller, only 17.5 percent:

> Notwithstanding the provisions of any law or regulation to the contrary, each local school district that participates in the Special Education Medicaid Initiative (SEMI) shall receive a percentage of the federal revenue realized for current year claims. The percentage share shall be 17.5% of claims approved by the State by June 30.[31]

The discrepancy is due to the state's manipulation of the Medicaid match structure. New Jersey has a 50 percent federal Medicaid match rate. So for $100 in claimed Medicaid payments for Anna, $50 is supposed to be paid by the state and $50 by the federal government. New Jersey only gives 35 percent of the federal portion of the match to Anna's school to help her (or $17.5, 35 percent of $50). But here is what makes the percentage even lower: New Jersey requires schools to absorb the costs of the state share rather than the state making those payments as intended.[32] So the schools get 0 percent of the state's $50 share. Thus, out of the total $100 that is supposed to go to Anna's school to help her, the school only receives 17.5 percent ($17.5 out of the $100 the school is supposed to receive).

---

[29] US General Accounting Office, *Medicaid in Schools: Poor Oversight and Improper Payments Compromise Potential Benefit*, GAO/T- HEHS/OSI-00–87 (2000), www.gao.gov/assets/110/108362.pdf.

[30] *Id.*

[31] The State of New Jersey, 2019 Detailed Budget at F-7, www.nj.gov/treasury/omb/publications/19budget/pdf/FY19BudgetBook.pdf.

[32] *Medicaid in Schools, supra* note 29, at 16.

It gets worse. The 2017 federal audit concluded that more than $300 million of the school-based Medicaid funds New Jersey claimed while working with PCG were unallowable and therefore that the state should refund that full amount, and that an additional $306.2 million in claims were unsupported. As part of its findings, the Inspector General determined that New Jersey "improperly incorporated into its payment rates more than $400 million owed to the school employees' pension fund despite not having made scheduled payments to the fund in nearly 20 years," and that "PCG improperly altered school employees' responses to timestudies to indicate that their activities were directly related to providing Medicaid services when the responses indicated the activities were unrelated."[33]

It gets even worse. New Jersey only forces schools in impoverished areas to participate in this revenue strategy. Schools with richer children can ask to opt out of the program, whereas schools with more poor children cannot.[34] The lower-income schools are required to work with PCG and develop target revenue goals. If Anna's school fails to meet its revenue quota of using poor children to claim Medicaid funds, New Jersey punishes the school with a reduction in state education funds. As the federal audit explains, "[E]ach school must reach 90 percent of the SEMI revenue budgeted by PCG each year or the school may lose State education aid."[35]

If Anna instead lives in Delaware, the 2000 GAO audit found that the state was taking 70 percent of the school-based Medicaid, New York and Pennsylvania were taking 50 percent, and Wisconsin and Michigan were taking 40 percent.[36] All those states have had statewide school-based Medicaid contracts with PCG.[37] In a sample contract proposal submitted to Nebraska in 2017, PCG states that it is "the nation's leading firm for assisting states administer and enhance school based Medicaid programs, while strictly adhering to state and federal compliance requirements," and that "[w]e have assisted over 15 statewide programs and 2500 districts level programs over the last 30 years in generating $5.2 [billion] in federal Medicaid reimbursement for our clients."[38]

---

[33] *New Jersey Claimed Hundreds of Millions in Unallowable or Unsupported Medicaid School Based Reimbursement, supra* note 3, at Results in Brief.

[34] Kimberley Harrington, Acting Commissioner, New Jersey Department of Education, Memorandum, Special Education Medicaid Initiative Fiscal Year 2018 Revenue Projections, www.nj .gov/education/specialed/memos/011717Meidcaid.pdf (explaining how only schools with fewer than 40 Medicaid eligible children can ask for a waiver from the program).

[35] *New Jersey Claimed Hundreds of Millions in Unallowable or Unsupported Medicaid School Based Reimbursement, supra* note 3, at 3. *See also* N.J.A.C. 6A:2A-5.3.

[36] *Medicaid in Schools, supra* note 29, at 16.

[37] Public Consulting Group, Technical Proposal in Response to State of Nebraska Request for Proposal for Contractual Services, RFP# 5331Z1, Transmittal Letter, Mar. 16, 2017, http://das .nebraska.gov/materiel/purchasing/5531/Public%20Consulting%20Group%20-%20Tech.pdf ("We currently administer statewide school-based Medicaid initiatives in thirteen states, including Arizona, Colorado, Delaware, Georgia, Indiana, Kansas, Michigan, New Jersey, New York, Pennsylvania, South Dakota, Wisconsin and West Virginia.").

[38] *Id.* at 2.

State Juvenile Courts Claiming Revenue by Removing Poor Children from Their Homes

Anna could have also ended up in a foster care placement due to juvenile delinquency allegations – and still be used as a source of revenue. If she lives in Ohio, the juvenile court receives payments if the judge determines Anna should be removed from her home, a revenue practice akin to the "kids for cash" scandal in Pennsylvania, where two juvenile court judges received payments in return for sentencing children to juvenile justice detention facilities.[39]

Title IV-E federal foster care funds are intended to help state child welfare agencies provide foster care services to abused and neglected children. But in Ohio, juvenile courts found a way to claim the federal foster care funds for themselves. To access the money, a juvenile court first signs a contract with the Ohio Department of Job and Family Services, the statewide agency that normally administers the state child welfare programs and the receipt of federal Title IV-E funds. Through the contract, the juvenile court becomes a subgrantee to be considered a Title IV-E placing agency. Then, if the court rules that a child is "unruly" or delinquent and orders the child removed from her home and put in eligible out-of-home placement, the court gets paid.[40] The more children the court removes from their homes, the more Title IV-E funds the court can receive. In Summit County – not the largest county in Ohio – the juvenile court was making more than $1.1 million in Title IV-E revenue annually through this strategy.[41] At least 34 county juvenile court systems in Ohio are now engaged in this revenue practice.[42]

To receive the money, Ohio juvenile courts have many placement options after ordering a child removal, including with for-profit companies and even out-of-state centers:

> Reimbursement may be claimed for youth placed in non-secure settings such as foster care, group homes, treatment foster care, residential treatment facilities and other child care institutions. There are restrictions on the size of eligible public facilities: they may not have more than 25 beds. But there is no restriction on the

---

[39] John Schuppe, *Pennsylvania Seeks to Close Books on "Kids for Cash" Scandal*, NBC NEWS, Aug. 12, 2017, www.nbcnews.com/news/us-news/pennsylvania-seeks-close-books-kids-cash-scandal-n408666.

[40] Ohio Dept. of Job and Family Services Subgrant Agreement, G-1415–06-XXXX, http://jfs.ohio .gov/ocf/2014–2015-Final-Juvenile-Court-Subgrant-Agreement.stm.

[41] Summit County Court of Common Pleas Juvenile Division, 2015 Annual Report, https:// juvenilecourt.summitoh.net/index.php/information/publications/reports/finish/17-annual-reports/1254-annual-report-2015.

[42] State of Ohio Title IV-E Juvenile Court Contact List, http://jfs.ohio.gov/ocf/JuvenileCourt ContactList.stm.

size of private facilities. Moreover, both in-state and out-of-state residential programs qualify, as do non-profit and for-profit organizations.[43]

One of the for-profit companies is what a news investigation describes as "a giant corporation called National Mentor Holdings, which, over the last three decades, has turned the field of foster care into a cash cow."[44] The investigative stories described National Mentor as "a $1.2 billion company with a history of trouble at its homes for at-risk children."[45]

There is a catch. Under Title IV-E, the juvenile courts only receive the revenue if they order the removal of children from poor families, not from well-off families. So the focus is on percentages: the higher the state "penetration rate" – the percentage of children removed from their homes who are poor and thus Title IV-E eligible – the more federal funds can be claimed. The state foster care agency's Bureau of Fiscal Operations has provided a slide show training for how the juvenile courts can maximize the funds, renaming the penetration rate the "Eligibility Ratio (ER) aka the participation, penetration or discount rate," and providing the equation used to maximize the funds:

The Eligibility Ratio (ER) is computed by taking:

The number of placement days experienced by Title IV-E program eligible children housed in allowable settings

DIVIDED BY

The total number of placement days experienced for all children in custody/care placements for the reporting period.[46]

The resulting ratio is used to claim the Title IV-E funds. So the greater the percentage of poor children compared to nonpoor children removed into foster care, the more revenue the juvenile courts can claim. The results are apparent in the numbers. Although Ohio's statewide poverty rate is 14.6 percent, the percentage of children removed into foster care who are poor reached 77 percent by 2014.[47]

---

[43] National Council of Juvenile and Family Court Judges, Juvenile Sanctions Center, Training and Technical Assistance Program Bulletin, *Using Federal Title IV-E Money to Expand Sanctions and Services for Juvenile Offenders*, Vol. 2 No. 2, 2004 at 4, http://docplayer.net/ 18586465-Using-federal-title-iv-e-money-to-expand-sanctions-and-services-for-juvenile-offenders .html.

[44] Aram Roston, *Foster Profits*, BUZZFEED, Feb. 20, 2015, www.buzzfeed.com/aramroston/ fostering-profits?utm_term=.ywWrAvyrY#.iqbK9abKM.

[45] Aram Roston, *"Culture of Incompetence": For-Profit Foster-Care Giant Is Leaving Illinois*, BUZZFEED, Apr. 17, 2015, www.buzzfeed.com/aramroston/mentorleavesillinois?utm_term=.koj zELqzv#.yxY4n1e4M.

[46] Ohio Dept. of Job and Family Services, Bureau of Fiscal Accountability, How to Develop the Allowable Cost Pool and Complete the Quarterly Billing Form (JFS 01797) for Title IV-E, http://jfs.ohio.gov/ocf/HowtoAllocateCosts022014_FinPart3.stm at 5, 56.

[47] Child Trends, Child Welfare Financing SFY 2014, Ohio, www.childtrends.org/wp-content/ uploads/2016/10/Child-Welfare-Financing-SFY2014_Ohio.pdf.

The Ohio juvenile courts sought help in maximizing revenue from children, through contacts with Justice Benefits, Inc.:

> Justice Benefits, Inc. ("JBI") specializes in federal revenue maximization for state and local political entities. JBI was incorporated in 1997 with the objective of helping state and local political entities access new federal funding opportunities. We specialize in Enhanced IV-E Administrative Claiming. JBI has been working with Ohio Juvenile Courts since 2003....
>
> JBI's IV-E training staff consists of former probation officers. Having this background allows the JBI staff to better relate to the Ohio Juvenile Court staff. JBI IV-E training staff have faced and solved the same day to day problems that Ohio County staff encounters on a daily basis.[48]

For example, Miami County, Ohio signed a contingency-fee contract where JBI helps the juvenile court maximize funds: "JBI is paid 22% on monies recovered through claims submitted by the Court, and will be paid from the Juvenile Court Title IV-E Fund."[49]

The more poor children the Ohio juvenile court orders removed, the more Title IV-E funds the court can claim, and the more money JBI can make through its contingency fee.

Because of the juvenile courts' potential conflict, the Supreme Court of Ohio's Board of Commissioners on Grievances and Discipline (Board) was asked in 2006 to address the legality of the revenue practice. But the Board punted the question to the Ohio Judicial Conference, who in turn asked its Juvenile Law and Procedure Committee to decide. So the question of whether it is legally permissible for juvenile courts to receive payments in return for ordering child removals was decided by a committee of juvenile court judges, who issued a legal argument that no conflict of interest or other legal concern was present.[50]

However, the contract document for the court subgrant agreements reveals that both the state and the juvenile courts realized the conflict exists. In the first section of the 24-page contract, the Ohio Department of Job and Family Services felt it necessary to admonish a juvenile court that it must agree "that it will not deliberately adjudicate a child unruly or delinquent for the sole purpose of receiving Federal Financial Participation (FFP) [federal Title IV-E funds]."[51] Further, a slide

---

[48] Web-Based System for the Ohio Juvenile Courts, Justice Benefits, Inc., http://jfs.ohio.gov/ocf/WebBasedRMSinformation.pdf.

[49] Miami County, Ohio, Commissioners Meeting Minutes Summary, Dec. 30, 2014, www.co.miami.oh.us/Archive/ViewFile/Item/379.

[50] Ohio Judicial Conference, Resolution to Support Optional Juvenile Court Participation as a Title IV-E Placing Agency, Prepared by the Juvenile Law and Procedure Committee, Nov. 17, 2006, www.ohiojudges.org/Document.ashx?DocGuid=400faab0-352d-474a-bcb9-d85a82f81bd7.

[51] Ohio Dept. of Job and Family Services Subgrant Agreement, https://council.summitoh.net/index.php/legislative-information/legislation/2011/finish/24/3429.

presentation prepared by the statewide agency's Bureau of Fiscal Operations also cautions juvenile courts of this conflict, including a more direct bullet point warning to courts: "No cherry picking" children for removals to receive more funds.[52] One juvenile court judge in Franklin County even went on record to explain his concern that "the more kids that are placed out of their homes, the more money the court gets, which might lead some people to question the court's motivation: helping the youngsters or getting the money?"[53] Further, the subgrant contract also indicates that the county commissioners can take a cut of the revenue that juvenile courts receive after ordering child removals, up to 25 percent.[54]

As more evidence of the conflict, the juvenile court in Cuyahoga County (which includes Cleveland) used the federal Title IV-E funds resulting from court-ordered child removals to give juvenile court system judges and staff more than $1.8 million in salary increases in 2017. The salary increases are laid out in a county council resolution: "To allow for the salary increases per County Council Resolution R2017–077 and the agreement that Juvenile Court pay for any 2017 salary increases in CY 2017.... Appropriations for this increase have been transferred in cash from Title IV-E Maintenance."[55] The salary increases were to be paid out the county general fund, but the juvenile court simultaneously transferred money from its Title IV-E revenue to pay the full amount back to the county general fund:

Fund Nos./Budget Accounts...

A. FROM: 20A635 – title IV-E Juvenile Court JT1717052 JC517318 – Title IV-E Juvenile Court FCM Transfer Out $ 1,830,389.04

TO: 01A001 – General Fund JC372052 – Juv Ctr – Judges Revenue Transfer $ 1,830,389.04

A cash transfer is requested to pay for the NCSC Juvenile Court Classification and Compensation Study completed in October 2015. Funding is coming from the Title IV-E Maintenance Fund, which as of June 30, 2017 had a cash balance of $5.8 million.[56]

As evident from the revenue amounts, there is no shortage of poor children in Cleveland from which the juvenile court can obtain Title IV-E payments in exchange for ordering child removals. As of 2017, the child poverty rate in Cleveland

[52] Ohio Dept. of Job and Family Services, Bureau of Fiscal Affairs, Overview of the Title IV-E Juvenile Court Program, http://jfs.ohio.gov/ocf/overviewoftitleive.pdf.

[53] Encarnacion Pyle, *Juvenile Courts' Role Debated*, COLUMBUS DISPATCH, Sep. 11, 2006, www .pressreader.com/usa/the-columbus-dispatch/20060911/282033322676879.

[54] Ohio Dept. of Job and Family Services Subgrant Agreement, Article III, C.1.

[55] County Council of Cuyahoga County, Ohio, Resolution No. R2017–0142, http://council .cuyahogacounty.us/pdf_council/en-US/Legislation/Resolutions/2017/R2017–0142C%20OBM %20Fiscal%20Items%20for%208-8-2017%20and%20amending%20R2017–0098.pdf.

[56] Ibid., 10.

reached 53.5 percent,[57] and for East Cleveland the child poverty rate reached 63.5 percent.[58]

In addition to failing to adequately address the conflict of interest, the Ohio Judicial Conference Juvenile Law and Procedure Committee also did not address Due Process Clause concerns when judges have an interest in the outcome of judicial hearings. The committee did not consider long-standing US Supreme Court precedent – from a case that started in Ohio during the prohibition era, *Tumey v. Ohio*:

> There, the mayor of a village had the authority to sit as a Judge (with no jury) to try those accused of violating a state law prohibiting the possession of alcoholic beverages. Inherent in this structure were two potential conflicts. First, the mayor received a salary supplement for performing judicial duties, and the funds for that compensation derived from the fines assessed in a case. No fines were assessed upon acquittal. The mayor-judge thus received a salary supplement only if he convicted the defendant. . . . Second, sums from the criminal fines were deposited to the village's general treasury fund for village improvements and repairs. . . . The Court held that the Due Process Clause required disqualification "both because of [the mayor-judge's] direct pecuniary interest in the outcome, and because of his official motive to convict and to graduate the fine to help the financial needs of the village." . . . It so held despite observing that "[t]here are doubtless mayors who would not allow such a consideration as $12 costs in each case to affect their judgment in it."[59]

Rather than address such Supreme Court precedent, the Ohio judges relied on their *parens patriae* powers to preemptively argue against potential legal challenges, giving themselves the green light to continue and expand the practice of claiming Title IV-E revenue through child removals.[60] Of note, Ohio juvenile court judges also submitted a similar argument in 1967 against recognition that children should be afforded constitutional rights, including the right to counsel:

> It is the unquestioned right and imperative duty of every enlightened government, in its character of *parens patriae*, to protect and provide for the comfort and well-being of such of its citizens as, by reason of infancy are unable to take care of themselves. The performance of this duty is justly regarded as one of the most important of governmental functions, and all constitutional limitations must be so understood and construed as not to interfere with its proper and legitimate exercise. . . .

---

[57] Northeast Ohio Coalition for the Homeless, *Just the Facts: Poverty and Homelessness in Our Community*, www.neoch.org/poverty-stats-2017/.

[58] Barb Hall, *New Census Data Shows 30 Percent Poverty Rate in 17 Cities in Ohio*, CLEVELAND PATCH, Jan. 12, 2017, https://patch.com/ohio/cleveland/new-census-data-shows-30-percent-poverty-rate-17-cities-ohio.

[59] *Caperton v. A.T. Massey Coal Co., Inc.*, 556 U.S. 868, 877–878 (2009) (discussing and quoting *Tumey v. Ohio*, 273 U.S. 510, 520–535 (1927)).

[60] Ohio Judicial Conference Resolution, *supra* note 50.

The present popularity of resorting to the constitutional safeguards of the liberties of the person presents an easy and plausible reason for ignoring the fact that children could not possibly grow to productive and law-abiding adulthood if they were entitled to those liberties which are the perquisites of physical, mental and emotional maturity.[61]

Luckily, the US Supreme Court ruled in favor of the children in that case. But courts have not yet considered possible legal challenges to the current revenue practices of the Ohio juvenile courts. Further, the receipt of federal foster care Title IV-E funds after ordering Anna's removal from her home is not the only revenue incentive in the Ohio juvenile courts, as explained in the following text.

After Ordering Child Removals, Juvenile Courts Seek Additional Revenue in Return for Ordering Support Obligations Against Impoverished Parents

After the juvenile court adjudicates Anna unruly or delinquent and orders her to be placed in out-of-home care, which trigger's the court's receipt of Title IV-E foster care funds, the court can then order Anna's impoverished parents to pay child support to reimburse the costs of the placement. Although still called child support, the money is not owed to the children but rather to the state. The court is incentivized to issue and enforce such orders against the parents because the orders trigger the ability of the juvenile court to obtain additional revenue.[62] Such funds are available under a different federal program, the Title IV-D child support program, intended to provide funds to help state child support agencies carry out their enforcement efforts. Courts have again found a way to claim the funds as revenue for themselves: if the juvenile courts sign contracts with the state child support agency, the courts can obtain the IV-D funds when ordering and enforcing child support against the poor parents. As examples, the Lucas County juvenile court received an additional three-quarters of a million in revenue in 2013 through the IV-D child support funds,[63] and Cuyahoga County's juvenile courts received more than $2.2 million in IV-D revenue in 2011.[64]

The juvenile courts' decisions to order child support against parents, and enforcing those orders to repay costs of care, cause yet more harm. The courts' revenue strategy pursues impoverished parents and undermines their struggles to improve their economic circumstances in the hopes of reunifying with their children. Through such practices, courts and state agencies are using foster children as

---

[61] Brief of the Ohio Association of Juvenile Court Judges as Amicus Curiae at 4, In re Gault 387 U.S. 1 (1967) 1966 WL 100788 at *3.

[62] Ohio Code 2151.36.

[63] Lucas County Juvenile Court, 2013 Annual Report, www.co.lucas.oh.us/Archive/ViewFile/Item/617.

[64] County Council of Cuyahoga County, Ohio, Resolution No. R2011–0104, http://council.cuyahogacounty.us/pdf_council/en-US/Legislation/Resolutions/2011/R2011–0104s.pdf.

collateral – where parents may not be able to get their children back unless they pay off the government costs ordered after the courts have removed the children. Some states will even permanently terminate parental rights if the parents can't afford the payments.[65]

Then, if one or both of Anna's parents is undocumented, the Ohio Sheriff's offices can receive revenue for incarcerating the parents. So, after the juvenile court orders Anna's removal from her home, and after ordering Anna's parents to pay support, a court could also decide to incarcerate the parents for nonsupport (which can include felony charges).[66] Then the county sheriff's office could receive revenue by jailing the undocumented parents, and could again contract with JBI to help maximize the funds, such as in Lucas County:

> After reviewing the operations, characteristics, policies and procedures used by the County, and particularly the Lucas County Sheriff's Office, Justice Benefits, Inc. (JBI) will identify and optimize all federal reimbursement opportunities that may exist through participation in new programs or expansion of current Federal Financial Participation programs. Of particular interest is the State Criminal Alien Assistance Program, which provides Federal assistance to local facilities incurring costs for incarcerating undocumented criminal foreign-born individuals meeting certain criteria. Upon the County signing an Initiative with JBI for the claiming of said federal funds, JBI will become entitled to twenty-two percent (22%) of all revenue paid to the County as a direct result of JBI's activities.[67]

The search for revenue from Anna is not done yet.

Juvenile Courts and Private Collection Agencies Seek Revenue Directly from Children

The juvenile court can even issue an order that Anna "reimburse any or all of the costs incurred for services or sanctions provided or imposed" (in addition to the other revenue practices in which the state takes her Social Security disability benefits and child support from her parents).[68] Because children like Anna and their parents are poor, they usually can't afford to pay back the costs in lump sum payments. So the juvenile court is given the authority to collect the resulting debt ordered against Anna, and can use private for-profit collection agencies to do so.[69] For example, the juvenile court in Columbiana County, Ohio hired Capital Recovery Systems, Inc. – "Home of the No-Cost Court Collections Program ©" – to

---

[65] POVERTY INDUSTRY, *supra* note 1, at 164–78.

[66] Ohio Code 2919.21.

[67] Lucas County, Ohio, Approval of Renewal Contract with Justice Benefits, Inc. for Federal Financial Participation Funding Opportunity Research for a Period of 1 Year for the Lucas County Sheriff's Office, July 26, 2016, https://lcapps.co.lucas.oh.us/carts/resos/18108.pdf.

[68] Ohio Code 2152.20

[69] *Id.*

collect such unpaid court costs and fines.[70] The juvenile court avoids paying any money to the collection agency by adding the collection fee as yet an additional amount owed by the child:

> The amount owed will increase once it has been turned over for debt collection. Capital Recovery Systems, Inc. does charge a fee to the Court of 30 percent of the costs collected. When an account is forwarded for collection, that fee will be added on to the account as additional costs to be collected from the parties so that the Court will not be incurring additional costs through this partnership.[71]

The juvenile court can also charge interest and an additional fee if the child struggles to make payments through a payment plan.[72] Then, if the child is old enough to drive, the juvenile court may take steps to suspend her driver's license due to unpaid court costs.

Youth involved in the foster care and juvenile justice systems already face almost insurmountable barriers, including frequent homelessness after they leave state custody. Pursing the youth for unaffordable court ordered costs, and taking their driver's license in the process, expedites the snowball effect of harm. As a Butler County, Ohio juvenile court clerk explained to a reporter, courts use license suspensions to go after the children who are "transient" because they don't consistently have a home:

> "This tool (suspension) is helpful as many of our population are transient, and you can't find a good address to pursue collections," he said. "These dollars from the inactive ledger continue to be recovered when individuals later pursue driving privileges or interact with the BMV. They then will respond to their suspension and the financial obligation which prompted it."[73]

Youth caught up in the juvenile system like Anna are supposed to be able to expunge and seal their juvenile records, but the juvenile court in Hamilton County (which includes Cincinnati) threatens juveniles that their court debts don't go away and that the failure to pay those fines and costs will block their ability to expunge their records:

Q. What happens if I don't pay my Court fines and costs?
A. Costs and fines do not go away unless they are paid. Juvenile Court has traditionally been responsive to the need of clients and allowed payment plans over a period of time.

---

[70] Capital Recovery Systems, Inc., www.caprecsys.com/.
[71] Morning Journal, *County Juvenile Court Partners with Collection Firm*, Sep. 14, 2014, www.morningjournalnews.com/news/local-news/2014/09/county-juvenile-court-partners-with-collec tion-firm/.
[72] Supreme Court of Ohio, Desktop Guide for Juvenile Court Clerks, www.supremecourt.ohio.gov/jcs/cfc/resources/juvcourtclerk.pdf.
[73] Denise G. Callahan, *Courts Looking at New Ways to Collect $18.4 Million in Fines and Costs*, JOURNAL-NEWS, Nov. 29, 2013, www.journal-news.com/news/courts-looking-new-ways-collect-million-fines-and-costs/67QPf4h4Cwp8eLlsHxNGyL/.

Costs and fines are debts just like any other financial obligation. Failure to pay fines and costs will prevent records being sealed or expunged.[74]

In several states, children can even be locked up again for not paying back the juvenile court costs and fines, resulting in yet more costs owed and further harm to the children through the impact of incarceration.[75]

Artificial Intelligence in Juvenile Courts

Looking toward the next wave of possible profit and revenue from vulnerable populations, artificial intelligence (AI) has entered the picture. In 2017, the Ohio juvenile courts began exploring a partnership with "IBM Watson" to bring AI into the judges' courtrooms: "Montgomery County, Ohio was the first to pilot the technology in a U.S. specialty juvenile court." According to IBM, "We signed [a juvenile court judge] up as a design partner and literally had our development and design team sit through his court." The judge and his colleagues "helped IBM develop the digital case file by blending the local court's experience handling tough children's cases with the capability of Watson's cognitive technology."[76]

The juvenile court is apparently aiming to reduce the time judges spend reviewing "so much information from so many different groups: probation officers, behavioral health providers, police departments, educators," and seeking to rely instead on IBM Watson: "The solution beats sifting through anywhere from 30 to 300 pages of paperwork in the five to seven minutes [the judge] may have for each of 30–35 juveniles seen during a typical treatment court docket."[77]

IBM Watson is now apparently aiming at juvenile courts across the country, serving as the main "presenting sponsor" in the 2018 National Conference on Juvenile Justice.[78] IBM is not new to seeking contracts to bring automation into state programs involving vulnerable populations, as explained in a review of Virginia Eubanks book, *Automating Inequality*:

Eubanks opens the book in Indiana in 2007, where the governor signed a contract with IBM to automate the food stamp and Medicaid application process by

---

[74] Hamilton County Juvenile Court, Frequently Asked Questions, Juveniles, www.juvenile-court .org/juvenilecourt/FAQs/FAQ_juveniles.asp.

[75] Jessica Feierman, Juvenile Law Center, *Debtors' Prison for Kids?*, 2016, https://debtorsprison.jlc .org/documents/JLC-Debtors-Prison.pdf.

[76] Chris Stewart, How to Develop the Allowable Cost Pool and Complete the Quarterly Billing Form (JFS 01797), Dayton Daily News, Aug. 3, 2017, www.mydaytondailynews.com/news/ local/hey-watson-local-judge-first-use-ibm-artificial-intelligence-juvenile-cases/ InVqz6eeNxvFsMVAe5zrbL/.

[77] Id.

[78] National Conference of Juvenile and Family Court Judges, 2018 National Conference on Juvenile Justice, www.ncjfcj.org/2018-national-conference-juvenile-justice (listing IBM Watson as the Presenting Sponsor).

replacing local caseworkers with online applications, statistical models, and a regional call center.

"What that system did was quite explicitly sever the link between local caseworkers and the district that they served," she says. "The result of that was *not* people getting off welfare and finding ways to self-sufficiency; the result was [a rise in] denials of benefits for basic human rights like food and medical care, a rise in extreme poverty in Indiana, and even death."

In 2009, Indiana had pulled out of the IBM contract, alleging improper rejections, missing documents and increased wait time.... An appeals court in 2012 found that IBM breached its contract with the state by failing to automate the system. Six years later, IBM is still litigating its battle with Indiana over the failed automation gambit.[79]

The cautionary tale should not be ignored as government programs serving children and the poor consider possible applications of new technologies. We need our states, agencies, and courts to be more human in order to be true in their purpose of serving the public good, not less so.

REALIGNING GOVERNMENT PURPOSE

States have lost their way. The revenue schemes are many, states have taken wrong turns into the intertwined web of money and harm, and private revenue contractors have helped guide them deeper and deeper down the wrong paths.

Even at state agencies and tribunals that exist to protect and serve the most vulnerable among us, the focus of agency leadership is increasingly all about the money rather than solely developing the best ways to serve their beneficiaries. States pursue short-term revenue strategies rather than long-term public good. Human service agencies create revenue maximization units at the center of their operations. Juvenile courts issue annual reports that highlight the amount of revenue they bring in.

This subversion of government purpose is undermining fiscal federalism, the intended partnership between states and the federal government in the funding and operation of America's largest aid programs. Fiscal federalism pairs the federal government's financial strength and ability to withstand economic downturns with the long-held view that state and local governments are better able to understand and serve the more localized needs of their vulnerable populations. So the idea is for the federal government to provide most of the funds and state governments to run the programs. However, when states use the vulnerable to maximize revenue rather than serving their best interests, the entire structure of fiscal federalism is broken.

---

[79] Sidney Fussell, *How Algorithmic Experiments Harm People in Poverty*, GIZMODO, Jan. 23, 2018, https://gizmodo.com/how-algorithmic-experiments-harm-people-living-in-pover-1822311248.

During times of economic turmoil when impoverished children and families need the most help, cash-strapped states may be even more likely to use the poor rather than serve them. The only beneficiaries are the contractors that profit from the harm. Poverty industry contractors now permeate every government level that administers programs for the vulnerable.[80] In terms of the flow of aid funds, contractors profit from helping county agencies and service providers claim funds from the states, from helping states audit and reduce payout of the funds to the service providers, from helping the states claim funds from the federal government, and from helping the federal government audit and reduce payout to the states.[81] Instead of collaborating to serve the public good, each level of government is pit against each other in the revenue quest. And to grease the poverty industry wheels, the contractors often hire staff directly from state and county human service agencies, and vice versa.[82]

A realignment of state and local government purpose toward maximizing the public welfare is needed, now more than ever. In normal times, federal agencies could be called on to increase oversight over state use of aid funds, and better enforce federal requirements – to help guide states back toward the right path. But these are not normal times. As states have fallen from their purpose, the agencies in the Trump administration have not just fallen but have actively undercut federal protections and imposed more hardships on the vulnerable. With the retirement of Justice Kennedy, the Supreme Court may transform from an already weak check to an enabler of governments' disavowal and dismantling of intended purpose.

Until elections hopefully help to stop our federal government from increasingly losing its way, states are largely on their own in developing their moral compass. Similar to how several cities and at least two states have now declared themselves sanctuaries in an effort to reduce harm to immigrant children and families, we need states and local governments to find in their soul the inherent purpose of serving the vulnerable rather than using them.

We cannot sit passively in our privileged false bubbles of nonexistent protection and wait for states to discover their soul. Disorganized reactionary flailing and yelling at each other on Twitter will not help. But through organized and sustained direct action, we can provide guidance and be catalysts in expediting the right path. Litigation, legislative reform, writing, teaching, speaking out, protesting, voting, running for elected office, helping a person in need, and training others to do the same can all play a role. Again, purpose matters, and we must all regularly self-reflect so that we do not put self-interest over cause. We need the press to expose and inform to serve the greater good, putting aside the self-interested chase for ratings and money. We need advocacy groups to coalesce in the pure pursuit of their

---

[80] POVERTY INDUSTRY, *supra* note 1, at 44.
[81] *Id.* at 44, 51–52.
[82] *Id.* at 40–41.

nonprofit missions rather than clambering to use the hardship of others for self-interested public relations. We need professors, scholars, and researchers to expend their efforts for societal benefit rather than solely on their careers. We need to protest with the aim of achieving necessary change and not simply providing fodder for Facebook.

For if we each are not individually true to our purpose, our collective states cannot be true. We are all vulnerable, and we are all interdependent – with each other and with the government institutions that are intended to help us.

When a foster child in West Baltimore is harmed, we are all harmed. So we need to help that child.

8

States' Evolving Role in the Supplemental Nutritional Assistance Program

David A. Super

INTRODUCTION

States have always been crucial to the Supplemental Nutrition Assistance Program (SNAP, formerly food stamps).[1] Even though the federal government has paid virtually all the program's benefit costs, state administration has always been indispensable for several reasons. State and local governments pay their staff considerably less than the federal government, making state administration less expensive.[2] States already administer other important antipoverty programs, notably family cash assistance and Medicaid, allowing them to coordinate the programs and minimize repetitive activities. And states have somewhat lower, and less polarizing, political footprints than does the federal government, moderating criticism of the program. In addition, giving states a stake in SNAP's administration often has co-opted them to support, or at least avoid attacking, the program.

From the perspective of states, administering SNAP has been an attractive deal. Even though federal merit systems' requirements prevent states from using SNAP administrative positions for patronage, getting a large number of state workers at only half the net cost is an attractive proposition. No doubt significant numbers of households mistakenly believe that the benefits they receive come from the state's coffers when they receive them through state offices. And because the Food and Nutrition Act makes no provision for anyone other than states to administer SNAP, a state's refusal to do so would mean turning away hundreds of millions or billions of dollars of federal funds and straining local charities far past the breaking point.

States' entrenched administrative role in SNAP has given them enormous influence over how the program operates. Some of this power comes directly from their

---

[1] Throughout this chapter, I will refer to SNAP and the Food and Nutrition Act of 2008 when speaking about all periods, even those when benefits were called food stamps and were issued under the Food Stamp Acts of 1964 or 1977.

[2] David A. Super, *Rethinking Fiscal Federalism*, 118 HARV. L. REV. 2544, 2567 (2005).

role as administrators. The oft-repeated claim that SNAP is a program controlled entirely by federal law has never been true. Over time, states' control over program operations has shifted somewhat from covert means to overt state options, but a major state influence has remained. Anyone who follows the program nationally can tell you in which states they would, or would not, prefer to live if they needed SNAP.

States also have exerted considerable influence over the program on the federal level. Much of the program's durability has come from its ability to transcend partisan politics with a culture of objective policy analysis. This culture derives in part from the peculiar nature of the US Department of Agriculture (USDA) and the House and Senate Agriculture Committees, which are deeply conservative but also dependent on the broader Congress to continue programs that transfer resources from taxpayers and consumers to agribusiness. Analytically defensible SNAP policy burnishes the image of the USDA and the committees as responsible stewards. Carrying out this mission have been a relatively pragmatic series of chairs and ranking members of the nutrition subcommittees and a career staff at the Food and Nutrition Service (FNS) that is deeply committed to professionalism. State human services agencies provided an obvious talent pool of public administrators knowledgeable about SNAP. These officials brought their appreciation of front-line administrative challenges, and their contacts with people still in state agencies, when they joined the federal service.

State human services agencies also have been a major source of the bureaucratic expertise on which federal policy makers have relied. Because of their official role implementing the program, federal officials and congressional staff routinely hold meetings with states' representatives from which other stakeholders are excluded. The policy decisions emanating from such meetings are all but impossible to dislodge. When antihunger advocates criticize conservative proposals, or right-wing groups attack liberal ones, state officials often hold the de facto deciding voice, adjudicating the claims for federal political officials less steeped in policy details. Savvy advocates learn to approach state agency representatives first with any proposals for federal policy change: if the states uniformly hate it, the proposal is probably dead, and if the states have concerns the advocates need to build a preemptive response into their initial pitches to federal administrators or congressional staff. State agencies have sufficient means of making federal administrators' lives difficult that FNS will often bow to states even on issues where it disagrees. And state human services officials' presumed expertise allows them unusual political access across the partisan divide even in times of increasing polarization: even if a senator is thoroughly estranged from her or his opposite-party governor, the state's SNAP director – who, of course, works for that governor – can readily get through.

Knowing that states have broad influence over SNAP does not tell us how they will exercise that influence. The values states seek to maximize in their influence on SNAP have shifted considerably over time in response both to general political, social, and economic currents and to changes in the program itself. Only rarely have they functioned as true laboratories of democracy with respect to SNAP, pursuing varying courses toward a common end.

States' SNAP agendas reflect the shifting influence and priorities among four main groups.[3] First, employers have sought a disciplined labor force. If SNAP is too generous, workers may decline onerous low-wage jobs. If it is too miserly during periods when employment is unavailable, the workers might move away and shrink the available labor pool. These employer interests were particularly important, especially in agricultural areas, during the program's early years. As agriculture automated and the national economy developed away from mass employment of low-skilled workers, these concerns faded away from SNAP policy discourse. They appear to be making a strong comeback in recent years, although the new emphasis on workforce discipline represents something quite different.

Second, a wide range of humanitarians support SNAP as a means of meeting one of the most basic of human needs. Some of these are simply compassionate voters with no particular connection to hungry people. Others may be involved in religious or other charity work and recognize that their efforts cannot scratch the surface in meeting peoples' needs without the nutritional foundation that SNAP provides. Organizations of low-income people played important roles in some states despite considerable barriers to their exercising political power.[4] State legislators from districts with large numbers of low-income people can be important voices for strengthening SNAP. Particularly in rural areas, these often include Republicans. Labor unions representing low-skilled workers have supported SNAP as a means of reducing employers' leverage, although labor interest waned rapidly after Congress excluded most strikers from SNAP in the late 1970s. Often humanitarians are found inside state human services agencies. Public employee unions have strongly supported SNAP. On the managerial level, SNAP directors often are among the most liberal senior executives inside state human services agencies: people with undeniable skills but too much empathy for low-income people to be placed in charge of programs dispensing state-funded benefits such as Medicaid.

A third, more diffuse, group that periodically influences state SNAP policy consists of efficiency-oriented economic elites. Businesses and affluent individuals seek lower state taxes, causing them to favor policies that maximize federal funding: a less-generous SNAP would increase pressure for state-funded programs to fill the gaps. Many businesses see low-income people more as a market than as a potential workforce. The more SNAP covers households' food needs, the more cash they have to pay their rent and utility bills and to buy other items. To the extent that these elites see low-income people as workers, they may regard SNAP benefits as lowering wage demands much as employers welcome the Earned Income Tax Credit (EITC)

[3] *See* David A. Super, *Laboratories of Destitution: Democratic Experimentalism and the Failure of Anti-Poverty Law*, 157 U. PA. L. REV. 541, 593–600 (2008).
[4] David A. Super, *Protecting Civil Rights in the Shadows*, 123 YALE L. J. 2806 (2014).

as reducing workers' reservation wage. SNAP's financing makes these elites natural supporters of the program – as long as their frame of reference is state specific.

A fourth group whose influence on state SNAP policies has grown dramatically over time has been ideologues seeking new battlegrounds. For them, state SNAP policy is more expressive than practical. Often, they seek to extend federal battles, especially during periods when federal policy is gridlocked. Initially, the most significant of these groups were on the left. More recently, a vast increase in right-wing funding, much of it coordinated by the American Legislative Exchange Council (ALEC), has led to a proliferation of state-facing organizations deeply hostile to SNAP.

This chapter charts the history of states' roles in SNAP as administrators, policy makers, and policy advocates on the federal level. It finds that shifts in the strengths and priorities of some of these groups, and in the emphasis each of them places on SNAP, have produced dramatic changes in state policies.

STATES AS DISCIPLINARIANS OF THE POOR

During the modern SNAP's earliest years,[5] the dominant policy model cast the states as disciplinarians of low-income people. Prior to one person, one vote, rural interests had outsized influence in state legislatures and were determined to prevent anything from diminishing farm and domestic workers' willingness to accept low wages. These attitudes contributed to the consistent parsimony of states' grant levels and eligibility rules in Aid to Dependent Children and later Aid to Families with Dependent Children (AFDC). The depth of this concern was evident in many states' decisions to set SNAP eligibility and benefit levels lower than permitted under federal law even though it would have cost the states nothing to provide benefits up to the federally defined level.

Aware of rural communities' antipathy for antipoverty programs, when Congress and President Nixon sought to make SNAP a national program in the early 1970s[6] they required that states participate statewide or not at all. By then, urban areas had developed sufficient political power, and areas already operating SNAP had seen enough of its benefits, that giving up the program to accommodate recalcitrant rural areas was unlikely. Still, several states had tense battles over statewide implementation of SNAP, and a few saw litigation.[7] A compromise in some states was to give counties primary administrative responsibility, with broad state oversight. Counties

---

[5] An earlier version of the Food Stamp Program existed during the Great Depression. It was sufficiently remote (temporally and politically) from the modern program, which began with pilot projects in 1963 and federal legislation in 1964 that lessons from it are not readily transferrable.

[6] Pub. L. No. 93–86, 87 Stat 221 (1973).

[7] *Madden v. Oklahoma*, 523 F.2d 1047 (10th Cir. 1975); Commw. *Dep't of Public Welfare v. Adams County*, 392 A.2d 692 (Pa. 1978).

also won the right to establish SNAP workfare programs even over their state's objections.

The modern SNAP was established in the midst of the civil rights revolution, at a time when states' rights were widely seen as a vehicle for perpetuating segregation and oppression. Accordingly, it had relatively strong civil rights protections earlier than other federal-state benefit programs. Distrusting exercises in discretion that state and local human services agencies had manipulated to disadvantage people of color, FNS began the development of highly specific substantive and procedural rules, initially contained in an FNS manual. Congress added far more detail to the federal statute in 1977,[8] and FNS took that opportunity to promulgate a detailed set of federal regulations after holding numerous hearings around the country to solicit information on problems in the program's current operations.[9]

Having standards is one thing, of course, but enforcing them is another. Federal statutes appeared to give FNS substantial leverage on noncompliant state and local agencies. In practice, however, each of the available tools was problematic. The Secretary of Agriculture could ask the Attorney General to sue a state for injunctive relief;[10] in practice, this has never happened as the rupture in federal-state relations that such a suit would bring has struck FNS as too drastic. FNS has the authority to withhold federal administrative funding from a noncompliant state.[11] FNS, however, has consistently believed states are spending too little on administering SNAP; reducing administrative resources further, especially for acts of nonfeasance, was unappealing. Moreover, creating a large hole in the state's human services budget could get the SNAP director fired – whether she or he was responsible for the problem – potentially putting the state's program in inexperienced hands at a time of crisis. Accordingly, FNS established an elaborate system of warnings designed to get the attention of officials senior enough to command the necessary resources to address the problem without destabilizing SNAP in the state. Even when FNS did withhold funds, it typically restored them once the state came into compliance. Because this bluff becomes less effective the more often it is run, FNS was hesitant to make formal findings of state noncompliance.

Simultaneously, however, private enforcement was becoming a realistic possibility. The Supreme Court's embrace of relatively liberal standards for private enforceability of programmatic statutes, together with the survival and growth of federally funded civil legal services, gave low-income households the chance to hold state and local agencies accountable for discriminatory, belligerent, or incompetent administration of SNAP. Coordinating much of this effort was the Food Research and Action Center (FRAC), a nonprofit group led by creative and energetic litigators

---

[8]   Food Stamp Act of 1977, Pub. L. No. 95–464 (1977).
[9]   7 C.F.R. Parts 271–290 (2018).
[10]   7 U.S.C. § 2020(g) (2016); 7 C.F.R. § 276.5 (2018).
[11]   7 U.S.C. § 2020(g) (2016); 7 C.F.R. § 276.4 (2018).

who saw access to food assistance as the next front in the civil rights movement.[12] Lawsuits FRAC brought or helped to coordinate challenged access to the program,[13] delays in state application processing,[14] the lack of prompt, effective fair hearings,[15] and the failure to pay retroactive benefits to households unlawfully denied assistance.[16]

The decline in power and commitment by employer groups seeking a dependent low-skill workforce, the promulgation of detailed regulations facilitating comparison of state and local offices' administration of the program, and the threat of recipient litigation and occasional federal sanctions pushed the disciplinarian model of state administration to the margins. A few traces of it remain. A handful of counties scattered around the country continued to operate workfare programs. Underfunding still led to periodic administrative problems, and the considerable discretion SNAP offices had in how much paperwork to demand of applicants likely led to significantly disparate experiences for households in different parts of the country.

Disciplinarian themes appeared in federal policy discourse when most strikers were ejected from the program in the late 1970s[17] and when Senator Jesse Helms won adoption of an employment and training (E&T) program for SNAP recipients in 1985.[18] The American Enterprise Institute's Charles Murray had tried to revive idea of disciplining the poor a year earlier when he proposed abolishing all anti-poverty programs operating above the county level, with the idea that local officials would have a better sense of the availability of work for claimants.[19] His work triggered a hail of criticism over his misuse of crucial data;[20] although he became an instant icon on the ideological right, his ideas had little immediate impact on policy.

It was a sign that the times had changed, however, when state SNAP administrators objected to the required high participation rates and low funding that E&T initially featured. In response to these complaints and an FNS study showing that E&T had no positive effects on employment or wages,[21] Congress moderated those participation rate requirements in the early 1990s. With their own experience of

[12] The author served as FRAC's legal director, albeit many years after the heyday of its litigation role.
[13] E.g., Tyson v. Maher, 523 F.2d 972 (2d Cir. 1975).
[14] E.g., Aiken v. Obledo, 442 F. Supp. 628 (E.D. Cal. 1977).
[15] E.g., Lambus v. Walsh, 448 F. Supp. 240 (W.D. Mo. 1978).
[16] E.g., Bermudez v. USDA, 490 F.2d 718 (D.C. Cir. 1973); Carter v. Butz, 479 F.2d 1084 (3d Cir. 1973).
[17] 7 U.S.C. § 2015(d)(3) (2016).
[18] 7 U.S.C. § 2015(d)(4) (2016).
[19] CHARLES MURRAY, LOSING GROUND AMERICAN SOCIAL POLICY 1950–1980 227–33 (1984).
[20] See, e.g., Robert Greenstein, Losing Faith in "Losing Ground," NEW REPUBLIC, Mar. 25, 1985, at 12.
[21] MICHAEL J. PUMA ET AL., FOOD & NUTRITION SERV., EVALUATION OF THE FOOD STAMP EMPLOYMENT AND TRAINING PROGRAM: FINAL REPORT (June 1990).

E&T's uselessness mirroring research findings, few states claimed much of the open-ended federal matching funds available to expand their E&T programs.

STATES AS MAXIMIZERS OF FEDERAL FUNDING

From the early 1960s to the 1980s, the value of low-income families' combined AFDC and SNAP benefits remained roughly constant after adjusting for inflation. This occurred because the creation and expansion of SNAP roughly offset the stagnation of AFDC eligibility and benefit levels. SNAP eligibility and benefit levels were tied, directly or indirectly, to the federal poverty level, which rose with inflation. Few states automatically adjusted their AFDC eligibility or grant levels for inflation, and many states would freeze or cut grant levels during the fiscal crises that accompanied recessions.

One effect of this shift in the composition of a roughly constant benefit package was a transfer of resources from the federal government, which paid all SNAP benefit costs, to states, which paid for 20–30 percent of AFDC benefits. This also led many state governments to start seeing SNAP as an important infusion of federal dollars into their local economies. A decade or so before Medicaid "creative financing" schemes began siphoning billions of addition dollars into state coffers,[22] a more low-key change began to emerge in state attitudes toward SNAP.

The evolving resource-maximizing view of SNAP manifested itself in a range of ways, some crudely self-interested. Many states cut, or failed to increase, AFDC benefits[23] in reliance on SNAP to offset 30–45 percent of the loss to households.[24] Other states went further and sought waivers from federal law to convert SNAP benefits into cash to make them full substitutes for partially state-funded cash assistance. After the Clinton administration showed no willingness to deny such waivers, a coalition of alarmed liberal and agriculture-oriented members of Congress enacted first an appropriations rider prohibiting new cash-out waivers and then made the restriction permanent with a provision in the 1996 welfare law.[25]

Most states, however, took a broader view of maximizing federal funds, seeking to increase SNAP benefits for their residents rather than seeking to directly fill state coffers. Several redesignated portions of cash assistance grants in ways that could

---

[22] David A. Super, Public Welfare Law 783–84 (Foundation Press 2016).
[23] See, e.g., *Quattlebaum v. Barry*, 671 A.2d 881 (D.C. 1995) (finding this explicit reliance did not violate 7 U.S.C. § 2017(b), which prohibits considering SNAP benefits in determining eligibility for other public program).
[24] SNAP benefits generally rise 30 cents for each dollar reduction in net income. 7 U.S.C. § 2017 (a) (2016). Net income for households with high shelter costs, however, is calculated with a deduction that grows as income declines, leaving many households with an effective marginal benefit reduction rate of 45 percent for unearned income such as AFDC benefits. *See id.* § 2014 (d)(6).
[25] 7 U.S.C. § 2026(b)(1)(B)(iv)(I) and (II) (2016).

prevent them from being counted as income in SNAP, thus increasing SNAP benefits.[26] Some sued USDA for permission to apply more lenient income-counting rules in determining SNAP benefits.[27] A dozen states quietly refused to follow FNS's policy of counting utility allowances from public housing authorities as income to resident households, while recipients and one state litigated the matter, prevailing after more than a decade.[28] With state human services agencies' encouragement, many members of Congress come to regard SNAP like other grants in aid, advocating policies that would send more money to their home states.[29]

Remarkably in light of subsequent events, states overwhelmingly opposed proposals by President Reagan and Senator Helms to convert SNAP into a block grant to the states. Although particular state officials would have gained more control over federal benefit dollars, they recognized that block grant funding would deteriorate over time to leave low-income households with less ability to purchase food absent increased state funding. Even in the more polarized environment of the mid-1990s, most governors and almost all state administrators expressed little or no support for proposals to block-grant SNAP even as they were eagerly lobbying to replace AFDC.

The most important manifestation of the benefit-maximizing mindset, however, appeared in states' exercise of discretion in program administration. More and more state human services agencies began to signal their front-line eligibility workers to be more lenient in granting SNAP benefits than they were for state-funded benefits. Deep-seated hostilities toward low-income people nurtured by some eligibility workers limited these signals' effectiveness, but overall SNAP became significantly more accessible, increasing participation.

Under other circumstances this shift might have gone unnoticed, but the late 1970s saw two other forces driving up SNAP participation: the recession of 1979–80 and the Food Stamp Act of 1977, which opened the program to many more low-wage workers and made participation more attractive by eliminating the

[26] See, e.g., *Maryland Dep't of Human Services v. USDA*, 976 F.2d 1462 (4th Cir. 1992) (discrediting one state's purported energy assistance program); COMM. ON WAYS & MEANS, U.S. HOUSE OF REPRESENTATIVES, COMM. ON WAYS & MEANS, 1994 GREEN BOOK 367 n. 5 (describing nine states' designation of parts of AFDC grants as energy assistance); *Commw. of Mass. v. Lyng*, 893 F.2d 424 (1st Cir. 1990) (refusing to exclude back-to-school clothing allowances from SNAP income).
[27] See, e.g., id.; *Dep't of Health & Welfare, State of Idaho v. Block*, 784 F.2d 895 (9th Cir. 1986) (finding energy assistance recipients entitled to standard utility allowance in computing SNAP shelter deduction); *State of New York v. Lyng*, 829 F.2d 346 (2d Cir. 1987) (declining to exclude from SNAP income allowances given to homeless people to allow them to obtain meals in restaurants); *South Dakota Dep't of Social Serv. v. Madigan*, 824 F. Supp. 1469 (D.S.D. 1993) (finding that public housing utility allowances do not count as income in determining SNAP benefits).
[28] See *Estey v. Comm'r, Maine Dep't of Human Serv.*, 21 F.3d 1198 (1st Cir. 1994) (finding utility allowances excludable); *West v. Bowen*, 879 F.2d 1122 (3d Cir. 1989) (same).
[29] For example, Senate Agriculture Committee Ranking Republican Richard Lugar inserted 7 U.S.C. § 2014(k)(2)(G) into the statute to exclude from SNAP income calculations township relief payments of a type found in his home state of Indiana.

requirement that households purchase (at a discount) their benefits. With SNAP operating under a funding cap, surging participation forced the Carter administration to make an embarrassing request for emergency legislation to keep benefits flowing.[30] In response to harsh congressional questioning about the surge in participation, the administration inaugurated an auditing system known as quality control (QC).

Although the Carter administration envisioned QC as one of many management tools to identify states' administrative deficiencies, when Ronald Reagan took over the White House and Republicans won control of the Senate, it quickly became much, much more. President Reagan and new Senate Agriculture Committee Chair Jesse Helms established severe automatic fiscal penalties for any state whose error rate exceeded 5 percent, as measured by QC's methods of imputation from a random sample. This level was dramatically lower than almost any state was achieving. Once the new system became fully effective with federal fiscal year 1983, more than 45 states faced sanctions each year. The amounts of these sanctions were staggering, far beyond most states' ability to absorb without action from their legislatures and likely deep cuts to their staffing levels. This presented the same dilemma that FNS had always faced concerning fiscal sanctions against states: if the state needed more, not less administrative resources, slashing its human services budget would only make matters worse. Here, however, FNS had far less room to maneuver: it was having to deal with the great majority of states all at once, the amounts at issue were generally much greater than FNS had even threatened on its own, no simple path to state compliance was evident, the statute gave the agency little discretion, and it was under immense pressure from Senator Helms, the Reagan White House, and its own political leadership (including former Helms staffer John Bode as Assistant Secretary) to take a hard line.

The Reagan administration's political leadership placed enormous pressure on FNS to reduce error rates, which in turn led many FNS regional offices to place enormous pressure on human services administrators. Previously cordial quarterly meetings between FNS Regional Administrators and state human services commissioners became tense standoffs over error rates. Accustomed to federal demands to implement this or that required SNAP policy, states were frustrated that FNS refused to specify what actions states could take to satisfy it. FNS insisted that only radically lower error rates would suffice. As SNAP directors and human services commissioners made their governors and legislatures aware of these potential sanctions, states' attitudes toward SNAP began to change. Several liberal SNAP directors and welfare commissioners were fired over QC error rates despite the fact that the vast majority of other states were in the same position. Some states concluded that SNAP expertise was crucial to solving a SNAP problem and promoted career civil servants with

---

[30] *See* David A. Super, *The Political Economy of Entitlement*, 104 COLUM. L. REV. 633 (2004) (describing drawbacks of funding caps).

commitments to low-income people not very different from those of their predecessors; others sought the sort of dispassionate accounting-oriented managers that had for some time run their Medicaid programs.

States' messages to front-line eligibility workers changed dramatically. Verification requirements multiplied, with those unable to produce the demanded documents summarily denied SNAP. These policies made accessing SNAP exceedingly difficult for people who have difficulty preserving important documents because of frequent moves, family breakups, or criminal victimization. The move to maximum verification was particularly ill-timed as the recession of 1981–82, deinstitutionalization, and the evisceration of state general assistance programs was creating a surge in homelessness.

Because the QC error rates that determined fiscal sanctions depended exclusively on improper awards of benefits and overissuances – not improper denials or underissuances – many states began to send eligibility workers' ill-disguised messages that, when in doubt, they should deny SNAP benefits. Indeed, because in a large portion of error cases the agency acted correctly given what it knew at the time, many eligibility workers came to view all applicants and recipients as potential sources of errors. Some states found creative means of driving home the single-mindedness of their demand for avoiding errors, frequently imposing collective punishment on local offices with high error rates even though QC samples were insufficient to generate reliable county-level estimates. One state required eligibility workers who had had cases containing QC errors to post pictures of bombs in their cubicles so that their colleagues could see who was responsible for the office's error rate.[31]

At the same time, Congress required states to compel almost all SNAP households to submit monthly reports on their circumstances whether anything had changed. The window for submitting these reports was extremely narrow: reports submitted too early were deemed incomplete and those submitted more than a few days after the end of the prior month were deemed late, in either case resulting in a suspension of benefits. If an eligibility worker was behind on paperwork or on vacation, if the SNAP office's mail sorting and distribution malfunctioned, or if its automated system failed, households that had complied perfectly were cut off,[32] without a pretermination hearing.[33] QC gave local SNAP managers an unappealing choice when they lacked the staff to process monthly reports timely: suspending the benefits of households that reported timely would be unlawful, but continuing benefits when some of their reports might contain changes that should affect their benefit level invited QC errors that could cost the manager her or his job.

[31] A scarlet "QC" might have been more fitting.
[32] Robert Greenstein & Marion E. Nichols, Ctr. on Budget & Pol'y Priorities, Monthly Reporting in the Food Stamp Program (Sept. 1988).
[33] 7 C.F.R. § 273.21(h) (2018).

Unsurprisingly, procedural terminations of eligible households proliferated.[34] States were required to report their rates of improper denials, but FNS generally did not audit those claims. The Government Accountability Office (GAO) and other outside groups found serious underreporting of improper denials.[35] FNS's response was tepid at best compared with the relentless campaign to lower error rates. Eventually, many antihunger advocates at both the federal and state levels concluded that lightening QC's heavy hand on state administration was the most important change that could be made in SNAP, ahead of liberalizations in eligibility and benefit computation rules.

QC dominated federal-state relations concerning SNAP for almost two decades. It sharply changed the nature of states' maximizing behavior from concern about the budgets of low-income households to fretting about their own. It also marginalized the threat of litigation by low-income households to enforce provisions of the federal statute and regulations: even if such litigation were to go badly, the sanctions a court might plausibly impose would pale compared to QC penalties.[36]

By the late 1980s, QC politics had begun to change at the federal level. More and more states had concluded that existing targets were essentially unmeetable, focusing their attention on federal legislation. Covington & Burling, which represented many states in litigating QC penalties, strongly urged its clients to pursue a legislative solution and represented them in that process. Several former governors and state legislators who had confronted QC sanctions had entered Congress. The two most powerful organizations of state governments – the National Governors Association and the National Conference of State Legislatures – heard concern from such a broad cross-section of states that they moved SNAP QC to the top of their legislative priorities.

On the other side, Senator Helms almost completely disengaged from SNAP when he lost the chair of the Agriculture Committee after Democrats won the Senate in 1986; indeed, he elected to displace Richard Lugar as the ranking member on the Foreign Relations Committee, which made it awkward for him to interfere in Senator Lugar's leadership on the Agriculture Committee. Assistant Secretary Bode and other USDA officials appeared to have wearied over fighting with states about QC. QC error rates had declined sharply, weakening the political imperatives that had led Congress to impose automatic sanctions. By this time, the only major active participant in SNAP policy making who did not seek to dial back QC sanctions was the Office of Management and Budget's (OMB's) poetically named budget

---

[34] *See, e.g.,* Anna Lou Dehavenon, *Charles Dickens Meets Franz Kafka: The Maladministration of New York City's Public Assistance Programs,* 17 N.Y.U. REV. LAW & SOC. CHANGE 231 (1989– 90)

[35] *See, e.g.,* GAO, FOOD STAMP PROGRAM: EVALUATION OF IMPROPER DENIAL OR TERMINATION ERROR RATES (1987). At the time, GAO was known as the General Accounting Office.

[36] David A. Super, *Are Rights Efficient? Challenging the Managerial Critique of Individual Rights,* 93 CALIF. L. REV. 1051 (2005).

examiner for SNAP, Les Cash. Although personally sympathetic to SNAP's goals, Cash understood OMB's institutional role as maintaining relentless pressure for better program administration. Many at OMB then also saw it as an institutional counterweight to cabinet departments and Congress, both of which are susceptible to capture by state governmental interests.

After protracted negotiations among states, Bode, and antihunger advocates, with congressional staff of both parties acting as mediators and Cash unseen but closely constraining what Bode could offer, a substantial revision of SNAP QC was added to the Hunger Prevention Act of 1988[37] that sought to cut in half the number of states sanctioned each year. It also added underissuances to recipients – but not the far more important improper denials – to error rate calculations. For budgetary reasons, however, it did not address the huge backlog of sanctions states had accrued up to that point.

After President George H. W. Bush lost the 1992 election, and most of his political appointees with responsibility for SNAP left for private-sector jobs, Andrew Hornsby, the former Alabama welfare commissioner, became acting FNS Administrator. Hornsby concluded that the risk of accusations of fiscal irresponsibility, and the watchful eye of OMB, would deter any regular presidential appointee from eliminating the huge backlog of state QC sanctions. Accordingly, he offered to excuse 85 percent of states' outstanding sanction balances in exchange for promises to "reinvest" the remaining 15 percent in efforts to improve state administration. States took him up on his offer en masse. A series of legislative and further executive actions eliminated or sharply reduced sanction liabilities for subsequent years. Antihunger legislation in 1993[38] further modified SNAP QC, sharply reducing penalty amounts by scaling them to the severity of violations but somewhat increasing the number of states sanctioned.

Although QC was no longer sanctioning 45 states a year, it was still sanctioning about half of them each year; many more were within or near the QC sample's margin of error. Only about 10 states each year could be confident that they would not face sanctions, with the rest continuing to obsess about their error rates. At the opening sessions of the American Association of SNAP Directors, where state delegations introduce themselves and talk briefly about the issues dominating their attention, almost every state discussed its error rate and typically nothing else.

While most antipoverty advocates were distracted by congressional battles over the 1996 welfare law, states and FNS career staff quietly began transforming SNAP in response to QC pressures. Given the pressure it was applying to state administrators, FNS felt uncomfortable refusing states' proposals to change SNAP rules in ways that might allow them to reduce errors. FNS therefore began granting waivers from some access-protecting regulations and abandoned enforcement of others. This allowed

---

[37] Pub. L. No. 100–435 (1988).
[38] Omnibus Budget Reconciliation Act of 1993, Pub. L. No. 103–624 (1993).

states more leeway to deny or terminate eligible households for minor technical mistakes. It also let states require households to reapply every three months to continue receiving benefits. Neither FNS nor the states explained how this squared with regulations requiring states to grant households the longest possible certification period up to one year and prohibiting certification periods less than six months absent extraordinary circumstances.[39]

The impact of these practices was concealed initially by caseload declines driven by an improving economy, the stigmatizing effect of debates over what became the 1996 welfare law, and the massive SNAP cuts that law contained. By 1998, however, the Center on Budget and Policy Priorities noticed that caseload declines were about twice what could be explained by the improving economy and the estimated impact of the welfare law.[40] Further, as more data became available it emerged that caseload declines were much steeper in two heavily overlapping groups of states: those achieving very large reductions in their QC error rates and those dramatically increasing their reliance on three-month certification periods. Flying in the face of the "welfare-to-work" rhetoric dominating human services debates in that period, these caseload reductions fell heaviest on working families with children. This reflected states' belief that these households had the greatest risk of causing QC errors because of the potential for their circumstances to change without the state agency learning and acting in time to adjust the household's benefits. In a clear face-off between ideological commitments to promoting work and states' desires to maximize protection against QC sanctions, the latter won overwhelmingly, with FNS's acquiescence.

Antihunger advocates saw this trend as both a serious harm in its own right and a grave threat to SNAP's stability and survival. AFDC had been dissolved in large part because it became associated with nonwork. Just as nobody cared that deliberate Reagan administration policies were the reason AFDC lacked substantial numbers of working recipients, nobody likely would care that SNAP's dwindling working poor participation was a byproduct of overzealous error-reduction efforts.

Because the existing QC system did indeed make households with complex or changeable circumstances greater error risks, states could be expected to impose burdensome requirements on working poor households – either to discourage their participation outright[41] or at least to minimize the risk of errors. Unless QC's error measurement could be adjusted to reflect the degree of difficulty of states' caseloads or states' QC anxieties could be largely laid to rest, burdensome requirements were likely to become standard. Advocates successfully lobbied OMB and the White House to direct FNS to implement a series of QC and programmatic changes to

[39] 7 C.F.R. § 273.10(f)(4)-(5) (1998).
[40] The author was general counsel at CBPP during this period.
[41] See David A. Super, *Offering an Invisible Hand: The Rise of the Personal Choice Model for Rationing Public Benefits*, 113 YALE L. J. 815 (2004).

remove the bullseye from the backs of working households. With President Clinton seeking to pivot from his impeachment to establishing a legacy, he embraced the opportunity to announce a package of initiatives to help working poor households receive food assistance. The Clinton Food Stamp Initiative of July 14, 1999, allowed states to liberalize the rules for households to own motor vehicles while receiving SNAP, reduced reporting obligations for working poor households (which had the effect of preventing many routine changes in circumstances from causing inadvertent errors), and moderated the QC system. The initiative and follow-on action that September established a formula for waiving QC sanctions that likely resulted from serving larger numbers of working families. States' error rates were recomputed for three subpopulations – working households with children, households with immigrant members,[42] and all others – with states' sanctions adjusted downward to reflect that share of the states' overall error rates resulting from disproportionate numbers of error-prone households. In addition, the tolerance for small errors was updated for inflation so that a recipient having a single extra work shift in a month would not be enough to cause an error.

The transformation in state attitudes was immediate and dramatic. The only states left with substantial QC sanctions were ones that undeniably did have serious problems with their programs' administration. These states had benefited from the united front of states sanctioned or at risk of sanctions, but now they had to face the realities of their own problems. Responding to the new priorities that the Clinton Initiative established, FNS offered these states plans under which part of their sanctions could be "reinvested" in improvements to program administration and part could be held "at risk," to be paid if the state's error rate remains high but waived if the state achieves significant progress. The "at risk" device sought to give human services administrators leverage with their state budget officers, governors, and legislatures to secure funding for more adequate staffing of SNAP eligibility determination. It often proved successful, allowing further reduction in error rates and thinning the ranks of states with seriously high error rates.

So rapid and complete was the change in state attitudes that states largely yawned in spring 2000 when FNS released the largest package of proposed SNAP regulatory changes in more than two decades. Along with changes required by the 1996 welfare law and those needed to codify the Clinton Food Stamp Initiative, this package included sweeping rollbacks of long-standing program access provisions. FNS had developed this package with state administrators in the mid-1990s as the culmination of the effort to reduce states' workloads and tighten access for potentially error-prone cases. It had languished in USDA's glacial clearance process and eventually been combined with the proposed rules to implement the 1996 welfare law.

---

[42] Although their modest numbers made them relatively small drivers in most states' error rates, the complexity of post-1996 eligibility rules for households containing immigrant members resulted in unusually large error rates for these households as well.

A handful of states submitted tepidly supportive comments and a few more raised minor technical quibbles. By contrast, antihunger advocates reacted with outrage that the Clinton administration was considering these changes while SNAP enrollment was already plummeting. Hundreds of comments, some exceeding one hundred pages, attacked the proposed regulations. Antihunger groups pressed Secretary of Agriculture Dan Glickman and senior OMB and Domestic Policy Council officials to intervene. Although former governor Clinton's White House always had an open door to representatives of state governments, no pressure in support of the proposed rules emerged. In the end, Les Cash's successor guided a thorough rewrite of the proposed rules to eliminate virtually all access-restricting provisions. Instead, the final rules further relaxed accounting pressures on working poor households and, correspondingly, potential QC errors for states.[43] State administrators' enthusiasm over these provisions swamped any disappointment over the rejection of the proposals they had negotiated with FNS at the height of the QC crisis.

Both antihunger advocates and state administrators wondered what George W. Bush's election would mean for the new federal-state détente in SNAP. They were relieved when he brought his human services commissioner from Texas, Eric Bost, to Washington to become USDA's undersecretary for food assistance programs. Although Texas had achieved very low error rates by driving working poor families off SNAP with three-month certification periods, Bost had previously served in other states and empathized with administrators facing QC sanctions. Using his knowledge of the program, his direct access to the president, and his considerable political skills, Bost persuaded the Bush administration to propose codification and expansion of some of the key Clinton program access initiatives and signed off on statutory QC reforms that were roughly the equivalent of what the Clinton administration had done administratively. Although improper denials and terminations remained outside the payment error rate on which sanctions were based, the legislation created a pool of bonus funds for states with outstanding performance in avoiding incorrect negative actions as well as for those that achieved high rates of timely application processing and participation among eligible households.[44] When this legislation passed with broad bipartisan support, states could feel confident that a new consensus had emerged to balance concern with payment accuracy and program access.[45]

---

[43] A *QC error* is defined as a substantial divergence between the benefits that should have been paid, if any, and the amount that were paid *due to a violation of program rules* by either the state agency or the household. If the program rules require fewer reports from households, fewer violations of reporting rules are possible.

[44] 7 U.S.C. § 2025(d) (2016).

[45] David A. Super, *The Quiet "Welfare" Revolution: Resurrecting the Food Stamp Program in the Wake of the 1996 Welfare Law*, 79 N.Y.U. L. REV. 1271 (2004).

The end of the QC wars led to a rapid, widespread acceptance of state options to improve access to low-wage workers.[46] Within a few years, almost every state was allowing working families to report on their circumstances only once every six months. Three-month certification periods largely vanished except for households genuinely expected to leave the area almost immediately. All but a handful of states stopped counting the value of motor vehicles as assets in determining SNAP eligibility, using either "broad-based categorical eligibility"[47] or another option that Representative Jim Walsh (R-NY) quietly added through an appropriations bill in 2000. Many adopted options to provide transitional SNAP benefits to people leaving welfare for work.

Indeed, even in the midst of the QC conflict and the philosophical upheaval that the 1996 welfare law occasioned, states continued to seek to maximize federal SNAP funding in ways that would not adversely affect their error rates. Only a small handful adopted various options the welfare law provided to expand disqualifications of otherwise eligible low-income people.[48] And after some initial skittishness, all but one state requested that their high-unemployment areas be waived[49] from the welfare law's three-month time limit on childless adults.[50] Indeed, most states had become such reliable SNAP maximizers that antihunger advocates relied on state options to eliminate counterproductive rules that were politically entrenched federally.

States' fund-maximizing largely represents a convergence of the humanitarian and elite efficiency-oriented perspectives on SNAP. The prospect of draconian QC penalties fractured that alliance for a time, but the alliance quickly reemerged with the end of overzealous QC enforcement. Groups that might have exploited that split lacked sufficient focus on SNAP: those advocating a disciplinary approach in prior

---

[46] Program Design Branch, Food and Nutrition Service, USDA, Food Stamp Program State Options Report at 1–8 (4th ed. Sept. 2004) https://fns-prod.azureedge.net/sites/default/files/snap/4-State_Options.pdf.

[47] The 1996 welfare law preserved a long-standing feature of SNAP law, "categorical eligibility," that eliminated the usual asset test for households in which all members received benefits under Title IV-A of the Social Security Act, which previously had contained AFDC and now housed the TANF block grant. 7 U.S.C. § 2014(a) (2016). Under AFDC, benefits generally meant a monthly cash assistance check for which eligibility depended on meeting an even more stringent asset test. TANF, however, allowed states to provide many other kinds of benefits without an asset test. Under "broad-based categorical eligibility," a state can give all members of a household access to an inexpensive service and treat the household as categorically eligible for SNAP as a result. Antihunger advocates had pointed out this opportunity to states in 1998, and FNS acknowledged its validity in its 2000 regulations, but many states delayed implementing until they were confident that USDA would continue to recognize this option.

[48] State Options Report, *supra*, at 18–21.

[49] Ed Bolen & Stacy Dean, Ctr. on Budget & Pol'y Priorities, Waivers Add Key State Flexibility to SNAP's Three-Month Time Limit (Feb. 6, 2018) www.cbpp.org/research/food-assistance/waivers-add-key-state-flexibility-to-snaps-three-month-time-limit.

[50] 7 U.S.C. § 2015(o) (2016).

decades had become deeply marginalized by the 1990s, and, although right-wing ideological opponents of antipoverty programs were becoming active in states, their primary focus was still on cash assistance funded under the Temporary Assistance for Needy Families (TANF) block grant that replaced AFDC.

STATES AS IDEOLOGICAL BATTLEGROUNDS

Responses to poverty combine practical and symbolic aspects. This has long been true of AFDC, which has served for some as a symbol of American generosity and for others as a monument to changing social norms. As open embraces of white supremacy became socially unacceptable, attacks on "welfare" served as a popular substitute. The result of symbolic political battles over AFDC was the program's decay and ultimate dissolution. The same uneasy partnership between practical and symbolic qualities exists in private charity as well: the stampede of volunteers seeking to help cook Thanksgiving dinner for the homeless is all about the symbolism of giving; the charities' struggles to ration grossly inadequate resources among myriad desperate applicants are typically guided by practical considerations.

State SNAP policy historically has been driven almost entirely by practical concerns, benign or otherwise. Those seeking to make symbolic or ideological points have focused on cash assistance, federal policy makers, or both. Over the past decade, however, that has changed dramatically. Progressive ideologues' attention remains fixed elsewhere, chiefly on enacting a single-payer health care system. Conservative ideologues, however, have begun to engage enthusiastically with state SNAP policy. This movement has provided a powerful counterpoint to the long-standing priority of maximizing federal funds.

This shift has several sources. Partly it reflects the radicalization of the Republican Party. Although many prominent Republicans – Richard Nixon, Bob Dole, Rudy Boschwitz, Bill Emerson, Richard Lugar, Saxby Chambliss, and Thad Cochran, among others – helped build and defend SNAP, today's Republican Party has forgotten or disparaged them. Even though a Republican president sent Congress a package of SNAP eligibility and benefit expansions as recently as 2002, support for antipoverty programs appears no longer to lie within the acceptable range of Republican thought.[51]

The shift from maximizing federal funds to maximizing ideological purity also reflects similar changes in other areas of antipoverty policy. Several Republican governors rejected welfare-to-work grants that bipartisan federal legislation created in 1997 despite the fit with the goals those governors were espousing. Resistance to the bipartisan No Child Left Behind Act similarly privileged states' rights ideology over receipt of federal education funds. And on a much grander scale, Republican states'

---

[51] Indeed, had Senator Cochran not recently retired, the author would have omitted him from this list to avoid embarrassing him politically.

refusal to accept the Affordable Care Act's Medicaid expansion, and refusal to establish state health insurance exchanges, sacrificed billions of dollars that would have benefited politically powerful hospitals and doctors.[52] Voluntarily reducing the flow of federal funds by operating a miserly version of SNAP is far less costly.

Perhaps the most significant reason state SNAP policy has become so ideological is the rapid growth of funding for right-wing state advocacy. A few states have long had conservative policy groups, but these were relatively small and only occasionally engaged seriously with antipoverty policy. Washington-based conservative advocacy groups such as the Heritage Foundation, the American Enterprise Institute, and the Cato Institute occasionally tried to influence state policy, but this often consisted only of issuing national reports or responding to specific requests in states.

All that changed with rise of ALEC. ALEC is well known for feeding model bills to conservative state legislators such as the "stand your ground" law that helped acquit Trayvon Martin's killer. ALEC meetings also provide a vehicle for connecting conservative donors with state-oriented advocacy groups. In addition to ALEC, which has steadily increased its opposition to antipoverty programs, state policy makers increasingly hear from the Secretaries' Innovation Group (SIG) and the Foundation for Government Accountability (FGA). SIG is an organization of right-wing former human services administrators; FGA broadly seeks to reduce eligibility and benefits in antipoverty programs. Although each remains hostile to programs under the TANF block grant, so few people remain on cash assistance,[53] and states' policies are already so restrictive, that it has lost appeal even as a symbolic target.

Right-wing advocacy groups' agendas typically lack unifying principles except reducing eligibility for SNAP and portraying SNAP recipients negatively. These groups are not, for example, pursuing the kind of "prowork" agenda that prior conservatives claimed: FGA advocates disqualifying otherwise eligible people who cannot find jobs for enough hours, but it also pushes to disqualify low-wage workers based on the value of the cars they drive to work. Even the Heritage Foundation's Robert Rector, by far the most important outside influence in shaping the 1996 welfare law's massive benefit cuts, found parts of FGA's agenda excessive.[54]

Many of their proposals seek to weaken public support for SNAP by implying serious moral deficiencies in low-income people without any serious evidence.[55]

[52] *See* David A. Super, *The Modernization of American Public Law: Health Care Reform and Popular Constitutionalism*, 66 STAN. L. REV. 873 (2014).

[53] IFE FLOYD ET AL., CTR. ON BUDGET & POL'Y PRIORITIES, TANF REACHING FEW POOR FAMILIES (rev. Dec. 13, 2017), www.cbpp.org/research/family-income-support/tanf-reaching-few-poor-families.

[54] ROBERT RECTOR ET AL., HERITAGE FOUNDATION, FIVE STEPS CONGRESS CAN TAKE TO ENCOURAGE WORK IN THE FOOD STAMPS PROGRAM (Apr. 19, 2018), www.heritage.org/hunger-and-food-programs/report/five-steps-congress-can-take-encourage-work-the-food-stamps-program.

[55] *See* David A. Super, *The New Moralizers: Transforming the Conservative Legal Agenda*, 104 COLUM. L. REV. 2032 (2004).

They demand that applicants be drug tested despite the lack of evidence of disproportionate substance abuse by SNAP recipients – and insufficient treatment facilities
for most. Similarly, despite USDA studies showing low fraud in SNAP,[56] these
groups demand aggressive, and loudly stigmatizing, antifraud campaigns. Ignoring
evidence that low-income shoppers obtain more nutrients per food dollar spent than
any other income group, FGA champions obesity-themed food purchasing restrictions. Similarly, FGA advocates finger-printing recipients even though several states'
experience with finger imaging was so thoroughly cost-ineffective that FNS no
longer allows federal matching funds for such contracts.[57] Another stigmatizing
proposal without practical potential would require SNAP recipients to have photographic identification cards: these serve no practical purpose as retailers cannot
require persons to present such cards because federal regulations allow households
to authorize representatives to buy food for them.[58] Capitalizing on stigmatization of
overweight persons and ignoring research evidence that SNAP recipients obtain
more nutrients per food dollar spent, they advocate restrictions on what SNAP
benefits may purchase, which would lead to many humiliating interactions at
checkout lines.

These groups' top priority, however, has been enacting state laws prohibiting
human services agencies from seeking waivers from the three-month time limit that
the 1996 welfare law imposed on many childless adults between the ages of 18 and
50. Although this provision's sponsors misleadingly characterized it as a "work
requirement," it disqualifies individuals without regard to how much effort she or
he has made to find work or how willing she or he is to perform unpaid work in
exchange for continued SNAP eligibility. As noted previously, the statute allows
states to request waivers from this requirement for areas with "insufficient jobs," and
in the late 1990s all but one state sought at least some waivers. Conservative groups
have won enactment of legislation in several states prohibiting such waivers and
have persuaded several additional governors to forbid their human services agencies
from requesting them. Notably, despite the prowork rhetoric of ALEC, FGA, and
SIG, none has made any discernible effort to press states to offer work slots to all
recipients facing termination under the time limit despite the additional federal
E&T funding available to states that do so.[59]

---

[56] Joseph Willey et al., Food & Nutrition Service, USDA, The Extent of Trafficking
in the Supplemental Nutrition Assistance Program: 2012–2014, at 12 (2017).
[57] Here the business interests that fund much right-wing state-level advocacy might be playing a
role: companies selling finger-printing services in the private market can boast of larger
"libraries" if they have collected the fingerprints of millions of SNAP recipients.
[58] 7 C.F.R. § 273.2(n)(3) (2018). Here broader Republican political priorities may play a role.
A recurrent objection to state laws requiring voters to present photographic identification at the
polls is that many low-income voters lack such identification; this argument can be blunted if
the state issues identity cards to many low-income people through SNAP.
[59] 7 U.S.C. § 2025(h)(1) (2016).

Although these policies could be mistaken for a reemergence of the model that sees the states as disciplinarians of the poor, they differ in both purpose and content. Agricultural employers wanted a large workforce that would depress wages. They thus saw an advantage in having meager programs to allow low-skilled workers to remain in the area when not needed on the farms. Current ideologues make no such distinctions, supporting any policy reducing benefits or stigmatizing recipients that seems to have potential political appeal. Indeed, ALEC's and FGA's top priority has been denying SNAP specifically to people in areas of high unemployment by blocking time-limit waivers there.

The new ideological approach to state SNAP policy is better understood as part of the same agenda of distraction and diversion that has produced fiercely antiimmigrant policies, a budding trade war, and frightening rhetoric about nonexistent crime waves. Condemning low-income people as morally unworthy may be the only viable strategy for deflecting criticism of fast-rising income inequality. Politicizing SNAP also provides Tocquevillian opportunities to develop right-wing civic virtues by practicing advocacy against antipoverty programs at the state and local level, making participants more reliable supporters of similar national efforts.

THE WAY FORWARD

For the foreseeable future, the tension between fund maximization and right-wing opposition to antipoverty programs is likely to shape states' roles in SNAP. However incoherent conservative proposals may be, attacks on antipoverty programs have proven political power, and the vast quantities of right-wing funds seeking activism to support will ensure that these positions will keep coming back.

On the other side, the forces that inclined states to seek to maximize SNAP federal funding – first and foremost for themselves, but also for low-income households – have weakened significantly in recent years. The generation of senior state administrators that remembers SNAP's early days, and that responded at least to the afterglow of the War on Poverty, have now left the scene. Many were pushed out prematurely in the conflict over error rates and were hence discredited with their successors. Those that survived the QC wars largely accepted the retirement incentives states offered to shrink their workforces during the Great Recession. In place of these administrators is a far more technocratic generation hired to reduce error rates and implement automated eligibility determination systems. Some are professional managers with little or no background in social work or experience working with low-income people.

State human services agencies have changed even more dramatically on their lower levels. Although social work–trained eligibility workers disappeared in most states long ago, eligibility workers at least had routine contact with SNAP recipients. Many, although by no means all, developed genuine empathy from these contacts. That model, however, is fast disappearing. The Great Recession simultaneously devastated state budgets, forcing large reductions in human services agencies' staffs and dramatically increased the number of households seeking SNAP. The traditional model assumed individual eligibility workers would serve caseloads of up to two hundred households; in numerous states, eligibility workers' caseloads far exceeded one thousand. The clear political infeasibility of securing the necessary resources from governors and legislatures caused human services administrators to go all-in on technology. Eligibility workers were herded into gigantic call centers where they would receive and process households' reports of changed circumstances, interview applicants and recipients over the phone, examine verification documents scanned in at kiosks in local communities – and rarely speak with the same household twice. Where politics precluded closing local human services offices, states established "statewide caseloads" that enabled eligibility workers to make changes in the benefits of a household living on the other end of the state. Eliminating continuing relationships between individual workers and recipient households inevitably reduces empathetic voices within state agencies. Indeed, right-wing groups continue to advocate for moving large parts of SNAP administration out of state agencies altogether, even though the Bush administration's two major attempts to privatize both ended in disaster.[60]

State government organizations that historically served a moderating function also are badly weakened. ALEC has pressed legislators to support it in preference to the bipartisan National Conference of State Legislatures, eroding the latter's funding and undercutting its claims to speak for state legislatures broadly. SIG has sought to weaken the American Public Human Services Association (APHSA) similarly. Hardline Republicans have blocked the National Conference of State Legislatures (NCSL), APHSA, and the National Governors Association from taking positions on numerous current public benefits issues important to states. Although the resulting dysfunction is most obvious in federal policy debates, it also has weakened policy coordination among states.

Rising inequality has fractured market after market, with some providers serving middle- and upper-income communities and others operating in low-income areas. Thus, many large businesses with broad political influence no longer receive significant business from low-income people. Trade associations of landlords, food stores, child care providers, and the like therefore may see the recipients of public benefits as outside their customer bases.[61]

Nonetheless, maximizing federal funds remains the dominant theme for most states. This can be seen in the opposition of many states to President Trump's proposals to require a state match for SNAP benefit costs and in states' general disinterest in House Republicans' various proposals to cap or block-grant SNAP spending. Of course, in a prior era one might imagine a bipartisan outcry from states

---

[60] David A. Super, *Privatization, Policy Paralysis, and the Poor*, 96 CALIF. L. REV. 393, 395 (2008).
[61] *See* David A. Super, *The Rise and Fall of the Implied Warranty of Habitability*, 99 CALIF. L. REV. 389 (2011) (describing changes in the low-income housing market).

over the administrative burdens of redetermining households' eligibility monthly and having to provide work programs for millions of people, as the House of Representatives' 2018 farm bill would require.[62]

Ironically, QC now constrains states' shift to ideological SNAP policy making. Right-wing governors are deterred from hiring conservative zealots lacking governmental experience by the danger that mismanagement will result in costly and embarrassing fiscal sanctions. Ideologically motivated privatization plans in Texas and Indiana, and aggressively harsh administration in Wisconsin, all resulted in ballooning error rates and fiscal sanctions. In many states, governors and legislatures may make ideological high-level SNAP policy decisions while technocratic SNAP directors continue pursuing fund maximization on lower-profile matters. This does mean, however, that creating state options to moderate harsh policies will have decreasing value as a compromise in federal policy making.

One recent episode illustrates both the continued draw of the fund-maximizing approach and the durability of the relationship between federal and state SNAP administrators. The USDA Inspector General attacked some states for manipulating sampling procedures to reduce their error rates.[63] The prospect of reigniting the QC wars was sufficiently repellent to all concerned that FNS and state administrators worked cooperatively in revising procedures to address these concerns. Whether similar cooperation remains possible on higher-profile issues is very much in doubt.

The demise of the disciplinarian model and the weakening of the fund maximization model of state SNAP are the result of shifts in the power of various interest groups and in the extent of their attention to SNAP. Further shifts are inevitable. If ongoing changes in the economics of food retailing cause large, powerful corporations to see low-income people as part of their consumer bases, the fund maximization model may revive. If President Trump moves the country sharply to the right, progressives may become even more distracted defending other laws and programs and leave SNAP policy increasingly to right-wing ideologues. If, by contrast, the country swings left in reaction to President Trump and Congress enacts a single-payor health insurance plan, perhaps hunger will become a major new priority for progressives and they may come to dominate state SNAP policy making. Other groups that have not traditionally been active in state SNAP policy making could well emerge.

The long-standing assumption that states played little meaningful role in make SNAP policy was never true. With the range of groups that have sought to shape state SNAP policies over the past several decades, states' roles are now gaining much wider recognition. We can and should judge the political and moral climate of a state by how it treats those struggling to secure enough food.

[62] David A. Super, *The New Republican Farm Bill Will Dismantle Our Programs to Feed the Needy*, L.A. TIMES, May 11, 2018, www.latimes.com/opinion/op-ed/la-oe-super-farm-bill-snap-20180511-story.html.

[63] OFFICE OF INSPECTOR GENERAL, FNS QUALITY CONTROL PROCESS FOR SNAP ERROR RATE (Audit Report 27601–0002-41 Sept. 13, 2015), www.usda.gov/oig/webdocs/27601-0002-41.pdf.

PART III

Advocacy

9

Federalism in Health Care Reform

Nicole Huberfeld

INTRODUCTION

History indicates that federalism in health care often does less for health, especially the health of the poor, than it does for intergovernmental relations and political expediency. States have exercised the police power to protect and regulate the health, safety, and welfare of the citizenry since the founding, but Congress has long established constitutional authority to regulate health care either directly through the commerce power or indirectly through spending and taxing powers. Even so, Congress has tended to act incrementally and to enact legislation that includes states in both minor and major statutory efforts such as, most recently, the Patient Protection and Affordable Care Act (ACA).[1] The legislative choice to include states in health reform is worthy of interrogation, yet rarely occurs. Does health care federalism only serve political ends, such as compromise to reach legislative agreement, or does a substantive reason exist to choose federalism in health care? Do states possess expertise in regulating health after years of front-line responsibility that justifies continued reliance on state governance? Is either level of government measurably better at shaping and implementing health law? While lawmakers seem to assume the answers to these questions point toward state control of health policy, these questions are seldom answered, let alone deeply explored.

States generally cannot and do not act alone, as even the boldest state experiments in health policy have involved the federal government's support. For example,

Thanks always DT and SRHT. *United States v. South-Eastern Underwriters Assn*, 322 U.S. 533 (1944); Nat'l Fed'n of Indep. *Bus. v. Sebelius*, 567 U.S. 519 (2012).

[1] Patient Protection and Affordable Care Act, Pub. L. No. 111–148 (2010), amended by Health Care Education and Reconciliation Act, Pub. L. No. 111–152 (2010).

Massachusetts initiated universal health insurance coverage in 2006 with approval from the Bush administration to use Medicaid funding to eliminate uninsurance among low-income residents.[2] This served as Congress's model for the ACA. While some states have worked through the years to improve the health of their citizenry, others have treated health care as a budgetary burden at best.

A noticeable pattern has emerged, with many of the same states making the same kinds of choices regarding health policy and participation in federal health programs they have made since before the New Deal. Yet, state power and flexibility arise repeatedly in debates about the kind of health reform that should occur and which level of government should be responsible for it. This choice is misleading because both the federal government and the states are long-standing participants in health law and policy and because states have been operating within a federal legislative framework for decades. While federalism tends to be understood to mean that states are in charge, for health reform this is inaccurate because states largely do not operate alone in the health care space.

Further, whether federalism is unto itself "good" for health remains an open question. Efforts at health reform that operate through the structural choice of federalism should be clear about what federalism can and cannot do. A thorough inquiry should acknowledge that American federalism is complex and dynamic, not a fixed, divided, dual sovereignty but rather a set of vertical and horizontal, intergovernmental and intrastate relationships within which each state separately bargains with the federal government for meeting its own needs. Bargaining can increase the variability that is expected in federalism structures. This variability may improve health but also may lower the national baseline, or allow a state to drop below a national baseline. This is especially relevant if the federal government attempts to improve conditions nationwide through health reform, as it did with the ACA's universal health insurance coverage.

In short, any assumption that states make better health choices is detached from history's lessons. This chapter considers the role of federalism in American health reform as it relates to social programs for the poor, in particular Medicaid. History shows that repeated efforts at protecting states' rights within federal health reform efforts have served multiple purposes that are not always designed to benefit the needy, for example, to make a political deal, improve health universally, decrease costs, or restrict access to the safety net for those deemed "undeserving." Without historical context, the debates of the twentieth century about the role of government in health care are bound to repeatedly arise with little to show for the (always) fraught effort.[3]

[2] *Massachusetts Health Care Reform: Six Years Later*, THE HENRY J. KAISER FAMILY FOUND. (May 2012), https://kaiserfamilyfoundation.files.wordpress.com/2013/01/8311.pdf.
[3] Nicole Huberfeld, *Federalizing Medicaid*, 14 U. PA. J. CONST. L. 431 (2011).

FROM POOR LAWS TO MEDICAL ASSISTANCE: HISTORICAL CONTEXT

The relationship between American federalism and health care is complex, with historical roots that manifest most noticeably in efforts to address the needs of the poor. Old ideas and patterns regarding who is deserving of assistance repeatedly arise in debates about access to medical care, especially when governmental assistance is at stake. The Elizabethan Poor Laws have a surprisingly strong presence throughout the development of modern health care programs. Elizabethan norms provided a model for the American colonies and later for state and federal laws addressing the needs of low-income individuals, and a direct descendant of the Poor Laws can be found in categorization of the poor as "deserving" and the parallel effort of preventing those deemed "able-bodied" from enrolling in social programs through rules such as work requirements. Such classifications of the poor are occasionally rejected (often by federal legislation), but more often than not states have been given latitude to decide which of the poor will gain access to medical care through government payment and the rules that attach to such funds. The structure of federalism, which is often expressed as state "choice" or "flexibility" in political dialogue, sometimes has acted as a proxy for other goals.

The 1601 Act for the Relief of the Poor ("the Poor Law") provided the "deserving" poor with money and services but channeled the "undeserving" or "able-bodied" poor to workhouses out of concern that they would become dependent on handouts and stop seeking gainful employment.[4] Deserving individuals included young children, people deemed disabled, widows, and others who could demonstrate inability to care for themselves such as the elderly. Local governments were given power to impose taxes so that they could support the deserving poor. These social program categorizations were replicated in the colonies, and they carried forward into the laws and policy choices of the states.[5] The states were responsible for their citizens' welfare, and many states chose to provide more help to those deemed worthy of government assistance. These categorizations and choices continued into early federal efforts to improve the health of the poor, such as the mothers' pensions law (the Sheppard-Towner Maternity and Infancy Act), later grant-in-aid programs such as Aid to Families with Dependent Children (welfare),[6] and Kerr-Mills (federal grants to states for elderly and other health care), which became Medicaid, discussed further below.

---

[4] See Marjie Bloy, *The 1601 Elizabethan Poor Law*, www.victorianweb.org/history/poorlaw/elizpl .html.

[5] See William P. Quigley, *Backwards into the Future: How Welfare Changes in the Millennium Resemble English Poor Law of the Middle Ages*, 9 Stan. L. & Pol'y Rev. 101, 102–3 (1998) (describing the "poor laws").

[6] See Theda Skocpol et al., *Women's Associations and the Enactment of Mothers' Pensions in the United States*, 87 Am. Pol. Sci. Rev. 686 (1993).

Before the early twentieth century, the federal government largely did not regulate health, safety, and welfare, except to supply medical care for war veterans.[7] States exercised police power to protect health and safety, which included providing for some of the needs of the poor. The default was state or local regulation. In the smaller communities of a largely agrarian society, and with no major medical improvements yet in existence, this approach was adequate; the sick and the dying needed a place to find comfort, but little else could be provided aside from sanitation. But, at the turn of the twentieth century, the industrialization and urbanization of America coincided with revolutions in medicine that started to involve more stakeholders and more money in health care and in policy. For example, the advent of aseptic surgery, as well as antibiotics, built on prevention of disease with sanitation measures, making medicine a field with potential to remedy human ailments.[8] Advances in sanitation and medicine roughly coincided with World Wars I and II, which deepened the need for scientifically based medical care for those injured in the war effort. The Great Depression also highlighted that states could not provide enough care or money to those in need of a safety net; at the moment that government support was needed the most, state budgets became much tighter because state and local taxes plummeted as employment declined.[9]

Key federal law developments occurred in a similar timeframe. The ratification of the Sixteenth Amendment to the US Constitution[10] gave Congress power to impose income taxes and elevated its ability to "provide for the general welfare" through spending.[11] Additionally, the US Supreme Court issued decisions recognizing broad authority for Congress over nationwide problems under the Commerce Power and the Taxing and Spending Power in this timeframe.[12] In short, the federal government arguably had neither Supreme Court–recognized power nor political reason to exercise authority over medical care before the early twentieth century. Yet, even when the federal government entered the health policy arena, state sovereignty has continued to be invoked during most federal health reform efforts to protect the culture and values of states. State sovereignty arises not only when negotiating the content of the health reform effort at hand but also through states' ongoing implementation of such laws.[13] In other words, federalism is a structural and substantive

---

7   Abbe R. Gluck & Nicole Huberfeld, *What Is Federalism in Health Care For?*, 70 Stan. L. Rev. 1689, 1706 (2018).

8   Paul Starr, The Social Transformation of American Medicine 143 (1982).

9   *See, e.g.*, David A. Super, *Rethinking Fiscal Federalism*, 118 Harv. L. Rev. 2544, 2641–42 (2005).

10 U.S. Const. amend. XVI (ratified 1913).

11 U.S. Const. art. I, §8, cl. 1.

12 *See, e.g., United States v. Butler*, 97 U.S. 1 (1936) (Congress's taxing and spending power under Article I, Section 8, clause 1 is a distinct enumerated power and does not solely modify the other enumerated powers); *NLRB v. Jones & Laughlin Steel Corp.*, 301 U.S. 1 (1937), *United States v. Darby*, 312 U.S. 100 (1941), and *Wickard v. Filburn*, 317 U.S. 111 (1942) (each finding congressional authority to regulate commerce that reaches into the states, reversing Lochner Era decisions severely limiting the commerce power under Article I, Section 8, clause 3).

13 *See, e.g.*, 82 Cong. Rec. 1404 (1937).

choice that lingers and that sometimes results in limited access to safety-net programs.

Such limitations tend to involve the categorization of the deserving and undeserving poor, and more specifically use of the words *able-bodied* to distinguish between the two. These phrases have a complicated past reflecting valuations of individuals' worth in society. For example, the words *able-bodied* were used to advertise and classify slaves as healthy, especially adult males who promised more laboring power and commanded higher prices at auctions[14] and who were also advertised as a "full hand."[15] Even after the Civil War, the words *able-bodied* were used to sort freed slaves for the social programs that supported them. For example, the Freedmen's Bureau classified freedmen as "able-bodied" to determine eligibility for and duration of federal assistance, which was time limited so that the freed slaves would not "forget how to work."[16] The words *able-bodied* also were used in the post–Civil War southern penal system, which funneled criminally convicted "able-bodied" freedmen into "convict lease" programs that provided involuntary, free labor to private industry in lieu of prison.[17] Being categorized as able-bodied was detrimental in each of these circumstances, in part because paying fairly for the work performed by either slaves or freedmen was the exception rather than the rule; yet, once freed, slaves were expected to fend for themselves, and their disadvantages were attributed by some to "race traits and tendencies."[18]

---

[14] Sales records were not kept in a uniform fashion, and other descriptors were used too, *see, e.g.,* Ulrich Bonnell Phillips, *The Economic Cost of Slave-Holding in the Cotton Belt*, 20 POL. SCI. Q. 257, 264–68 (1905) (discussing a lack of durable records for slave sales and historians' reliance on estate sales such information); but *able-bodied* was common enough to appear on posters advertising slave sales.

[15] *See generally,* Christopher R. Adamson, *Punishment after Slavery: Southern State Penal Systems 1865–90*, 30 SOCIAL PROBLEMS 555 (1983) (exploring convict leasing as a method of controlling freed slaves and substituting free labor). Adamson states:

> The very terminology of slavery was retained under the convict lease system. Employers used the slaveholders' classification of laborers, according to their ability to work, into first, second, third, fourth, and fifth class hands. Able-bodied males were referred to as "full hands"; women and children prisoners were known as "half-hands." Company employers were reluctant to rent "dead hands"-prisoners too old or too sick to work.

Id. at 560 (citations omitted).

[16] *See* GEORGE R. BENTLEY, A HISTORY OF THE FREEDMEN'S BUREAU 144 (1970) (writing that "the [Freedmen's] Bureau was generally careful not to let able-bodied men and women subsist long on its charity and thus forget how to work. It kept its relief subordinate to its labor program.").

[17] *See id.; see also* DOUGLAS A. BLACKMON, SLAVERY BY ANOTHER NAME: THE RE-ENSLAVEMENT OF BLACK AMERICANS FROM THE CIVIL WAR TO WORLD WAR II 50, 64, 348 (2009).

[18] *See, e.g.,* FREDERICK L. HOFFMAN, RACE TRAITS AND TENDENCIES OF THE AMERICAN NEGRO 95 (1896) (asserting that an "immense amount of immorality" was responsible for higher rates of disease and death among southern freed slaves, and concluding not that the "conditions of life" but that "race traits and tendencies" were the root cause of differences between whites and blacks).

Federal social programs that developed as a result of the Great Depression in the New Deal era continued some of these the post–Civil War practices. Before the New Deal, southern states dreaded the power of the federal government to end the vestiges of slavery, such as legal segregation, through national legislation.[19] Southern legislators fought the Social Security Act of 1935 (SSA) effectively, forcing a compromise on agricultural and domestic workers – who were predominantly former slaves and their descendants – by keeping them out of the SSA's reach.[20] Senator Byrd's southern resistance[21] pinned support of the SSA on opposition to paying "able-bodied Negroes to sit around in idleness."[22] Southern Democrats foiled efforts at enacting national health insurance for the same reason,[23] and other New Deal legislation was negotiated to reflect "due regard to local and geographic diversities."[24] In short, the term *able-bodied* has been used in American policy making, at federal and state levels, to deny certain populations available governmental assistance, regardless of their need.

Between the New Deal and the Great Society, the federal role in medical care for the poor grew incrementally as efforts to pass national health reform arose, were defeated, and alternative legislation passed. For example, after President Truman's national health insurance plan failed, the Hill-Burton Act offered an alternative: federal funds to build hospitals in medically underserved areas that required recipients to provide some charity care but allowed segregated hospitals to be funded.[25] Incremental alternatives were stopgaps that never quite alleviated the financial burden of increasingly expensive modern medicine for either individuals or states.

---

[19] *See* Marc Linder, *Farm Workers and the Fair Labor Standards Act: Racial Discrimination in the New Deal*, 65 Texas L. Rev. 1335, 1364–66 (1987) (detailing the history of deliberately excluding people of color from the SSA and other New Deal legislation and underpaying those who were eligible for social security under the law, so that "the actual discriminatory impact of the Social Security Act on blacks corresponded closely to the hopes of southern congressmen.").

[20] Edwin E. Witte, The Development of the Social Security Act 143–44 (1962). Witte wrote regarding resistance to the Social Security Act: "[S]ome southern senators feared that this measure might serve as an entering wedge for federal interference with the handling of the Negro question in the South. The southern members did not want to give authority to anyone in Washington to deny aid to any state because it discriminated against Negroes in the administration of old age assistance." *Id.*

[21] David G. Smith & Judith D. Moore, Medicaid Politics & Policy 6 (2d ed. 2008). Desire for "cheap agricultural and domestic labor" thwarted pension protections drafted into the SSA for agricultural and domestic workers, as Senator Byrd led a coalition of southern legislators who opposed federal "interference" in the "Negro question" against provisions of the SSA setting federal pension standards. *Id.* at 8–9.

[22] Linder, *supra* note 20, at 1364 (quoting *Jackson Daily News* regarding Mississippians' strong negative reactions to the proposed SSA).

[23] Timothy Stoltzfus Jost, Disentitlement? 83 (2003).

[24] Linder, *supra* note 20, at 1373, n. 259 (citing committee reports from 1937).

[25] *See* David Barton Smith, *Addressing Racial Inequities in Health Care: Civil Rights Monitoring and Report Cards*, 23 J. Health Pol. Pol'y & L. 175, 181 (1998) (describing an Alabama senator's intentional limitation of federal reach in crafting Hill-Burton).

By the time President Kennedy was elected, the medical needs of the elderly brought debate about governmental assistance in health care back to national prominence and led to enacting Medicare and Medicaid. These major federal programs have different governance structures and now account for more than 40 percent of the population's insurance coverage, making each relevant to considering the role of federalism in health care for the poor.

In crafting the Medicare program, Congress essentially took one category of deserving poor and provided special treatment for them by creating a national program, delinked from the variability of state laws, that would address the elderly's growing poverty rates, which were closely associated with medical care.[26] Enacted as part of President Johnson's War on Poverty, Medicare was a new approach, a fully national program for the elderly (and, later, permanently disabled) that offered then-comprehensive health insurance coverage. The federally funded and administered structure of Medicare was partly the result of lobbying by the elderly, who did not want access to medical care to fluctuate depending on the economics and policy preferences of states, and partly the desire of states to not be responsible for their medical costs.[27] Though detractors demonized it as "socialized medicine," Medicare was enacted on July 30, 1965 and required that hospitals receiving federal funding desegregate.[28] Medicare has grown into a popular and politically protected program over the course of its 50-plus years.

Where Medicare was markedly different, Medicaid was remarkably consistent with prior health laws, even though President Johnson signed them into law on the same day. Medicaid followed the path of the Poor Laws by providing medical assistance only to the deserving poor – families with children, people with disabilities, seniors – the same populations served by federal grant-in-aid programs in the years between the SSA and the Great Society as well as by states' welfare programs.[29] Medicaid built on existing federal-state partnerships by inviting states to make health policy choices in various aspects of implementing the new program, though with stronger federal rules than prior programs.[30] States' rights were baked into the law because states historically were responsible for health but also due to southern states' resistance to federal interventions and a political desire to get them on board (through the offer of state flexibility within new federal rules).[31] Medicaid carried

---

[26] Robert Stevens & Rosemary Stevens, Welfare Medicine in America 23–26 (2d prtg. 2004).

[27] Gluck & Huberfeld, *supra* note 8, at 1711–13.

[28] *See* Smith, *supra* note 26, at 83 (discussing the combined role of Title VI of the Civil Rights Act and Medicare in desegregating hospitals).

[29] Stevens & Stevens, *supra* note 27.

[30] Edward Berkowitz, *Medicare and Medicaid: The Past as Prologue*, 27 Health Care Fin. Rev. 11 (2005–6).

[31] *See* Laura Katz Olson, The Politics of Medicaid 21–50 (2010) (tracing political features of historical resistance to national health reform in the context of Medicaid's creation).

forward the deserving/undeserving, able-bodied distinction that has guided American social programs since the colonial era.

This brief march through health reform indicates that, more often than not, state flexibility has been incorporated into federal interventions not because states are effective at crafting or implementing health policy but rather to make a deal. The same could be said for the Children's Health Insurance Program (CHIP), a politically popular federal block grant to states to cover more children than Medicaid (often administered as part of Medicaid), negotiated by the Clinton administration after a major effort at health reform failed.[32] As the next part discusses, this is true for major elements of the ACA as well. The question is why? Allowing states to be responsible for health and welfare was a congressional choice rather than a constitutional certainty after a certain point in jurisprudential history, yet federalism keeps showing up in health reform efforts.

HEALTH CARE FEDERALISM, GOVERNANCE CHOICES, AND HEALTH REFORM

Since the 1940s, the Supreme Court has held that Congress has constitutional authority to regulate national industry and to influence national policy in ways that bring federal power into the field of health care. Yet, since the Court started to read congressional authority expansively, Congress has exercised its authority often in a limited fashion, enacting incremental legislation that invites states to participate in national programs. An early but important example occurred in 1944, when the Court affirmed Congress's exercise of the commerce power over national insurance markets.[33] Congress reacted with the McCarran Ferguson Act, which gave power to regulate insurance back to the states.[34] Such legislative decisions reflect deep tensions regarding the role of federal and state government, distribution of taxpayer dollars, and which populations benefit from social programs. The debate over health care's driving principle – individual endeavor or collective effort; welfare or social insurance; freedoms or rights – is ongoing in the United States.

Even though Congress has power to enact nationwide, uniform legislation, states have been partnering with the federal government in health care for nearly a century, influencing the shape of laws and policy as well as the implementation of health reform efforts. The ACA fits this mold. Though some have characterized it as federal capture of health care,[35] in fact, key features of the ACA, such as Medicaid

---

[32] 42 U.S.C. § 1397aa.

[33] *United States v. South-Eastern Underwriters Ass'n*, 322 U.S. 533 (1944).

[34] 15 U.S.C. § 1011 (1945).

[35] *See, e.g.*, Jonathan H. Adler, *Cooperation, Commandeering, or Crowding Out? Federal Intervention and State Choices in Health Care Policy*, 20 KAN. J. L. & PUB. POL'Y 199, 199 (2011); Richard A. Epstein, *Bleak Prospects: How Health Care Reform Has Failed in the United States*, 15 TEX. REV. L. & POL. 1, 10–11 (2010).

expansion and health insurance exchanges, rely on federalism.[36] The ACA ended federal categorization of the "deserving" poor in health care by creating a federal baseline of universal health insurance coverage.[37] The law's principle of universality is arguably the most meaningful federal health reform since 1965.[38] The ACA facilitates universal coverage by regulating private health insurance and expanding the public health insurance of Medicaid, focusing on the needs of low-income populations who were much less likely to be offered, or be able to afford, employer-sponsored health insurance.

To that end, the ACA created standards for group and nongroup private health insurance that prevented past exclusionary practices, such as eliminating preexisting condition exclusions, requiring guaranteed issue, and offering premium assistance through tax credits for purchasing private insurance on exchanges.[39] Premium assistance is available for individuals earning between 100 and 400 percent of the federal poverty level (FPL), as research indicated that those earning less than 400 percent of the FPL were not likely to be able to obtain employer-sponsored health insurance. Those earning less than 250 percent were even less likely to have health insurance as an employment benefit, which the ACA addressed through cost-sharing reductions for this population.[40] The ACA's private insurance regulations level the playing field so that individuals who were prevented from obtaining insurance for health reasons could apply for comprehensive coverage, and those who were prevented from purchasing insurance for financial reasons could pay premiums to buy coverage. The ACA created these federal standards but then invited states to administer them, in part because states have regulated insurance for years under the McCarran Ferguson Act and developed regulatory mechanisms accordingly. Two-thirds of states ultimately chose not to develop their own exchange platform, relying instead on the federal exchange but often in a hybrid arrangement that still leaves some insurance regulation in the state's control.[41]

The ACA amended Medicaid to include nonelderly, childless adults earning up to 138 percent of the FPL for the first time, creating a mandatory new category of eligibility for states to include in their Medicaid programs (sometimes called the "eighth category" of eligibility).[42] The expansion was structured to target very

---

[36] Gluck & Huberfeld, *supra* note 8, at 1703–5, 1726–31.

[37] Near-universal coverage is more accurate, as undocumented immigrants were excluded. Pub. L. No. 111–148, § 1323(f)(3), 124 Stat. 119, 184 (2010). Medicaid covers emergency services that hospitals provide to undocumented immigrants, but they cannot enroll through such services, though a state can opt to cover pregnant women and children. 42 U.S.C. § 1396b(v).

[38] *See* Nicole Huberfeld, *The Universality of Medicaid at Fifty*, 15 YALE J. HEALTH POL'Y L. & ETHICS 67 (2015).

[39] 42 U.S.C. §§ 300gg–300gg-4.

[40] *See, e.g.*, Carmen Denavas-Walt et al., INCOME, POVERTY, AND HEALTH INSURANCE COVERAGE IN THE UNITED STATES: 2009, at 22–28, 26 tbl.9 (2010).

[41] Gluck & Huberfeld, *supra* note 8, at Part V.

[42] 42 U.S.C. § 1396a(a)(10)(A)(i)(VIII).

low-income populations who cannot obtain employer-sponsored health insurance, cannot afford private insurance, and were otherwise left out of the safety net. The federal government fully funded the expansion at the outset of implementation (January 1, 2014) and slowly decreases funding to a 90 percent federal match in 2020 – a match that is higher than federal law offers for other Medicaid beneficiaries. The ACA as drafted did not allow states to opt out of the expansion of Medicaid eligibility. Instead, the ACA created a national baseline of eligibility for Medicaid that intentionally ended old categorizations of the poor to achieve universal coverage. But, the Supreme Court in 2012 held that HHS could not penalize states that refuse to expand.[43] Thus, the Court's decision in *NFIB* v. *Sebelius* effectively rendered Medicaid expansion optional, although the Medicaid Act and the ACA were not modified.

The federalism of the ACA thus varies in implementation from the law as enacted; states have created individualized features that vary from the law's national baseline and from its universality principle. States have negotiated with HHS for approval of demonstration projects under SSA section 1115, which was designed to encourage improvements in welfare programs and predates Medicaid.[44] In the Medicaid program, states typically seek 1115 waivers to improve coverage, delivery of care, or benefits – common measures of successful health policy – which the Secretary of HHS has authority to allow so long as the proposal is budget neutral to the federal government and the "experimental, pilot, or demonstration project . . . is likely to assist in promoting the objectives" of Medicaid.[45] The negotiation of waivers to implement the ACA has demonstrated that states very effectively negotiate with the federal government within the federalism structure of the ACA. The ACA's implementation contradicts the Supreme Court's view of states needing the judiciary's protection under the Tenth Amendment.

States have proven adept at seeking concessions from HHS within the ACA's federalism design.[46] Some sought waivers to expand Medicaid eligibility and make use of new federal funds soon after the ACA was enacted. For example (in order of expansion), Minnesota, Connecticut, the District of Columbia, California, Washington, and New Jersey used the ACA's offer of federal funds to expand Medicaid before January 1, 2014 to take advantage of newly available federal money that augmented existing state health policies. All except Connecticut operated expansion through demonstration waivers by 2012.[47] In 2015, New York and Minnesota expanded beyond the ACA's baseline through the Basic Health Plan option offered

[43] *Nat'l Fed'n of Indep. Bus.* v. *Sebelius*, 567 U.S. 519 (2012).
[44] President John F. Kennedy Special Message to the Congress on Public Welfare Programs, Feb. 1, 1962, www.presidency.ucsb.edu/ws/?pid=8758.
[45] 42 U.S.C. § 1315.
[46] *See* Gluck & Huberfeld, *supra* note 8, at Parts III & IV.
[47] Kaiser Family Found., *States Getting a Jump Start on Health Reform's Medicaid Expansion* (Apr. 2, 2012), www.kff.org/health-reform/issue-brief/states-getting-a-jump-start-on-health/.

by the ACA, which allows states to include more nonelderly adults and legal immigrants in Medicaid.[48] These states operated within the intended federalism structure of the ACA to operate in harmony with federal health reform, yet to the advantage of the state's policy choices and budget. They also offer early examples of the waiver possibilities in the ACA's health reform enterprise, and other state-based choices fit this model as well. For example, states have obtained waivers to use Medicaid managed care to address social determinants of health[49] and to design accountable care organizations that are designed to improve beneficiary health through care coordination.[50]

After *NFIB* v. *Sebelius*, states used their new leverage to negotiate with HHS for individualized waivers with adaptations that arguably varied more widely from the ACA as drafted. For example, Arkansas was the first "red state" to receive HHS approval for a demonstration project to expand Medicaid by a waiver that funneled the expansion population into the exchange to purchase private insurance with federal Medicaid money. The Arkansas "premium assistance" model introduced privatization into the ACA's Medicaid expansion. Other states learned from Arkansas's success, with each seeking more variation from the ACA's baseline in negotiating waivers with HHS, such as requiring premiums for the expansion population, or limiting nonemergency medical transportation, or offering a more generous benefit package to those who could pay more.

Waivers that were approved late in the Obama administration and early in the Trump administration demonstrate different facets of health care federalism. On one hand, the negotiations that have encouraged states to engage with HHS demonstrate a dynamic federalism that has facilitated implementation – albeit slowly through a one-by-one process rather than all at once as intended – of a law that those states may have rejected otherwise. On the other hand, this federalism has allowed some states to make exclusionary policy choices – such as the stigmatizing categorization of the poor – by allowing a return to policies that the ACA eradicated. The motivation for allowing such state choices was wildly different for the Obama and the Trump administrations, making it hard to draw conclusions regarding the value of the federalism in the implementation of health reform.

The Obama administration pursued the goal of universal coverage, with the attitude that, after *NFIB*, working with states to expand Medicaid was paramount

[48] Pub. L. No. 111–148 § 1331.
[49] *See* Letter to Lori Coyner, Medicaid Director, Oregon Health Authority from CMS, CMCS Director Vikki Wachino, Jan. 12, 2017 (approving Oregon Health Plan waiver), www.oregon .gov/oha/HPA/HP-Medicaid-1115-Waiver/Documents/Oregon%20Health%20Plan% 20STCs_2017-2022.pdf.
[50] *See* New Jersey Department of Human Svcs., Division of Medical Asstc. & Health Svcs., Accountable Care Organizations, www.nj.gov/humanservices/dmahs/info/aco.html.

because getting people covered to achieve universality was the driving concern.[51] Even so, HHS had certain boundaries it would not cross, such as work requirements as a condition of eligibility and partial Medicaid expansion. As with every prior administration, state requests to impose work requirements were denied, though states were told they could offer voluntary job placement programs to Medicaid beneficiaries (and some have done so).[52] Partial expansion, meaning eligibility only for those earning up to 100 percent of the FPL, was rejected because the ACA's statutory language does not permit it and it would be detrimental to low-income individuals who churn in and out of minimum-wage jobs and would have to pay much more out of pocket for private insurance. The Secretary approved waivers with provisions that were controversial in 2015 and 2016. Indiana, for example, requested premiums with lockout features for nonpayment; nonpayment for nonemergency medical services; reduced retroactive eligibility; and work requirements. HHS approved all these except for work requirements. Early reports on Indiana's waiver indicate that nonenrollment and disenrollment occur with these waiver provisions. If the goal of health reform is universal coverage, then allowing variability has both positives and negatives. A state like Indiana may not have been willing to expand without these concessions, but they are concessions that violate the primary principle of the ACA.

The Trump administration's openly anti-ACA posture seems to influence its waiver approvals; yet, these negotiations continue the dynamic federalism started with the Obama administration and may have the effect of encouraging more states to opt into Medicaid expansion. President Trump issued an Executive Order upon entering office that instructed federal agencies to minimize the impact of the ACA and "afford the States more flexibility."[53] Shortly thereafter, the Secretary of HHS and Administrator of the Centers for Medicare and Medicaid Services (CMS) issued a letter to governors stating that the Trump administration's policy was to interpret Medicaid as serving the "most vulnerable populations," the implication being that "working age, nonpregnant, non-disabled adults" were disfavored beneficiaries. The letter put the "undeserving" on notice that they are not welcome in Medicaid.[54] Congress did not have enough votes to repeal the ACA in 2017, but on January 11, 2018, CMS issued a new policy inviting states to create work requirements through waiver requests. CMS stated that:

> [The agency] support[s] state demonstrations that require eligible adult beneficiaries to engage in work or community engagement activities ... to determine whether

---

[51] *See* Abbe R. Gluck & Nicole Huberfeld, *The New Health Care Federalism on the Ground*, 15 IND. HEALTH L. REV. 1 (2018) (detailing qualitative data from interviews with key officials in ACA implementation).

[52] *See, e.g.,* Letter to Arkansas Governor Asa Hutchinson from Secretary of Health and Human Services Sylvia Burwell, Apr. 5, 2016 (on file with author).

[53] Exec. Order 13765, Jan. 20, 2018, 82 Fed. Reg. 8351 (Jan. 24, 2017).

[54] Dear Governor Letter, Secretary of HHS Tom Price and CMS Administrator Seema Verma, Mar. 2017, www.hhs.gov/sites/default/files/sec-price-admin-verma-ltr.pdf.

those requirements assist beneficiaries in obtaining sustainable employment or other productive community engagement and whether sustained employment or other productive community engagement leads to improved health outcomes. This is a shift from prior agency policy regarding work and other community engagement as a condition of Medicaid eligibility or coverage, but it is anchored in historic CMS principles that emphasize work to promote health and well-being.[55]

A federal court ruled that the first such waiver HHS granted was an arbitrary and capricious exercise of administrative authority, in part because Kentucky predicted 95,000 people would lose coverage due to this condition of eligibility yet HHS did not evaluate that mass disenrollment. The court found Medicaid's purpose in the language of the law, "provid[ing] medical assistance," which the court stated was not the same as "health and well-being" because providing medical assistance does more than improve health, it also pays for medical care.[56] The court vacated Kentucky's waiver, but 10 more states had waiver approvals or requests at the time. HHS has been clear – through articulated policy and by opening a new comment period on Kentucky's waiver application – that it intends to implement this new policy.

The details of 1115 waivers are less important here than the ideas driving them. Work requirements reinsert the distinction between the deserving and undeserving poor in Medicaid, which the ACA discarded and the Medicaid Act, as amended by the ACA, does not permit. While policy changes with each new administration, the president is still obligated to "take care that the laws be faithfully executed," meaning that coverage of the eighth category cannot be eliminated by administrative action because the ACA is still the law.[57] Yet, policies that will limit enrollment of the newly eligible population in expansion states are being approved. For example, work requirements have a predictable disenrollment effect (Arkansas, the first state to implement work requirements, disenrolled 18,000 in a few months), and other waiver features such as paying premiums and provisions that demote premium nonpayers to a lesser benefit package (i.e., no dental or eye care) will also disenroll and affect the health of the expansion population.[58] These policies have the effect of restigmatizing populations as both deserving and undeserving: deserving because they are portrayed as helpless and vulnerable, undeserving because they are portrayed as lazy, irresponsible, and needing to have "skin in the game."[59]

---

[55] State Medicaid Director Letter 18–002, Jan. 11, 2018, www.medicaid.gov/federal-policy-guidance/downloads/smd18002.pdf.
[56] *Stewart* v. *Azar*, Civil Action No. 18–152 (JEB) (D.D.C. June 29, 2018).
[57] U.S. Const. art. II, §3.
[58] *See, e.g.*, MaryBeth Musumeci et al., *Approved Changes in Indiana's Section 1115 Medicaid Waiver Extension*, Kaiser Family Found., Feb. 9, 2018, http://files.kff.org/attachment/Issue-Brief-Approved-Changes-in-Indianas-Section-1115-Medicaid-Waiver-Extension.
[59] *See, e.g.*, Seema Verma & Brian Neale, *Healthy Indiana 2.0 Is Challenging Medicaid Norms*, Health Aff. Blog, Aug. 29, 2016, www.healthaffairs.org/do/10.1377/hblog20160829.056228/full/.

Yet, states are exploring expansion precisely because the Trump administration is open to work requirements. This ultimate red-state twist could bring about total Medicaid expansion, which could have the ironic effect of shoring up rather than undermining the ACA. Total Medicaid expansion would mean that the ACA is implemented nationwide (14 states are still opted out of Medicaid expansion as this chapter goes to press). But this form of expansion comes at a steep cost to the Medicaid program and to some of its beneficiaries, who will find that paperwork and other administrative burdens limit their ability to enroll or remain enrolled in a program that historically requires states to enroll everyone who is statutorily eligible. This impoverished population will find itself in the same situation it was in before the ACA, unable to obtain health insurance through public or private means because they are deemed undeserving.

This leads to a key question: if a national policy of universal coverage is normatively beneficial, are federalism compromises worth the costs they impose to achieve that national baseline? From a theoretical and historical perspective, the answer to the first part of the question is yes: national baselines have made a difference for the health of all Americans and especially the poor, but success is more assured if the program is universal because targeting the needs of the poor can stigmatize a program and its beneficiaries.[60] Although a national baseline approach has not achieved universal coverage or a nonfragmented health care system yet, each major federal effort at health care has made strides in this direction to date. Take Medicare as an example. Policy makers believed Medicare would morph into universal health coverage when it was drafted, but Medicare was also a basic mechanism for protecting the elderly from the high risk of impoverishment from medical expenses – a basic role of health insurance, to protect against financial risk. Though it has not become the basis of universal coverage, as an antipoverty measure Medicare is successful. At the time of Medicare's enactment, around 30 percent of the elderly lived in poverty; by Medicare's 50th anniversary, around 9 percent of the elderly were living in poverty.[61] This national social insurance program has been an effective antipoverty policy, especially in combination with the SSA. Is that because federalism was written out of Medicare's design? The causation is hard to prove, but simplification in governance, administration, uniformity, and universality surely have played roles.

By comparison, in 1965, 19 percent of the nonelderly population lived in poverty, and as of 2016 12.7 percent did, which matches the pre-recession poverty rate from 2007. This rate has been fairly steady for decades (though a drop was documented

[60] Theda Skocpol, *Targeting within Universalism: Politically Viable Policies to Combat Poverty in the United States*, in THE URBAN UNDERCLASS (Christopher Jencks & Paul E. Peterson eds., 1991).
[61] Ezekiel Emanuel, *Opening Remarks for Symposium on the Law of Medicare and Medicaid at 50*, YALE J. HEALTH POL'Y, L. & ETHICS, 27, 30 (2015).

from 2014 to 2016).[62] Children have even higher rates of poverty, about 21 percent as of 2016, yet children comprise more than half of Medicaid (and CHIP) enrollees.[63] State variation in Medicaid takes many forms, from the initial choice to opt in (all states participate in Medicaid as of 1982), to payment levels for health care providers, to other state choices regarding the generosity of coverage benefits. Medicaid was not structured to be universal like Medicare was – Medicare demonstrates intentional universalism, and Medicaid exhibits incremental, unplanned universalism – and intentionally universal social programs are stronger politically.

Universal programs are harder to tear down because everyone benefits from them; the polity has a sense of stewardship. Medicare's great success in reducing medical risk and thus poverty for the elderly is rooted in its universalism, as people feel that they have worked to earn what Medicare provides because it is funded in part through payroll taxes – any citizen who works and pays those taxes for 40 quarters automatically qualifies at age 65.[64] Medicaid, as was previously discussed, drew on Poor Laws, welfare programs, and their categorization of the poor, distinguishing between those who qualified as deserving and those who did not. Nevertheless, despite its unplanned universalism, Medicaid has achieved a hidden, near universality, which largely existed even before the ACA added a new category of eligibility. Despite targeting only the deserving poor for its first five decades, Medicaid covers half of all births, more than a third of all children, and is the primary payor for long-term care – anyone who lives long enough is highly likely to become a Medicaid beneficiary.

The ACA created a plan for universal coverage, but it is not a fully universal program in the way that Medicare is because it patches together existing public and private insurance, amending a variety of federal laws and keeping states in the picture to achieve the goals of the law. The ACA's universalism lies somewhere between Medicare and Medicaid, which means it is a weaker law than the intentional universality and uniform programmatic structure of Medicare. The ACA strengthened Medicaid's safety net and appears to have made the program more

---

[62] Jessica L. Semega et al., *Income and Poverty in the United States: 2016*, UNITED STATES CENSUS BUREAU (2016), www.census.gov/content/dam/Census/library/publications/2017/demo/P60-259.pdf.
[63] *See id.* at 18. The report shows that children are disproportionately represented among those living in poverty:

In 2016, children represented:

- 23.0 percent of the overall population.
- 20.0 percent of people in families with income at or above 200 percent of their poverty threshold.
- 28.3 percent of people in families with income between 100 percent and less than 200 percent of their poverty threshold.
- 32.6 percent of people in families below 50 percent of their poverty threshold.

Id.
[64] 42 U.S.C. § 1395c.

visibly popular, or at least less vulnerable, as exhibited by the outcry when Congress proposed variations of weakening the program in 2017. Medicare and Medicaid both contain statutory entitlements, meaning that by law a person who meets eligibility standards must be enrolled in the program – effectively creating a statutory right to health care. For Medicaid, this also means that states are entitled to unlimited federal funding so long as they comply with the Medicaid Act's rules.[65] In contrast, CHIP explicitly does not create an entitlement, so states can cap enrollment, a method for dealing with the program's federal funding limits.[66] Thus, on the universality spectrum, CHIP is relevant only as an add-on to Medicaid.

The ACA has been intensively studied in its early implementation, though evidence on the role of states in spreading universal coverage is somewhat limited, and understanding how implementation differs from the law as drafted is helpful in deciphering the data. Medicaid expansion was designed to be implemented by states working from a federal baseline of universal coverage. Opting out was not part of the law's architecture, though the usual state choices within Medicaid remained (states have a great deal of policy flexibility). Exchanges were designed to be implemented by states, with the federal government operating as a backup for states that could not or would not create exchanges. But the majority of states chose not to operate their own exchanges, creating an unanticipated burden on the federal exchange. The ACA's federalism structure was turned on its head by *NFIB*, and it is not possible to know what implementation would have looked like – or if it would have been successful on its own terms – due to that interruption.

Yet, because the majority of states have implemented Medicaid expansion, studies have tracked and analyzed the effects of expansion. Such studies show that Medicaid expansion increases coverage, which in turn increases access to care, improves the health and financial security of beneficiaries, and may improve population health.[67] Individuals, health care professionals and institutions, and states benefit economically from Medicaid expansion.[68] Individuals are more likely to be able to obtain and keep a job when enrolled in Medicaid because they are healthier and

---

[65] 42 U.S.C. §§ 1396–1, 1396b.

[66] 42 U.S.C. § 1397bb(b)(5).

[67] Olena Mazurenko et al., *The Effects of Medicaid Expansion under the ACA: A Systematic Review*, 37 HEALTH AFF. 944 (2018). The authors studied all literature that included "peer-reviewed empirical studies [examining] the association between the ACA-related Medicaid expansion and any of the major goals of the ACA, among them changes in health insurance coverage, access to care, health care costs, and patient outcomes." *Id.* at 945. Other literature reviews with different methodologies have found similar results; *see, e.g.*, Larisa Antonisse et al., *The Effects of Medicaid Expansion under the ACA: Updated Findings from a Literature Review*, KAISER FAMILY FOUND. (Mar. 28, 2018), http://files.kff.org/attachment/Issue-Brief-The-Effects-of-Medicaid-Expansion-Under-the-ACA-Updated-Findings-from-a-Literature-Review.

[68] Mark Hall, *Do States Regret Expanding Medicaid?*, BROOKINGS, Mar. 26, 2018, www.brookings.edu/blog/usc-brookings-schaeffer-on-health-policy/2018/03/26/do-states-regret-expanding-medicaid/.

less concerned about the narrow range of jobs with health insurance benefits.[69] Community health centers in rural areas of expansion states have experienced a significant decrease in the number of uninsured patients as well as increased screening and detection of chronic and serious illnesses.[70] In California, the percentage of uninsured patients in emergency departments decreased by half and the odds of frequent emergency department use declined for Medicaid patients.[71] None of this addresses the rising costs of care, but that was not the ACA's primary project, coverage was, though the decline of uninsurance is making it easier for hospitals to be fiscally stable and remain open, especially in rural areas.[72]

A common refrain when states opt out of Medicaid expansion is that Medicaid is a failed program or that it costs too much, but these arguments are disproven by data. The hard question is what explanation remains when money and programmatic viability are removed, and this is where history and patterns of state participation in health reform are relevant. Early adopter states tended to engage eligibility expansion on the ACA's terms, often taking advantage of their own developed administrative expertise, and they tended to be states that engaged in health care reforms over time. Historically, certain states have been more willing than others to take new federal money when offered as part of a cooperative federalism scheme. For example, the early expansion states had already expanded Medicaid to nonelderly adults. These same states made the most of Kerr-Mills funding before Medicaid was enacted, and they also took federal funds for predecessor programs.[73]

Given the *NFIB* option to reject Medicaid expansion, states that have been historically reluctant to engage in social programs have also rejected Medicaid expansion or other federalism choices that are perceived as aligning with the ACA, such as state-run exchanges. While these rejections have been written off as political, many are much more complicated than red-state/blue-state politics, with deep roots in the history of health care and welfare. These state choices are not experiments in health policy, they are not based on economics, and they weaken the health reform aim of ending exclusion in health law and policy.

Thus, the deep tensions regarding the role of government in health care, and health care's driving principle, continue. If the debate over health care's driving principle were resolved in favor of recognizing a statutory right to health care for

---

[69] *See* Douglas Jacobs, *The Social Determinants Speak: Medicaid Work Requirements Will Worsen Health*, HEALTH AFF. BLOG, Aug. 6, 2018, www.healthaffairs.org/do/10.1377/hblog20180730.371424/full/.

[70] Megan B. Cole et al., *Medicaid Expansion and Community Health Centers: Care Quality and Service Use Increased for Rural Patients*, 37 HEALTH AFF. 900 (2018).

[71] Shannon McConville et al., *Frequent Emergency Department Users: A Statewide Comparison before and after Affordable Care Act Implementation*, 37 HEALTH AFF. 881 (2018).

[72] Richard C. Lindrooth et al., *Understanding the Relationship between Medicaid Expansions and Hospital Closures*, 37 HEALTH AFF. 111 (2018).

[73] STEVENS & STEVENS, *supra* note 27.

everyone, then the structure of the program would possibly matter less.[74] Would the ACA have been simpler to implement without state buy in? It seems clear that the answer is yes. But the political expediency of health care federalism's structure is hard to measure, and seemingly even harder to get rid of when no right to health is driving the conversation.

CONCLUSION

A movement to have a purely federal, universal health care program, a Medicare for all, gained momentum in 2018. It seems more promising than such notions have for a while, but it is not new – presidents from Teddy Roosevelt to Bill Clinton all tried to create national health insurance. President Obama succeeded at crafting universal insurance coverage, but the political resistance to implementation of the ACA has been potent. What are the health care federalism lessons for health reform efforts going forward? History indicates that allowing states to make health policy choices may do less for health in all its dimensions than it does for intergovernmental relations and political expediency.

The constitutional structure of vertically divided governance that is expressed through federalism made decentralized decision making a key attribute of health care for most of US history. But it has been hard to divorce from the notion that the able-bodied are not deserving of governmental assistance and that state flexibility historically has allowed for discrimination against certain populations. This exclusionary approach was discarded by the ACA, but the reinvigorated federalism of optional Medicaid expansion has spotlighted and facilitated choices that do not serve any of the standard measures of health. Policies of disenrollment through conditions of eligibility contradict existing law, and the return to Elizabethan norms and the renewed use of the term *able-bodied* is concerning because it has little regard for the history of discrimination behind it.

---

[74] No constitutional right to health care exists except for prisoners due to the Eighth Amendment's prohibition on cruel and unusual punishment. *See Estelle v. Gamble,* 429 U.S. 97 (1976).

10

Poverty Lawyering in the States

Andrew Hammond

INTRODUCTION

Fifty years ago, legal aid lawyers challenged Alabama's "substitute father" rule. This rule, used in several states, permitted Alabama caseworkers to deny welfare benefits to children if their mother lived with a man or even had a romantic relationship outside the home. The Supreme Court in *King* v. *Smith*, 392 U.S. 309 (1968), agreed with the legal services attorneys and the lower court that Alabama's practice violated the Social Security Act. In a unanimous decision, Chief Justice Warren concluded that "destitute children who are legally fatherless cannot be flatly denied federally funded assistance on the transparent fiction that they have a substitute father." In doing so, the Supreme Court struck down, for the first time, a state welfare provision based on federal law.

Fifty years after *King*, it is worth assessing the state of poverty lawyering. Lawyering in this area has always been deeply entangled with the actions of individual states. These states act under, within, and against rules emanating from Congress and fashioned in greater detail by agencies and courts. However, 50 years on from *King* v. *Smith*, poverty lawyering is even more state-focused. The increasingly state-based nature of the work has wide-ranging implications for legal practice and the development of doctrine.

The classic formulation of poverty law was to use federal law, either statutory (e.g., *King* v. *Smith*) or constitutional (e.g., *Shapiro* v. *Thompson*, *Goldberg* v. *Kelly*), to invalidate a punitive state law or practice. That work continues and may even experience a resurgence during the current administration. But the classic account of coordinated, strategic federal litigation fails to capture the varied practice that characterizes poverty lawyering in the states today. In particular, the classic account leaves out the thicket of constraints that have grown up around this area of practice, especially in the last 20 years.

Today, many lawyers who represent poor Americans face significant constraints in their practice.[1] Attorneys who accept federal funds from the Legal Services Corporation (LSC) cannot lobby for legislative change. They cannot file class actions. They cannot represent prisoners or noncitizens. Some previously LSC-funded lawyers formed their own organizations to practice outside of these strictures. In light of these federal restrictions and other constraints, this chapter seeks to map the terrain of poverty lawyering to date. Such an effort reveals some of the misguided assumptions about the interchangeability of federal and state advocacy. It also shows how lawyering in the states both supports and weakens federal work.

But first, a definition. My working definition of *poverty law* is the law generated by federal and state legislatures, agencies, and courts as lawyers, advocates, activists, and poor people challenge the rules, regulations, and practices that people with limited means and few resources inevitably encounter in their lives. That law can touch on consumer law, criminal law, family immigration law, and landlord-tenant law. The list goes on and on. One irrefutable area of substantive poverty law is the law regulating how government at all levels distributes public benefits and services, especially medical, food, cash, housing, and disability assistance.

We can debate where this law began. The earliest candidate is the common law tradition of poor relief. One could quibble that the United States has always had some modicum of public assistance, typically administered by municipalities, that resembles the poor relief of English society since the seventeenth century. An obvious candidate is the New Deal brought about by Franklyn Delano Roosevelt's election to the presidency in 1932 and his subsequent three reelections. FDR and his allies in Congress enacted the Social Security Act of 1935, which laid the groundwork for national antipoverty policy. However, the Social Security Act's legacy – an impressive one, at that – lies largely in its creation of old-age insurance.[2]

Poverty law, though, is ultimately that which emanated from a collision of an expanded federal government and its far more ambitious and intrusive domestic policy with the social movements of racial justice, gender equality, and others of the 1960s and 1970s. Movements of people thought of and fought for a new, enhanced role and function of national government. Medicaid, Supplemental Nutrition Assistance Program (SNAP) (formerly food stamps), and disability assistance for poor people (i.e., Supplemental Security Income) all date to this era. Lawyers were not able to regularly challenge welfare practices in court until this period. Following

---

[1] Throughout this chapter, I use various terms to label lawyers practicing in this area, including "antipoverty lawyers," "legal services," "legal aid," and "public interest lawyers" recognizing that each of these carry different connotations from the others, but preferring those shades of meaning, which reflect the diversity of practice, over the inadequacy and redundancy of a single term.

[2] For the definitive account of the first generation of federal and state welfare administration following the enactment of the Social Security Act, see KAREN TANI, STATES OF DEPENDENCY: WELFARE, RIGHTS, AND AMERICAN GOVERNANCE, 1935–1972 (2016).

this flurry of activity, poverty law developed around the precise mechanics of how to apportion those responsibilities among federal, state, and local governments as well as civil society or private enterprise, and how to reconcile government action with fundamental legal principles like equal treatment, nondiscrimination, and procedural fairness.

THE PURPOSE(S) OF POVERTY LAWYERING

Poverty lawyering reflects the range of practice in public interest lawyering generally. There is a robust scholarly literature on the proper role and function of lawyers in social movements and working with marginalized populations. Some scholars have characterized poverty lawyering as ultimately a legitimation project, one that assuages poor people who perceive law as systematically stacked against them. Others concede that systemic work can cause some lawyers to neglect the interests and goals of clients and community-based organizations.[3] More recently, scholars like Catherine Albiston, Laura Beth Nielsen, Deborah Rhode, and Rebecca Sandefur have conducted empirical research, surveying the lawyers who practice in this area.[4] What follows builds on this literature with an up-to-date account of poverty lawyering.

Enforcing State Obligations under Federal Law

Lawyers representing poor clients work to improve their clients' access to public benefits. This work might entail representing clients in administrative hearings, appeals of those hearings, and court proceedings. Over time, antipoverty organizations and even individual attorneys usually develop enough connections with state agencies and local offices that they can contact the agency or relevant caseworker

---

[3] For the classic account of this view, see Derrick A. Bell, *Serving Two Masters: Integration Ideals and Client Interests in School Desegregation Litigation*, 85 YALE L. J. 470, 478–92 (1976). For a recent formulation, see Sandra R. Levitsky, *To Lead with Law: Reassessing the Influence of Legal Advocacy Organizations in Social Movements*, in CAUSE LAWYERS AND SOCIAL MOVEMENTS 157–58 (Austin Sarat & Stuart A. Scheingold eds., 2006). For a persuasive, revisionist account of legal aid that predates the War on Poverty, see FELICE BATLAN, WOMEN AND JUSTICE FOR THE POOR: A HISTORY OF LEGAL AID, 1863–1945 (2015).

[4] Deborah Rhode, *Public Interest Law: The Movement at Midlife*, 60 STAN. L. REV. 2027, 2028 (2008) (pointing out that "[d]espite the importance of American public interest legal organizations as a force for social progress, they have attracted little systematic research"). See Catherine Albiston, Su Li & Laura Beth Nielsen, *Public Interest Law Organizations and the Two-Tier System of Access to Justice in the United States*, 42 LAW & SOCIAL INQUIRY 990 (Fall 2017) (hereinafter *Two-Tier System*); Catherine R. Albiston & Laura Beth Nielsen, *Funding the Cause: How Public Interest Law Organizations Fund Their Activities and Why It Matters for Social Change*, 39 LAW & SOCIAL INQUIRY 62 (Winter 2014). Although this research does not focus exclusively on antipoverty organizations, much of their research applies to poverty lawyering.

directly to resolve the matter without resorting to formal process. Many state agencies and local offices are contending with inadequate training, massive case-loads, and incomplete data. Agencies will want to avoid the prospect of attorneys doggedly challenging their decisions. As a result, repeated formal challenges to agency determinations often cause the agency to seek out the attorneys filing those actions to create some informal process. Sometimes, the agency will change its policy in light of these challenges.

Despite the significant discretion states enjoy in designing and administering public benefits programs, these programs still operate within a federal framework. As a result, public interest lawyers can resort to federal statutes, regulations, and guidance in ways that benefit the lawyers' clients. Attorneys can use these sources of law as a way to persuade states to change their policies to comport with the federal regime. Attorneys can also alert federal agencies to look into state practice. Attorneys sometimes file Freedom of Information Act (FOIA) requests with both federal and state agencies to get a better understanding of government practice.

Attorneys also can file lawsuits on the basis of that law in federal and state court. Admittedly, the opportunities to enforce federal requirements on state and local agencies vary widely across programs. Some of this variation derives from which decisions the federal government has devolved to states. Other variation derives from judicial doctrine, such as whether the federal courts have determined there is a private right of action to enforce federal requirements of a particular social pro-gram.[5] Sometimes the mere threat of the lawsuit can convince states to change their policy or practices. Other times, the filing of a lawsuit can lead the state to settle the matter outside of court. If an earlier, related case led to a court order, such as a settlement agreement or a structural injunction, attorneys may be able to use that decision as a vehicle for continuing to oversee state practice and enforce federal law. Of course, it takes time and resources for attorneys to continue the requirements of a settlement agreement and convince the court to maintain meaningful oversight.[6]

Pushing States to Use Flexibility within Federal Law

Public interest attorneys can also use the flexibility in federal law to push states to make their policies and programs more responsive to the needs of low-income people. For instance, the Food and Nutrition Service identifies 28 "state options"

[5] *See, e.g., Briggs* v. *Bremby*, 792 F.3d 239, 246 (2nd Cir. 2015) (holding that SNAP recipients can enforce statutory time limit provisions in the Food Stamp Act through Section 1983). Congress has been effective at impairing prison litigation. See Brian J. Ostrom et al., *Congress, Courts and Corrections: An Empirical Perspective on the Prison Litigation Reform Act*, 78 NOTRE DAME L. REV. 1525, 1525–26 (2003) (noting the 40 percent decline in prison litigation in the four years following enactment of the Prison Litigation Reform Act).
[6] *See generally*, Jason Parkin, *Aging Injunctions and the Legacy of Institutional Reform Litigation*, 70 VAND. L. REV. 167 (2017).

that allow state governments to alter the SNAP program in their particular jurisdiction.[7] Some of these policies make the program more accessible to senior citizens and people with disabilities. Others simplify deductions for housing costs and child support. For Medicaid, states have to cover certain mandatory populations and provide certain services. However, the federal government will also subsidize states' decisions to cover certain optional populations and optional services. With the Temporary Assistance for Needy Families (TANF) block grant, states have significant discretion in structuring their program, including the ability to define what activities qualify as "work."[8] To be sure, some states use federal law's flexibility in this area to make programs less accessible, but each of these programs offer advocacy opportunities for antipoverty organizations and attorneys.

Indeed, another area of state flexibility is the extent to which federal law permits states to waive federal requirements altogether. Section 1115 of the Social Security Act authorizes the Secretary of Health and Human Services to "waive compliance" with certain federal requirements of public benefits programs including TANF and Medicaid in particular circumstances. The Secretary of Agriculture can also waive certain federal requirements for the SNAP program.[9]

Much of the academic literature around waivers, let alone the media coverage and political rhetoric, make them seem cheap and frictionless. If scholars do focus on the transaction costs, they focus on the federal level, where agencies consider whether to grant the state request. That Washington-centric account is incomplete. It fails to account for the work that goes into persuading a state to ask for a waiver in the first place, how to structure the waiver request, and how to implement state policy in light of the waiver.

To advocate for the waiver, public interest attorneys must identify who in the Governor's Office advises on this issue, either formally or informally, as well as the relevant decision makers in the impacted state agency. Legislators may also get involved. Once the state has decided to request a waiver from the federal government, states must make important choices in the application. Some of these choices can include deciding what areas of the state and to which populations the waiver will apply, as well as how the state's policy will depart from federal law. Although drafting the waiver request is rarely difficult as a technical matter, attorneys often spend considerable time and resources trying to pressure the state to fashion the waiver in such a way so as to benefit their clients.

Once the federal government approves the state's waiver, the state usually needs to promulgate regulations, publish subregulatory policy, and disseminate manuals to instruct state workers. Attorneys typically have begun discussions about

---

[7] The Food and Nutrition Service publishes an annual State Options Report detailing how states use this flexibility, www.fns.usda.gov/snap/state-options-report.
[8] *See* Noah Zatz, *Welfare to What?*, 57 HASTINGS L. J. 1131 (2006).
[9] *See* Section 6(o)(4) of the Food and Nutrition Act of 2008, as amended.

implementation with the state and figured out their own ways to monitor the implementation even before the waiver is approved. Conversely, antipoverty lawyers often challenge waivers that they believe violate federal law and harm their clients' access to services, such as recent waivers to impose work requirements on Medicaid recipients.[10]

Convincing States to Exceed Federal Effort

While much of poverty law operates within a framework of federal statutes and regulations, states can also create programs and legal regimes separate and apart from federal law. Lawyers can push states to legislate or create programs that go beyond federal law. Some of these proposals may be low-cost or no-cost proposals, but are nonetheless difficult to pass in state legislatures. Often, these proposals revolve around an attempt to prevent private actors from discriminating against poor people. For instance, local government bodies can enact a Source of Income ordinance that prohibits landlords from refusing to rent to tenants who pay rent with a housing subsidy like a Section 8 voucher. Legislatures can pass a "ban the box" statute, which prevents employers from asking individuals about their criminal record. Sometimes these proposals mirror federal legislation but extend those protections to a different group. For instance, some states have enacted a Domestic Workers Bill of Rights, extending state minimum wage laws and other labor protections to those workers.

Some proposals, though, require significant state funds. Many states offer a state Earned Income Tax Credit (EITC) that relies on federal income tax reporting. Many states have created separate cash assistance programs that run parallel to the federally required TANF program. These state-funded, state-run programs extend cash assistance to some immigrant families and others excluded under federal law. The last 15 years have seen an explosion in state pre-K programs that draw on federal funds but still require sizable state outlays. As I discuss in the following section, relying on states to finance safety-net programs exposes these programs to the structural instability of state budgets.

Choosing the Tools

Much of the activity of antipoverty lawyers discussed previously implies the use of certain lawyering skills. For legislative advocacy, lawyers may draft legislation, lobby, testify, and otherwise negotiate the legislative process. For administrative advocacy, lawyers may draft regulatory language, comment on proposed regulations, and interpret promulgated regulations and published guidance. Sometimes lawyers are called on by other advocates and service providers to interpret new statutes and

---

[10] *See Stewart v. Azar*, No. 18-cv-152 (D.D.C. Jan. 24, 2018).

regulations. In all this legislative and administrative advocacy, the extent to which legal aid lawyers and other advocates can access the relevant decision makers in each stage of this process varies across states, issues, and agencies. What's more, this advocacy occurs in the context of myriad demands on legal aid organizations' limited resources.

Litigation happens when relationships break down. Poverty law is no exception. When antipoverty lawyers encounter a state legislature or a state agency repeatedly hostile to their clients' demands, these lawyers must consider litigation. The investigation and legal research to bring a case often involve a significant investment of the antipoverty organization's resources. Cases also raise expectations among allied organizations and clients. They also may contribute to a deteriorating relationship with state policy makers. As previously mentioned, the threat of litigation can reinforce advocacy efforts.

If legal aid attorneys do decide to pursue litigation, they often look for pro bono assistance from private firms.[11] Although firms occasionally donate substantial resources to impact litigation in the area of poverty law (and other areas), firms can be reluctant to commit to litigating complex disputes out of concern that they are not using their attorneys in a way that maximizes profits.[12] Moreover, there are some types of poverty law cases, particularly when they involve government relying on private industry for services, where a firm may have a "hard" conflict. For instance, the defendant corporation is an institutional client. Or a firm may have a "business conflict": the firm believes it would be bad for their business if they sued, say, IBM.[13] Furthermore, some activities of the legal aid organization may run counter to the firm's own interests.[14] Even if the case clears the firm's conflicts check and the firm decides to devote significant resources to assist public interest lawyers, the firm as funder can exert influence disproportionate to its substantive expertise, making legal aid organizations reluctant to disagree on litigation strategy

---

[11] DEBORAH L. RHODE, PRO BONO IN PRINCIPLE AND IN PRACTICE 12 (2005) (describing how historically lawyers provided minimal pro bono service and little financial support for legal aid organizations).

[12] The American Bar Association replaced its Canons of Professional Ethics in 1969 with the Model Code of Professional Responsibility and then replaced the Model Code with the Model Rules of Professional Conduct in 1983. Among the other changes to arguably the most important source of ethical guidance for American lawyers, the Model Rules stepped back from the commitments of Canon 8 ("A Lawyer Should Assist in Improving the Legal System"). Canon 8 included ethical considerations exhorting lawyers to "endeavor by lawful means to obtain appropriate changes in the law" where that lawyer "believes the existence or absence of a rule of law, procedural or substantive causes or contributes to an unjust result" including "legislative and administrative changes."

[13] *See* VIRGINIA EUBANKS, AUTOMATING INEQUALITY 39–83 (2017) (detailing Indiana's privatization of its welfare administration by contracting with IBM and the subsequent political fallout and litigation); Norman W. Spaulding, *The Prophet and the Bureaucrat: Positional Conflicts in Service Pro Bono Publico*, 50 STAN. L. REV. 1395, 1395 (1998).

[14] Some legal aid organizations are involved in efforts to make state tax systems more progressive, which often means increasing attorneys' taxes.

when the firm is footing the bill for that particular case (and may be a major donor to the legal aid organization).

THE CONSTRAINTS ON POVERTY LAWYERING

Lawyers' Constraints

All lawyers face limitations in their practice, but public interest lawyers face constraints specific to poverty law. Some of these constraints stem from the restrictions placed by Congress on attorneys funded by the LSC. The restrictions imposed by Congress on LSC organizations do not only apply to state-based lawyering but because much of poverty law is made and administered at the state level it bears mentioning here.

Since the federal government began funding poverty lawyers through the Economic Opportunity Act of 1964, Congress has placed restrictions on how those lawyers practice. Building on demonstration projects funded by the Ford Foundation, Congress authorized a federal Legal Services Program in the Economic Opportunity Act of 1964.[15] Originally housed in the President's Office of Economic Opportunity, federal legal services eventually became funded through its own dedicated federal agency, the LSC. However, when Congress created that agency through the Legal Services Corporation Act of 1974, it prohibited LSC-funded organizations from using either federal or private funds for certain activities. President Nixon had vetoed an earlier version of that bill when it arrived at his desk as part of comprehensive child care legislation. These activities included political activities (including voter registration), lobbying legislatures and agencies except in limited situations, criminal cases except for cases in tribal courts, habeas corpus actions, labor organizing activities, abortion-related litigation, and proceedings involving desegregating schools, military service, or assisted suicide. In 1982, Congress reduced LSC funding by 25 percent and imposed additional restrictions.

Congress restricted LSC-funded programs further through the 1996 Appropriations Act. Congress limited the types of cases that can be brought by prohibiting LSC-funded attorneys from bringing class actions. Congress also limited the clients

---

[15] Alan Houseman identifies five ways in which federal legal services departed from previous legal aid programs: (1) a notion of responsibility to all poor people as a "client community;" (2) the right of clients to control decisions about the solutions pursued for their problems; (3) representation included law reform work, defined as a "commitment to redress historic inadequacies in the enforcement of legal rights of poor people caused by lack of access to the institutions that created those rights;" (4) a "responsiveness to legal need rather than to demand;" and (5) a full range of services akin to what private attorneys provide paying clients. *See* Alan Houseman, *Civil Legal Assistance for the Twenty-First Century*, YALE J. L. & POL'Y 369, 374–75 (1998). *See also* Catherine Albiston, *Democracy, Civil Society, and Public Interest Law*, WIS. L. REV. 187 (2018) ("As public interest law expanded dramatically in the 1960s and 1970s, it came to mean much more than pro bono representation of the poor.").

LSC-funded lawyers could represent by prohibiting them from representing prisoners, public housing residents who faced drug-related criminal charges, and noncitizens except in limited circumstances.[16] LSC-funded organizations were further restricted from lobbying. They could not solicit clients in person. They could not work on matters related to redistricting or the census.[17] Despite these restrictions, it is remarkable how the LSC managed to survive, despite multiple proposals by members of Congress and successive presidential administrations to eliminate it.[18]

The consequences of the LSC restrictions and its decline in funding have shaped poverty lawyering in the states. There are national organizations who, among other functions, serve as support centers to legal aid organizations, like the National Center for Law and Economic Justice, the National Health Law Program, and the Sargent Shriver National Center on Poverty Law.[19] But these organizations do not receive LSC funding because they refuse to practice under the federal restrictions. This is not to say that these organizations are the only places with nationally recognized experts. Indeed, many subject matter experts remain at state-based organizations. Often, national support centers regularly consult with these experts in specific states.

Nonetheless, with the poverty law bar split between LSC-funded and non-LSC–funded organizations, public interest lawyers have to work harder to share their knowledge and coordinate their activities. These restrictions disconnect non-LSC–funded organizations from neighborhood legal services.[20] As Albiston and Nielsen put it in their study of public interest organizations, there is "a vigorous network of national organizations engaged in impact litigation, legislative advocacy, media strategies, and appellate practice" that "are predominately located in large cities on the coasts or in Chicago, in relatively progressive counties, and in counties with

---

[16] For a discussion of unmet legal need among immigrants, see Geoffrey Heeren, *Illegal Aid: Legal Assistance to Immigrants in the United States*, 33 CARDOZO L. REV. 619 (2011).

[17] Initially, LSC-funded attorneys could not claim fees for any case they successfully litigated, but Congress restored that restriction in the 2010 Appropriations Act, Pub. L. 111–117. *See also* David Luban, *Taking Out the Adversary: The Assault on Progressive Public-Interest Lawyers*, 91 CALIF. L. REV. 209, 224 (2003) (arguing that LSC restrictions were designed to remove any form of advocacy beyond individual representation); BRENNAN CTR. FOR JUSTICE, RESTRICTING LEGAL SERVICES: HOW CONGRESS LEFT THE POOR WITH ONLY HALF A LAWYER 9–13 (2000).

[18] Peter Edelman, SO RICH, SO POOR 17 (2012) (attributing LSC's persistence to the "staunch support" of the American Bar Association). The LSC also successfully challenged some of the restrictions. *Legal Servs. Corp. v. Velasquez*, 531 U.S. 533, 536–38, 541–49 (2001) (holding that prohibitions on LSC-funded attorneys representing clients in challenges against federal welfare law violate free speech under the First Amendment).

[19] In the interest of full disclosure, I have practiced at the Shriver Center as a Skadden Fellow and as a staff attorney.

[20] See Catherine Albiston et al., *Two-Tier System* at 1017 (concluding that "political attacks and legislative constraints have limited the scope of [public interest organizations'] activities, and developed a striking, empirically documented divide between local and regional organizations that provide direct services and national organizations that seek law reform").

less poverty."[21] In this higher tier of public interest practice, none of these groups accept LSC funds, and "they depend far less than local or regional organizations on any form of government support." In the second tier of practice, there is a group of local and regional organizations that "rely heavily on state and federal governmental support," are "primarily engaged in direct service cases, and are less likely to engage in the systemic reform activities of legislative advocacy or appellate practice than their more nationally-orientated counterparts."[22] This context is particularly acute in rural areas.[23] The reality of a two-tier poverty law bar flies in the face of the animating idea behind the creation of federal legal services: that the demands of individual clients should alert and inform lawyers and government to needed changes in federal and state law.

Reliance on any significant funding stream can comprise a nonprofit organization's independence and its ability to respond to its clients' needs.[24] Antipoverty attorneys do have access to other ways to fund their work, but the LSC restrictions have teeth because other possible sources of legal aid funding cannot match that consistent national support.

Beginning in the 1980s, state and local governments started appropriating funding for legal aid organizations, and such combined funding now rivals LSC funding. Relatedly, legal aid organizations now receive revenue through Interest on Lawyers Trust Accounts (IOLTA) programs. Starting in the 1980s, state legislatures, courts, and bar associations instituted IOLTA programs to collect pooled interest on small amounts or short-term deposits of client trust funds used for court fees, settlement proceeds, and other client needs from bank accounts. By 2000, every state, the District of Columbia, and Puerto Rico had an IOLTA program.[25] IOLTA has become the second-largest source of funding for LSC-funded organizations, but low interest rates and banking fees have kept IOLTA revenues fairly low. As with state finances, the procyclical nature of interest rates makes it a less-than-ideal funding source for legal aid. Finally, if they succeed in their lawsuits, public interest attorneys can collect reasonable fees for their work.

---

[21] *Id.* at 1016.

[22] *Id.* at 1016.

[23] *Id.* at 1015 (concluding that, based on a national sample of public interest organizations, "rural counties, and especially relatively poor rural counties, are less likely to have a [public interest law organization], and even if they do, that [organization] is more likely to focus on direct services, less likely to have an appellate practice, and less likely to engage in systemic law reform strategies such as legislative advocacy, amicus brief work, or concerted media strategies").

[24] *See* Catherine Albiston, *Democracy, Civil Society, and Public Interest Law*, WIS. L. REV. 212 (2018) (arguing that "as public interest law organizations are currently constituted and funded, they may lack sufficient independence to function as effective civil society organizations").

[25] The Supreme Court upheld the IOLTA program in *Brown v. Legal Foundation of Washington*, 538 U.S. 216 (2003). Under the cy pres doctrine, residual funds from a class action suit can also be distributed to a nonprofit including legal aid organizations.

Donations of time and money by the private bar, while vital, are also unlikely to replace sustained government funding. Like most businesses, law firms struggle during economic downturns, when the need for legal services among low-income people will be greatest and when political pressure to cut public benefits at the state level will be greatest. And as previously discussed, support from firms sometimes comes with its own limitations, not the least of which that private attorneys who are not expert in poverty law may be less qualified to handle these cases.[26] While pro bono involvement has increased since the 1980s, it is still quite narrow and shallow.[27] Only one in five attorneys met the 50-hours-a-year goal set by the American Bar Association. Economic downturns also contribute to declines in charitable contributions from foundations and private donors. Law school clinics can co-counsel for legal aid attorneys, but those partnerships also raise questions about competence relative to full-time, specialist public-interest attorneys.[28]

Setting funding to one side, poverty lawyers practice in an era of increasingly divergent state law. As states depart from federal regimes through state statute, waivers, and parallel programs, attorneys face statutory and regulatory regimes distinct from the regimes encountered by their counterparts in other states. Indeed, as discussed earlier in this chapter, to be effective, poverty lawyers must embrace and exploit flexibility at the state level to best serve the interests of their clients. But the result is that attorneys do not always have model legislation or complaints they can borrow from other jurisdictions.

States' Constraints

Even if this part of the American bar did not practice under any statutory constraints and the laws governing poor people were more uniform across states, poverty lawyers would still run into significant state-level barriers to practice. Compared to the federal level, states' fiscal, legislative, and bureaucratic capacities make them less auspicious arenas of action.

As the political scientist Kimberly Morgan put it, "[R]edistributive programs of the welfare state cannot exist without a politically secure and stable source of finance."[29] State budgets are neither politically secure nor stable. As with the federal budget,

[26] *See* Rebecca L. Sandefur, *Lawyers' Pro Bono Service and American-Style Civil Legal Assistance*, 41 Law & Soc'y Rev. 79, 97 (2007) (calculating that it takes 59 pro bono attorneys to handle the workload of a single, year-round legal aid attorney).
[27] Am. Bar Ass'n Standing Cmte. on Pro Bono & Pub. Serv., Supporting Justice (Apr. 2018) (surveying 47,000 attorneys in 24 states and estimating that in 2016 American attorneys provided an average of 36.9 hours of pro bono).
[28] *But see* Sameer M. Ashar, *Deep Critique and Democratic Lawyering in Clinical Practice*, 104 Calif. L. Rev. 201, 228 (2016) (characterizing many clinics as preferring limited and direct representation over other advocacy).
[29] Kimberly J. Morgan, *Constricting the Welfare State: Tax Policy and the Political Movement Against Government*, in Remaking America at 27 (2009).

state budget processes are highly contested. Many states reserve budget decisions for every other year – in part, because doing it every year would derail any other lawmaking. Unlike the federal government, however, 49 out of the 50 states cannot run a deficit.[30] Governments that cannot run deficits must produce balanced budgets, which put unyielding pressure on countercyclical programs. During economic downturns, the demand for antipoverty programs increases, precisely when state revenue declines. I have shown in the case of TANF that the fiscal realities of state governments make them structurally deficient administrators of countercyclical programs.[31] Whether these deficiencies are determinative will depend on the program, but every program that relies in part on state financing will be subject to these budgetary constraints.

In addition to fiscal constraints, states lack some of Congress's capacity to legislate on these issues. First, state legislatures are less likely than Congress to have professional committee staff. Even fewer states employ nonpartisan staff to research and analyze proposed legislation. This lack of subject-matter expertise has implications in a whole range of policy areas, but for antipoverty policy this lack of legislative knowledge hinders considered action. The field's complexity derives from the federal-state nature of these programs, the budgetary ramifications of tax and transfer programs, and the use of administrative data to evaluate impact.

Furthermore, the legislators face different constraints than members of Congress. Many legislatures meet for only a few months a year. Others meet every other year. The infrequency of legislative sessions, the modest pay, and the professional connections that come with elected office push many legislators to have jobs in addition to their elected posts. For many, this is their first legislative office and the highest office they will achieve. Several state legislatures have instituted term limits, preventing legislators from developing expertise. As a result, many legislators will not know enough about any particular area of law or policy unless they have some prior training or professional experience in that area. And even among the potential areas of expertise, antipoverty policy will typically rank lower than other areas like education and criminal justice. Few state legislators will have the benefit of professional staff, whether partisan or nonpartisan. Those who have personal staff, rarely have staff that can assist the legislator with research and bill drafting.

Into this vacuum of legislative know-how step sophisticated parties with vested interests. Retailers, industry, and state and municipal workers spend significant time, resources, and political capital in each legislative session. By contrast, the lack of legislative capacity also presents an opportunity for public interest lawyers and their organizational allies to draft, shepherd, and block bills.

---

[30] Nicholas Bagley, *Federalism and the End of Obamacare*, 127 YALE L. J. F. 1, 9–10 (2017) ("With the exception of Vermont, the states are legally obliged to balance their budgets every year.").

[31] For further discussion of state budgetary pressures, see Andrew Hammond, *Welfare and Federalism's Peril*, 92 WASH. L. REV. 1721, 1744–46 (2017).

The paucity of expertise in statehouses parallels the lack of expertise in state administrative agencies. Just as the lack of legislative capacity at the state level empowers lobbyists, the lack of bureaucratic capacity empowers consultants. Furthermore, the boom-bust cycle of state finances makes reliance on third-party providers for the administration of benefits all the more desperate. It is not surprising that states increasingly rely on the private sector for consulting and service provision for their safety-net programs.

It is worth asking why the federal government has not privatized in the ways states have. Part of the reason must be that the fiscal pressures, though present, are not as immediate. The mandate in states to balance budgets annually or biannually creates interest and pretext for politicians to characterize privatization schemes as purportedly cost-saving measures. There is also more gridlock in the federal system that makes wholesale privatization of core services unlikely. Additionally, greater technical expertise and know-how in parts of the federal bureaucracy, like the Social Security Administration and the Internal Revenue Service, may also dampen privatization pressures.

This emphasis on states' constraints should not obscure some advantages of state advocacy over advocacy on the federal level. Sometimes, it is easier to form a successful antipoverty coalition in a particular state than at the national level. Working across multiple states allows advocates to take advantage of particularly auspicious political moments that may be distinct from whatever is transfixing Washington, DC. State constitutions can be independent sources of rights. Enforcing those rights through litigation has produced mixed results, such as the decades-long struggle to reduce homelessness in New York City. While there are certainly reasons to prefer state-based work, poverty lawyering in the states operates under constraints specific to states.

CONCLUSION

The constraints that characterize poverty law in the states present opportunities for enterprising lawyers.[32] States' fiscal, bureaucratic, and legislative weaknesses create a target-rich environment for poverty lawyers. Given all these constraints, it is difficult for states to meet their legal obligations. As a result, at any point in time for some number of public benefits recipients and applicants, state and local governments are in violation of some federal law or regulation.

Take for example, the SNAP time limit. Adults between the ages of 18 and 49 who are not working 80 hours a month, not disabled, and are not raising children can

---

[32] For more on this perspective, see Steven L. Winter, *Cursing the Darkness*, 48 U. MIAMI L. REV. 1115, 1120 (1994) (explaining how "every constraint is also an enablement" and that the "social and political context can also create possibilities for reform through litigation quite beyond those sanctioned or even hinted at by the governing legal standards").

only receive SNAP for three months in a three-year period. To meet the disability exemption, many will need third-party verification. This is an extraordinarily difficult policy to implement. For those SNAP recipients who do not meet a federal exemption, a state must verify each recipient's work situation including hours and wages on a *monthly* basis. All this for a program that has been characterized by expansion and a relaxation of conditions. Indeed, SNAP's expansionary period has lasted so long that many caseworkers and even supervisors were not working in the SNAP program before the Great Recession – the last time the time limit was in force in every state.

For attorneys, the challenges in poverty law are less likely to involve crafting a novel legal theory and more likely to revolve around those to be expected with private enforcement of public law. For instance, legal aid lawyers spend a great deal of time and energy finding clients willing to challenge the state in court. If the attorneys are proceeding as a class action, they also need to find clients who can adequately represent a class of plaintiffs. Attorneys must often wage protracted discovery fights with the state and sometimes with county-level or other local officials. Furthermore, what is happening inside a state agency is difficult to know from the outside, especially for advocates whom the state sees as hostile. This is not to say that these challenges are insurmountable. Rather, it is to say that if we care about whether practices and programs that serve poor people comport with fundamental principles like due process and equal protection, we should care about the mechanisms for private enforcement, especially at the state level where government capacity is characteristically deficient.

By moving from purposes to practice to constraints, this chapter risks ending on a mournful note or even a critique of poverty lawyering. That is not my intention. This chapter stands as one attorney's honest assessment of the state of the practice – one that can just as easily be interpreted as a call for more lawyers to do this challenging, varied work. Attorneys who have practiced in this area for decades are some of the unsung heroes of the American bar. These lawyers practice under pressure-filled and deteriorating conditions, zealously representing people who cannot afford an attorney but have meritorious claims in the oldest, wealthiest democracy on earth.

11

Conclusion

A Way Forward

Peter Edelman

Where do we go next? I have three suggestions. One is to enlarge the frame of our work on poverty and race, including a focus on the ever-widening chasm of inequality, and all of it pressing toward the center stage of national attention. A second is to consolidate our work about income, jobs, and cash assistance into a unified frame, which I call a three-legged stool. And the third is to think from a perspective of place, and what that tells us about our antipoverty work.

A LARGER FRAME FOR OUR WORK

We need a banner, a message, a theme, a politics for ending poverty. The substance of ending poverty is complex, but making it a top national priority requires finding a unifying concept. Experience tells us that poverty by itself is not enough to achieve center stage.

I suggest that the unifying banner is economics – the pocketbook. Of course the idea is not new. President Clinton rode to victory with the theme, "It's the economy, stupid." The idea was that voters would believe he was promising to help everyone who needed it. The thought succeeded in reaching people and was a major factor in his election. In office it was more complicated. The expansion of the Earned Income Tax Credit (EITC) in his first term and the economic boom in his second term were positive, to the point that official poverty was down to 11.3 percent when he left office, almost to the 1973 historic low level of 11.1 percent. However, his so-called welfare reform hurt millions of single mothers and their children, and he cozied up to Wall Street. Of course, the cry of economics is hawked by politicians of all stripes, but it is also the way for us, done right.

Our flag of economics goes further than helping the poor and near poor. It is the way to repair our politics generally, and it is also the mechanism by which we can get poverty in front and center in the political process. In the spring of 2018 we saw the successes of Conor Lamb in Pennsylvania and Stacey Abrams in

Georgia – individuals seemingly representative of differing wings within the party but sounding quite alike on economic issues. The pocketbook speaks to all lower levels of incomes and all races and ethnicities, and does not differentiate on gender. The vessel of economics carries a wide variety of goods, but it can sail toward a politics of economic justice.

In the light of the last few decades especially, the flag of economics has to include inequality. We need a politics of FDR updated to the twenty-first century. His words ring out now with a special truth, more than any time since then. He talked of "economic royalists" and "the privileged princes of the new economic dynasties, thirsty for power," and said, "for many the political equality we once had ... [is] meaningless in the face of economic inequality."[1]

This is a fight about power. It is a fight between great power in the hands of a few enormously wealthy individuals and corporations and the rest of us. There are more of us than there are of them, but we can only win if we build from the bottom up, to reach people everywhere and add up to the mass that can take the country back.

The specific content of this chapter is about poverty and near poverty, but the most powerful strategy to win on those issues is to perfect and protect our democracy.

The 2016 election was very much about economics but not in the way it should have been. What happened was not a pretty picture. President Obama had tackled the economics of the Great Recession and made important progress that deserved more credit than he received. He did emphasize economics, and we saw some real wage growth and a drop in poverty. But the gains didn't address the deep-seated financial insecurity and lack of confidence for the future that was gripping too many lower- and middle-income people. Perhaps things would have gone better if he had trumpeted his accomplishments more effusively, but in any event the remaining gaps created a political challenge for Secretary Clinton that she did not meet. She did not convince voters that she would close the gaps, while President Trump in contrast was masterful in manipulating the anger of the people who still felt the hurt.

The debacle was not a new development. Its seeds were sown in the early 1970s. As one example of what happened, income and employment levels for African American men had risen steadily from the end of World War II, but suddenly turned down in 1973 and went in the wrong direction and kept on going. People of all races and genders were stricken, although black men were hit most dramatically.

What happened, of course, was deindustrialization. The good jobs went to other countries or were replaced by automation. New jobs replaced those that were lost, but they were low-wage jobs. They paid poorly at the outset and stayed that way, barely keeping up with inflation. Now half of all jobs in the country pay $38,000 annually or less (if the person has full-time, full-year employment). A quarter of all

---

[1] President Franklin D. Roosevelt, Acceptance Speech at the Democratic Convention (June 27, 1936).

jobs pay just above the poverty line for a family of four, or a little more than $26,000.[2] Families must have two workers to have even a chance of supporting themselves, and single mother-headed families with minor children confront poverty that exceeds 40 percent.

Better jobs do exist, but they are limited in supply and require postsecondary education. The lost industrial jobs did not require even a high school diploma, but those jobs paid so well that workers nonetheless joined the middle class and sent their children to college in droves. The good jobs of the twenty-first century, in such numbers as there are, require specialized high school and postsecondary education that is not available everywhere, especially in inner-city neighborhoods and rural areas.

Deindustrialization meant leaner profits for businesses, and they took steps to protect themselves. Unions lost ground in part due to intensified opposition by management, and companies began to oppose health and safety regulations and minimum wage increases. The attack on unions and regulations weakened the capacity of workers to fight for higher wages and protection in the workplace. Bad went to worse.

All this was part of a structural change that was difficult to repair, to say the least. Democrats led in enacting the Comprehensive Employment and Training Act (CETA) program in 1973 that did create jobs, but President Reagan ended it and whatever good the program had done was gone. No one really tackled the crisis head-on.

Family incomes deteriorated a little more each year. It was like the frog in the pot of water. If the frog encounters a boiling temperature when put into the pot, it will jump out. If the temperature is raised gradually, it will stay in the pot and die when the boiling level is reached.

A version of that parable is something like what happened in 2016. From the early 1970s into the Great Recession, the hurt grew subtly, bit by bit. The people fumed but didn't blow up. But when the Great Recession receded and most of America returned to work while many in the Rust Belt did not, the slow burn turned into rage. It was finally like the frog thrown into the boiling water. The people were furious and, realizing that neither party had addressed their plight, they turned to Trump.

His election put our democracy at risk in multiple ways, but as a consequence also evoked a national wake-up call of potentially enormous power. At a very high price (just think of the retirement of Justice Anthony Kennedy), we have an opportunity to turn the country around, an opportunity to do things right now. At the heart of it is economics – the pocketbook.

---

[2] *See* Elyse Gould, Economic Policy Institute, The State of American Wages 2017 (2018).

Economics as the political framework and as a substantive foundation for people in and near poverty must have four components, covering audience, message, and organizing.

One, the focus must consist of people with incomes up to at least twice the level of the poverty line and a commitment to fight inequality on incomes at both the bottom and the top. Both substantively and politically, the effort must include people at the bottom up to that level that encompasses almost 100 million people (and must include people with incomes down to zero). For a family of three, twice the poverty line is roughly $40,000 annually, and for a family of four it is about $50,000. That nearly one in three people in this country lives below these thresholds is largely the result of the United States turning into a low-wage nation.

Substantively, this income level encompasses the low-wage families who are just one paycheck from poverty, as is often said. In fact people slide in and out of poverty. Those who are above the poverty line and those who are below it are for the most part the same people. Most people who live in poverty are there for a spell and then escape (although typically not beyond the 200 percent level). Our public policies should reach up to the 200 percent level and, in some cases, even higher.

And beyond raising income at the bottom we must tackle inequality at the top. As FDR said, "[P]olitical equality ... [becomes] meaningless in the face of economic inequality" is as true today as it was in 1936. Destructive inequality exists at both ends and it must be attacked at both ends. To make matters worse, President Trump's unspeakable tax law created floods of red ink as far as one can see and then some. This is not only immoral, but also means that Republicans will continue to clamor for deep cuts in programs for the poor and near poor to pay for the gifts handed to the rich.

Two, race, gender, and others subject to discrimination must be major and visible players in both politics and substance. Structural economic injustice has had a disproportionate impact on women and people of color. But it is vital to create a broad solidarity across all races and both men and women around a critical analysis of the economy, while noting that there has been deeper disadvantage due to racism and sexism.

Some antipoverty strategists tend to underplay racial or gender disparities. After all, hunger is hunger whether one is black or brown or white, or male or female. Indeed, one might point out that in sheer numbers more white people are poor than people of color and therefore might argue that we do better politically when we emphasize that fact.

There is some sense in that, but we must call out the racism. People of color receive public benefits disproportionately only because the disparity of poverty is in part the result of racism, whether outright, institutional, or implicit. Discrimination, whether in schools, employment, health care, housing and homelessness, mass incarceration, or elsewhere (and in tandem), creates poverty and perpetuates it. We must call all of it out and fight back.

But it is not either one or the other. We also want people to understand that poverty strikes all races. It is important for everyone to know that whites constitute a larger number of those in poverty than people of color. Too many people who are not poor assume that those in poverty are mainly people of color. This widely believed supposition supports stereotypes and fuels racially motivated opposition to addressing poverty.

The larger version of this question is even more challenging. That is the issue of identity politics versus the claim that Democrats cannot win unless they underplay racial and other identity issues. Of course, some important pocketbook policies that assist everyone also help people of color disproportionately. Minimum wage, housing vouchers, Supplemental Nutrition Assistance Program (SNAP) (formerly food stamps), and so on, help everyone, although people of color do receive more because more of them live in poverty. Nonetheless, there must be visible color in the political message to get more people of color to vote.

This is win-win, in my mind. Emphasizing ideas that cross lines of color is very important – that is one reason for using economics as the flag – but it is not enough. On the merits and to get people with identity issues to the polls, those issues must be addressed explicitly. The issue of identity politics versus ideas that appeal to all has to be both-and, not either-or. Perhaps the both-and approach will drive some white voters away, but it is the right thing to do anyway (and I believe the ensuing turnout will be an increase of votes on the progressive side).

Most important, we have failed to convince people of all races that the enemy is those who use their economic and political power to satisfy their own selfish interests and hurt millions and millions of others. When we talk about the pocketbook, we have to reach people all across the board and get them to understand that their economic injury is coming in significant measure from the top.

Three, economics as our flag will strengthen our advocacy on specific issues. Education, health care, housing, disability, and the like have their own politics, but connecting them to the overarching idea of economics will add to our case.

Good schools and access to postsecondary institutions strengthen the economy. Strong health care produces more effective workers. Affordable housing reduces evictions and stabilizes workforces. Better child care and child development are helpful to current employers and in the future will have more effective workers as the years pass.

Child care is an especially good example, and we see advances there. Organizing and educating for greater support for caregiving can only be enhanced if we emphasize its importance as a pocketbook matter.

The Center for Community Change has put together a group of 20 local partner organizations in 16 states that cuts across parent groups, provider associations, immigrant coalitions, faith-based federations, and multiissue community organizations. Most have leadership that comes from women of color. The aims are to lift up early education as a public good, increase parent subsidies for the cost of caregiving, raise wages for early educators, improve child care quality, and promote race and gender equity within the child care system.

The outcomes of these actors are impressive: major budget increases in at least five states (making the subject a high priority in three gubernatorial campaigns), a significant increase in federal funding in 2018, and a new legislative proposal for a national child care entitlement that has more than one hundred cosponsors in the House of Representatives.

Four, we cannot succeed at scale without organizing at the community level. Lawyers and other policy advocates need to work more closely with local organizers and community builders and vice versa. Organizers and community leaders provide the details necessary to translate community wishes into legislative proposals or litigation put forth by advocates; and advocates, with ideas that originated in communities, need constituents in large numbers to authenticate proposals to the decision makers.

Movement lawyers were reasonably plentiful in the 1960s, both in civil rights and poverty work, and later on behalf of women, environmental issues, and the LGBT community. In the poverty movement specifically, Ed Sparer at Mobilization for Youth Legal Services in New York and George Wiley at the National Welfare Rights Organization collaborated across the country to build a genuine movement toward ending poverty. Both died much too young.

The movement aspects of advocacy dwindled in the late 1970s and in the Reagan years, and the nature of the work changed, too. American apartheid ended even though segregation did not, but the next phase of constitutional advocacy was deemed by the Supreme Court not to be "de jure" but just "disparate impact" and "de facto" and therefore was not responsive. The Supreme Court also said poverty issues did not merit any scrutiny beyond that given to ordinary business economic regulations, and Congress barred federally funded lawyers from engaging in class actions and legislative advocacy. Civil rights lawyers had plenty of work but it was mainly in the form of statutory litigation against discrimination and legislative work principally carried out by inside actors. Organizing on welfare and other poverty issues lost steam, too.

We are seeing a new wave of movements, beginning with Occupy and then Black Lives Matter, followed by the #MeToo Movement, the DREAMers Movement, International Indigenous Youth Council, March for Our Lives, and more. Cutting across all of those specific efforts, the resistance movement carries on the fight to push back against all that President Trump is doing. Connecting these and longer-standing organizers and community builders, on the one hand, and advocates, on the other hand, will produce better outcomes. We have a new opportunity to do movement work.

It isn't just movement lawyering, though. Helped by social media, the resistance movement showed that it could spontaneously catalyze hundreds of lawyers to push back on the Muslim bans and the separation of children from their parents on the

Mexican border. But there are opportunities in communities all across the country to contribute pro bono to make a difference, and these opportunities need not take the form of litigation. Take housing, for example. We can forestall evictions by working in collaboration with residents and organizers. Local zoning, protesting lack of rigor in code enforcement, expanding the supply of affordable housing, and much more are areas in which lawyers can do much more than fighting off eviction of particular clients, important as that is.

Perhaps it is not necessary to say, but the work has to be everywhere and at all levels. Lawyers and other advocates, state and local elected leaders, and civic leaders must all work locally as well as nationally to build from the bottom toward a renewed democracy. The threat to our democracy is quite real.

INCOME, JOBS, AND CASH ASSISTANCE

We are seeing new ideas to address poverty on a large scale. This is exciting. It is the first time we are seeing bold positive ideas on income since the major improvement in the EITC in 1993. One, the Universal Basic Income (UBI), would create a guaranteed annual income and, two, others propose guaranteed job creation schemes. Both are very important but, depending on how they are designed, each presents major problems.

The heart of an appropriate antipoverty strategy is for people to have jobs – jobs that yield an adequate income. Cash assistance must be part of such a three-dimensional strategy but it is not the main event. Jobs are. But creating jobs without cash assistance is also deeply flawed.

The job part of the strategy means increased income as part of the wage itself (minimum wage and laws to treat unions fairly) and wage supplements in cash or cash equivalents (EITC, child and long-term care, housing vouchers, and health care). And actual job creation. But a cash assistance regimen must also be part of a total strategy, and it should be connected to work.

The new ideas are both audacious, but some of their proponents are going at them in a tunnel-vision way instead of with a holistic approach. The UBI proponents seem to show little interest in job policies, and some of those pushing job creation appear to lack interest in cash assistance. Not seeing the forest for the trees, the ideas being put forward raise both structural problems and political concerns.

As currently described by most of its supporters, UBI is troubling on three counts. One, as I said, it seems focused solely on getting money to people. A consequent disconnect between the UBI and the labor market means it would not help them find and maintain jobs. Two, depending on how it is constructed, it could be unnecessarily expensive. Three, and most important at this fraught time, it invites a bastardized version of the idea put forth by Paul Ryan and others who would use it to get rid of existing programs and replace them with a vastly less well-funded UBI.

On the job creation side a number of people are pushing a proposal to create a massive number of varied federal jobs that pay $15 an hour and apparently do not contemplate raises and promotions. Again in brief, the idea is to employ unemployed, underemployed, and low-income individuals employed in jobs that will raise their incomes by doing constructive work for $15 an hour.

This has three defects. One, mirroring the UBI lack of context, the advocates seem not to see the need for accompanying cash assistance as part of a three-dimensional strategy. Two, as of now the jobs are not defined. Some advocates do mention examples of possible jobs but not in a systematic way, and, with the one-size-fits-all $15 an hour model, it appears that the ideas of promotions and careers seem off the table and unconnected to professional norms. And three, again as of now, it is not clear how the program would be organized and managed.

My critique of UBI is not just that we need to pay attention to jobs but also to what kind of jobs we want to create. We aren't interested in just any job even though it does generate some income. Assuaging people's sense of insecurity is surely import-ant, but we can do better. People need to feel independent and valuable, productive and making a difference. I worry that the $15 an hour approach misses the mark, and the mark is important.

As to UBI's tunnel view on cash, the problem revives an old argument. As the Democratic candidate for president in 1972, Senator George McGovern proposed a "demogrant." It was part of a proposal for a far-reaching reform of the entire tax system, raising income and estate taxes on wealthy individuals, increasing taxes on big corporations, and simplification everywhere. For those at the bottom, McGovern proposed that each member of a family would get $1,000 annually. A four-person family would therefore receive $4,000 if they had no income, an amount that would be reduced to zero when the family's income reached the phase-out level of $12,000. Inflation since 1972 is about sixfold, so the $4,000 for a four-person family would be $24,000 now or just about the poverty line for a family of that size. The $12,000 level where the benefit would reach zero would be approximately $72,000 now.

Beginning in the fall of 1970 I had worked closely with George Wiley and the National Welfare Rights Organization to defeat President Nixon's Family Assistance Plan. The plan had been whittled down in its journey through Congress, and we concluded that it did not provide enough for its recipients and also acquired work requirements. A new front opened when McGovern brought out his more generous plan, but while it was better it nonetheless troubled us. In retrospect, two presiden-tial candidates competing over whose guaranteed income proposal was more gener-ous now seems preposterous, but we found both to be unsatisfactory. Among other things, the demogrant as proposed did nothing about jobs.

My friend, Frank Mankiewicz (with whom I had worked for Robert Kennedy), was managing McGovern's campaign, so I turned to him to complain about the problems with the "demogrant." Frank set up a meeting with James Tobin, the Nobel Prize winner and Yale professor, and Ed Kuh, a former adviser to Robert

Kennedy and MIT professor whom I knew well, and others. We argued for something like two hours.

My argument was that jobs had to be the central focus. That encompassed a host
of matters that included assuring low-income people a living wage, especially
including job creation, and particularly focused on people of color because they
were the ones having particular difficulty in finding work. I said cash assistance was,
of course, necessary but it had to be connected to the world of jobs.

My main point was to argue for a robust job creation initiative that focused special
attention on people living in areas with high unemployment. Robert Kennedy and
others had proposed a substantial job creation program as part of the War on Poverty
reauthorization in 1967, but they did not succeed on the Senate floor because
President Johnson opposed it. I found it unacceptable that George McGovern's
friend, Robert Kennedy, along with Frank Mankiewicz who was running
McGovern's campaign would not have a major job creation proposal as part of
the campaign.

It was the economists against me. As economists, they were professionally interested in a system based on money. Simple, they said. No bureaucracy. Just pay out
the money. As H. L. Mencken said, "For every complex problem there is an answer
that is clear, simple, and wrong." This is the essence of the UBI idea when it is
proposed as the sole answer to poverty.

I lost. The economists' idea was elegant. But wrong. (By the time of the Democratic convention, the party's platform said it favored "a decent job for every
American." Too late and without specificity, although the whole issue was hardly
what brought McGovern down.)

THE THREE-LEGGED STOOL

There is much more to ending poverty than income. We need to tackle education,
health and mental health care, housing and homelessness, ending mass incarceration, place-based strategies whether in inner cities or rural areas, civil legal aid,
economic development and entrepreneurship, attacking discrimination of all kinds,
and more. But when we talk about income, we need to focus on three legs: deep
poverty and cash assistance, wages and wage supplements to achieve a living
income, and a system to prepare people for quality jobs plus job creation.[3]

Deep Poverty and Some Form of Cash Assistance to Help

We have a terrible problem caused by TANF: the enormous gap of income at the
very bottom. There are 18.5 million people with incomes below half the poverty line,
below $10,000 a year for a family of three. Much of that stems from the loss of cash

[3] *See generally,* PETER EDELMAN, SO RICH, SO POOR (2012).

Peter Edelman

assistance, which, of course, is TANF. The consequence of the near disappearance of TANF is that there are fewer than three million recipients nationally, under 1 percent of the nation's population, with almost half of those people located in California and New York. TANF's disappearance leaves about seven million people with income only from SNAP in a typical month, which pays only about a third of the poverty line, or a little more than $6,000 a year for a family of three receiving the maximum benefit in 2018. Having SNAP to afford food is crucial, but by itself it is woefully inadequate.

The problems with our public benefits are not the same as they were in 1972. The income supplementation that helps low wage workers now did not exist then. Help for them has been built gradually over the years, albeit not perfectly, with the EITC and the Child Tax Credit (CTC). Those benefits still need improvement, but the glaring gap is the huge hole at the bottom.

A national minimum benefit for TANF to fill the hole would be useful but anything that smells of welfare will be hard to sell, at least for now and maybe on a continuing basis. So we have to talk about other ideas. That's why a well-designed UBI or something like it is very important. However, if the idea is the version of a UBI that would replace all our current programs, it is extremely dangerous as national policy right now and would still be problematic in a more benign political time.

Like the economists I debated in 1972, and even more so now, an elegant computer modeling of a guaranteed income would be inadequate and, currently, toxic. If the UBI is presented as an all-purpose answer right now, Paul Ryan would love it. He would love to enact UBI in return for EITC and CTC and SNAP and housing vouchers and everything else that we have now. The total benefit tendered to recipients would inevitably be less than the sum of the current programs. Ryan has in effect already made that offer, only with a different name on it. We cannot fall into this trap.

That's the first problem.

The second is what I argued in my debate in 1972. It is imperative that our main focus be on jobs that produce a living income. This problem of the UBI could be alleviated by making it the cash aspect of a larger job-centered approach (although in effect it would then no longer be a UBI).

What would be involved is extensive. It starts with the minimum wage. Child care and help with transit to get to work are vital. People with little work experience need training and support. Conservatives claim that people prefer public benefits to having a job and therefore must be subjected to work requirements. This is simply not correct. People greatly prefer to work. But that does not mean they are necessarily ready to succeed immediately in a job search and in the workplace. They may need treatment for substance abuse and/or mental health services. People with minimal work records need concrete job training and subsidized employment, and "soft" supports like learning to write a resume, appropriate clothing, and punctuality. The work of Toby Herr in Chicago shows that a person with limited work experience may need a "buddy" to navigate the working world, sometimes for a substantial time. Many people with modest work experience fail at more than one job before they stabilize and successfully stay with a job.[4] And job creation must be part of a full picture, as I'll discuss shortly.

The right is not interested in the facts, so they just say work requirements will take care of the problem. But some on the left miss the point, too. Having a cash assistance system as the totality of an antipoverty strategy is wrong, too. Having policies like child care, transportation help, and the EITC and the CTC all incentivize work and are vital. But if we really want to reach people with little work experience we need even more. Some of the UBI adherents seem not to understand that, and seem not to have much interest in policies that relate to jobs.

The third problem would be if the proposal is for a universal program with a tax attached to it for people with higher incomes. I have no personal antipathy to that idea, but the politics would be brutal because the gross figure would be thrown around in ways that would make it seem insanely expensive.

With cash assistance in a job-centered approach, we should push for a child allowance or a family allowance or, better, a broader construct of some kind that would not be limited to children or families with children. The latter would have the advantage of having a basic income for all that would include young people struggling to get into the labor market and older people not yet old enough to collect Social Security. Recipients would receive the full amount, with the benefit decreasing gradually as income increases up to a total phaseout point. The program should be administered at the federal level to avoid bureaucratic attitudes at the state and local level, and should be run in the most client friendly method. In fact, the program could be built out from the EITC, starting benefits at zero income and adding people with no children into it. Whatever the frame, it should be managed by the Internal Revenue Service or the Social Security Administration.

Even in a relatively hospitable political time, I would not abandon what we have achieved unless the atmosphere changed radically. It was developed with sweat and blood over a long period and it works reasonably well except for people at the very bottom. Building onto our current framework, we could add a base income for people of $6,667 annually for a family of three, plus SNAP. The total would be about two-thirds of the poverty line, with a formula to reduce the payment as income goes up. The payment would be complemented by the EITC and the CTC for those who find work, with housing vouchers available to all who qualify for them and help with child care to all who need it. Arguably, even without a cash payment for those at the bottom, a guarantee of SNAP, help with child care, and housing

---

[4] *See generally*, Toby Herr & Suzanne L. Wagner, Project Match, Persistent Nonworkers among the Long-Term Unemployed: The Implications of 20 Years of Welfare-to-Work and Workforce Development Research (2011).

vouchers could constitute the baseline, if that is more acceptable from a political viewpoint. It would be calibrated so it would always be more attractive to work than to rely solely on benefits.

Whatever the combined cash and in-kind portion adds up to, it must not be considered in a vacuum. There must be a framework. Wherever people can be helped to get available jobs, a structure has to be created to help them. Where people live in places with few jobs, an honest and just approach would help people move out of the area if they prefer, as well as pursue economic development where they live now. People who prefer to stay would have a limited income on which to subsist unless they find a job.

The facts are otherwise now. People in deep poverty live disproportionately where there is little work: the Mississippi Delta, the Black Belt in Alabama, Appalachia, the colonias in South Texas, and on Indian reservations. Due to the damage TANF has caused, large numbers of people in those places subsist only on SNAP, period. Extended families do what they can but life is grim. And all of it is essentially out of sight to the rest of the country.

One thing is certain. We need to convince the rest of the country to help the shocking number of people who live in extreme poverty. This is not easy, but Robert Kennedy went to Mississippi and saw the children who were suffering from serious malnutrition, and from that day on he told people all over the country what he had seen. The ultimate result was the SNAP program we now have.

Living Income from Work and Work Supplements

I started with deep poverty because it is so serious. Our overall policy aim, though, must be jobs that produce a living wage and have the fewest possible people who receive cash assistance and SNAP as the major source of their income. And this should be done without work requirements. Incentives to work should be built in. The vast majority of the poor want to work. People living in poverty get most of their income from working. Seventy percent of the income of people who live in poverty comes from work, typically only part-time or part of the year or both, but there are some who have little or no income and we must help them. Their income must be increased.

This brings us to the second leg of the stool, which is about income from work and from benefits connected to work, beginning with those on the very bottom up to 200 percent of the poverty line.

We have made progress but we have much more to do. To begin, we need to emphasize what we have accomplished. If we did not have the public policies we have in place, we would have almost 90 million people in poverty instead of the 41 million we have. We need to remind people of that, frequently and strongly. Paul Ryan and others repeat over and over that our public policies are a failure. They say that because we have 41 million people in poverty our public policies are a failure.

We know that repetition of lies begins to find acceptance after they are repeated again and again. We need to repeat the facts just as often.

The list of the programs that are effective is lengthy: Social Security, SNAP, EITC, CTC, housing vouchers, unemployment insurance, Supplemental Security Income (SSI), Social Security Disability Income (SSDI), workers compensation, paid leave, and more (including Medicare and Medicaid, which are not counted for purposes of whether someone is poor). Without all those we would have twice as many people in poverty.

Why are there still 41 million people in poverty? The biggest cause is that we are a low-wage nation.

Apart from the special need to help people at the very bottom, we need to raise wages and wage supplements, and there is much to do to make that happen. Altogether, improvements in all the existing programs can add up to a substantial increase in income, but there is no national understanding of the importance of this fact. We are raising the incomes of millions of working families – including people who voted for President Trump, I am sure – but they do not understand how important this is and who made it happen, let alone the need for more investment in these programs. In and of themselves, these programs make up an extremely important progressive strategy against poverty.

The minimum wage is the most obvious item and the only one that has visible politics, both nationally (although not successful in recent years) and at the state and local levels, which has produced significant success. Advocates of the other programs generally do their work more narrowly and more quietly, except perhaps for child care and paid leave.

The challenge is to tie all of this into a visible package. Of course, the biggest task now is to protect these programs from budget cuts and destructive policies like work requirements. But we need to do more. Other than emphasizing the minimum wage, candidates don't include these policies in stump speeches. Some talk about child care and paid leave, which certainly speaks to people, but do not mention other relevant programs. Candidates should emphasize all the policies together and make such an important difference. We do not hear that now.

It struck me that Secretary Clinton's emphasis on child care and the CTC did not move the needle much. Her arguments sounded wonky – programs that seemed out of context. The larger point would have been to explain that the programs are part of a strategy that, in the aggregate, would significantly increase people's incomes and improve their lives. That would have had political oomph.

The nearly 60 million people with incomes between the poverty line and twice that line should be voting Democrat, but too many are voting either Republican or not voting at all. Democrats are now pushing Medicare for all, free tuition for college, and a $15 an hour minimum wage, all of which are major steps. But there is another major item. For years, Democrats have fought successfully to raise the income of people stuck in low-wage jobs, and they will keep on fighting. Having done so, it should now be a major plank in the Democratic platform and in the playbook of every Democrat running for office.

A National Framework for Employment, Including Job Creation

The third leg of the stool is job creation and its role in a larger overhaul of our labor market. We can't have a useful discussion of job creation if we don't nest it in a larger context.

Other than the historic New Deal job creation programs during the Great Depression, job creation at scale has not occurred with the exception of the CETA program that I mentioned earlier. Important pilot projects like New Hope in Wisconsin took place in the nineties and Congresswoman Jan Schakowsky and Congressman George Miller introduced important job creation bills in the Great Recession (and there was Robert Kennedy's 1967 proposal mentioned previously). By contrast, while President Obama's 2009 Recovery Act boosted demand for labor, it had only a modest (and successful) job creation initiative that was tied to TANF but nothing more. Between Obama's omission and the Republican control of Congress thereafter, the TANF-related program expired quickly.

Particularly in the light of the election of President Trump and the ensuing call from many quarters for more far-reaching proposals on a number of subjects, members of Congress, outside advocates, and policy analysts have begun to come up with various job creation ideas.

Even before 2017, numerous people had realized that income from wages and wage supplements was not increasing satisfactorily and that people in high-poverty areas were not finding jobs at all. Ideas for job creation began to appear that would create reasonably paid jobs, tighten the labor market, and be especially important for people living in areas with high unemployment. For example, Senator Cory Booker and Representative Bonnie Watson Coleman have introduced a bill for 15 pilot job creation projects in areas in high-unemployment communities, both rural and urban. It is a worthwhile beginning.

Booker and others are doing what they should do – legislating. At the same time, a far-reaching and more futuristic discussion is taking place, which is also important. One set of people proposes $15 an hour for an open-ended number of jobs without definitive career pathways or specific suggestions of how the program would be operated. The other group argues for what I call "national needs" jobs – jobs doing things our country needs: infrastructure, caregiving, housing, green energy, health care, and so on. Both ideas would require significant funding if and when they operate at scale, so if a major initiative begins to get traction its supporters will need to be clear about the cost and how to find the money as well as lay out the details of the proposals.

Other than CETA, we have never had a national policy to create jobs other than during recessions. The ambitious jobs proposals I've just mentioned are a new idea.

It should be routine to have job creation programs during recessions, and we know how to do it even if we don't often do it. But that is quite different from job creation in times of low unemployment nationally. Jobs created in recessions generally are temporary, but most such jobs would not make sense as careers.

Before I delve further into the ideas, it might be helpful to understand that we already use job creation in various ways. Understanding them opens up a larger map so we can see where job creation fits in and reveals that we really have no overall systematic framework for job creation.

The larger map shows that job creation in the sense of paid work experience begins in high school. We don't call it job creation, but it is. I am talking about high school, where we call it career and technical education (CTE), which at its best includes paid work experience. It tends to be symbiotic with places where employers are clamoring for employees. If you go to the Nashville area, you'll see highly sophisticated manufacturing employers operating in tandem with schools (and postsecondary institutions) to educate young people for excellent jobs. The students are paid for their work and, just as important, their CTE curriculum also contains the complete program necessary to go to a four-year university if that is their preference. Those students have the opportunity to obtain the best jobs of the twenty-first century. (Apprenticeships are a variation. Drawn from Germany and other European countries, they are a form of paid work experience or job creation on the way to permanent employment. We have done little of it in our country, but we should.)

But it's all spotty. Young people of color don't get the same opportunities, even in the job-abundant Nashville area, and girls don't get treated justly either. And in areas where employers aren't clamoring so much for employees, they are less hungry for recruiting young people regardless of color. Of course, the engineers and computer whizzes and the electricians and plumbers could go somewhere else if the particular place isn't hiring, except somebody has to get them started. Every school system has the responsibility to offer a first-class CTE program, but too many don't. So much of our country is divided – the places where things are fine and the places where they are not. Education is not different.

The picture remains spotty as young people grow up. What about the young people who have dropped off the pathway, not finishing high school and sometimes acquiring a criminal record? Look at YouthBuild. The heart of what they do is job creation, focusing on building houses (although they are paid more like stipends than the wage of full-fledged employees). We need to invest far more than we do to help young people get back on the track. Job creation is a part of that effort.

AmeriCorps changes lives. People of all ages can participate. It's community service and, while we don't say it out loud, it's job creation (although more as a stipend than a wage). Community service takes a variety of forms – Teach for America and City Year are partially funded by AmeriCorps – and also serves as a bridge into the labor market.

Then there is a workforce development structure that has been in place since the 1960s with federal assistance. These services are meant for people of all working ages. This system does not include job creation although other than that some of the local agencies do their work quite well, executing job training where useful, offering counselors who help people, finding jobs, and arranging child care and transit. Some do not.

Subsidized employment would fit in here, filling in the lack of job creation in the toolkit in workforce development. It is a kind of job creation that helps people to obtain a steady and reasonably paid job as a transition to permanent work. Funding of subsidized jobs is very important. It is not a new idea, but it has been re-engineered in the last few years. Senators Ron Wyden and Chris Van Hollen and Representative Ro Khanna all have bills on subsidized employment, already introduced or on the way. These will be important contributions and could serve both for-profit and nonprofit employers.

Finally in the current menu of what exists or is being proposed in Congress is the idea of having jobs programs in places of high unemployment. Senator Booker's bill is an example of that. Indeed, the Booker and the subsidized employment bills could be brought together because many or perhaps all those who benefit would be temporary employees on their way to permanent work. The Booker bill is place based while the subsidized employment bills are not.

We need to pay attention to all of this and build on it. We have existing job creation programs and they deserve much more funding than they receive now. So before we talk about spending billions for jobs that aren't connected to any framework, we need to look at the ones we have.

Beyond what I've laid out, I favor a job creation program that would involve real jobs where workers would work side by side with existing workers – no difference. Even though we are close to full employment nationally at the moment, there are big gaps in specific places and among people who have historically been left behind, and there are millions who do have jobs but are paid shockingly low wages. And as important as they are, the minimum wage, the EITC, and the other wage supplements are not getting us to where we need to be.

Beyond our current national needs, some observers believe that the continuing march of technology will dry up many of the jobs we now have. They say we must be prepared with new jobs. Perhaps, and if so, it adds another support for job creation. (Personally, I am something of a doubter. I remember vividly that in 1963 the Department of Labor released a widely publicized report that prophesied a looming technological revolution that would cause a mass loss of jobs. We still have more or less enough jobs. The problem is that they're lousy jobs.)

Current public investment in national needs is grossly inadequate in many areas and getting worse and worse as our population ages. We read about it every day, and it's far from just infrastructure. Of course, we will have to pay for what we need and that will require a serious national discussion, but we should spend on what we need (and only what we need).

So I would create jobs that our country needs. Some commentators believe a policy like the UBI is the answer to the disappearing jobs. I do not agree. People maintain their dignity by working, especially if their work is on tasks that make our nation a better place. There is so much to do. If people have a choice between receiving a check or doing something useful, most would do the latter. Cash assistance is needed, but as an auxiliary to jobs.

UBI is not the answer if there is a shortage of jobs. The idea of money in lieu of jobs is not what we need. We need jobs. The $15-an-hour-jobs devotees and I agree on that. Where we differ is on how the jobs should be created. Here is an example of what I would suggest (and my colleagues and I at the Georgetown Center on Poverty and Inequality have written at length about it): caregiving.[5]

We have an enormous need for caregiving, for children (including child development, not just caregiving), for the elderly, and for people with disabilities. There is an existing framework in place in governments at all levels, and a delivery system run by people who live in communities and don't work for governments. Public funds to run it are essential, with copayments by recipients or families based on their ability to pay, while the delivery of services occurs at the local level by nongovernment employees.

Beyond the expansion of caregiving jobs along with improved wages and quality of service, the program would recruit for applicants among low-income people wherever they live. Applicants would be trained as any employee would be. This is crucial.

All this is certainly ambitious, and it would not be put into place instantaneously. It would take time to grow the system, both substantively and financially, but it could be carried out within a framework that already exists. That is vital.

This is different from the jobs of the Depression. Those were meant to be temporary. Hiring people now for $15 an hour in a program that mimics the Civilian Conservation Corps or the Works Progress Administration will for the most part not do for permanent employment. A permanent job has to be permanent, not a rerun from a Depression design. If we want real jobs that offer careers with promotions, they have to be just that: careers with possible promotions and built-in structures that operate side by side other employees.

Nor should caregiving be the only area of national need we pursue. Infrastructure is obvious, but to be done right requires a commitment to recruit low-income people in the same way I propose for caregiving. The Affordable Care Act and the new Medicaid have engaged in this kind of job creation, although not with enough focused effort on the training and hiring of low-income people. Housing is a great possibility. The need is enormous. YouthBuild has been doing it for years and with

---

[5] *See generally,* Nina Dastur et al., Georgetown Law Center on Poverty and Inequality, Building the Caring Economy: Workforce Investments to Expand Access to Affordable, High-Quality, Early and Long-Term Care (2017).

great success although not at the scale that it deserves. And there are surely permanent jobs in environmental careers and green energy, among other growing industries.

In the meantime, current programs with job creation features must be improved and built up further. Promoting multiple pathways to success is essential. Career and technical education must be brought up to speed everywhere. Apprenticeships must be expanded. AmeriCorps should grow with increased stipends. Organizations like YouthBuild should expand. Subsidized employment should be legislated into existence and grown.

BEYOND THE THREE-LEGGED STOOL: HIGH-POVERTY PLACES

Everything I've discussed comes together exponentially in places of concentrated poverty. Comparing poverty in 2018 with 1968, inner-city neighborhoods and rural areas still have serious problems and some are even worse off. Every aspect of poverty converges there and the sum of its parts is even more troubling. Looking ahead, particular attention must be paid to place-based solutions.

Improving employment and income is number one, but there is much more to do and they all play a role in getting more jobs for residents. Schools including children aged zero to five, health and mental health care, housing, mass incarceration, community safety, the systemic effect of racism, and more are all important in and of themselves and crucial to increase employment in the area. We have to work on all of it simultaneously.

There is some good news here. The Bedford-Stuyvesant project in Brooklyn, New York on which I worked with Robert Kennedy ran as one large organization that was supposed to do everything. To be sure, entities like these did a great deal, but it was difficult to manage all the responsibilities when they were placed under one roof. In addition, the idea of a community development corporation was almost by definition anchored in housing and economic development. As time passed, the vast majority of the 2,000-plus community development corporations (CDCs) focused solely on developing low-income housing, and not on scale. Not bad, certainly, but not the multifaceted organizations that were envisioned.

In recent years, new kinds of multifaceted initiatives have begun to pop up, including President Obama's Promise Neighborhoods legislation. Instead of a single organization doing everything, the new social entrepreneurs operate on principles of partnership, creating relationships both inside and outside of the neighborhoods, and bringing multiple kinds of expertise to meet residents' needs. Instead of centering activities solely on housing and occasional community development, the new creators feature different kinds of hubs and build out their partnerships like spokes on a bicycle.

The hubs are schools, Head Start programs, community health centers, "modern" settlement houses, and mental health professionals, to name a few. The spokes are anything that might help people – job training and placement, financial literacy, housing assistance, legal aid, parenting education, family counseling, public benefits, and much more. Characteristically, the hubs and spokes operate at scale, reaching hundreds and sometimes thousands of people, so they make a notable difference. Some of the services relate to parents to make things better in the here and now, and some relate to the futures of children, for the next generation.

These initiatives are not magic. They can't conjure up a job that does not exist. They can't build affordable housing if there isn't funding. They can't find income if a family is not eligible for any public benefit. They can't create accessible transit if there is none. And all too often now, undocumented people can't be saved from being terrified when they have all too many reasons to be so.

To address these structural problems, lawyers, organizers, and other advocates need to connect to these new initiatives. More broadly, the new entities need to have connections to all relevant outside forces. If one lesson of the last five decades is the idea of hubs and spokes, another is that the leadership in a high-poverty place cannot obtain everything needed within its own boundaries. It should have a local governance of some kind, but it needs external partners whether they are governments and their agencies, educational systems and institutions, businesses, unions, foundations, or faith organizations. Those who would reduce poverty in places where it is most serious must get themselves connected to these external resources.

But even where the outside is not as responsive as it should be, there is much that can be done.

In Tulsa, Steven Dow leads the Community Action Program (CAP) Tulsa, which has its "hub" in a Head Start program that serves 2,300 children at 11 sites and 350 families that receive home visits. Just running a Head Start program of that scope is impressive, but CAP has expanded in other directions, making it a set of programs that is far broader. CAP Tulsa has a large contract with Family and Children's Services (FCS), with 27 family specialists and 11 mental health specialists. Each morning an FCS social worker meets children and parents ready to help if asked and noting if something seems amiss that could be a reason for following up. Every family has a support person who is an MA or BA social worker, and FCS offers many classes for parents as well. When called on, a multiplicity of partners is summoned to deliver the needed help.

CAP Tulsa is one of the best examples in the country for what are called two-generation or "2-Gen" programs that combine child development and family support. FCS is a partner with CAP Tulsa from the moment a child starts at Head Start. They conduct a family needs and strengths assessment with all parents at the very beginning. They organize and encourage parents to join social groups that result in important friendships and peer education. The mental health team works with about a third of the children, usually in tandem with their parents.

Career Advance works with the parents, especially on preparing for a job or a better job, with about half of the parents participating. Some of the steps are small but important: helping parents get a GED or study English as a second language, or simply assisting families with house cleaning. Smart Singles is a group that helps to identify healthy relationships and educate parents on domestic issues that could be barriers to success. Healthy Women, Healthy Future is taught by faculty from the University of Oklahoma, College of Nursing, and helps young women decide whether to get pregnant and how to handle a pregnancy.

Learning at Home, the home visiting program, has 17 staff members serving 350 families at any one time. The team does 90-minute home visits every two weeks for families who have children up to three years old, spending about a third of the time in child interaction with the parents – reading, singing, and playing with the children – and the rest of the time with the parents, providing developmental information and addressing issues of family well-being.

Concerned with the economic well-being of parents, and seeing an opportunity with the enactment of the Affordable Care Act, CAP Tulsa created a program – the beginning of Career Advance – to train parents for health care jobs. By now it has a track record, but the experience shows how difficult it is to succeed. Many interested parents were not remotely ready to do community college work. CAP had to back up and develop what turned out to be a four-tier developmental education system, with the largest tier delivering elementary school–level instruction in English and math. Each accepted person is given an academic coach, a career coach, a financial coach, and a life coach. By now some hundreds have obtained jobs despite the struggle. It is working.

Logan Square Neighborhood Association (LSNA) in Chicago is more than half a century old. It has grown with the times – initially a traditional settlement house for an Eastern European clientele and now serving mainly Latinos – and is doing work at the cutting edge. With 51 member organizations and 225 partner organizations, LSNA organizes and advocates on affordable housing, education policy, voting, and immigrant integration, but its national claim to fame is its Parent Mentor program.

Parent Mentors are parents, mostly women, from the neighborhood schools who have children in third grade or lower and are recruited at the start of the school year. They are generally low-income immigrants from Spanish-speaking homes who typically have not been working outside the home and are not active in the community. Once trained, the parents spend two hours a day in the classroom working directly with children, followed by a workshop to build leadership skills. They receive a $500 stipend at the end of the year. There are about 200 parent mentors in the nine neighborhood schools at any one time, and since the program began in the 1990s more than 2,000 parents have participated.

The track record is wonderful. Some become teachers or coordinators in the programs or work in a school as a cafeteria worker or bus monitor. Others start small day care centers, work in community centers, or do something else in the neighbor-hood. Many get GEDs. Logan Square gets the mothers involved in public issues, especially issues of direct interest in their community. The mothers have testified frequently in the state legislature and have gone to Washington, DC to lobby on immigration reform. The program has been replicated elsewhere in the state and around the country and it deserves to be spread even further.

The Northside Achievement Zone (NAZ) is in North Minneapolis and is one of the Promise Neighborhoods created by President Obama to improve outcomes for children and families in neighborhoods of concentrated poverty. Built out from a previous nonprofit organization and headed by Sondra Samuels, a long-respected leader living in the neighborhood, the program is located in an African American neighborhood troubled with high poverty, unemployment, and extensive violence.

Having grown up in the city, I found myself especially disturbed when I visited the environs of NAZ. It is close to downtown, within eyesight of the tall buildings, but it might as well be a thousand miles away. It reminded me of Alcatraz, where the inmates could see San Francisco with no possibility of getting there.

That said, NAZ is making a difference. The preexisting organizations already there were doing good work, but there was no ecosystem pulling them together. Working with its partners, NAZ created a family-friendly structure. The family coaches are like home visitors, recruiting families initially and continuing to visit them at home and in the neighborhood. They do informal coaching and connect families to Zone partners who have expertise in education, parenting, child care, housing, jobs, and financial literacy.

The Zone is two-generational and includes parent involvement in strategies for children, services directed at parents, classes at NAZ's Family Academy, and an emphasis on parents as leaders. The academy's classes track the age of the children: College Bound Babies (three and under), Ready to Succeed (ages four and five), College Bound Scholars (kindergarten through fifth grade), and Family Foundations for all parents. Zone staff do not tell parents how to parent, but rather offer a toolbox of strategies.

In just a few years, NAZ has matured, nurturing and supporting a group of strong partners with knowledge and capacity that would be impossible to create as a single organization. It has already made a tangible difference for hundreds of families.

Of course, there are challenges that are beyond NAZ and the local community. The city and its powerbrokers (and the state) should be ashamed for what they have allowed to happen. Jobs, especially good jobs, are a major problem, for which the business community must take some of the blame. And it is difficult to improve the neighborhood schools when they are controlled by the system's central office. The police are a continuing problem as well. Affordable housing is a governmental responsibility in part. Mass incarceration is a huge barrier. Racism is a continuing and malignant force. Still, the Zone is making an identifiable difference in the lives of many people, even if it has not yet been able to affect the level of poverty in the neighborhood as a whole.

For a long time Rosanne Haggerty has been one of America's great advocates for ending homelessness. Some years ago, though, she began to realize housing alone is not enough, noting that it needs to be situated in healthy and safe neighborhoods and people need to be able to pay their rent. She began looking at how homelessness might be prevented in the first place. Never one to make a small plan, she found herself in the Brownsville neighborhood in Brooklyn, New York, a place of deep poverty where becoming homeless was a common experience.

Brownsville is tough, for sure. In a neighborhood of 88,000 people, 36 percent have incomes below the poverty line and 44 percent of working-age residents are out of the workforce altogether. Its concentration of public housing is the largest in the country and it has the highest homicide per capita of any precinct in the city, with perpetrators as young as 12.

Haggerty did a reconnaissance and found that there were many public agencies and nonprofit organizations that serve neighborhood people, but in pieces, not as whole people or families. She thought she should look for a way to connect the agencies and organizations and get them to serve people comprehensively. She called it the Brownsville Partnership.

She began by focusing on homelessness prevention for people on the brink of being evicted. Using tips from various social service agencies and going door to door, she and her staff found people on the edge and coordinated with various partners to keep them in their homes. Whether the key to preventing an eviction is a lawyer, public benefits, a health or mental health professional, a job, a charity, or all of the above, the Partnership prevented more than 800 evictions and connected more than 350 residents to jobs.

Haggerty realized that the heart of the problem runs much deeper – a lack of jobs. She and her staff decided to embark on a campaign to find five thousand jobs for residents of Brownsville as the central element of the work of the Partnership's efforts. It has not been easy work, but she has almost realized this goal.

Haggerty is determined to serve people in deep and chronic poverty whose needs often demand extra attention, make employers less welcoming, and require additional funding to address. Building relationships with high schools and community colleges has been slow, and more partners addressing education and training, health and mental health and addiction issues, domestic violence, housing issues, and criminal justice are needed. Still, she has persevered.

Complementing the jobs work, the Partnership largely shifted from direct services to more of a switchboard function, serving as a hub for the partner groups. Eviction issues were picked up by a legal organization located in the Partnership's building. An improved communication system set up a monthly partner meeting and improved coordination of the work. Place-related partners worked on improving safety in public housing blocks, restoring a century-old park, and reclaiming a historic market street that had become blighted and dangerous. Other specific projects include food systems, early childhood supports, and a youth corps to improve public spaces and solve community challenges.

Looking forward, Haggerty is seeking partners for a tech incubator and sites for new mixed-income housing. She is working toward a collaboration with the community, the police, and mental health professionals to reduce harm to children exposed to violence and to assist volatile families. She is also working on improving financial services starting with a free-tax preparation site at the Partnership building.

There is a great deal of action at the Brownsville Partnership.

The New Haven Mental health Outreach for MotherS (MOMS) Partnership in Connecticut emerged from the leadership and entrepreneurship of another remarkable individual: founder Megan Smith, a professor of psychiatry, child study, and public health at Yale Medical School.

Battling mental illness is the hub of this partnership and its strategy is centered on stress management groups. A total of 20.6 million children live with a parent with mental illness, and the incidence is disproportionately high for children in low-income families. Coping with the serious stresses of daily life that come with poverty or near poverty takes an enormous toll. These daily struggles do not necessarily spell psychosis for the adults involved, but they make life miserable, and that misery often spills over onto children, with long-term implications.

Using multiple strategies of community outreach, Community Mental Health Ambassadors (who are former participants) recruit mothers to enroll in the groups, which meet twice a week in two-hour sessions over a period of eight weeks. The staff starts by assessing needs; moms are then assigned to classes depending on their measure on the depression scale. The groups focus on cognitive behavior therapy but the classes are decidedly down to earth, offering mothers techniques to manage stress and take time for themselves, and educating mothers about resources in the community. They also provide babysitting. Participants who live in public housing get $20 Walmart gift cards for each session they attend. Others receive a basic needs bag that contains items that the moms request.

MOMS also offers job-readiness classes that help with resumes and mental health–oriented interview training, focusing on the stresses and fears that relate to the job-seeking process. A former participant can come by one of the Partnership's sites any time she is stressed or needs to talk. A clinician is available to talk and to direct her or her child to other services in the community. One former group member offers financial literacy classes, too.

The groups are obviously not the solution for every problem, but participants in the stress management groups say they are now better parents and better spouses. Of course, such problems like the lack of jobs, basic skills, affordable child care, and affordable housing, as well as mass transit, domestic violence, addiction, and so on, do not go away magically, but those who have participated in the groups say they have benefited.

Smith also does research, testing ideas that she hopes to adopt more widely. An experimental social networking app connects new mothers around the common experience of childbirth to deal with the isolation and internal depression that often comes from that experience. The initial purpose of the app was to help with postpartum depression, but it has developed to promote relationships on a larger scale. Very quickly, the moms began exchanging information and advice, building new friendships. Part of the experiment was to send out challenges to the moms – activities they could do with their baby out in the community, like meeting other moms at an art museum. The mom would receive a certain number of tokens for accomplishing a task, and a batch of those could be cashed in for Walmart cards. Counselors would be available to help with emotional issues, and for a biweekly screening for depression.

A social cessation app, Momma Live Long, is designed to decrease the chances of a mother returning to smoking after delivery. Each mom receives a cell phone and a sensor for carbon monoxide that can be read remotely by a technician. Moms who don't smoke get monetary rewards. If they crave a cigarette, they can press "I crave" and get a supportive quote and social support other from mothers on the app.

As one satisfied customer at the Partnership said, "I would tell the world about MOMS."

The Alameda Health Consortium in California is part of the community health centers that were and are one of the most important components of the War on Poverty going back to the 1960s. To say the national program is thriving is an understatement. It now serves about 28 million people in 1,300 health-center organizations, with a total of 9,200 delivery sites.

Community health centers are a model of partnerships nationally, and the Alameda Health Consortium is an outstanding example of a partnership. The consortium has eight centers with 75 clinic sites, and serves almost 200,000 people.

A group of school-based health centers that help children and families operates as a partnership within the Consortium. In all, there are 160 school-based clinics in the county. Staffing at each clinic ranges from three to ten people. All offer medical, dental, and behavioral health services, health education, and youth development – a far cry from the school nurse of my childhood.

A student who comes in for first aid is often testing the waters about the clinic's other programs, and a visit for first aid generally leads to broader participation. The Consortium's aim is that all students should graduate healthy and ready for college academically, physically, socially, and emotionally. Thus, each school-based clinic also strives to change policy and atmosphere in the school and to help families outside of school. The volume of their work is large. For example, just one of the eight school sites run by La Clinica de la Raza handles 25,000 individual visits annually.

Trauma that students have experienced constitutes a major theme of the work. La Clinica school sites conduct a universal screen for depression, substance abuse, and trauma on students who come into the clinic. The sites then offer 10-week group sessions and one to three individual sessions with a licensed clinician to parents and children who want to participate. The staff also offers training for the teachers to help them understand what trauma looks like and how to respond in nonpunitive ways. The incidence of trauma is widespread: a study of 23 students found that 19 had experienced at least at least one traumatic event, and the average was four.

La Clinica also has gender-specific culturally based healing circles. Boys and girls of African descent and girls of Latino descent benefit the most. They start with a daylong retreat that begins with sharing the trauma they have experienced, then identifies the similarities among them, and finally sets standards for how they will interact. This creates a safe space for resolving situations, using a restorative model to analyze what harm has been done and how to repair it. As a consequence, school disciplinary actions have decreased significantly.

Of particular note are the medical-legal partnerships that La Clinica has begun with the East Bay Community Law Center. Lawyer Rosa Maria Loya Bay rides circuit among four of the school-based health centers and even makes house calls when needed. When a student comes to the school-based clinic, the health professional asks questions to ascertain if the student or his or her family have legal issues. The health professional might uncover education or juvenile justice issues facing the student, or housing or immigration problems confronting the family.

The clinic staff then refers the matter to Bay.

There is a steady flow of students, often because of behavior in school that results in arrest but stems from trauma. Immigration problems are a growing category of referrals. Bay may represent the youth or their families or refer the case to her colleagues or other attorneys. A student younger than 18 needs permission from a parent to undertake a full intake and be represented. The organization also runs general civil legal clinics and immigration clinics every two weeks at each school, which parents can attend.

The community health clinic partnerships are long-standing and differ based on local needs. The school-based clinics in Alameda County are an outstanding example among such clinics and an example of the power of hubs and spokes in the health world generally.

Dixon Slingerland, the founder of the Youth Policy Institute (YPI) in Los Angeles, is significant to me personally beyond the superb work of YPI. Before coming to Los Angeles, Slingerland worked for many years in Washington, DC for David Hackett, Robert F. Kennedy's best friend. RFK would be proud of him.

YPI, now containing one of President Obama's Promise Neighborhoods, is all about families, especially young people. YPI has been operating since 1996 and it was a success long before it was designated a Promise Neighborhood. YPI works in 18 schools, runs three charter schools, and also manages two Los Angeles Unified District schools. It also operates family centers outside of schools, offering job training and a multitude of other services. YPI has nearly 1,600 employees, of whom three hundred are full-time, and a total yearly budget of almost $50 million. It has 137 program sites and annually serves more than 115,000 children and adults.

Slingerland has long pursued a place-based saturation strategy, understanding that success is possible only if education, health, and employment are addressed simultaneously. The heart of the work is child-centered and nested in a family-centered frame.

"There is no silver bullet," he says. "You have to do it all and do it well, do it with partners both in schools and elsewhere, track it well, and measure outcomes for children and families in combined ways. It's enormously complex. We have to spend a lot of time on relationships." He says YPI runs schools only when necessary; they partner with more than a hundred schools (beyond those connected with the Promise Neighborhood) and have at least five staff members in each. They have a full-service community schools coordinator, a family advocate, tutors (before and after school and in the summer), college and career advisers in the high schools, and instructors for specific subjects. They provide resources that the school district cannot provide and help support the priorities of each principal.

Slingerland is passionate about structural change, always thinking and acting on a big scale. He is making a difference and it goes without saying that he will keep at it.

CONCLUSION

Reducing poverty, racism, and inequality in our nation requires more space than I have been allotted here. I left out discussion in depth of many relevant subjects – education, housing, health and mental health care, mass incarceration, and more. I have, however, tried to address what I think are three vital aspects of moving forward.

The first was to pursue a larger frame for our work. Two was to pull together our thinking about issues of income, jobs, and cash assistance. And three was to look at our efforts from a perspective of place.

Against this background, we need to reexamine the roles of lawyers, advocates, organizers, journalists, and academics, including collaborative work among the various groups. If the actors broaden their outreach into a larger frame, will it add value to the outcomes they obtain? If we retool the modus operandi of each actor both in her own work and in collaborating with people with different skills, will it make a difference? If we use a wider lens, will we create a more effective politics and better substantive results?

We have accomplished more than many think. Yet after a half century of explicit effort, we have much more to do. We have to do better.

Index

Lightning Source UK Ltd.
Milton Keynes UK
UKHW020045180321
380546UK00007B/83